Out in Theory

Out in Theory

The Emergence of Lesbian and Gay Anthropology

Edited by Ellen Lewin
and William L. Leap

Foreword by Esther Newton

UNIVERSITY OF ILLINOIS PRESS
URBANA, CHICAGO, AND SPRINGFIELD

© 2002 by the Board of Trustees
of the University of Illinois
Gayle Rubin retains copyright to chapter 1
Deborah Elliston retains copyright to chapter 11
Manufactured in the United States of America
1 2 3 4 5 C P 6 5 4 3 2

∞ This book is printed on acid-free paper.

Library of Congress Cataloging-in-Publication Data
Out in theory : the emergence of lesbian and gay anthroplogy / Edited by Ellen Lewin and
William L. Leap.
p. cm.
Includes bibliographical references and index.
ISBN 978-0-252-02753-6 (cl. : acid-free paper)
ISBN 978-0-252-07076-1 (pbk. : acid-free paper)
1. Lesbians—Identity.
2. Gays—Identity.
3. Lesbians—Social life and customs.
4. Gays—Social life and customs.
5. Homosexuality.
6. Gay and lesbian studies.
I. Lewin, Ellen. II. Leap, William L.
HQ75.5.O936   2002
305.9'0664—dc21   2001007366

Contents

FOREWORD
Esther Newton   vii

ACKNOWLEDGMENTS   ix

Introduction
Ellen Lewin and William L. Leap   I

I
*Studying Sexual Subcultures: Excavating the Ethnography of
Gay Communities in Urban North America*
Gayle Rubin   17

2
*Reading Sexualities across Cultures: Anthropology and
Theories of Sexuality*
Evelyn Blackwood   69

3
*"These Natives Can Speak for Themselves": The Development
of Gay and Lesbian Community Studies in Anthropology*
Elizabeth Lapovsky Kennedy   93

4
*Another Unhappy Marriage? Feminist Anthropology and
Lesbian/Gay Studies*
Ellen Lewin   110

5
*Studying Lesbian and Gay Languages: Vocabulary,
Text-making, and Beyond*
William L. Leap   128

6
The Iceman Cometh: Queering the Archaeological Past
Robert A. Schmidt   155

7
*Bareback Sex, Risk, and Eroticism: Anthropological
Themes (Re-)Surfacing in the Post-AIDS Era*
Benjamin Junge   186

8
We're "Not about Gender": The Uses of "Transgender"
David Valentine   222

9
A Queer Itinerary: Deviant Excursions into Modernities
Martin F. Manalansan IV   246

10
*Do We All "Reek of the Commodity"? Consumption
and the Erasure of Poverty in Lesbian and Gay Studies*
Jeff Maskovsky   264

11
*Anthropology's Queer Future: Feminist Lessons from
Tahiti and Her Islands*
Deborah Elliston   287

CONTRIBUTORS   317

INDEX   321

Foreword

Esther Newton

Apropos of the recent day when my book, *Mother Camp: Female Impersonators in America* (1973) was prominently spotlighted in a display case in the University of Chicago library, my partner teased, "You were stuffed and mounted." In conjunction with a well-funded and pleasant conference convening queer historians and other scholars (who were impressed and grateful to receive such abnormally plushy treatment), the library had put together an exhibit documenting what turned out to be the extensive history of the study of homosexuality by students and faculty at the university. The other scholars at the exhibit beamed, congratulated me, and shook my hand while the library folks snapped pictures of us in front of the display of *Mother Camp*. I was honored and a bit stunned. "Stuffed and mounted" was certainly an appropriate anthropological image, encapsulating perhaps the scientific, colonial, educational, and macho in the discipline's past. I imagined myself alert but strangely immobile in one of those dioramas at the Museum of Natural History. And if, explaining the display to the public, there were to be a caption—or, to employ a more postmodern image, perhaps an electronic zipper— I would like the text of it to be any page from this wonderful book.

Thirty-five years earlier, in that same city of Chicago, I had been thrilled by performances of the gaudy, daring female impersonators whom I saw in gay bars. Although in the year 2000 I was being lauded as a pioneer who had bushwhacked through the wilderness of homophobia and made a path others would eventually follow, at the time I had no idea where I was going, certainly no notion that some day a book such as *Out in Theory* might be conceived of, much less published. They say that pioneers take the arrows— and we did—but at the time I was just stubborn. I foresaw neither wounds nor vindication. I only knew that outside the university, in the neighborhoods of Chicago, was a gay community of which I was a part, whose stories and aspirations could and should be translated into the terms I had been learning as a student of anthropology, terms like *culture, performance,* and *ritual.*

If eventually I would like this book of anthropological essays to be in my hypothetical diorama, now, at its inception, *Out in Theory* should have a deb- utante party, for it represents not only a presentation of gay and lesbian an- thropology to "society" (by which I mean the so-called mainstream of anthro- pology and also intellectuals who have other interests and may not appreciate our value) but also its coming of age. Confident and poised, these essays are the culmination of at least a century (as Gayle Rubin's essay in the volume shows) of scholars and intellectuals' patient and difficult work on the ethno- graphic and theoretical questions involved in the anthropology of alternative sexualities and genders. Until the 1980s, this work and the people doing it were disconnected and completely marginalized, so progress was slow. But with the emergence of the Society of Lesbian and Gay Anthropologists (SOLGA) everything changed. What constitutes a social, political, and intel- lectual emergence? In the case of SOLGA, it was the process by which those of us who are older were able to connect with each other and, most thrilling- ly for queer scholars, whose relations with youth are always impeded, to con- nect with a new generation. Scholars of different ages and perspectives present the good results of that emergent process here. This book reflects on the twen- tieth century and points toward the future.

SOLGA has been so important to the current flowering of gay and les- bian anthropology that these essays, I think, represent not only individual achievements but also the achievements of the scholarly community SOLGA has become. No one deserves more credit for intellectual and day-to-day leadership of anthropologically minded queers than the editors of this and previous landmark books, Ellen Lewin and Bill Leap. I have every expecta- tion that the essays herein will be read widely in the social sciences and cultural studies, assigned to thousands of students, and years from now will be stuffed and mounted to loud and sustained applause.

Acknowledgments

This volume began as a session that we co-organized, "Anthropology and Homosexuality: A Critical Retrospective," for the scientific program of the 1996 meetings of the American Anthropological Association in San Francisco. Some of the papers in that session explored the emergence of lesbian/gay–focused theory-building within cultural/social anthropology, archaeology, and linguistics. Other papers surveyed interests currently defining this new "subfield" in anthropology and examined efforts to extend some of these discussions beyond a strictly lesbian/gay domain. Audience support for the session was substantial, encouraging us to organize the papers into a companion volume to our earlier collection, *Out in the Field.* We planned the new collection to have a focus on theory-building within a distinctively lesbian/gay anthropology and to examine connections between this work and other areas of concern in anthropology.

Out in Theory is the result of a four-year engagement with this task. We have worked hard to maintain the spirit of the San Francisco session, and the collection includes many of the papers originally presented there along with several that were delivered in a related session held at the AAA meetings in Washington, D.C., the following year. Several papers presented in the 1996 session have been published in other sources and are not included here: Gilbert Herdt on the contributions of fieldwork in New Guinea to the formation of the new subfield, Sue-Ellen Jacobs and Wesley Thomas on berdache/two-spirit studies, Steve Murray on gay-male centered theory-building, and Deb Amory on experimental ethnographic writing. In addition, discussions of topics not addressed in either AAA session have been added: Ben Junge on HIV-related studies and Rob Schmidt on emerging interests in lesbian/gay archaeology as well as a foreword by Esther Newton. Moreover, and appropriately to work in sexuality and gender studies elsewhere in anthropology, discussion throughout the collection now highlights efforts to move beyond a strictly lesbian/gay–inquiry and situate discussions of same-sex desire in broader terms. We intend that the sense of lesbian/gay "theory-building" that emerges here is equally far-reaching in its scope.

Our students and colleagues—for Ellen at the University of Iowa and for Bill at American University—have done much to help us as we organized the collection, solicited written papers, evaluated submissions, and negotiated the final selection for the collection. In Iowa City, Ellen Lewin was fortunate to have the support of Natalya Tchernyaeva, Katharina Mendoza, and Michelle Feijo. In Washington, D.C., Bill remains especially appreciative of the support given to this project by anthropology doctoral candidates Mindy Michels, Christa Craven, Frank McKeown, and by other graduate students in his "Cultural Constructions of Gender" seminars.

We also acknowledge the patience and helpful support that Liz Dulany and the rest of the University of Illinois Press editorial and production staff have given to each phase of the collection's development. Helpful reviews of individual chapters by Louise Lamphere and Mary Weismantel did much to solidify the volume's coherence. Any shortcomings that remain after these meticulous comments are, of course, entirely our responsibility.

Finally, we acknowledge the support to this project, and to our work in lesbian/gay anthropology, which we continue to receive from our partners, Liz Goodman and Angui Madera. Ellen wants to dedicate this book to Annabel, who had a special place in her heart for anthropologists—if not for theory. Bill is happy there is a book to dedicate and looks ahead to the next joint venture that Lewin and Leap plan to pursue.

Out in Theory

Introduction

Ellen Lewin and William L. Leap

We have heard in recent years about anthropology being a discipline "in crisis" in terms of its subject matter, its allegiance to (exotic) field research, and its overly cautious commitments to theory-building. Such statements suggest that anthropologists are moving through a moment in intellectual history that resembles what Thomas Kuhn (1962) called a "paradigm shift." Some of the issues addressed in this "shift"—particularly the increasingly visible shift of anthropology's research focus from remote, exotic locations to cultures of the contemporary United States—reflect the changing political and economic climate in which anthropologists work and might be considered adaptive corrections rather than profound points of change. But other issues go to the heart of the anthropological enterprise and represent a rethinking of the nature of the relationship between anthropologists and the people we study. In some cases, these discussions have led to reconsiderations of the ethical implications of our work, particularly by those who voice concerns about anthropology's complicity in global systems of inequality. In other cases, the wider political climate brings topics formerly overlooked into the foreground of anthropological conversation, sometimes prompting massive reconfigurations of theory and method.

In recent years, conventional wisdom in anthropology has been particularly challenged by two (somewhat overlapping) groups of scholars—those who question the stance of the discipline in relation to its "subjects" and those who interrogate the androcentrism of established anthropological scholarship. Broadly speaking, these represent two distinct genealogies. One strand grew out of the social movements of the 1960s and early 1970s and foregrounded questions of equality and justice that are once again receiving widespread attention within the discipline. For example, *Reinventing Anthropology* (Hymes, ed. 1972) and *Anthropology and the Colonial Encounter* (Asad, ed. 1973), two of the influential volumes from the earlier period, raised questions about anthropology's continuing complicity in U.S. colonial processes and proposed that anthropological inquiry become more concerned with social critique and social disclosure. To begin this process, contributors to these volumes argued, anthropology needed to broaden its focus to include studies of the powerful as well as the powerless—the "studying up" approach advocated by Nader (1972)—both to avoid exploiting those who could not repel our advances and to begin to unravel the otherwise concealed processes of regulatory control in contemporary societies.

Just a few years later, the pathbreaking collections *Woman, Culture and Society* (Rosaldo and Lamphere, eds. 1974) and *Toward an Anthropology of Women* (Reiter 1975) launched a critique of male dominance in anthropological research that brought into being what would become the subfield of feminist anthropology. Contributors to these volumes pointed to the near-invisibility of women from the ethnographic record and the distortions imposed on anthropological theory as a result of these absences. Furthermore, the contributors argued (albeit from somewhat dissimilar theoretical stances) that women's devaluation in Western cultures discouraged making women a focus of inquiry. They also maintained that careful consideration of the ethnographic record would show similar patterns of misogyny among most, if not all, of the world's cultures. Drawing on pervasive assumptions about universal attributes of women, the scholars reasoned explicitly or implicitly that women anthropologists ought to take up the study of women because there would be less social distance between themselves and the focus of their work.[1]

More recently, the assault on business-as-usual in anthropology has been led by scholars influenced by the critical stances of postmodern, postcolonial, and cultural studies. In volumes such as *Writing Culture* (Clifford and Marcus, eds. 1986) and *Anthropology as Cultural Critique* (Marcus and Fischer 1986), contributors pushed discussions of anthropological inquiry beyond definitions of subject-matter and drew attention to problems of representation and voice as these emerge in ethnographic writing. But contributors overlooked recent feminist treatments of such themes and neglected gender and sexuality in other ways. In response, several essays in *Women*

Writing Culture (Behar and Gordon, eds. 1995) proposed a more detailed interrogation of the politics of authorship in anthropology while underscoring the particular challenges feminist stances present to scholars in the field.

Out in Theory is also the product of a moment of disciplinary reflection. We have assembled this collection some five years after the publication of *Out in the Field* (Lewin and Leap, eds. 1996), our first attempt to examine how lesbian and gay subjectivities have affected research practice, theory-building, and issues of representation in ethnography. When we began editing that collection in 1990, the small and informal Anthropological Research Group on Homosexuality (ARGOH) had just become the much larger and more institutionalized Society for Lesbian and Gay Anthropology (SOLGA). In 1998, as we began our work on the present collection, SOLGA moved from being informally associated with the American Anthropological Association (AAA) to being an official section of the association. These changes in SOLGA's professional visibility (and the continuing evolution of our publication projects) were prompted by a substantial florescence of lesbian/gay–oriented scholarship throughout anthropology and by the emergence of distinctively bisexual and transgender studies as well.[2]

Anthropological publications on these themes were now beginning to appear bearing the imprint of mainstream academic presses in addition to that of the "specialty" publishers that had been attentive to lesbian/gay academic interests for some time. In addition, the number of papers and sessions on lesbian, gay, and related topics was now on the increase at national and regional meetings of anthropological organizations, and so was the visibility of lesbian and gay, bisexual and transgendered participants at professional meetings and in the other domains of academic and professional life.[3]

Anthropological conferences specifically focused on lesbian, gay, and related concerns also began to appear during this period. American University's annual Lavender Languages Conference and the biannual meetings of the International Association for the Study of Sexuality, Culture, and Society are only two examples. Even though opportunities to obtain funding for research on lesbian and gay topics grew much more modestly, more graduate students began choosing to concentrate their studies in the anthropology of lesbian, gay, bisexual, and transgendered people, and more anthropology departments became willing to provide an academic "safe space" for these students and for the faculty willing to work with them. Through SOLGA, these conferences, and other mechanisms, anthropologists with interests in lesbian and gay themes began to locate colleagues with similar interests and to join with them in various forms of scholarly dialogue. Non-gay colleagues also became more eager than they once were to hear about this work. As a result, papers on lesbian and gay topics began to be solicited for conferences and edited collections not solely focused on lesbian, gay, and related themes (e.g., Behar and Gordon, eds. 1995; Ferguson and Gupta, eds. 1997; and Markowitz and Ashkenazi, eds. 1999).

By the time we completed the editing of this collection in the fall of 2000, lesbian and gay studies, and to some extent bisexual and transgendered studies as well, was well on its way to becoming a distinct field of specialization within anthropology and had also become sufficiently complex to require some form of codification.[4] We organized this collection accordingly. Our goals are several: to explore the reasons behind the emergence of this specialization (including a careful review of the scholarly and personal events that preceded it); to summarize the issues and debates that give this inquiry its distinctiveness; and to assess the effects of the emergence of this "new" specialization on other anthropological subfields concerned with gender, power, and related themes elsewhere in anthropology and on the work in lesbian/gay studies that are unfolding in other academic domains.

After *Out in the Field:* The Concerns of This Collection

We (and several authors included here) began to take stock of these developments, and the new expressions of lesbian/gay visibility they inspired, when we organized our earlier volume, *Out in the Field.* That project was similar in its focus to *Women in the Field* (Golde 1970), a collection that did much to encourage the emergence of a feminist anthropology. Our goal in *Out in the Field* was to examine the dilemmas, conflicts, and sources of cohesion created by being an anthropologist and being lesbian or gay. In other words, we wanted to focus more on the personal experiences of the contributors, as field workers and creators of ethnographic representations, rather than on the discipline as a whole. By doing so, we wanted *Out in the Field* to draw attention to efforts that many lesbian and gay anthropologists had undertaken to claim their own sex/gendered subjectivity within their research and writing in spite of the stigma associated with homosexuality—and homosexuals—within many areas of the profession.[5]

Largely unexplored in that collection, however, was an inventory of topics that lesbian/gay anthropologists were exploring through their research and writing and the connections with academic disciplines outside anthropology that those topics have constructed. Also unexplored were the boundary lines defining and delimiting positionality in lesbian/gay anthropology. We assumed, for example, that certain issues establish a common ground between lesbian and gay experience, but we did not specify what that common ground contained. And we said even less about the ways in which bisexual and transgendered experiences might overlap with this more privileged, taken-for-granted, lesbian/gay terrain. Finally, although Esther Newton, Kath Weston, and other contributors addressed these questions in terms of their own work, *Out in the Field* did not address larger, more complex questions about the politics of ethnographic descriptions and the right to claim authority in lesbian/gay ethnography.

Viewed against that background, contributors to the present volume faced several tasks. First, many had to take on anthropologists' long-standing practice of overlooking (or declining to elaborate) lesbian, gay, and other non-heterosexual "meanings and understandings" during fieldwork and in ethnographic writing. Second, contributors had to address the willingness of lesbian and gay as well as heterosexual colleagues to assume a single set of meanings as being associated, unproblematically, with homosexuality. Many lesbian, gay, and heterosexual anthropologists have been guilty of simplifying the multidimensionality of sexual and gender identities and behaviors, of collapsing any experience with such individuals into a limited set of categories. Third, given the attention now being paid to this issue throughout the discipline, contributors were obliged to examine the politics of representation relevant to their area(s) of lesbian/gay anthropology. Finally, faced with a long legacy of silencing and invisibility, contributors had to present their discussions in terms that would convince other lesbian and gay anthropologists, as well as anthropologists not personally concerned with lesbian and gay experiences, that ethnographic discussions of these themes can be productive, meaningful, and rewarding.

So, in *Out in Theory* we seek to situate lesbian and gay anthropology in the larger history of the discipline while also developing a set of ideas about the directions this specialization might be expected to take as it continues to grow and diversify in the years to come. Essays by Gayle Rubin, Evelyn Blackwood, and Elizabeth Lapovsky Kennedy explore the origins of lesbian and gay anthropology as embedded in the broader intellectual inclinations characteristic of social and cultural anthropology. Ellen Lewin considers how the interests of feminist anthropology helped define the field, and William L. Leap and Robert A. Schmidt take up similar themes for language and gender studies and for archeology.

Each of these essays, while certainly subfield/disciplinary–specific, also makes clear that lesbian and gay anthropology's relationship to the larger discipline is more than just derivative. Lesbian and gay anthropologists have been key players in the intellectual developments that have framed anthropology as a whole, both in the past and the present, even if the recognition of their central roles is only now coming to light. Now that lesbian and gay anthropology has become a more visible part of the anthropological landscape, the focus of such inquiry has broadened considerably. Essays by Benjamin Junge, David Valentine, Martin F. Manalansan IV, Jeff Maskovsky, and Deborah Elliston show how HIV studies, transgendered concerns, globalization and modernity, dynamics of race and class, and the indeterminacy of queer theory are also now being addressed—often, not harmoniously—within the enterprise of "lesbian and gay" anthropology.

With this broadening of focus have come renewed reflections on the anthropological canon as well as fresh understandings of some of the discipline's more established concerns (e.g., studies of kinship and family, language and gender, ethnicity, community, and nationality). Thus, one of the challenges facing contributors to this volume, in addition to tracing the origins of some areas of lesbian and gay anthropology and/or outlining directions in which each area was moving, was to think about how lesbian and gay anthropology has begun to reshape concerns across the discipline as a whole. Particularly important here are the contributors' discussions of the various meanings assigned to the terms *lesbian* and *gay* in anthropological and other research and their explorations of the connections between a lesbian and gay-centered anthropology and more recent developments in queer theory. The resulting synthesis of anthropology and lesbian/gay studies offers possibilities for reconsidering anthropological expectations about the universality of heterosexuality that drive social and cultural anthropology and, as Leap and Schmidt show, linguistics and archaeology as well.

Rethinking Culture

The concept of culture, not surprisingly, is a primary focus for much of the discussion in this volume. But whose concept of culture are we discussing? Culture is no longer a subject matter uniquely controlled by anthropology, and culture theory is no longer the exclusive terrain of anthropological theory-making. Indeed, since "cultural studies" (now an academic discipline in its own right) has provided the intellectual homeland for much of the work in lesbian/gay studies, assuming that references to "lesbian/gay culture" conform to anthropological definitions of this term are simply out of step with, if not entirely irrelevant to, current directions in lesbian and gay inquiry.

Nowhere are the differences more apparent among notions of culture advanced in anthropology versus cultural studies than in current debates over the locations of cultural experience as it applies to lesbians and gay men. For one thing, scholars in cultural studies usually locate culture within broader domains of race, class, and/or sexuality, whereas anthropologists use culture as the more inclusive location within which (in terms of which?) claims to race, class, and sexuality are then explored. Moreover, scholars in cultural studies often derive lesbian and gay subjectivity out of forms and practices of cultural consumption. Anthropologists, however, are more likely to treat lesbian and gay subjectivities as forms of cultural production—that is, as gendered stances that emerge in response to the particulars of social and political conditions.

Cultural studies–based discussions of culture-as-consumption are not concerned with the individuality of the social actor as an empirically demonstrable set of ideas or actions but with more abstract notions of perspective, voice, appellation, and gaze grounded in the perspective of the analyst. Anthropologists, in contrast, are very much interested in "the particulars"—once called the "emic" perspective—of the social actor. Understandably, then, although a text in cultural studies is a manifestation of multiple, intersecting, and often conflicting streams of social discourse, themselves the products of the interaction of social institutions and intellectual traditions, in anthropology a text is a product of a speaker's context-based choice-making, sensitive to larger ideologies but reflective of the speaker's local understandings of those larger themes. Similarly, while cultural studies explores postcolonial experiences and other components of late modernity in terms of the general disruptions of diaspora, displacement, and dysphoria, anthropological perspectives on the postcolonial and the late-modern focus instead on the articulations between the global and the local and emphasize forms of engagement/resistance to globalization that emerge under local conditions—of which diaspora is one, but only one, part.

It may be unfair to describe the theory of culture in cultural studies in such generic and general terms. However the representations of culture proposed under most segments of the cultural studies canon are, in various ways, at great distance from the conditions of everyday life that these representations seek to explain. In contrast, although again with certain exceptions, anthropology's theories of culture remain more closely aligned with local conditions, given our continuing interests in constructing situated descriptions of "raw data" and developing situated understandings of those details. Although some critics may complain about anthropology's narrowness of focus in this regard, anthropological understandings of culture bring valuable commentary to the discussions of lesbian and gay cultures taking place in cultural studies or in any other academic field. The intent of such commentary is not to preempt discussions of culture in other academic disciplines but to allow anthropology's rich perspectives on the particulars of social settings and the individuality of social actors to enhance those discussions. As Kennedy (chapter 3) shows, such has certainly been the case for anthropological studies of lesbian and gay community compared to work in community studies undertaken by researchers in other disciplines. Hence Maskovsky's discussion (chapter 10) of the tensions between class and racial divisions and assumptions of sexual sameness within inner-city "gay" experience in Philadelphia raises a question yet again, Whose assumptions are giving focus to these conversations? And, as Junge (chapter 7) points out, anthropological emphasis on the particulars of the erotic moment has drawn attention to cultural dynamics of sexual pleasure and sexual practice that more broadly focused, prevention-oriented inquiry has consistently ignored.

Beyond Lesbian and Gay

Many theorists have noted that *lesbian* and *gay* are not context-free categories but express subjective understandings of gender, sexuality, and social location closely linked to the historical emergence of North Atlantic capitalism and to the politics of cultural pluralism during the late modernist period (D'Emilio 1983; Foucault 1978; Weeks 1985). Unfortunately, much work in lesbian and gay studies overlooks the historical location of these categories and refers quite casually to *lesbian* and *gay* identities and desires outside of, as well as within, North Atlantic domains. Whatever the intentions of the researcher, such usage invokes cross-cultural parallels and equivalences that are fictional and often distort the details of situated gendered construction that the research is trying to explore.

We might avoid problems with inappropriately applied labeling in a number of ways, although each "solution" seems to present its own new dilemmas. One approach would be to use phrases like "same-sex identities and desires." But in taking that route, one inevitably makes additional assumptions about the cross-cultural significance of "sexual" similarities and differences, as about the universality of "identities" and "desires," that are difficult to confirm ethnographically. That is, an emphasis on the "sexual" character of particular behaviors situates the discussion in a distinctly Western paradigm.

To avoid this particular hazard, some scholars have advocated using "native" terminology to identify these constructions in situationally relevant ways. That practice, however, tends to lock the inquiry within the boundaries of descriptive relativism that makes cross-cultural similarities difficult to achieve. For example, can we really claim that the male-bodied, female-behaviored *alyhu* is the Mojave equivalent of the North Atlantic "gay" man— and if so, what else are we suggesting when we assert such equivalence? And because the definition of the native category is still phrased in the researcher's language, references to the Mojave *alyhu* (Devereaux 1937) or Polynesian *mahu* will still encounter the limitations of the English-language terminologies discussed earlier.

Gilbert Herdt (1994) has suggested that "third sex" and "third gender" are more suitable categories than *lesbian* or *gay* for cross-cultural gender comparisons. He notes, however, that readers need to remember that "third" really means "more than two" and that multiple sexes and genders are really being referenced when such terminology is employed. Unfortunately, some researchers working within this frame tend to overlook Herdt's caution and use "third gender" as an inclusive category for all forms of nonreproductive, nonheterosexual, gendered identities, rendering "third sex" and "third gender" as synonyms to "same-sex" or "lesbian" or "gay" and not as an alternative usage at all.

Several essays in this collection have to address these problems of terminology, and they remind us that these problems may be indissoluble features of the cross-cultural enterprise, even when the focus of research lies within seemingly familiar terrain at home. Moreover, as Schmidt, Manalansan, and Elliston argue, meanings of some sex and gender constructions relevant to each local setting are always likely to remain unidentified and unacknowledged, whatever solutions to issues of terminology a researcher endorses. Hence, an important part of cross-cultural "lesbian/gay/third sex/ third gender/same-sex desire and identity/homosexuality" studies is the documentation of the locally "inconceivable" as well as any additional categories which, although acknowledged within the lexicon, are still excluded from the primary points of sex/gender reference.

Within the North American context, these categories include persons who self-identify as bisexual or transgender but whose place in lesbian and gay studies—and lesbian/gay politics—has never been secure. More generally, there remain the questions of whether bisexual and transgender issues should be part of "lesbian and gay anthropology" or assigned their own research focus and whether bisexual and transgender studies raise the same kinds of questions about sex and gender as are being addressed in lesbian and gay anthropology.

Confronting Queerness

In his lengthy review of *Out in the Field,* Don Kulick (1997) questions our concern with "outness" and our deployment of this experience as a key focus of that collection. Kulick argues that "coming out" is a generationally situated phenomenon and thus more relevant to the life experiences and career paths of older anthropologists (i.e., many of the contributors to that volume) than it is to younger, presumably more theoretically up-to-date, scholars. For younger anthropologists, Kulick asserts, being openly lesbian and gay is not a controversial status because they became comfortable with their sexuality long before they began to make decisions about anthropological careers. A more suitable paradigm for *Out in the Field,* he suggests, would have been one that spoke more directly to the concerns of younger lesbian and gay anthropologists, and that paradigm is queerness, queer theory, and, ultimately, a queer(ed) anthropology.

Our reasons for framing our earlier work outside the queer paradigm were several. In the early 1990s, queer theory had not penetrated anthropology in nearly the same degree that it had literary studies, cultural studies, and other fields. Very few anthropologists claimed to be queer theorists, and few published under that banner in professional journals. Other anthropologists—young and old—pointedly rejected the queer label as being too closely tied to the detached theorizing of literary studies and cultural studies.

Queer theorists, for their part, acknowledged their debt to Gayle Rubin's profound theorizing of sex/gender systems (1975, 1984) and embraced Esther Newton's *Mother Camp* (1972) as an important forerunner of queer interests in performativity, masquerade, and interpolation of witness (Sedgwick

1993). But beyond these citations, self-identified queer scholars tended to keep their distance from anthropological research and to exclude such work from their publications, their conferences, and their professional networks. In particular, their formulations were only infrequently informed by "empirical" approaches. Typically, queer theorists saw invocations of "the real world" as evidence of an unhealthy preoccupation with facts and data. Anthropologists, not surprisingly, were reluctant to allow their speculations to drift too far from the categories their informants understood to be meaningful.

Given this history, we were not convinced that queer theory was part of lesbian and gay anthropology or that such connections were likely to emerge. Instead, we saw lesbian and gay anthropologists struggling to assert the rightful place of anthropological theorizing of culture, gender and sexuality, and power within the larger interdisciplinary conversation of which queer theory was also a part. To do that, lesbian and gay anthropology needed to preserve some distance from queer theory.

Moreover, insofar as *Out in the Field* drew on the accounts and reflections of anthropologists who identified as lesbian or gay, the models that made sense to our authors had to be the guide to the broader organization of the volume. Questions of outness were central in these narratives, as were related issues of professional responsibility and ethical obligation. And contrary to Kulick's observation, the concern with outness was not just the consequence of our authors' cultural orientation or age or a by-product of having come out as lesbian or gay in the years before queer politics. In contrast, the experiences related in many of the chapters were stark reminders of the impact such identification could and did have on real people's careers and its continuing significance for their professional status.[6]

We maintain the position claimed in our earlier volume as we finish the work on the present collection. Although now there may be additional indications of a queer presence in anthropology, those anthropologists associated with such a perspective are still not using queerness to build bridges between anthropological inquiry (or personal politics) and the theory-building of queer theorists in other fields, nor are they doing so to offer an ethnographic critique of their claims. Instead, for those anthropologists, the term *queer* acknowledges a location within a complex gender politics that transcends differences in bodies, erotic practices, and desires identified by such terms as *lesbian, gay, bisexual, transgender,* and the like. At this stage of theorizing, it is difficult to tell where such an inclusive, generic focus will lead or to assess how helpful to studies of culture, gender, and sexuality that focus will be. Indeed, and consistent with that difficulty, although we had no trouble finding anthropologists willing to prepare essays on lesbian, gay, and trans-gendered themes for this collection, we were unable to locate a scholar willing to address connections between anthropology and queer theory.

At the same time, outness continues to be a site of experience relevant to professional and personal experiences of lesbian and gay anthropologists. Even a casual survey of the career paths of anthropologists who have studied lesbian/gay topics reveals a pattern of unemployment, underemployment, and concealment that has done violence, in many instances, to productivity and intellectual fulfillment. In short, those who want to do work in lesbian and gay anthropology are painfully aware that such work carries a demanding price tag and that part of the cost may be the possibility of gaining secure academic employment. It is not surprising then, given this reality, that many who have undertaken lesbian and gay studies in anthropology have done so from the relatively comfortable position of post-tenure. There are others, of course, who simply made the sacrifice and carried on with their research on lesbian/gay topics. Still others—more than we can possibly document—took the more prudent path into other areas of research and writing. As the scholars whose narratives informed the report of COLGIA reminded us repeatedly, conducting lesbian/gay research is tantamount to coming out—whether one is actually lesbian/gay or not. Although doing research in New Guinea, for example, does not lead to the assumption that one must be a native of that region, studying lesbian/gay topics is imagined as only possible for a "native."

The subtext that underlies all the essays in this volume is that directly engaging with lesbian/gay lives, behaviors, identities, or cultures as one's ethnographic focus requires a level of courage and fortitude not needed in other areas of investigation. Like the personal experience of lesbians and gay men, that coming out, no matter its risks, is the only way to effectively destigmatize their identities and show that they are people, too, anthropologists who study lesbian/gay existence must also come out. By coming out, we can approach the matter of legitimizing our work, of situating it securely in the anthropological canon, and of beginning meaningful dialogue with anthropologists who study other topics. In a fundamentally comparative discipline, after all, it is in breaking down the divisions between subfields, as well as in erecting them, that progress will be made.

Notes

1. The assumption that women share attributes that minimize the impact of cultural differences has been controversial to say the least. In particular, a rich literature on the question of "insider" and "outsider" perspectives in anthropology in general, and in feminist anthropology in particular, has appeared in recent years (e.g., Behar and Gordon, eds. 1995; Limón 1991; Narayan 1993).

2. Although we note the broader and more inclusive characterization—lesbian, gay, bisexual, transgender—that has become the norm in referring to this field, our concern in this volume is primarily with the lesbian and gay part of the story. That story has a long, better-documented history in which nomenclature is somewhat less ambiguous and politicized. In particular, there is continuing disagreement among scholars in the field over whether bisexual and transgender are truly independent categories or extensions to "lesbian" and "gay" (see Valentine this volume for more on this difficult issue).

3. See, for example, collections of articles by lesbian and gay scholars that testify to the particular experiences these individuals have had in their professions and in the academy more generally.

4. A particularly authoritative marker of this growing legitimation was the 1993 publication of Kath Weston's review article on "lesbian and gay anthropology" in the esteemed *Annual Review of Anthropology.* Weston's review made clear not only that lesbian and gay anthropology (like area studies) was beginning to be a field in its own right, by virtue of its particular ethnographic focus, but that it had also begun to split into a number of subfields that have diverse historical and theoretical underpinnings.

5. The Commission on Lesbian, Gay, Bisexual, and Transgender Issues in Anthropology (COLGIA), organized by the American Anthropological Association in 1993 to assess the status of LGBT individuals in the profession and the viability of anthropological research on LGBT issues, conducted a number of data-gathering efforts that documented a pervasive pattern of (at best) marginalization and (at worst) overt discrimination in the educational and professional lives of lesbian and gay anthropologists. The commission's research revealed, for example, that failure to progress through graduate school, particularly because of the inability to secure adequate mentoring, is a common problem for lesbians and gay men. Lesbian and gay faculty report problems with such vital areas of professional life as having families join them in the field, academic schedules, and promotion and tenure decisions as well as (perhaps more mundane) difficulties related to housing, health benefits, and social relations with colleagues. The commission also documented widespread suspicion of (or anxiety about) lesbian/gay issues as the focus of research or curriculum, in part related to a perception that doing such research or teaching marked one as queer.

6. When members of the AAA's Commission on Lesbian and Gay Issues in Anthropology (COLGIA) took testimony from lesbian, gay, bisexual, and transgendered anthropologists regarding their experiences of discrimination, younger respondents

voiced concerns about employment, job security, tenure, and professional advancement. They admitted that they wanted to work in lesbian and gay anthropology and also admitted their fears that a close association with such interests would make them unmarketable (Leap and Lewin 1999). In other words, no matter how profound the intellectual implications of queerness may be, younger anthropologists are still concerned with issues of outness insofar as they continue to shape directions in lesbian and gay anthropology and directions in lesbian/gay anthropologists' actual careers. However much we might prefer to have discovered that anthropology as a profession and as an academic discipline has transcended such mundane cruelties as homophobia, the undeniable reality of lesbian and gay anthropologists' personal histories is that it has not. Under such circumstances, if *Out in the Field* had offered an open endorsement of queer theory we would have contradicted the politics of real-life experience as lesbian and gay anthropologists describe it. (See McNaron [1997] and Mintz and Rothblum, eds. [1997] for examples from other disciplines.)

References Cited

Asad, Talal, ed. 1973. *Anthropology and the Colonial Encounter.* New York: Humanities Press.

Behar, Ruth, and Deborah A. Gordon, eds. 1995. *Women Writing Culture.* Berkeley: University of California Press.

Clifford, James, and George Marcus, eds. 1986. *Writing Culture: The Poetics and Politics of Ethnography.* Berkeley: University of California Press.

D'Emilio, John. 1983. *Sexual Politics, Sexual Communities: The Making of a Homosexual Minority in the United States, 1940–1970.* Chicago: University of Chicago Press.

Devereaux, George. 1937. "Institutionalized Homosexuality among the Mohave Indians." *Human Biology* 9(4):498–527.

Foucault, Michel. 1978. *The History of Sexuality: An Introduction.* Vol. 1. New York: Random House.

Golde, Peggy. 1970. *Women in the Field: Anthropological Experiences.* Chicago: Aldine.

Gupta, Akhil, and James Ferguson, eds. 1997. *Anthropological Locations: Boundaries and Grounds of a Field Science.* Berkeley: University of California Press.

Herdt, Gilbert. 1994. "Introduction: Third Sexes and Third Genders." In *Third Sex, Third Gender: Beyond Sexual Dimorphism in Culture and History,* ed. Gilbert Herdt, 21–83. New York: Zone Books.

Hymes, Dell, ed. 1972. *Reinventing Anthropology.* New York: Pantheon.

Kuhn, Thomas. 1962. *The Structure of Scientific Revolutions.* Chicago: University of Chicago Press.

Kulick, Don. 1997. "Review of *Out in the Field.*" *Journal of the History of Sexuality* 8(2):330–34.

Leap, William L., and Ellen Lewin. 1999. *Final Report of the Commission on Lesbian, Gay, Bisexual, and Transgender Issues in Anthropology.* Arlington: American Anthropological Association.

Lewin, Ellen, and William L. Leap, eds. 1996. *Out in the Field: Reflections of Lesbian and Gay Anthropologists* Urbana: University of Illinois Press.

Limón, José. 1991. "Representation, Ethnicity, and the Precursory Ethnography: Notes of a Native Anthropologist." In *Recapturing Anthropology: Working in the Present,* ed. R. G. Fox, 115–35. Santa Fe: School of American Research Press.

Marcus, George E., and Michael M. J. Fischer. 1986. *Anthropology as Cultural Critique: An Experimental Moment in the Human Sciences.* Chicago: University of Chicago Press.

Markowitz, Fran, and Michael Ashkenazi, eds. 1999. *Sex, Sexuality, and the Anthropologist.* Urbana: University of Illinois Press.

McNaron, Toni A. H. 1997. *Poisoned Ivy: Lesbians in Academia: Degrees of Freedom.* New York: Routledge.

Mintz, Beth, and Esther D. Rothblum, eds. 1997. *Lesbians in Academia: Degrees of Freedom.* New York: Routledge.

Nader, Laura. 1972. "Up the Anthropologist: Perspectives Gained from Studying Up." In *Reinventing Anthropology,* ed. Dell Hymes, 284–311. New York: Pantheon.

Narayan, Kirin. 1993. "How Native Is a 'Native' Anthropologist?" *American Anthropologist* 95(3):671–86.

Newton, Esther. 1972. *Mother Camp: Female Impersonators in America.* Chicago: University of Chicago Press.

Reiter, Rayna R. 1975. *Toward an Anthropology of Women.* New York: Monthly Review Press.

Rosaldo, Michelle, and Louise Lamphere, eds. 1974. *Woman, Culture and Society.* Stanford: Stanford University Press.

Rubin, Gayle. 1975. "The Traffic in Women: Notes on the 'Political Economy' of Sex." In *Toward an Anthropology of Women,* ed. Rayna R. Reiter, 157–210. New York: Monthly Review Press.

———. 1984. "Thinking Sex: Notes for a Radical Theory of the Politics of Sexuality." In *Pleasure and Danger: Exploring Female Sexuality,* ed. Carol S. Vance, 267–319. New York: Routledge.

Sedgwick, Eve Kosofsky. 1993. "Queer Performativity: Henry James' The Art of the Novel." *GLQ* 1(1):1–16.

Weeks, Jeffrey. 1985. *Sexuality and Its Discontents: Meanings, Myths, and Modern Sexualities.* New York: Routledge.

Weston, Kath. 1993. "Lesbian/Gay Studies in the House of Anthropology." *Annual Review of Anthropology* 22:339–67.

ONE

Studying Sexual Subcultures: Excavating the Ethnography of Gay Communities in Urban North America

Gayle Rubin

> Our own society disapproves of any form of homosexual behavior for males and
> females of all ages. In this it differs from the majority of human societies. Some
> people resemble us in this respect, but a larger number condone or even encour-
> age homosexuality for at least some members of the population. Despite social
> and legal barriers to such behavior, homosexual activities do occur among some
> American men and women. (Ford and Beach 1951:125)

Over the past several decades, anthropology has played a prominent
yet inconsistent role in the study of sexual communities and erotic populations. Anthropology has been a major force in contemporary theories of sexuality, particularly in the critiques of gender and heterosexuality as naturalized universals (Reiter, ed. 1975; Rosaldo and Lamphere, eds. 1974).
Comparative ethnographic data have helped undercut the moral legitimacy
of anti-homosexual bias (Ford and Beach 1951; Ortner and Whitehead, eds.
1981). Anthropologists have made substantial contributions to the social
science literature on homosexuality (for an excellent overview, see Weston

1993). Anthropological work has helped to undercut the intellectual foundations of "perversion" models of sexual variation.

For much of the twentieth century, sexual practice that varied from a norm of fairly straightforward, generally monogamous, and preferably marital heterosexuality with a possibility of procreation was cast not only as undesirable but also physically unhealthy, socially inferior, or symptomatic of psychological impairment. Such perversion models presumed the pathology of sexual variety. These assumptions of disease and dysfunction could be explicit or implicit, but they were ubiquitous. They were particularly characteristic of medical and psychiatric literatures, which in turn were hegemonic professional discourses of sexuality.

The social sciences—particularly anthropology, sociology, and history—can often articulate a countervailing intellectual tendency toward accepting the moral equality of social diversity. Anthropology has facilitated potent shifts toward ideological leveling in many registers, including the sexual, by refusing to accept Western industrial civilizations as the measure of human achievement, by treating different cultural systems as equally legitimate, by attacking the foundations of racial ranking and the concept of race itself, by situating epistemological assumptions within culturally specific frameworks, and by showing how systems of moral value are produced by particular social contexts. Particularly in the second half of the twentieth century, anthropology and the other social sciences contested medicine for control over the study of sexuality and helped displace perversion-based models with frameworks grounded in the appreciation of the diversity of human cultural practice.

Nonetheless, anthropology remains enmeshed in its own social locations and has been considerably less self-reflective about the resulting implications for sexual bias than other forms of rationalized condescension. It is ironic that so influential a discipline has also been oddly parochial in resisting the study of sexuality. In particular, the institutions of the discipline have often failed to encourage, and have in some respects obstructed, research on homosexuality, especially in Western urban contexts. The resulting discrepancy between anthropology's strong intellectual contributions and weak institutional presence in contemporary scholarship on homosexuality and other sexual populations has had significant repercussions. Many scholars who work on gay, lesbian, bisexual, or transgender issues, for example, assume that such research began in the 1990s, is derived almost entirely from French theory and is primarily located in fields such as modern languages and literature, philosophy, and film studies.[1] Many anthropologists, in turn, are unaware of the extensive history of social science attention to sexualities and may think of gay research as something accomplished mainly in the ethereal realms of aesthetic critique.

Nonetheless, the study of homosexuality and other non-normative sexualities has a long and distinguished lineage in the social sciences. This essay is an attempt to excavate some of that history, specifically in terms of the ethnographic study of gay, lesbian, and other minority sexual populations in the metropolitan areas of North America, and suggest some of the ways in which that body of work contributed to the articulation of new theories and paradigms of sexuality in the early to mid-1970s.[2]

The Urban Problem

> Anthropology . . . has been mainly concerned up to the present with the study of primitive peoples. But civilized man is quite as interesting as an object of investigation, and at the same time his life is more open to observation and study. . . . The same patient methods of observation which anthropologists like Boas and Lowie have expended on the study of the life and manners of the North American Indian might be even more fruitfully employed in the investigation of the customs, beliefs, social practices, and general conceptions of life prevalent in Little Italy on the lower North Side in Chicago, or in recording the more sophisticated folkways of the inhabitants of Greenwich Village and the neighborhood of Washington Square, New York. (Park, Burgess, and McKenzie 1967 [1925]:3)[3]

As a neophyte graduate student in anthropology in the early 1970s I spent many hours in the library at the University of Michigan, looking for material on the anthropology of homosexuality. There were rich data about same-sex contact in some non-Western societies, the most obvious of which included extensive literature on ritualized semen exchanges among males in New Guinea and nearby Pacific Island cultures, and institutionalized roles for intermediate genders, principally among indigenous people of North America. There were also the occasional reports of homosexual practice or same-sex unions, for example, in some African societies.[4] Data on contemporary sexual communities such as gay Greenwich Village, Fire Island, or West Hollywood, however, were scarce, and anthropological interest in such populations difficult to detect.

The two major compendia then available on the anthropology of sexuality were Ford and Beach's *Patterns of Sexual Behavior* (1951) and Marshall and Suggs's *Human Sexual Behavior* (1971). *Patterns of Sexual Be-*

havior was an indispensable text in comparative sexology. It was widely cited and highly influential in establishing the extent of cultural variation in sexual practices. Ford and Beach included a chapter on homosexuality in which material was presented chiefly in terms of whether societies approved or disapproved of homosexual conduct. By noting that the level of disapproval that obtained in the United States in the 1950s was not universal and was even somewhat extreme, Ford and Beach expressed implied, if muted, criticism of the prevailing intolerance. Their overview and references provided a wonderfully useful finding guide for locating data on same-sex contact in the ethnographic literature for other societies, especially in the Human Relations Area Files.

For the United States, however, Ford and Beach relied on the major sex surveys available at that time, notably the first volume of the Kinsey report from 1948, George Henry's two-volume opus on sex variants (1941), and Katherine Bement Davis's survey of the sex lives of twenty-two-hundred women (1929). The discussion in Ford and Beach reflects those sources by focusing on individuals and types of sexual activity. It reiterates, for example, how many of Kinsey's respondents had practiced "mutual handling of the penis" or what percentage had engaged in anal copulation. Given that social groups are the more customary units of anthropological interest, the absence of any awareness of organized communities of homosexuals in the United States is striking. Ford and Beach brought to the study of homosexuality a strong measure of cultural relativism but little recognition of the social complexity of urban sexual populations.

By contrast, when *Human Sexual Behavior* was published two decades later, Marshall and Suggs were well versed in the social life of urban homosexuals yet considerably less adept at maintaining a consistent stance of ethnographic relativism. They noted that "some homosexuals congregate or regularly visit for residence or recreation specific districts that have shown more tolerance for deviant behavior," and that "some Western homosexuals have developed entire subcultures, with their own patterned behavior" (1971:234). "Just as the homosexual advertisements in the *Berkeley Barb* appear with those of the voyeur, the sadist, the masochist, and the fetishist," they stated, "so it is difficult to interpret such behavioral manifestations as the 'fairy balls,' or the transvestite 'beauty contests' of some urban areas as anything more exalted than sociopathic manifestations of personality disturbances *complicated by membership in a pervasive subculture*" (235, emphasis in the original).

Furthermore, according to Marshall and Suggs, "Medical and psychiatric data together with interpretations by some analysts and by logic indicate that some contemporary Western sexual deviants must be regarded as socially and personally maladjusted, in some cases so very ill as to endanger society" (231). A scant two years before homosexuality was officially reclassified as nonpathological and removed from the list of psychosexual disorders by the American Psychiatric Association, they could flatly state, "Social approval of active homosexuality is tantamount to declaring that society has no interest in, or obligation to make well, the sociopsychologically deviant so as to prevent a disturbing behavior pattern from spreading in its midst—or that the society is not concerned with its own survival" (Marshall and Suggs 1971:236; see also American Psychiatric Association 1952, 1968, 1980, 1987, 1994; and Bayer 1981).

Marshall and Suggs concluded by claiming a new level of ethnographic objectivity and scientific neutrality in the study of sexuality: "With all the effort devoted to the study of manifold aspects of sex throughout the decades since Ellis, Krafft-Ebing, Freud, and others, *only now have we begun to arrive at a relatively culture-free perspective of this most basic aspect of human behavior*" (242, emphasis added). Their laudable attempt to approach sexual variation with an open mind and a minimum of cultural baggage, however, floundered on the presumption of homosexuality as intrinsically pathological. Far from establishing a nonethnocentric study of human sexuality, *Human Sexual Behavior* demonstrates the extent to which ethnographic reflexes were still trumped by common prejudice and psychiatric hegemony as late as 1971. It is ironic that during the two decades bracketed by these two anthropological texts the work of establishing a social science approach to sex, of producing ethnographic studies of contemporary sexual populations, and of challenging the privileged role of psychiatry in the study of human sexuality was mostly accomplished by sociologists.

The University of Chicago and the Discovery of Sexual Worlds

The refashioning of homosexuality as a social phenomenon, rather than a purely psychological one, was established by two means—first by the definition of *homosexuality as a social problem* (ambiguously framed as one of either a problem of the social adjustment of homosexuals or the elimination of prejudice against homosexuals), and second, the public recognition of *the existence of a homosexual world*. Starting in the immediate postwar period and up through the sixties homosexuality as a social issue emerged in a number of different bodies of discourse. (Escoffier 1993:5, emphasis in the original; see also Escoffier 1998:79–98)

The idea that sexuality was social and an appropriate object of social science inquiry was powerfully articulated during the 1950s and 1960s in a small literature in the sociology of deviance. The assumptions, questions, and implications of this body of work challenged those of psychiatry, displacing interest in the etiologies of individual disorders with curiosity about the institutional structures and socialization mechanisms of deviant subcultures. As Jeffrey Escoffier has observed, the "discovery" of homosexual social worlds was central to the reclassification of homosexuality as a social rather than a medical issue. Ethnographic attention to homosexual subcultures shifted attention from individuals to communities and from illness to routine.

Many key scholarly figures of this transition were trained in sociology at the University of Chicago, including John Gagnon, William Simon, Albert Reiss, William Westley, and, less directly, Howard Becker and Erving Goffman. There were, of course, many other notable researchers who also contributed to this process, especially Evelyn Hooker, a psychologist, and Alfred Kinsey, whose background was in biological science. In addition to Chicago, other institutions, such as UCLA, where Hooker was on the faculty, and Indiana University, where the Kinsey Institute was located, served as major intellectual loci for redefining sexuality and resituating sexual deviance.[5] Nonetheless, the centrality of urban ethnography, the sociology of deviance, and the peculiar concentration of individuals trained in social science at Chicago deserve attention.

Social research at the University of Chicago had been famous for its pioneering work in urban sociology since the publication of *The Polish Peasant in Europe and America* (1918–20) by W. I. Thomas and Florian Znaniecki. Thomas is perhaps best known for his role in establishing urban research based on detailed field observation, but he also published a sexological treatise in 1907. His *Sex and Society: Studies in the Social Psychology of Sex* (1907) assembled a collection of earlier journal articles. *Sex and Society* is not grounded in original research but is primarily a commentary based on previously published data, much of it ethnographic. Thomas extensively cites many familiar turn-of-the-century anthropological tomes, such as those of Westermarck, Tyler, Spencer, Lubbock, and Morgan; he also invokes early sexological compendia, such as the work of Havelock Ellis. *Sex and Society* is as a reminder that data on sexual practice were central to late-nineteenth-century anthropology and social theory; similarly, anthropological concerns, findings, and scholarship powerfully shaped early sexology. The overlap between these fields was substantial and their differentiation still embryonic.

W. I. Thomas had also served on the Chicago Vice Commission, one of several investigatory bodies established as a result of interrelated anti-vice crusades that flourished in the United States in the early part of the twentieth century. In addition to the temperance movement, there were also enormous social mobilizations against prostitution (the "social evil") and "white slavery" as well as active campaigns to raise the age of consent for girls and curb the social freedoms of young, working-class women.[6] It is ironic that much of what we know about "vice" in U.S. cities in the early twentieth century results from data collected to assist in attempts at its elimination.

Moreover, the surveillance of prostitution by anti-vice organizations produced observational data on homosexuality. New York's Committee of Fifteen (founded in 1900) documented prostitution in New York City, as did its successor the Committee of Fourteen, "an anti-prostitution society whose investigators kept much of the city's nightlife and streetlife under surveillance from 1905 to 1932. . . . In the course of their search for prostitutes, they [investigators for the Committee of Fourteen] regularly encountered gay men. . . . The reports they filed about those encounters provide exceptionally rich evidence about the haunts of gay men, gay street culture, and the social conventions that governed gay men's interactions with other men and the reactions of the investigators themselves to them" (Chauncey 1994:367).[7] Like its New York counterparts, the Vice Commission of Chicago documented the existence of homosexual underworlds in Chicago as it gathered intelligence on female prostitution (Heap 2000:16; Vice Commission of Chicago 1911).

Despite his service on the Vice Commission and his position on the faculty at the University of Chicago, W. I. Thomas was a casualty of these turn-of-the-century, anti-vice crusades. He was fired in 1918 after being arrested in a hotel with a woman to whom he was not married and charged with violating the Mann Act. The Mann Act, enacted in 1910 and also known as the White Slave Traffic Act, prohibited the interstate transportation of women or girls for "immoral purposes." Although its ostensible purpose was to protect women from coerced prostitution, in practice the Mann Act resulted in restrictions on female travel, harassment of unmarried heterosexual couples, and the establishment of the FBI as a permanent office of the federal bureaucracy (Langum 1994).[8]

Although the case against Thomas was dropped, publicity about the morals charge ended his career at Chicago. "His dismissal was . . . a cruel and considered blow, which was pushed through with thoroughness. The University of Chicago Press, which had published the first two volumes of *The Polish Peasant,* was ordered by the president to terminate the contract and cease distribution of the volumes published. . . . Thomas's name was to be expunged from the university" (Bulmer 1984:59–60, quotation on 60).[9] Thomas never again held a regular academic appointment, spending the rest of his career as a freelance researcher.

Despite Thomas's departure, however, urban ethnography continued to thrive at Chicago throughout the 1920s and 1930s under Robert E. Park and Ernest Burgess. Recreation and leisure activities were an inescapable element of the urban landscape. Park devoted considerable attention to the relationship between the dynamics of metropolitan life and "vice." In a 1915 essay on the urban environment, he noted that "commercialized vice is indigenous" to cities and that conditions peculiar to city life "make the control of vice especially difficult" (Park, Burgess, and McKenzie 1967 [1925]:32–33). Indeed, the city drew individuals who did not fit into the life of small towns and rural areas:

> The attraction of the metropolis is due in part . . . to the fact that in the long run every individual finds somewhere among the varied manifestations of city life the sort of environment in which he expands and feels at ease; finds, in short, the moral climate in which his peculiar nature obtains the stimulations that bring his innate dispositions to full and free expression. It is, I suspect, motives of this kind . . . which draw many, if not most, of the young men and young women from the security of their homes in the country into the big, booming confusion and excitement of city life. In a small community it is the normal man, the man without eccentricity or genius, who seems most likely to succeed. The small community often tolerates eccentricity. The city, on the contrary, rewards it. . . . In the city many of these divergent types now find a milieu in which, for good or for ill, their dispositions and talents parturiate and bear fruit. (41–42)

The concentration of specializations made possible by city size and gravitational pull results in what Park famously called "moral regions" of a city:

> The population tends to segregate itself, not merely in accordance with its interests, but in accordance with its tastes or its temperaments. The resulting distribution of the population is likely to be quite different from that brought about by occupational interests or economic conditions. Every neighborhood, under the influences which tend to distribute or segregate city populations, may assume the character of a "moral region." Such, for example, are the vice districts, which are found in most cities. A moral region

is not necessarily a place of abode. It may be a mere rendezvous, a place of resort. . . . We must then accept these "moral regions" and the more or less eccentric and exceptional people who inhabit them, in a sense, at least, as part of the natural, if not the normal, life of a city. It is not necessary to understand by the expression "moral region" a place or a society that is either necessarily criminal or abnormal. It is intended rather to apply to regions in which a divergent moral code prevails, because it is a region in which the people who inhabit it are dominated, as people are ordinarily not dominated, by a taste or a passion or by some interest. . . . It may be an art, like music, or a sport, like horse-racing. . . . Because of the opportunity it offers, particularly to the exceptional and abnormal types of man, a great city tends to spread out and lay bare to the public view in a massive manner all the human characters and traits which are ordinarily obscured and suppressed in smaller communities. (43, 45–46)

In these comments, Park notes the existence of populations organized around non-normative sexualities, observes that they are spatially located and socially distinct, recognizes their indigenous criteria for moral legitimacy, and provides a rationale for their study.

Students of Park and Burgess fanned out into Chicago to study saloons, speakeasies, gangs, slums, hobos, and a wide range of urban activity, life, and leisure (Anderson 1998 [1923]; Creesey 1968 [1932]; Reckless 1969 [1933]; Zorbaugh 1976 [1929]). None of the published work of this period was primarily focused on homosexuality, but as Chad Heap observes, "Students also examined the increasing presence of homosexuality in the city, chronicling a wide range of same-sex relations and networks associated with specific urban locations and populations" (2000:17). Heap singles out Nels Anderson's *The Hobo* and Zorbaugh's *The Gold Coast and the Slum* as two published works that contained descriptions of same-sex activities and networks (17). Fortunately, much of the unpublished research on homosexuality has been preserved in the Burgess Papers at the University of Chicago. Contemporary scholars such as Allen Drexel, Chad Heap, David K. Johnson, and Kevin Mumford have been exploring the Burgess archives and finding extraordinarily rich documentation on homosexual life in Chicago before World War II (Drexel 1997; Heap 2000; Johnson 1997; Mumford 1996, 1997).

The traditions of urban ethnography continued at Chicago after World War II. Joseph Gusfeld conveys something of the spirit of this work with the following comment: "We used to say that a thesis about drinking written by a Harvard student might well be entitled 'Modes of Cultural Release in West-

ern Social Systems'; by a Columbia student it would be entitled, 'Latent Functions of Alcohol Use in a National Sample'; and by a Chicago student as, 'Social Interaction at Jimmy's: A 55th St. Bar'" (Gusfield 1982, cited in Galliher, 1995:183).[10] But the post–World War II cohort did more than add to the
literature on diverse concentrations of urban delinquents. Several of its members also developed a pervasive critique of the prevailing assumption that
something was intrinsically wrong with deviants and misfits. They showed
how such populations became morally discredited and how they constructed
alternative structures of community and meaningful lives within them.

Dismantling Deviance

> The attitudes we normals have toward a person with a stigma, and the actions we
> take in regard to him, are well known, since these responses are what benevolent
> social action is designed to soften and ameliorate. By definition, of course, we
> believe the person with a stigma is not quite human. On this assumption we exer-
> cise varieties of discrimination, through which we effectively, if often unthink-
> ingly, reduce his life chances. We construct a stigma theory, an ideology to ex-
> plain his inferiority and account for the danger he represents, sometimes
> rationalizing an animosity based on other differences, such as those of social
> class. . . . We tend to impute a wide range of imperfections on the basis of the
> original one. (Goffman 1963:5)

> When do we accuse ourselves and our fellow sociologists of bias? I think an
> inspection of representative instances would show that the accusation arises . . .
> when the research gives credence, in any serious way, to the perspective of the
> subordinate group in some hierarchical relationship. The superordinate parties in
> the relationship are those who represent the forces of approved and official mo-
> rality; the subordinate parties are those who, it is alleged, have violated that mo-
> rality. . . . We provoke the suspicion that we are biased in favor of the subordi-
> nate parties . . . when we tell the story from their point of view. (Becker 1970
> [1967]:125)

In an essay entitled "Chicago's Two Worlds of Deviance Research:
Whose Side Are They On?" John Galliher details the impact of a cohort of
sociologists who did their graduate work at Chicago after World War II and
proceeded to significantly reshape studies of deviance and crime. One of the
key figures in repositioning "deviance" was Howard Becker.[11] Becker's influence was derived from his choice of research topics, his bold reconcep-
tualizations of the field, his work as an editor of the journal *Social Problems*

in the early 1960s, and his service as president of the Society for the Study of Social Problems. His 1966 presidential address, later published in *Social Problems,* was the famous "Whose Side Are We On?" (Galliher 1995:169).

In it, Becker challenges social researchers to include the perspectives of all parties, not only those of the accepted authorities. "It is easily ascertained that a great many more studies are biased in the direction of the interests of responsible officials than the other way around" (Becker 1970 [1967]:127). A key concept was what Becker dubbed "the hierarchy of credibility." He noted that "in any system of ranked groups, participants take it as a given that members of the highest group have the right to define the way things really are. . . . thus credibility and the right to be heard are differentially distributed through the ranks of the system. As sociologists, we provoke the charge of bias . . . by refusing to give credence and deference to an established status order, in which knowledge of truth and the right to be heard are not equally distributed" (126–27).

In his research and theoretical writings, Becker in various ways declines to observe that moral hierarchy and engages instead in what might be called a project of "moral leveling."[12] He comments, for example, "In the course of our work . . . we fall into deep sympathy with the people we are studying, so that while the rest of the society views them as unfit in one or another respect for the deference ordinarily accorded a fellow citizen, we believe that they are at least as good as anyone else" (Becker 1970 [1967]:124; see also Goffman 1963 for a similar leveling effect). Giving equal consideration to the opinions of disreputable deviants, respectable citizens, and authoritative officials was extraordinarily subversive.

Although Becker's early research on "outsiders" focused on marijuana users and jazz musicians, he discussed homosexuality in the context of deviance and "deviant careers" (1973:30–38, 167–68). In *Stigma: Notes on the Management of Spoiled Identity* (1963) Erving Goffman also used homosexuality to exemplify the broader workings of stigma. His interest was in how individuals and groups become discredited, tainted, and discounted and how they construct or learn to participate in alternative values, social affiliations, and "moral careers."

It was John Gagnon and William Simon, two other Chicago-trained sociologists, who would undertake the most comprehensive rethinking of specifically sexual deviance, including a sweeping reevaluation of homosexuality. After their graduate work, they were hired to conduct research at the Institute for Sex Research at Bloomington, Indiana. Gagnon arrived in 1959, and Simon was engaged in 1964. The confluence of the intellectual heritage of Chicago social research and the Kinsey Institute's focus on sexuality was fortuitous. Gagnon and Simon quickly grasped the implications of their sociological perspectives for the conduct of sex research and the reshaping of sexual theory. During the course of the 1960s and early 1970s, they produced a body of work that virtually reinvented sex research as social science. They also aggressively contested the hegemony of psychiatry and the paucity of its interests. Reminiscing about this period years later, Gagnon commented, "Each of the research projects [undertaken by them] was an attempt to *bring the field of sexuality under the control of a sociological orientation. The novelty of what we did then was to lay a sociological claim to an aspect of social life that seemed determined by biology or psychology. . . . The research project on gay men . . . began with a distrust of etiological theories and a vision of sexual lives as determined by social factors"* (1992:231, emphasis added).

This insistence on treating sexuality in all its forms as a social phenomenon addressable by social science was perhaps their most influential and breathtaking accomplishment. Simon and Gagnon promoted the application of ordinary sociological questions and techniques to the study of homosexuals as well as to a range of other sexual populations and topics. As Kenneth Plummer observed, "One of the central ideological thrusts in their writings is their wish to take the study of human sexuality out of the realm of the extraordinary and replace it where they believe it belongs: in the world of the ordinary" (1981:24). Simon and Gagnon reformulated the research project to ask not why a particular individual was homosexual but how that person became socialized into homosexual life and the social content of that particular "deviant career."

The researchers were critical of etiological obsessions and the naturalization of heterosexuality:

> The study of homosexuality today, except for a few rare and relatively recent examples, suffers from two major defects: (1) it is ruled by a simplistic and homogeneous view of the psychological and social contents of the category "homosexual," (2) At the same time it is nearly exclusively interested in the most difficult and least rewarding of all questions, that of etiology. . . .
> It is this nearly obsessive concern with the ultimate causes of adult conditions which has played a major role in structuring our concerns about beliefs about and attitudes toward the homosexual. Whatever the specific elements that make up an etiological theory, the search for etiology has its own consequences for research methodology and the construction of theories about behavior . . . the problem of finding out how people become homo-

sexual requires an adequate theory of how they become heterosexual; that is, one cannot explain homosexuality in one way and leave heterosexuality as a large residual category labeled "all other." (Simon and Gagnon 1969 [1967]:14–16)

They also highlighted the arbitrary quality of the assumption of homosexual pathology:

> In practically all cases, the presence of homosexuality is seen as prima facie evidence of major psychopathology. When the heterosexual meets these minimal definitions of mental health, he is exculpated; the homosexual—no matter how good his adjustment in nonsexual areas of life is—remains suspect. . . . Obviously, the pursuit of a homosexual commitment—like most forms of deviance—makes social adjustment more problematic than it might be for a conventional population. What is important to understand is that consequences of these sexual practices are not necessarily direct functions of such practices. It is necessary to move away from an obsessive concern with the sexuality of the individual, and to attempt to see the homosexual in terms of broader commitments that he must make in order to live in the world around him. Like the heterosexual, the homosexual must come to terms with the problems which are attendant upon being a member of the society: he must find a place to work, learn to live with or without his family, be involved or apathetic in political life, find a group of friends to talk to and live with, fill his leisure time usefully or frivolously, handle all the common and uncommon problems . . . and in some manner socialize his sexual interests. (17–19, 24)

In short, a sociological approach to homosexuality would "trace out the patterns of living in their pedestrian aspects as well as those which are seemingly exotic" (24).

Gagnon and Simon also conducted and promoted social research, including ethnographic studies, on other sexual populations. They wrote widely on many sexual topics, including pornography and lesbianism; coauthored two influential anthologies, *Sexual Deviance* (1967) and *The Sexual Scene* (1970); and produced a magisterial summation of their social and theoretical approach to sexuality in *Sexual Conduct* (1973).[13]

Sexual Deviance is an extraordinary collection of classics that have almost been lost, and the anthology should be brought back into print. In addition to sections on sex offenses, lesbians, and prostitutes, *Sexual Deviance* contains most of the key originating articles on the ethnography of contemporary homosexual life. Among these are Evelyn Hooker's "The Homosexual Community" (first presented as a paper in 1961); Maurice Leznoff and

William A. Westley's article by the same name (first published in *Social Problems* in 1956); Albert J. Reiss's study of teenaged hustlers, "The Social Integration of Peers and Queers" (also originally published in *Social Problems,* in 1961); and Nancy Achilles' remarkable discussion of San Francisco gay bars, "The Development of the Homosexual Bar as an Institution" (which was based on her unpublished 1964 M.A. thesis for the Committee on Human Development at the University of Chicago).

The three essays that provide overviews of urban gay populations span a period of observation from roughly the mid-1950s to the early 1960s and three cities: Los Angeles, San Francisco, and an unspecified "large Canadian city" (presumably Montreal). Leznoff and Westley's study was the earliest and in some respects the most rudimentary. It documented that there were "known homosexual meeting places within the city such as specific bars, hotel lobbies, street corners, and lavatories" and discussed the way in which "queens" (whose homosexuality was open and somewhat flagrant) exercised social leadership functions (Leznoff and Westley 1967 [1956]:195–96, 194–95).

The most interesting aspects of the article are the authors' observations about the relationships among social status, economic location, community participation, and homosexual disclosure. Leznoff and Westley observed two basic strategies for managing homosexual stigma and the attendant legal and social sanctions. Some number of their research population "passed" as heterosexuals, both at work and in social relationships. Others who were openly homosexual in mid-1950s' Canada tended to "work in occupations where the homosexual is tolerated, withdraw from uncompromising heterosexual groups, and confine most of their social life to homosexual circles" (189).

Leznoff and Westley called these two crowds the "secret" and the "overt." They noted an inverse relationship between overt disclosure of the stigmatized homosexual identity and class status and social mobility: "The overt homosexual tends to fit into an occupation of low status rank; the secret homosexual into an occupation with a relatively high status rank" (191). Furthermore, "the homosexual tends to change his orientation from 'overt' to 'covert' as he becomes upwardly mobile" (192). In the intervening decades, as the punitive costs of overt homosexuality have diminished this relationship has undoubtedly altered but still can be discerned in muted and mutated forms. A larger arena of economic and social practice now permits open disclosure of homosexuality, although acknowledged homosexuality is still hazardous for individuals in a wide range of careers and positions, such as military personnel, politicians, members of the judiciary, entertainers, professional athletes, teachers and educators, and among the clergy of most denominations.

Hooker's research depicts a slightly later, much larger, more differenti-ated, and evidently less anxious community. She noted a much more devel-oped territoriality. Although the Los Angeles homosexual community of the late 1950s and early 1960s lacked "a territorial base with primary institu-tions serving a residential population," homosexuals were "nevertheless, not randomly distributed throughout the city, nor are the facilities of institutions which provide needed services and functions as focal gathering places . . . [where] heavy concentrations of homosexuals result in large cluster forma-tions. In these sections, apartment houses on particular streets may be owned by, and rented exclusively to, homosexuals. . . . The concentrated character of these areas is not generally known except in the homosexual community, and in many instances by the police" (Hooker 1967 [1961]:171–72).

Hooker also noted the central importance of the "gay bar" among the pub-lic institutions of homosexual social life and the relationship of this impor-tance to anti-gay stigma:

> Because most homosexuals make every effort to conceal their homosexual-ity at work, and from heterosexuals, the community activities are largely leisure time or recreational activities. The most important of these commu-nity gathering places is the "gay bar" . . . but there are also steam baths ca-tering almost exclusively to homosexuals, "gay" streets, parks, public toi-lets, beaches, gyms, coffee houses, and restaurants. Newsstands, bookstores, record shops, clothing stores, barber shops, grocery stores, and launderettes may become preferred establishments for service or for a rendezvous, but they are secondary in importance. (173)

Hooker counted sixty gay bars in Los Angeles around 1960 and observed in passing the harassment of these bars by police and the alcoholic beverage control authorities (173).[14]

The essay by Nancy Achilles explores the institutional centrality of the gay bars of the early 1960s in greater depth. The most important service of gay bars, she comments, consisted of:

> the provision of a setting in which social interaction may occur; without such a place to congregate, the group would cease to be a group. . . . Articulating with various commercial and political institutions of the larger society, the bar may obtain legitimate and illegitimate goods and services for its clien-tele. As each bar develops a "personality" of its own and becomes an institu-tion in its own right, it fulfills more specialized and nonsocial functions. A particular bar, for example, may serve as a loan office, restaurant, message

reception center, telephone exchange, and so forth. . . . The bar is the homosexual equivalent of the USO or the youth club. (Achilles 1967:230–31)

This institutional importance of gay bars made their control by police and
state alcohol authorities politically significant. "If there is one particular issue
which calls forth a unified protest from the homosexual Community, it is that
of police activity. Many homosexuals remain passive until a favorite bar or
close friend is threatened by the police. . . . The greatest sense of group cohesion in the homosexual Community is expressed in reaction to the police."

Moreover, as Achilles notes, some of the important legal battles to establish the right of homosexuals to congregate in public were fought over
regulations governing liquor licenses. Consequently, in attempting to retain
their licenses and serve a homosexual clientele, "It is often the bars themselves which make the most salient plea for the homosexual's civil rights,
for it is most often the bars which undertake a defense in cases involving the
law" (234–35).

Considerable bar specialization was evident by the early 1960s:

The gay world is one marked by a galaxy of social types, each one compris-
ing a sub-group within the Community. Often a bar will cater to one particular sub-group, and the bartender will be representative of its social type.
For example, one bar will be known as a "leather bar," where the customers
are the exaggeratedly masculine type, sporting motorcycle jackets and boots.
Another bar may be popular with the effeminate "queens". . . . A female
behind the bar indicates a primarily Lesbian clientele. The same applies to
more subtle distinctions; in the discreet gilt and mahogany bars of the financial district, the bartenders wear black ties and speak with Oxford accents.
(Achilles 1967:240)

Some of the spatial distribution of gay sites could be specified by the early
1960s. Achilles noted that several bars were "located in the Tenderloin district of San Francisco, and several others in the industrial section and its
adjacent waterfront" (242, probably a reference to South of Market and the
old Embarcadero). Her research was undertaken a decade before the Castro
became a significant location in the city's homosexual geography and when
local gay sites were indeed heavily concentrated in the Tenderloin/Polk area
and the South of Market (242).

Finally, Achilles used the notion of a "gay bar system," noting that "the
individual bars may open and close rapidly and regularly, but the system and
its participants remain the same" (239). Achilles' study was evidently con-

ducted during a period of relative stability in the system, and perhaps that led her to overestimate its permanence. "The bars come and go, like a chain of lights blinking on and off over a map of the city, but the system remains constant" (244). This observation is insightful if unduly functionalist and overly generalized to other periods. Within a decade of Achilles' research, gay settlements in major North American metropoles would undergo substantial and visible expansions of territory, economic diversification, and institutional proliferation. Certainly in San Francisco, the "gay bar system" was not stable. It underwent explosive growth, and during the mid-1980s it contracted and shrank. Such changes are significant, result from changes in the urban environment, and indicate new kinds of institutional formation or attrition within urban gay populations (Garber ca. 1990; Garber and Walker 2000; Rubin 1994, 1997, 1998, 2000). Nonetheless, Achilles' research remains an invaluable description of a vanished time. Yesterday's sociology has become today's history.

One of the very real problems of the ethnographic work on gay communities from the 1950s and 1960s (a problem shared with most other ethnography from the period) is a lack of temporal awareness and the consequent misidentification of transient conditions as universal ones. For example, Simon and Gagnon stated, "In contrast to ethnic and occupational subcultures the homosexual community—as well as other deviant subcommunities—has very limited content" (1969:21). That view, common at the time, made perfect sense when gay life was both more secretive and less institutionally elaborated than it would become in the 1970s. Writing from a later vantage point, Harry and DeVall could observe, "The Gagnon and Simon thesis of cultural impoverishment was a time-bound hypothesis that had a measure of validity for certain gay settings . . . and for earlier decades. However, the growth of gay institutions during the last fifteen years, the rise of a sense of collective identity, the creation of a sophisticated political culture, and the efflorescence of a variety of gay recreational styles has significantly expanded the content of that culture" (154).[15]

Such debates demonstrate the importance of longitudinal observation and sensitivity to the diachronic dimensions of social structures as well as the hazards of elevating contingencies into principles. But these discussions and their resulting refinements would not have even been possible without the kind of data on homosexual settlements found in *Sexual Deviance*.

Sexual Deviance also included Albert Reiss's fascinating essay on commercial sexual transactions between adult homosexual men and young "hustlers" who do not consider themselves "queer." "The adult male client pays a delinquent boy prostitute a sum of money in order to be allowed to act as a fellator. The transaction is limited to fellation and is one in which the boy develops no self-conception as a homosexual person or sexual deviator, although he perceives adult male clients as sexual deviators, 'queers' or 'gay boys'" (1967 [1961]:199). This pattern of conduct lead Reiss to distinguish between "homosexual behavior" and the "homosexual role" and to think about the mechanisms by which boundaries between "homosexual acts" and "homosexual identities" were maintained by the rules governing such transactions (225).

The exchange of money, for example, demarcated "queers" (who paid) from "peers" (whose heterosexual masculinity was protected by being paid). The sexual acts were limited, at least in principle, to oral sex, with the boy as penetrator and the homosexual, penetrated. The sexual acts should be "affectively neutral," and only the homosexual participants could acknowledge sexual gratification as a goal. "It should be kept in mind that self gratification is permitted in the sexual act. Only the motivation to sexual gratification in the transaction is tabooed. But self-gratification must occur without displaying either positive or negative affect toward the queer. In the prescribed form of the role relationship, the boy sells a service for profit and the queer is to accept it without show of emotion" (Reiss 1967 [1961]:214–19).

Finally, violence could be used to reassert boundaries should any of these expectations be violated. Should the "queer" fail to pay, treat the "boy" with overt affection, or attempt penetration, the boy is entitled or even required to defend his masculinity and heterosexuality by beating up the client:

> Put another way, a boy cannot admit that he failed to get money from the transaction unless he used violence toward the fellator and he cannot admit that he sought it as a means of sexual gratification. . . . the *violence is a means of enforcing the peer entrepreneurial norms of the system.* . . . The fellator risks violence, therefore, if he threatens the boy's self-conception by suggesting that the boy may be homosexual and treats him as if he were. . . . The prescriptions that the goal is money, that sexual gratification is not to be sought as an end in the relationship, that affective neutrality be maintained toward the fellator and that only mouth-genital fellation is permitted, all tend to insulate the boy from a homosexual self-definition. So long as he conforms to these expectations, *his "significant others" will not define him as homosexual;* and this is perhaps the most crucial factor in his own self-definition. (224–25, emphasis in the original)

In this system of sexual signification, an individual could engage in homosexual acts without assuming the identity of a homosexual. Moreover, the borders between "gay" and "non-gay" were maintained by purely conventional means that included a set of customary expectations regarding money, sexual position, emotional affect, and physical violence. In retrospect, the categories of heterosexual and homosexual were already demonstrably arbitrary and thoroughly destabilized in this 1961 account, decades before "queer theory." Reiss's essay is yet another example of how work in what was then called "sexual deviance" had already incorporated several conceptual innovations, the implications of which would eventually contribute to a major shift in the theoretical paradigms governing research on sexuality.[16]

By dismembering deviance in general and sexual deviance in particular and by producing ethnographic studies of urban gay life, this small sociological literature would have many reverberations. It would be a major influence in the earliest ethnographic research conducted by anthropologists on gay communities in urban North America. In the mid-1970s it would also help instigate a profound, extensive, and aggressive reappropriation of sexuality as a topic by sociologists, historians, and anthropologists.

From Sexual Deviance to Social Construction

The development of a social-constructionist interpretation of homosexual history is one of the major intellectual achievements of the Stonewall generation of lesbian and gay scholars. (Escoffier 1990:44)

But many of Boswell's critics are truly dogmatic in their social constructionism. . . . The response of the rabid constructionists seems to be to ignore anything that doesn't fit their schemata.

As I am curious to read what you are calling "rabid constructionists," perhaps you could provide some citations?

Well, "rabid" was polemical of course. Foucault, who started it all, and his epigones—Jeffrey Weeks, David Greenberg, Ken Plummer, David Halperin, just to mention the Anglo-Americans—who have done fine work all, but seem to have this persistent theoretical bias.[17]

It is frustrating for those of us who have been toiling in this particular vineyard since the turn of the 1960s and 1970s to have our early efforts in understanding sexuality in general, and homosexuality in particular, refracted . . . through post-Foucauldian abstractions . . , and then taken up as if the ideas are freshly minted. I am struck . . . by the reception of queer theorists . . . in recent writing about the body and sexuality (especially in queer studies) in the Anglo-Saxon world,

when, . . . they are not saying anything fundamentally different from what some
of us have been trying to say for twenty-five years or so, inspired in large party
by a reading of Mary McIntosh's "The Homosexual Role," which was first published in 1968. (Weeks 1998:132)

Despite considerable controversy, "social construction of sex theories" became an indispensable paradigm for social science research on sexuality during the last decades of the twentieth century (Escoffier 1990, 1992,
1998; Hansen 1979; Katz 1983; Padgug 1979; Plummer 1975, 1981, ed.,
1992, ed.; Rubin 1984; Vance 1989a, 1991; Weeks 1977, 1981, 1985, 1986,
1991, 1998, 2000). The persistence of its attribution primarily to the work
of Michel Foucault, particularly volume one of his *History of Sexuality,* is
as puzzling as it is frustrating, given the very clear lineages and citational
trails that link early social construction scholarship to previous work in sociology, anthropology, and social history. Two sociologists, Kenneth Plummer and Mary McIntosh, were significant conduits through which the sociology of sexual deviance was absorbed into emerging work in gay history.

Plummer is a major figure. When *Sexual Stigma: An Interactionist Account*
was published in 1975 it joined Gagnon and Simon's *Sexual Conduct* as a con-
summate reappraisal of the sociology of sex. Plummer was aware of and cited all the individuals discussed earlier, although he seemed to take much inspiration more directly from Blumer's *Symbolic Interactionism* (1969), Berger
and Luckmann's *The Social Construction of Reality* (1967), and Goffman's
Stigma. Plummer applied their approaches directly to sexuality, particularly
male homosexuality. He later edited two important anthologies—*The Making of the Modern Homosexual* (1981) and *Modern Homosexualities* (1992)—
and currently edits the journal *Sexualities.* In his introductory essay in *The
Making of the Modern Homosexual,* Plummer provides a brief history of some
of the key ideas of social construction, singling out the work of Kinsey, Simon and Gagnon, and Mary McIntosh as particularly formative. A reprint of
the McIntosh essay originally published in 1968 in *Social Problems* is also
included in the volume.

Mary McIntosh's "The Homosexual Role" is a pivotal essay that links
preexisting work in sociology to the evolving gay histories, social theories,
and sexual political activism of the early 1970s (Plummer 1975, 1981; Weeks
1977, 1998, 2000). McIntosh provides a dazzling synthesis of the theoretical implications of Kinsey's research, cross-cultural data on homosexuality
from anthropology, and the sociological literature on sexual deviance. She
notes, for example, the difficulty in studying homosexuality because "be-

havior patterns cannot be conveniently dichotomized into heterosexual and homosexual," a perspective brilliantly elucidated by Kinsey in *Sexual Behavior in the Human Male,* particularly the extensive and subversive chapter on male homosexuality (Kinsey, Pomeroy, and Martin 1948:610–66).[18] Moreover, because homosexuality had been understood as a "condition," "the major research task has been seen as the study of its aetiology." In a particularly memorable formulation, McIntosh comments, "One might as well try to trace the aetiology of 'committee chairmanship' or 'Seventh Day Adventism' as of 'homosexuality.' The vantage point of comparative sociology enables us to see that the conception of homosexuality as a condition is, in itself, a possible object of study" (McIntosh [1968] in Plummer, ed. 1981:31).

McIntosh proposes "that the homosexual should be seen as playing a social role rather than as having a condition" (33). In addition, the social role itself is culturally and historically specific. McIntosh reviews ethnographic data on homosexuality (drawn primarily from the Human Relations Area Files and other cross cultural data discussed in Ford and Beach's *Patterns of Sexual Behavior*) to establish the cultural specificity of the "homosexual role." "In all these societies," she notes, "there may be much homosexual behavior, but there are no 'homosexuals'" (35–36).

McIntosh's greatest contribution, however, was to historicize this "homosexual role." A social role involving a type of person we could call "a homosexual," she maintains, is a fairly recent phenomenon: "Thus a distinct, separate, specialized role of 'homosexual' emerged in England at the end of the seventeenth century, and the conception of homosexuality as a condition which characterized certain individuals and not others is now firmly established in our society" (38). That claim opened a new field of historical inquiry into the conditions and mechanisms and specifications of the development of new kinds of sexual practice, identity, and meaning. This key insight—that homosexuality had a history—was profound in its implications. The "discovery" of homosexual social worlds had led to a reconsideration of homosexuality as a social rather than a medical problem. Similarly, the "discovery" of the extent of historical change in what we think of as homosexuality helped precipitate the articulation of a new theoretical framework, what we now call "social construction of sexuality."

Jeffrey Weeks was quick to grasp the implications of McIntosh's sketchy historical outline as well as the ideas developed in work of Plummer, Gagnon, and Simon. A generation of gay historians and anthropologists met these thinkers and the perspectives embedded in their work through Weeks's early articles and his first book, *Coming Out: Homosexual Politics in Britain, from the Nineteenth Century to the Present* (1977). The first bibliographic entry of *Coming Out* reads: "My general approach has been influenced by the following: Mary McIntosh, 'The Homosexual Role,' *Social Problems,* vol. 16, no. 2, Fall 1968; Kenneth Plummer, *Sexual Stigma,* London 1975; J. J. Gagnon and William Simon, *Sexual Conduct: The Social Sources of Human Sexuality,* London 1973" (239).

Coming Out was the first major social history of homosexuality and also one of the earliest crystalizations of the premises of the social construction of sex paradigm. It was the first comprehensive investigation of the position that homosexuality was not a transhistorical category but rather a form of same-sex behavior that involved particular types of historically specific persons, identities, and communities. As Weeks put it, "We tend to think now that the word 'homosexual' has had an unvarying meaning, beyond time and history. In fact it is itself a product of history, a cultural artefact designed to express a particular concept. . . . The term 'homosexuality' was not even invented until 1869. . . . and it did not enter English currency until the 1890s. . . . They [new terms such as *homosexuality* and *gay*] are not just new labels for old realities: they point to a changing reality" (3).

One such shift was the emergence of urban homosexual subcultures. *Coming Out* highlighted the historical and theoretical significance of such developments:

> Homosexuality has everywhere existed, but it is only in some cultures that it has become structured into a sub-culture. . . . A sub-culture does not arise in a vacuum. There needs to be both the felt need for a collective solution to a problem (group access to sexuality in this case) and the possibility of its satisfaction. And it is the growth of towns with large groupings of people and relative anonymity which provides the possibility of both. . . . By the mid-century [nineteenth] the sub-culture is much more complex and variegated. The records of the court cases from this period show the spread of a homosexual underworld in the major cities (especially London and Dublin) and the garrison and naval towns. In the 1840s, London had brothels that supplied young boys as well as young girls. . . . A network of meeting-places developed, often located around public lavatories after the mid-century, the occasional public bath, private meeting places and clubs, and straightforward cruising areas. In London, the Regent's Street Quadrant, the Haymarket and areas toward Trafalgar Square and the Strand were favourite haunts for male (as for female) prostitutes, while in the 1880s, the circle of the Alhambra Theatre was a well-known picking-up area, as was part of the Empire Music Hall, the Pavilion, the bar of the St James's and a skating rink in Knightsbridge. (Weeks 1977:35–37)

The notion that homosexuality had a history was one of the central insights grounding early articulations of social construction frameworks. Previous work in gay history had tended to assume an unvarying homosexuality subjected to variable legal sanctions and cultural assessments. The new gay history, of which Weeks's work was so exemplary, discovered instead a mutable homosexuality that had discontinuities sufficient enough to make problematic even the application of labels such as "lesbian," "gay," or "homosexual" to persons in other historical periods or cultural contexts. That which we might be tempted to identify as "homosexual" might refer to an assemblage of institutional elements and social relations alien to a modern or Western notion of sexual, much less "homosexual," conduct.

Gay history was recast from the history of homosexuals, or even a unitary notion of homosexuality, to histories of homosexualities or homoerotic sexual practice whose precise social and cultural relationships and valences had to be determined in particular contexts rather than assumed on the basis of those obtaining in modern Western industrialized societies. In addition, the realization that homosexuality was historically and culturally protean had broader implications: a corollary was that other sexualities also had histories.[19] Volume 1 of Michel Foucault's *History of Sexuality,* entitled *An Introduction,* was published in France in 1976 and in English translation in the United States in 1978. In it, Foucault proposed an expansive model in which all of the sexual "perversions," as well as the concept of sexual perversion, had histories. Eventually, Jonathan Katz, who previously had done trailblazing work in gay history, published an essay and a book on "the invention of heterosexuality" (1976, 1983, 1990, 1995).

Like Weeks, I have profound appreciation for Foucault's work. I do not intend to impugn his originality and brilliance or to suggest that his innovations should be situated in some lineage of Anglo-American sociology. There were innumerable theoretical currents within French academia and politics that comprised the intellectual context for Foucault.[20] Nor do I wish to imply a rigid separation between French, British, and U.S. academic developments. Clearly, there was a great deal of cross-fertilization as well as convergent theoretical evolution. Moreover, much French "theory" in the 1960s and 1970s was rooted in disciplines such as anthropology, linguistics, and history, even if many of the ideas therein were most successfully introduced into U.S. contexts through philosophy or literary criticism (Dosse 1997).[21]

I do wish to caution, however, against an all-too-common and oversimplified attribution of many ideas, including social construction of sexuality, to a short list of French thinkers or to a sudden revelatory flash circa 1978.

Most component parts that led to social construction and then to queer theory had been in circulation for decades and across a broad range of disciplines, although much of that history appears to be forgotten or seems to be remembered by only a few sociologists. It is interesting in this regard to peruse the citations and index entries of two more recent books on queer theory, Annamarie Jagose's *Queer Theory: An Introduction* (1996) and William Turner's *A Genealogy of Queer Theory* (2000).

Both volumes give accounts of the origins, sources, and development of queer theory, although Turner's is more explicitly historical and more conversant with the role of gay history in the evolution of the queer theory conceptual apparatus. Jeffrey Weeks is cited and discussed in both books, although Foucault receives more attention. The entries for Weeks in Turner's index fit on one line, whereas the entries for Foucault take up almost an entire page. The bibliographies of both books include Kenneth Plummer and Mary McIntosh, although Plummer is not discussed in the text and there is only a single brief mention of McIntosh (Turner 2000:66). The names of John Gagnon and William Simon do not appear in either bibliography, nor do any of the other authors in *Sexual Deviance.* It seems that the acknowledged debt of Weeks and Plummer to McIntosh has ensured her inclusion in lineages of queer theory, but then the trail goes completely cold. The entire sociological tradition in which her own work can be situated is absent.[22]

Turner comments that "Foucault acquired an unearned reputation as the originator of 'work on the social construction of sex' because *The History of Sexuality* had the effect of helping to legitimate the historical study of sex" (63). I tend to agree with that assessment. Foucault's legitimating effect stemmed not only from the undoubted quality of his work but also from his reputation as a major thinker and the fact that in the mid- to late 1970s his homosexuality was little known in the United States. Concurrent developments within gay history were sexually stigmatized, intellectually segregated, and more readily ignored by mainstream academicians.

As Turner perceptively observes, "The similarities in the accounts of Weeks and Foucault stemmed from their coincident movement in the same direction, not from Weeks's following Foucault. The relationship among the writings of Weeks, Katz, and Foucault suggested epistemic change, the intellectual manifestation and perpetuation of social, political, and economic changes that produced similar results at disparate locations for disparate scholars" (67).[23] Many scholars were arriving independently at similar formulations within a short period around the mid-1970s, drawing on the available data and applying existing theoretical frameworks to sexuality. As Simon and Gagnon had done a decade earlier in sociology, the theoretical move of "social construction" was to treat sexuality as ordinary and assume it could be productively addressed using conventional tools, notably those of social history and cultural anthropology. A few short additional examples illustrate some of the preexisting work that made the emergence of "social construction of sexuality" theories not only possible but also highly likely. The question is not why so many people began to approach the study of sexuality in this way at that time but why they did not do so sooner and with less controversy. As Carole Vance observed, "The specialness of sex is highlighted by this comparison, since a quite ordinary and accepted insight about cultural construction in most areas of human life seems very difficult to understand without distortion when applied to sexuality" (1989a:17).

The arguments between social constructionism and essentialism vis-à-vis sexuality are conceptually similar to those in economic anthropology between substantivism and formalism. As Polanyi noted in the 1950s, economic formalism presumed a consistent type of economic actor who could be found in all human societies, a universal set of economic motivations always shaping economic behavior, and an economic domain that in all cases acted upon the societies in which it was located. "Approaching the economy in any of its widely varied aspects, the social scientist is still hampered by an intellectual heritage of man as an entity with an innate propensity to truck, barter and exchange one thing for another. This remains so in spite of all the protestations against 'economic man' and the intermittent attempts to provide a social framework for the economy" (Polanyi, Arensberg, and Pearson 1970 [1957]:239).

Polanyi observed that such assumptions about economic action were instead a specific product of a particular social form: "This view of the economy . . . grew out of the Western milieu of the eighteenth century and it is admittedly relevant under the institutional arrangements of the market system, since actual conditions here roughly satisfy the requirements set by the economistic postulate. But does this postulate allow us to infer the generality of a market system in the realm of empirical fact? The claim of formal economics to an historically universal applicability answers in the affirmative" (240).

Polanyi argued the negative. He proposed instead that economic motivations were a product of social institutions and varied accordingly. Moreover, economies are what he famously called "instituted processes," that is, human economies are "embedded and enmeshed in institutions, economic and noneconomic. . . . The study of the shifting place occupied by the economy in society is therefore no other than the study of the manner in which the economic process is instituted at different times and places" (250; see also Sahlins 1972). The decentering of "economic man" and the insistence on economic motivations as structurally produced and specific to the societies in which they are located is conceptually similar to the subsequent process of thinking about how sexuality is socially structured, institutionally shaped, and widely variable. If the psychology of economic decision making was not universal, why not the psychologies of desire? If "the economy" is an instituted process, why not sexuality?

Marxist-inflected British social history was also influential in shaping ways of thinking that were applied first to gender and then to sexuality. E. P. Thompson, in the preface to *The Making of the English Working Class,* comments:

> This book has a clumsy title, but it is one which meets its purpose. *Making,* because it is a study in an active process, which owes as much to agency as to conditioning. The working class did not rise like the sun at an appointed time. It was present at its own making. *Class,* rather than classes. . . . By class I understand an historical phenomenon, unifying a number of disparate and seemingly unconnected events, both in the raw material of experience and in consciousness. I emphasize that it is an *historical* phenomenon. I do not see class as a "structure," nor even as a "category," but as something which in fact happens . . . in human relationships. (1963:9)

Thompson's insistence on class as a historically constructed formation rather than a universal classification and his emphasis on the produced quality of what appear to be unvarying human experiences prefigure subsequent approaches to gender and sexuality. A superb example is his essay on "Time, Work-Discipline, and Industrial Capitalism," which was first published in 1967. There, Thompson "deconstructed" the modern experience of time and showed the ways in which the requirements and accomplishments of industrialization profoundly reshaped something as timeless as time (1993 [1967]).[24]

By the early 1970s, feminist anthropologists and historians were among those actively dismantling the prevailing notions of gender along similar lines, and a tendency to extend such analyses to sexuality was immanent in much of this material.[25] One example is the work of Judith Walkowitz on the social history of Victorian prostitution. In her work, prostitution is no longer an unchanging and universal vice, the "oldest profession," but rather a shifting institutional complex. An entire chapter of *Prostitution and Victorian Society* is devoted to "The Making of an Outcast Group: Prostitutes and Working Women in Plymouth and Southampton" (192–213).[26] The emphasis is on changing social formations and on their produced quality.

These examples could be readily multiplied. Throughout the 1970s a number of works created a new theoretical paradigm by applying, with increasing consistency and effectiveness, the ordinary tools of history, anthropology, and sociology to sexualities. By the summer of 1979, the *Radical History Review* put out a special issue on "Sexuality in History" that included two theoretical essays articulating the emergent "social construction" perspective: Bert Hansen's "The Historical Construction of Homosexuality" and Robert Padgug's "Sexual Matters: On Conceptualizing Sexuality in History" (Hansen 1979; Padgug 1979).[27] As Carole Vance observed, "Social construction theory in the field of sexuality proposed an extremely outrageous idea. It suggested that one of the last remaining outposts of the 'natural' in our thinking was fluid and changeable, the product of human action and history rather than the invariant result of the body, biology, or an innate sex drive" (Vance 1989a:13). Social construction work has refined the theoretical bases for social approaches to sexual behavior. Although it built upon developments in history, anthropology, and sociology, social construction insisted on more thoroughly social approaches than its predecessors.[28]

Since then, the new theoretical consolidation has inspired a vast outpouring of work that has continuously destabilized universal sexual categories and increasingly placed sexualities into history, society, and culture.[29] Yet it is important to remember that such perspectives were grounded in older literatures and have grounded in turn a newer body of work that includes what is now called queer theory.

From Sociology to Anthropology

Anthropologists have ignored homosexuality in Western societies, and, what is worse, have barely taken note of it as it manifests itself in primitive groups. . . . Ford and Beach (1951) could only generally distill from anthropologists' reports societies which simply (1) have homosexuality present or not (as ethnographers saw it) and (2) have condoned or condemned it. Such has been the Science of Man's attention to a most obvious aspect of human behavior. (Sonenschein 1966:75)

When John Gagnon and William Simon were at Indiana University in the 1960s, they hired David Sonenschein, a graduate student in the anthropology department, to conduct a study on the gay male community in Chicago. Sonenschein wrote the earliest articles from within anthropology that pointed to the need to do research on contemporary homosexual populations in industrialized countries. His essay on "Homosexuality as a Subject of Anthropologic Inquiry," written in 1966, is a remarkably prescient document. It reviewed the state of anthropological research on the subject, sketched a program for future work, and summarized many of the repetitive themes and problems that have bedeviled ethnographic work in this area.

Like virtually all social scientists who ventured into the area of sex before the early 1970s, Sonenschein had to confront the hegemonic models:

> Rather than to establish a claim of validity or rationale that would enable an anthropologist to professionally approach the subject of homosexuality (or to make him feel more comfortable in doing so), this paper is presented more as a simple plea for research and as a departure point for discussion. . . . Quite obviously, homosexuality has traditionally and predominantly been considered as a research problem for psychology. . . . The three main considerations in dealing with homosexuality by psychologists have been (1) its origin or cause (2) its ongoing operation, and (3) its treatment and ultimate cure. All research has assumed the locus of the individual as the basic, final, and exclusive unit of study. (Sonenschein 1966:73)

Sonenschein went on to observe the existence of the small but important sociological literature that had appeared by the mid-1960s and would be anthologized in *Sexual Deviance,* the first of the Simon and Gagnon collections, published the year after Sonenschein's essay:

> Stemming from recent attention to delinquency and the development of a sociology of delinquent behavior, various writers have had occasion to use, for example, theories relating to reference group behavior and to consider homosexuals as forming a minority group. . . . With these newer considerations, later writings have assumed a somewhat greater depth and broadness of scope. . . . The dynamics of social roles and interactions within and among homosexual communities provide excellent opportunities for the applications of small group . . . methods. (75)

Sonenschein pointed to the relative neglect of the subject within anthropology. In reviewing the limited literature available on the subject, he noted behaviors in non-Western cultures that were "homosexual-like" or "would appear in our society as homosexual tendencies," but he stopped short of describing shamans or berdache as homosexuals. He distinguished between homosexual behavior and cross-gender practices, a distinction that is still all too often neglected.

Sonenschein noted that "homosexuality emerges as being in reality a group phenomenon as well as an individual one" (76) and called for "the application of an anthropological investigation of homosexuality in contemporary Western society" (77):

> [T]he anthropological approach assumes that homosexual groups and individuals transmit, learn, share, create, and change the content of various forms (such as speech, dress, behavior, artifacts) so as to establish and maintain what can be called a relatively distinct "culture." . . . Here, all the interests of cultural and social anthropologists would prevail: social organization, economics, communication, social control and norms, world-views and myths, demography, social and cultural change, material culture, enculturation and socialization. (76–77)

Sonenschein concluded with the observation that most previous data on homosexuals were based on a population of *patients,* some in therapy by court order, and that anthropological research would result in a different perspective on homosexuality. He advised attention to homosexual subcultures. "Among humans," he noted, "at least in the Western Urban tradition, homosexual behavior manifests itself in special kinds of culturally distinct groups and artifacts" (80).

Virtually all the major points in this essay with regard to homosexuality can be applied to many other forms of contemporary erotic diversity. During the 1960s Sonenschein had set out a research program for the anthropological study of homosexuality and, by extension, other sexual populations in modern, Western, urban societies. With one equally extraordinary exception—Esther Newton's *Mother Camp*—it would take quite a while for Sonenschein's insights to have an impact on the field of anthropology.

Mother Camp

It should be noted that by "women" I mean the signs and symbols, some obvious and some subtle, of the socially defined category in American Culture. On the cross-cultural level, it is obvious that female impersonators look like American "women," not like Hopi "women" or Chinese peasant "women." What is not so obvious is the relationship *within* American culture between biology, concepts of biology ("nature"), and sex-role symbols. It seems self-evident that persons classified as "men" would have to create artificially the image of a "woman," but of course "women" create the image "artificially" too.

> On the one hand there is the "gentleman deviant." . . . At this pole we find the "masculine," and "respectable" homosexuals, the leaders of most homophile organizations and so on. At the opposite pole there are the persons who most visibly and flagrantly embody the stigma, "drag queens," men who dress and act "like women." Professional drag queens are, therefore, professional homosexuals; they represent the stigma of the gay world. Not surprisingly, as professional homosexuals, drag queens find their occupation to be a source of dishonor, especially in the relation to the straight world. Their situation in the gay world is more complex. The clever drag queen possesses skills that are widely distributed and prized in the gay world: verbal facility and wit, a sense of "camp" (homosexual humor and taste). . . . In exclusively gay settings such as bars and parties, drag queens may be almost lionized. (Newton 1972:3, 5)

In the early 1970s, only two anthropologists—Sonenschein and Esther Newton—could be found among the slightly more numerous sociologists producing ethnographic work on gay populations. Newton's 1972 *Mother Camp,* a monograph on female impersonators, was the first book-length ethnography of a modern, Western, urban gay population. *Mother Camp* focuses on the more specialized subgroup of professional female impersonators, but Newton's observations of gay community life, social structure, and economics were insightful, original, and provocative.

Mother Camp was based on Newton's 1968 dissertation for the department of anthropology at the University of Chicago, where her advisor was David Schneider. Newton was fortunate to be at Chicago and especially to work with Schneider. She has recalled the extraordinary and unusual quality of Schneider's support for graduate students with then-unconventional demographics:

> [Schneider was] a blessing for those of his students like me who were marginal and offbeat, for in addition to the white males whom everyone thought would succeed, Schneider was attracted to students like closet gays and struggling women who could not easily attract the support of the powerful. I well recall when Schneider reported to me on the year-end departmental review of my progress; the professors relayed to me through Schneider that my wearing pants manifested a lack of commitment to the anthropological vocation. . . . In the Schneiders' living room, by contrast, I was told that wearing dresses was neither here nor there on the ultimate scale of value. (Newton 2000:217)

Schneider was also supportive of unconventional research topics:

> When I showed David some field notes and my excitement, he encouraged me to make female impersonators the subject of my doctoral dissertation. . . . He helped me to develop the intellectual tools to do the work, and just as important, he was prepared to back me up with his departmental clout. . . . Gays were then looked on within social science as the object solely of psychological, medical, or even criminological study. . . . What he [Schneider] imparted to me, more in his office and his home than in the classroom, was that female impersonators (about whom he knew nothing more than what I told him) were a group of human beings and so necessarily had a culture worth studying. The insight that gays were not just a category of sick isolates, but a group, and so had a culture, was a breathtaking leap whose daring is hard to recapture now. (Newton 2000:216)

Newton noted in her discussion of field methods in *Mother Camp* that there was "to date no full ethnography of the homosexual community, much less the drag world, so that from the beginning I was 'flying blind.' Moreover, very few ethnographies (except for the early community studies) have been attempted in America, so that my model of field work procedure was largely based on non-urban precedents" (1972:132). When Newton began to discuss her work with Schneider, however, he directed her to the literature in the sociology of deviance dealing with sexuality (Newton, personal communication). There was little anthropological literature upon which to draw, but Newton cited and productively used the ethnographic work of Hooker and Sonenschein, the perspective on stigma of Goffman, the sex research of Kinsey, the general theoretical orientation of Simon and Gagnon, the economic observations of Leznoff and Westley, and the notion of a "deviant career" developed with such thoroughness by Becker and others. If there was little help in anthropology, there was a great deal in the extant sociology of "deviance."

Mother Camp is a deceptively straightforward book whose sophistication and subtlety becomes more remarkable with each reading. It is laden with astute observations about the social organization of gay life in the 1960s, the social and physical architecture of gay performance, and the internal stylistic and sexual differentiation of gay populations as well as specific theatrical techniques of professional female impersonation. But *Mother Camp* is most profoundly effective in three areas. It prefigures notions of gender as "performed"; provides an analysis of the political economies of homosexuality in the 1960s; and links types of performance to economic stratification, political orientation, and hierarchies of social status.

Newton's work focused on a small group of female impersonators who were paid, worked onstage and in theaters, and considered themselves to be entertainment professionals. Thus there was always a performance aspect to their drag. Newton broadened this notion of gender performance by observing that all drag, "whether formal, informal, or professional, has a theatrical structure and style" (37). This distinguishing characteristic of drag, she argued, was its "group character." The performance of gender required an audience. Moreover, she saw how the gender reversal of drag "questions the 'naturalness' of the sex-role system *in toto;* if sex-role behavior can be achieved by the 'wrong' sex, it logically follows that it is in reality also achieved, not inherited, by the 'right' sex" (103). Moreover, "drag implies that sex role, and by extension, role in general is something superficial, which can be manipulated" (109).

It is fascinating that Newton used stage performance to make points about ordinary activities that anticipate the more refined formulations in contemporary work on gender, particularly that of Judith Butler. Butler uses more philosophically developed notions of performativity, drawn in part from speech-act theory, and takes gender analysis to new levels of precision. But she cites Newton's *Mother Camp* and also uses drag and gender inversion to make points about the way gender is interactively produced (Butler 1990, 1993; see especially 1990:136–37).

Although Butler's work has facilitated a contemporary reevaluation of Newton's early articulations of the relationships of gender to drag and performance, *Mother Camp*'s contributions to the political economies of sexualities have been largely ignored. Newton built on the observations of Leznoff and Westley to take exploration of the relationships between sexual disclosure and economic position to new levels of intricacy. She elaborated on the distinction between secret and overt homosexuals, but used the slightly modified terminology of "overt" and "covert":

> The overts live their *entire* lives within the context of the [gay] community; the coverts lives their entire *nonworking* lives within it. That is, the coverts are "straight" during working hours, but most social activities are conducted with and with reference to other homosexuals. . . . Overt-covert distinctions correlate to some extent with social class, but by no means invariably. . . . Covert means only that one cannot be publicly identified by the straight world and its representatives, such as bosses, co-workers, family, landladies, teachers, and the man on the street. One hides, or attempts to hide, one's homosexual identity *from straight people.* In Goffman's terminology,

one attempts to manage one's discreditability through control of personal front and restriction about one's personal life. (Newton 1972:21–22).

At the time of Newton's study in the late 1960s, gay communities in North America were less economically developed and institutionally differentiated than they would become in the 1970s. Thus she observed that the gay community "has an economics but no economy. Strictly speaking, the gay world has no class system. Nevertheless, gay life has recognizable social strata that are accorded differential value. People speak about 'high-class,' 'middle-class,' and 'low-class' bars, parties, clothes and people" (28). And the category of "low-class" was not a purely economic designation; rather, "low-status homosexuals who [were] socially avoided and morally despised by the middles and uppers" were often those who, "in their flamboyant stylization and distinctive adaptations to extreme alienation" (29), were extremely overt in self-presentation. There was a set of assumed relationships between class, stigma, and overtness and a resulting set of mechanisms intended to create boundaries and manage the dangers of proximity to economic or social ruin.

All these vectors intersect in the large status difference between two kinds of drag performers: professional impersonators on the one hand and "street fairies" on the other. "Street fairies are jobless young homosexual men who publicly epitomize the homosexual stereotype and are the underclass of the gay world. . . . The stage pattern, on the other hand, *segregates* the stigma from the personal by limiting it to the stage context as much as possible. The work is viewed as a profession with goals and standards" (Newton 1972:8). Female impersonators were, in effect, "professional homosexuals" who could make a living from overt expression of stigmatized identities. On the one hand, they represented the stigma of homosexuality; on the other, they were public figures celebrated for their glamour and occupied a relatively high-status position among those performing drag.

Professional performers looked down on street fairies and attempted to maintain social distance from them. Street drag was "tacky," meaning "cheap, shoddy, or of poor quality. . . . 'Tacky' is a pejorative term. No single word was used more consistently by the older, more show-business oriented performers to describe the appearance of lower-status street oriented performers. . . . 'Tacky' is thus indirectly a class descriptive term" (Newton 1972:49).

Such disapproval of obvious expressions of stigmatized and discrediting homosexuality was situational and mobile:

This may be viewed as a hierarchy of stigmatization, or "obviousness." Any particular group will tend to draw the line just below itself. For instance, female impersonators are considered by most homosexuals to be too overt. They are consistently placed on the low end of the continuum of stigmatization, and one of the first things that female impersonators must learn is not to recognize anyone on the street or in any other public place unless they are recognized first. Yet female impersonators who believe themselves to be less overt try to avoid public association with female impersonators whom they consider "too obvious," and very few female impersonators will associate publicly with "street fairies," boys who wear make up on the street, because "there's no point in wearing a sign. I believe I can pass." Those on the low end resent those above them. (Newton 1972:25).

The marginal conditions of the pre-Stonewall gay economy made the maintenance of a high-status performing career somewhat perilous. The performance venues themselves were stratified. At the low end was the gay bar, always vulnerable to the police. "Any gay bar is living on borrowed time, and neither the owners nor clientele can count on permanence. Therefore, gay bars operate by and large on a quick-money policy. This is most extreme where police pressure is most intense and less pronounced where owners can count on some degree of stability. But quick-money policy means that owners invest little in plant, keep overhead and operating expenses low, and try to reap quick profits" (Newton 1972:115). As a result, the bars tended to be small facilities in poor condition, the salaries for performers low, and "job tenure [was] nil" because the "bar could be closed at any time" (116).

Higher up on the scale of status, facility, and compensation was the "tourist club," where a mostly straight clientele comes to see "exotic" entertainment. Such clubs have a larger base of customers and are subject to far less punitive police attention:

[They] are stable institutions by gay bar standards. The stability . . . allows the tourist bar to be at least three times the size of the average gay bar. Not only is the stage larger to accommodate a larger and more lavish show, but the floor space is larger to pack in more people. . . . From the point of view of the performer, working in a tourist club means working in a bigger and more elaborate show. . . . In terms of physical amenities (dressing room), stage facilities (lighting, curtains, band), and actual time spent on stage, the show at the tourist club is probably easier on the performers. However, performers in a tourist club are freaks or clowns up for display to a hostile audience. (Newton 1972:118)

Thus tourist bars offer greater compensation and conditions of work at the cost of potentially damaged self-esteem.

The social marginality and scarcity of job sites for impersonators meant that even higher-status performers often lived precariously close to disaster. "The manager is the man the impersonators most fear," Newton observes, "for he has a great deal of control over them, ultimately hiring and firing. The impersonators have no way to fight back; no way to appeal. . . . None of the performers worked under contract, so that they could be (and were) fired at a moment's notice. No one knew when the ax might fall. Requirements for job holding were nowhere formalized or even made explicit, although performers knew that seriously antagonizing the manager in any way could mean dismissal" (123–24). As a result, the actual line of demarcation between the more respectable and prosperous impersonators and the more disreputable and impoverished street fairies was perilously thin. Many professionals had been street fairies before becoming impersonators, and "if they lost their jobs or quit, they had no place to go but back to the street. When stage impersonators talked about quitting, they said they wanted to 'go legit.' But when I asked a street performer what drag queens do when they are out of work, he said, 'They get their butts out on the street, my dear, and they sell their little twats for whatever they can get for them'" (10). The actual economic instability and permeable boundaries contrast with the carefully cultivated symbolic differentiation between stage and street.

Newton's descriptive richness and analytic elegance wove together and elaborated on many of the themes of the work that preceded her own. These include Park's observations on the importance of cities for sexual subcultures, Hooker and Achilles' emphasis on the social centrality of bars to gay communities and the role of the police in setting the parameters of homosexual social institutions, and the political economies of the closet and sexual disclosure first articulated by Leznoff and Westley. Newton explores in much more luxuriant detail the complex internal differentiation of gay populations noted by previous observers. She productively expands on Goffman and Becker's dismemberment of the moral hierarchies of deviance, Simon and Gagnon's appropriation of the study of sexuality into the disciplinary reach of the social sciences, and the prefiguring of social construction theories implicit in Simon, Gagnon, and Reiss. *Mother Camp* cites Becker, Goffman, Hooker, Gagnon, Simon, Sonenschein, Leznoff, and Westley. Newton skillfully brought their tools and tactical moves to bear in what is ultimately a masterful synthesis linking gender, class, stigma, self-presentation, and the political economies of marginal sexualities in the period before Stonewall.

Newton's work is situated within a long sociological tradition and stands at the beginning of a newer lineage of anthropologists. Although *Mother Camp* should have signaled a new wave of work on homosexuality within anthropology, it was instead largely ignored and followed by thundering silence and a painfully long hiatus. For many years *Mother Camp* stood alone, an exceptional document with no apparent successors or company. Not until almost a decade later did more anthropological work on modern homosexualities begin to emerge. It would be almost two decades before there was much anthropological literature on urban gay communities in the United States.[30]

In 1979 Deborah Goleman Wolf's study of *The Lesbian Community* was published. The same year, Stephen Murray's important essay on homosexuals as "quasi-ethnic" communities was published, albeit in a journal of sociology. In 1980 Kenneth Read's *Other Voices: The Style of a Male Homosexual Tavern* appeared. A great deal of important work was published during the 1980s, for example, Blackwood's edited collection *The Many Faces of Homosexuality* (1986) and a burgeoning literature on AIDS. Gilbert Herdt's *Guardians of the Flutes* (1981) was a milestone in the anthropology of homosexual practice, although it was not about a modern urban population.

It was only in the 1990s, however, almost two decades after the publication of *Mother Camp,* that a substantial literature began to accumulate. Just how sudden that shift was can be seen by two articles in the *Annual Review of Anthropology.* In 1987 a review essay on "The Cross Cultural Study of Human Sexuality" could still comment that "the most glaring omission in professional research on sexual practice is certainly in the area of homosexuality. Although early attempts were made to describe same sex patterns of arousal and attraction, this topic quickly went 'underground' and is only today receiving the serious attention it deserves" (Davis and Whitten 1987:71). By 1993, the growth of lesbian and gay research within anthropology was so dramatic that the journal included Kath Weston's review essay on the subject, a mere six years after the 1987 review complained about the paucity of such material.

Publications since 1990 would include Weston's *Families We Choose: Lesbians, Gays, Kinship* (1991) and Herdt's edited collection *Gay Culture in America* (1992). Three landmark studies by anthropologists were finally published in 1993 after many years of anticipation: *Boots of Leather, Slippers of Gold: The History of a Lesbian Community* (in Buffalo) by Elizabeth Kennedy and Madeline Davis, *Lesbian Mothers* by Ellen Lewin, and

Esther Newton's study of *Cherry Grove, Fire Island.* Since 1993, an expo-
nential increase has occurred in the number of publications, resulting in a
rich and substantial ethnographic literature on gay, lesbian, bisexual, transgender, and other erotically demarcated populations.

Legacies and Lessons

My work is deeply indebted to scholars such as Esther Newton, John
Gagnon, and William Simon. They allowed me to contemplate doing ethnographic work on sexual communities in urban North America at a time
when such projects were outside the accepted parameters of anthropological research. The corpus of ideas they conveyed had sources I did not know
but provided intellectual frameworks for thinking as a social scientist about
marginal and stigmatized erotic populations. When I finally did encounter
Robert Park and Howard Becker, for example, they were shockingly familiar because their fingerprints were all over other texts I had read.

My research on urban gay communities has given me an ever-greater appreciation of older ethnographic texts, and I continue to be impressed by their
conceptual sophistication and descriptive richness. The importance of bars
to gay and lesbian social life in the mid-twentieth century may not seem at
first glance very interesting or exciting. Gay bars are so familiar that it is easy
to forget that bars in the modern sense did not really exist in the United States
until after the repeal of Prohibition, when taverns and cafes were restruc-
tured as licensed premises; that liquor license regulations have powerfully
shaped urban social practice; and that the escalating price of urban real es-
tate and increasing availability of Internet-based contact may be undermining the viability and centrality of bars as gay social institutions. Gay bars
may be vanishing or at least eclipsed institutions, but they have been as characteristic of mid-twentieth-century homosexuality as were Big Men to political systems of highland New Guinea or large-scale trading circuits to the
indigenous people of the South Pacific. Knowing this about gay bars, and
thinking about their shifting significance, is not as trivial as it may first appear. Similarly, the complicated intersections of class, race, social status,
income, sexual orientation, gender identity, job segregation, and stylistic
expression beg for further exploration.

Because the idioms of previous decades may seem dated, their theoretical subtlety and originality is often underestimated. Many ideas articulated

in these texts continue to resonate in contemporary scholarship, however, even when their sources are obscured. The work of these authors permeates social construction paradigms and helped to assemble them. This literature has been key in wresting intellectual authority over sexuality from its monopolization by medicine and psychiatry, firmly establishing the intellectual (if not institutional) claims of social science in the field of sexual studies. Finally, in both theoretical innovations and ethnographic contributions, the texts discussed here have been major forces in displacing "perversion" models of sexual variation, which presume pathology, with "diversity" models, which imply moral equality and leveled legitimacy.

It is common to mistake the place where we first encounter a theoretical revelation as its original manifestation and to confuse one's own intellectual biography with some more public sequence of events. In this essay, I hope that I am not inadvertently making the same error and confusing my paths of discovery with a general history. I certainly do not want to be proposing some new, oversimplified tale of origin for those I have criticized. Nonetheless, much of what we now take for granted in the anthropology of sexuality and homosexuality owes a great deal to an odd assortment of urban sociologists, historians of homosexuality, and brave, pioneering ethnographers who went where almost no one had gone before and undertook considerable risks to their careers to do so. There is a great deal to learn from looking back and seeing how much they did. If their contributions have been so readily forgotten, this is less a commentary on the work itself than on the extraordinary limitations of the intellectual and institutional circumstances in which they operated.

Notes

Although this essay is rooted in the literature chapter of my dissertation (Rubin 1994), I have delivered several versions as lectures. These include papers at the 1996 annual meeting of the American Anthropological Association and the 1998 annual meeting of the American Sociological Association and invited lectures at the University of California, Los Angeles (1997), California State University at Northridge (1997), and the University of Missouri, St. Louis (1995).

I am indebted to many individuals who have contributed to this essay and the ideas behind it. Conversations with Jeffrey Escoffier, John Gagnon, the late William Simon, Barrie Thorne, Howard Becker, and Esther Newton have been particularly informative about the context of social research at the University of Chicago and its importance to contemporary studies of sexuality. Barrie Thorne directed me to some helpful articles and provided me with copies. My editors, Ellen Lewin and William

Leap, have exhibited patience and encouragement beyond the call of duty. Mitchell Duneier, Jeffrey Escoffier, John Gagnon, Esther Newton, PJ McGann, and Carole Vance all read earlier drafts, and I am deeply grateful for their suggestions and comments. Jay Marston has been a constant source of support and inspiration. The writing of this essay was assisted by a fellowship from the Sexuality Research Fellowship Program of the Social Science Research Council with funds provided by the Ford Foundation.

1. Jagose (1996) and Turner (2000) both provide excellent overviews of queer theory, although neither discusses most of the literature discussed below.

2. Since this essay was originally drafted, several publications have appeared that address some of these same issues. See, for example, Epstein (1996); Stein and Plummer (1996); Gagnon (1999); Nardi and Schneider, eds. (1998a, 1998b); Rubin (1995); Schneider and Nardi, eds. (1999); Simon (1999); Weeks (1998); and Weston (1998).

3. The original essay appeared in journal form in 1915.

4. For New Guinea and Oceania, see, for example, Herdt (1981, 1984); Kelly (1976); and Williams (1936). For North America, see, for example, Brown (1997); Devereaux (1937); Jacobs, Thomas, and Lang, eds. (1997); McMurtrie (1914); Roscoe (1991); Whitehead (1981); and Williams (1986). See also Evans-Pritchard (1970) and Herskovitz (1937).

5. I do not mean to underestimate the enormity of the contributions of Kinsey and Hooker, both of whom deserve a much more extensive treatment beyond the scope of this essay. Many others have of course written on Kinsey's impact, with Paul Robinson's analysis (1976) among the most insightful. In 1998 the first issue of the journal *Sexualities* devoted a special section to a symposium on the fiftieth anniversary of the publication of the first Kinsey report (Nardi and Schneider, eds. 1998b). One of the best overviews of Hooker's impact is *Changing Our Minds: The Story of Dr. Evelyn Hooker* (1991), a documentary film directed by Richard Schmiechen. Most of Hooker's work was in article form, and it is unfortunate that these have so far not been assembled and published as a collection.

6. Detailed studies of various aspects of the sexual politics of the period can be found in Brandt (1985); Connelly (1980); D'Emilio and Freedman, eds. (1988); Langum (1994); Odem (1995); and Peiss (1986). For white slavery, see especially Connelly and Langum.

7. Chauncey's entire note on sources (366–70) provides a useful overview of such material, particularly for New York.

8. "The Mann Act," Langum comments, "resulted in the Bureau's first major field office, in Baltimore, and a dramatic increase in manpower. . . . the Mann Act provided the real takeoff for the FBI. One historian of the FBI wrote that 'the enforcement of the Mann Act began the transformation of the Justice Department's police bureau from a modest agency concerned with odds and ends of Federal law enforcement to a nationally recognized institution, with agents in every State and every large city'" (1994:49).

9. Other famous targets of Mann Act prosecution included Jack Johnson, Chuck Berry, and Charlie Chaplin (Langum 1994).

10. Barrie Thorne (in a personal communication) has conveyed something of this tradition in noting its "unshockability," which allowed for virtually anything to be studied, no matter how disreputable the topic or population. This unshockability opened research vistas that criteria of respectability would have made inaccessible.

11. Becker points out the difficulty in assigning such shifts in intellectual frameworks to any individual. "I wasn't the only one interested in saying things about deviance. Kai Erikson (1962) had been saying the same thing. John Kitsuse (1962) was saying the same things. Lemert had said it years before. There were a number of people whose ideas were in the air. Probably what I did was to make a very clear and simple statement as to what it was about. At least I think it's a clear and simple statement" (Becker with Debro [1970] in Becker 1986:33). Although I think Becker is unduly modest (and characteristically generous), most such conceptual innovations do have complex genealogies and multiple origins. I risk in this essay an unintended oversimplification, particularly as I am trained in neither sociology nor intellectual history. Nonetheless, the writings of Becker (and Goffman) seem to have been particularly effective in communicating this body of ideas. My larger point is that there was an intellectual culture whose tendencies were absorbed and creatively applied by a number of thinkers and which ultimately had an impact on reevaluating homosexuality.

Chapoulie credits much of that culture to Everett Hughes: "More than a dozen years after his death in 1983, Everett C. Hughes is generally recognized as one of the links between the founders of 'The Chicago School'—W. I. Thomas and Robert E. Park, to whom we might add Ernest W. Burgess and the philosopher George Herbert Mead—and the group of sociologists trained at the University of Chicago in the 1940s and 1950s, who are often labeled collectively as symbolic interactionists. This group, notable for its studies of institutions, work and the professions, art, deviance, and medicine, includes such researchers as Erving Goffman, Howard S. Becker, Anselm Strauss, and Eliot Freidson, who have also contributed to making fieldwork—the ethnographic method—one of the most fruitful research approaches in the social sciences" (1996:3). Chapoulie also notes that by the end of the 1950s, the ethnographic approach had become unpopular at Chicago, resulting in the departures of Hughes and many of his students (19). See also Reinharz (1995).

Chapoulie also notes the importance of journals such as *Social Problems* and *Urban Life and Culture,* which were associated with this group of scholars and published extremely important work in the sociology of sexuality during the 1960s and 1970s. I leave fuller exploration of the role of these individuals and journals to those more qualified to produce histories of sociological work. My point here is to help ensure greater appreciation of their contributions by anthropologists, queer theorists, and others whose training may not have provided exposure to this material. See also Becker (1964).

12. The phrase *moral leveling* is indebted to Paul Robinson, who uses the phrase *sexual leveling* in his discussion of Kinsey (1976:58–59).

13. It is notable that *Sexual Conduct* was published in the Observations series edited by Howard Becker for Aldine.

14. Of relevance to my research on gay male leather communities (but not to this particular essay) is the fact that Hooker was aware of a particular "motorcycle crowd, or leather set" that resisted stereotypical gay "effeminacy" (1967 [1961]:182).

15. Stephen Murray makes similar points. He notes that "insofar as 'community' is a technical term in the social sciences and insofar as there can be said to be 'communities' in North American cities, there are 'gay communities'" (1979:165).

16. Some of these theoretical strategies in turn are rooted in Kinsey, Pomeroy, and Martin's *Sexual Behavior in the Human Male,* published in 1948, and in which the distinction between sexual acts and named sexual identities was widely used. Kinsey's role was critical and should not be underestimated, although his contributions lie outside the main line of argument in this particular essay. His work, however, clearly had an impact on the sociologists discussed here.

17. Posts to Queer Studies List <QSTUDY-L@UBVM.cc.buffalo.edu>, July 28–29, 1994. The first post was from Michael J. Sweet, the second from Gayle Rubin, and the subsequent response from Sweet.

18. Some of Kinsey's many insightful comments are worth remembering: "Concerning patterns of sexual behavior, a great deal of the thinking done by scientists and laymen alike stems from the assumption that there are persons who are 'heterosexual' and persons who are 'homosexual,' that these two types represent antitheses in the sexual world, and that there is only an insignificant class of 'bisexuals' who occupy the intermediate position between the other groups. It is implied that every individual is innately—inherently—either heterosexual or homosexual. It is further implied that from the time of birth one is fated to be one thing or the other, and that there is little chance for one to change his pattern in the course of a lifetime" (1948:636–37). Moreover, "Males do not represent two discrete populations, heterosexual and homosexual. The world is not divided into sheep and goats. Not all things are black nor all things white. It is a fundamental of taxonomy that nature rarely deals with discrete categories. Only the human mind invents categories and tries to force facts into separated pigeon-holes. The living world is a continuum in each and every one of its aspects. The sooner we learn this concerning human sexual behavior the sooner we shall reach a sound understanding of the realities of sex" (639).

19. For less abbreviated versions of this history of the development of social construction theory, see Vance (1989a, 1991) and Escoffier (1990, 1992).

20. A very small example can be seen in Althusser and Balibar's *Reading Capital,* published in France in 1968 and in English translation in 1970. In it, Althusser proposes a concept he calls the *"differential forms of historical individuality"* (251, emphasis in the original). "We can say that each relatively autonomous practice thus engenders forms of historical individuality which are peculiar to it. . . . For each practice and for each transformation of that practice, they are the different forms of individuality which can be defined on the basis of its combination structure" (252). The production of subjectivity was a major concern of many French intellectuals

throughout the 1960s, and it is not a huge leap from the production of subjectivity in general to the production of sexual subjectivity in particular. See also Eribon (2001) and, more broadly, Dosse (1997, vols. 1 and 2).

21. In his preface to *The Order of Things,* Foucault commented: "This book first arose out of a passage in Borges, out of the laughter that shattered, as I read the passage, all the familiar landmarks of my thought—*our* thought, the thought that bears the stamp of our age and our geography—while breaking up all the ordered surfaces and all the places with which we are accustomed to tame the wild profusion of existing things. . . . This passage quotes a 'certain Chinese encyclopaedia' in which it is written that 'animals are divided into: (a) belonging to the Emperor, (b) embalmed, (c) tame, (d) sucking pigs, (e) sirens, (f) fabulous, (g) stray dogs, (h) included in the present classification, (i) frenzied, (j) innumerable, (k) drawn with a very fine camelhair brush, (l) *et cetera,* (m) having just broken the water pitcher, (n) that from a long way off look like flies.' In the wonderment of this taxonomy, the thing we apprehend in one great leap, the thing that, by means of the fable, is demonstrated as the exotic charm of another system of thought, is the limitation of our own" (1970:xv). This is a deeply anthropological moment, albeit generated by fiction rather than the equally startling details of ethnoclassification.

22. Although this essay addresses the amnesia in queer studies of its social science antecedents, it is also important to note a similar memory lapse within sociology with respect to its contributions to sex research. For example, in Gary Alan Fine's edited collection on post–World War II Chicago sociology, neither John Gagnon nor William Simon are mentioned at all. This absence is striking, given the significance of their work on human sexuality. Reiss and Westley are mentioned, but only in connection with work on criminology, deviance, and methodology. Their forays into the ethnographic study of homosexuals are not noted. This suggests that despite their critical perspectives on stigma, sociologists, too, are not immune to the undertow of sexual discreditization.

23. I have made a similar point (Rubin, with Butler 1995). I also concur with Turner: "The almost complete triumph of the social constructionist position, in turn, would contribute crucially to the conditions of possibility for queer theory, which assumes the radical historical variability of sexual identity categories" (2000:69).

24. I am grateful to Charles Tilly for bringing this wonderful essay to my attention.

25. A fuller discussion of the issue lies outside the scope of this essay, but feminism and various forms of Marxism were significant areas in which these larger epistemic shifts had been developing. See also Stein and Plummer (1996).

26. Judith and Daniel Walkowitz were making a similar argument as early as 1973.

27. This entire issue constitutes a watershed in scholarly journal publication. In addition to Padgug and Hansen, there are essays on families by E. P. Thompson and Ellen Ross, an article on lesbian history by Blanche Wiesen Cook, Ann Barr Snitow's essay on romance novels, a piece on sexual meanings and gay identities by Jeffrey Weeks, a critique of sociobiology in the context of the history of biological science by Donna Haraway, and several other distinguished contributions.

28. Vance (1991) contrasts social construction with some of the earlier anthropological literature on sexuality, which was less consistent in its application of social analysis and retained certain biomedical assumptions.

29. A small sample of the relevant work would include the following: Altman et al. (1989); Bérubé (1990, 1993, 1996); Chauncey (1982–83, 1994, 1995); D'Emilio (1983a, 1983b, 1989a, 1989b, 1992); D'Emilio and Freedman, eds. (1988); Duberman, Vicinus, and Chauncey, eds. (1989); Duggan (1993, 2000); Escoffier (1990, 1992, 1998); Foucault (1978); Freedman (1987); Halperin (1990); Halperin, Winkler, and Zeitlin, eds. (1990); Katz (1983, 1990, 1995); Kennedy and Davis (1993); Peiss, Simmons, and Padgug, eds. (1989); Plummer, ed. (1981, 1992); Rubin (1984); Snitow, Stansell, and Thompson, eds. (1983); Vance (ed. 1984, 1989a, 1989b, 1990a, 1990b, 1990c, 1990d, 1991); Vicinus (1982, 1992); Walkowitz (1980a, 1980b, 1982, 1992); Weeks (1977, 1981, 1985, 1991, 1998, 2000); and Winkler (1990).

30. Since 1970 sociologists have undertaken a number of important ethnographic and analytic projects. The first and most famous of these was Laud Humphreys's *Tearoom Trade: Impersonal Sex in Public Places* (1970). During the late 1970s, several books appeared almost simultaneously. Joseph Harry and William DeVall's *The Social Organization of Gay Men,* John Allan Lee's *Getting Sex,* and Barbara Ponse's *Identities in the Lesbian World* all appeared in 1978. The following year saw the publication of Martin Levine's wonderful anthology *Gay Men: The Sociology of Male Homosexuality.* Also published in 1978 was Bell and Weinberg's *Homosexualities.* Although that volume was mostly based on survey research, it included as an appendix, "Ethnography of the Bay Area Homosexual Scene." In 1983 Susan Kreiger's *The Mirror Dance* appeared.

References Cited

Achilles, Nancy. 1967. "The Development of the Homosexual Bar as an Institution." In *Sexual Deviance,* ed. John Gagnon and William Simon, 228–44. New York: Harper and Row.

Altman, Dennis, et al. 1989. *Homosexuality, which Homosexuality?* International Conference on Gay and Lesbian Studies, Amsterdam. London: GMP Publishers.

Althusser, Louis, and Etienne Balibar. 1970 (1968). *Reading Capital.* London: New Left Books.

American Psychiatric Association. 1952. *Diagnostic and Statistical Manual, Mental Disorders.* Washington, D.C.: American Psychiatric Association.

———. 1968. *Diagnostic and Statistical Manual of Mental Disorders.* 2d ed. Washington, D.C.: American Psychiatric Association.

———. 1980. *Diagnostic and Statistical Manual of Mental Disorders.* 3d ed. Washington, D.C.: American Psychiatric Association.

———. 1987. *Diagnostic and Statistical Manual of Mental Disorders.* 3d ed. rev. Washington, D.C.: American Psychiatric Association.

———. 1994. *Diagnostic and Statistical Manual of Mental Disorders.* 4th ed. Washington, D.C.: American Psychiatric Association.

Anderson, Nels. 1998 (1923). *On Hobos and Homelessness.* Chicago: University of Chicago Press.

Bayer, Ronald. 1981. *Homosexuality and American Psychiatry: The Politics of Diagnosis.* New York: Basic Books.

Becker, Howard S., ed. 1964. *The Other Side: Perspectives on Deviance.* New York: Free Press.

———. 1970 (1967). "Whose Side Are We On?" In Becker, *Sociological Work: Method and Substance.* New Brunswick: Transaction Books, pp. 123–134.

———. 1973. *Outsiders: Studies in the Sociology of Deviance.* New York: Free Press.

Becker, Howard S., with Julius Debro. 1986. "Dialogue with Howard S. Becker (1970): An Interview Conducted by Julius Debro." In *Doing Things Together: Selected Papers,* ed. Howard S. Becker, 25–46. Evanston: Northwestern University Press.

Bell, Alan P., and Martin S. Weinberg. 1978. *Homosexualities: A Study in Diversity among Men and Women.* New York: Simon and Schuster.

Berger, Peter, and Thomas Luckmann. 1967. *The Social Construction of Reality: A Treatise in the Sociology of Knowledge.* Garden City: Doubleday.

Bérubé, Allan. 1990. *Coming Out under Fire: The History of Gay Men and Women in World War Two.* New York: Free Press.

———. 1993. "'Dignity for All': The Role of Homosexuality in the Marine Cooks and Stewards Union (1930s-1950s)." Paper given at the "Reworking American Labor History: Race, Gender, and Class" conference, Madison, Wis.

———. 1996. "The History of the Bathhouses." In *Policing Public Sex: Queer Politics and the Future of AIDS Activism,* ed. Dangerous Bedfellows, 187–220. Boston: South End Press.

Blackwood, Evelyn, ed. 1986. *The Many Faces of Homosexuality: Anthropological Approaches to Homosexual Behavior.* New York: Harrington Park Press.

Blumer, Herbert. 1969. *Symbolic Interactionism: Perspective and Method.* Englewood Cliffs: Prentice-Hall.

Brandt, Allan M. 1985. *No Magic Bullet: A Social History of Venereal Disease in the United States since 1880.* New York: Oxford University Press.

Brown, Lester K. 1997. *Two Spirit People: American Indian Lesbian Women and Gay Men.* New York: Harrington Park Press.

Bulmer, Martin. 1984. *The Chicago School of Sociology.* Chicago: University of Chicago Press.

Butler, Judith. 1990. *Gender Trouble: Feminism and the Subversion of Identity.* New York: Routledge.

———. 1993. *Bodies That Matter: On the Discursive Limits of "Sex."* New York: Routledge.

Changing Our Minds: The Story of Dr. Evelyn Hooker. 1991. Documentary film directed by Richard Schmiechen. Frameline.

Chapoulie, Jean-Michel. 1996. "Everett Hughes and the Chicago Tradition." Trans. Howard S. Becker. *Sociological Theory* 14(1): 3–29.

Chauncey, George, Jr. 1982–83. "From Sexual Inversion to Homosexuality: Medicine and the Changing Conceptualization of Female Deviance." In *Homosexual-*

ity: Sacrilege, Vision, Politics, ed. Robert Boyers and George Steiner. Special issue of *Salmagundi* 58–59 (Fall-Winter): 114–46.

———. 1994. *Gay New York: Gender, Urban Culture, and the Making of the Gay World, 1890–1940.* New York: Basic Books.

———. 1995. "Christian Brotherhood or Sexual Perversion? Homosexual Identities and the Construction of Sexual Boundaries in the World War One Era." *Journal of Social History* 19 (Winter): 189–211.

Connelly, Mark Thomas. 1980. *The Response to Prostitution in the Progressive Era.* Chapel Hill: University of North Carolina Press.

Creesey, Paul G. 1968 (1932). *The Taxi-Dance Hall: A Sociological Study in Commercialized Recreation and City Life.* New York: Greenwood Press.

Davis, D. L., and R. G. Whitten. 1987. "The Cross-Cultural Study of Human Sexuality." *Annual Reviews in Anthropology* 16: 69–98.

Davis, Katherine Bement. 1929. *Factors in the Sex Life of Twenty-two Hundred Women.* New York: Harper and Brothers.

D'Emilio, John. 1983a. *Sexual Politics, Sexual Communities: The Making of a Homosexual Minority in the United States, 1940–1970.* Chicago: University of Chicago Press.

———. 1983b. "Capitalism and Gay Identity." In *Powers of Desire,* ed. Ann Snitow et al., 100–113. New York: Monthly Review Press.

———. 1989a. "Gay Politics and Community in San Francisco since World War II." In *Hidden from History: Reclaiming the Gay and Lesbian Past,* ed. Martin Bauml Duberman, Martha Vicinus, and George Chauncey, Jr., 456–73. New York: New American Library.

———. 1989b. "The Homosexual Menace: The Politics of Sexuality in Cold War America." In *Passion and Power: Sexuality in History,* ed. Kathy Peiss, Christina Simmons, and Robert Padgug, 226–40. Philadelphia: Temple University Press.

———. 1992. *Making Trouble: Essays on Gay History, Politics, and the University.* New York: Routledge.

D'Emilio, John, and Estelle B. Freedman, eds. 1988. *Intimate Matters: A History of Sexuality in America.* New York: Harper and Row.

Devereaux, George. 1937. "Institutionalized Homosexuality among Mohave Indians." *Human Biology* 9(4): 498–529.

Dosse, Francois. 1997. *History of Structuralism,* vol. 1: *The Rising Sign, 1945–1966;* vol. 2: *The Sign Sets, 1967-Present.* Minneapolis: University of Minnesota Press.

Drexel, Allen. 1997. "Before Paris Burned: Race, Class, and Male Homosexuality on the Chicago South Side, 1935–1960." In *Creating a Place for Ourselves: Lesbian, Gay, and Bisexual Community Histories,* ed. Brett Beemyn, 119–44. New York: Routledge.

Duberman, Martin Bauml, Martha Vicinus, and George Chauncey, Jr., eds. 1989. *Hidden from History: Reclaiming the Gay and Lesbian Past.* New York: New American Library.

Duggan, Lisa. 1993. "The Trials of Alice Mitchell: Sensationalism, Sexology, and the Lesbian Subject in Turn-of-the-Century America." *Signs* 18(4): 791–814.

————. 2000. *Sapphic Slashers: Sex, Violence, and American Modernity.* Durham: Duke University Press.

Duggan, Lisa, and Nan D. Hunter. 1995. *Sex Wars: Sexual Dissent and Political Culture.* New York: Routledge.

Epstein, Steven. 1996. "A Queer Encounter: Sociology and the Study of Sexuality." In *Queer Theory/Sociology,* ed. Steven Seidman, 145–67. Cambridge: Blackwell.

Eribon, Didier, 2001. "Michel Foucault's Histories of Sexuality." Trans. Michael Lucey. *GLQ* 7(1): 31–86.

Escoffier, Jeffrey. 1990. "Inside the Ivory Closet: The Challenges Facing Lesbian and Gay Studies." *Outlook* 10 (Fall): 2–26.

————. 1992. "Generations and Paradigms: Mainstreams in Lesbian and Gay Studies." In *Gay and Lesbian Studies,* ed. Henry Minton, 112–27. New York: Harrington Park Press.

————. 1993. "Reading the Social: Homosexuality and the Sociological Imagination in the Fifties and Sixties." Paper given at the Center for Lesbian and Gay Studies, CUNY.

————. 1998. *American Homo: Community and Perversity.* Berkeley: University of California Press.

Evans-Pritchard, E. E. 1970. "Sexual Inversion among the Azande." *American Anthropologist* 72: 1428–34.

Ford, Clellen S., and Frank A. Beach. 1951. *Patterns of Sexual Behavior.* New York: Harper and Row.

Foucault, Michel. 1970. *The Order of Things.* New York: Pantheon.

————. 1978. *The History of Sexuality,* vol. 1: *An Introduction.* Trans. Robert Hurley. New York: Pantheon.

Freedman, Estelle. 1987. "Uncontrolled Desires: The Response to the Sexual Psychopath, 1920–1960." *Journal of American History* 74(1): 83–106.

Gagnon, John. 1992. "An Unlikely Story." In *Authors of Their Own Lives: Intellectual Autobiographies of Twenty American Sociologists,* ed. Bennett M. Berger, 213–34. Berkeley: University of California Press.

————. 1999. "Sexual Conduct: As Today's Memory Serves." *Sexualities* 2(1): 115–26.

Gagnon, John, and William Simon, eds. 1967. *Sexual Deviance.* New York: Harper and Row.

————. 1970. *The Sexual Scene.* Chicago: Aldine, Trans-Action Books.

————. 1973. *Sexual Conduct: The Social Sources of Human Sexuality.* Chicago: Aldine.

Galliher, John F. 1995. "Chicago's Two Worlds of Deviance Research: Whose Side Are They On?" In *A Second Chicago School? The Development of a Postwar American Sociology,* ed. Gary Alan Fine, 164–87. Chicago: University of Chicago Press.

Garber, Eric. ca. 1990. "A Historical Directory of Lesbian and Gay Establishments in the San Francisco Bay Area." Ms. Gay and Lesbian Historical Society of Northern California.

Garber, Eric, and Willie Walker. 2000. "Queer Sites in San Francisco: A Listing of Gay Bars, Restaurants, and Other Sites." Database. Gay, Lesbian, Bisexual, and Transgender Historical Society of Northern California.

Goffman, Erving. 1963. *Stigma: Notes on the Management of Spoiled Identity.* Englewood Cliffs: Prentice-Hall.

Halperin, David M. 1990. *One Hundred Years of Homosexuality and Other Essays on Greek Love.* New York: Routledge.

Halperin, David M., John J. Winkler, and Froma I. Zeitlin, eds. 1990. *Before Sexuality: The Construction of Erotic Experience in the Ancient Greek World.* Princeton: Princeton University Press.

Hansen, Bert. 1979. "The Historical Construction of Homosexuality." *Radical History Review* 20 (Spring–Summer): 66–75.

Harry, Joseph, and William B. DeVall. 1978. *The Social Organization of Gay Males.* New York: Praeger.

Heap, Chad C. 2000. *Homosexuality in the City: A Century of Research at the University of Chicago.* Exhibition catalog. University of Chicago Library.

Henry, George. 1941. *Sex Variants: A Study of Homosexual Patterns.* 2 vols. New York: Paul B. Hoeber.

Herdt, Gilbert. 1981. *Guardians of the Flutes: Idioms of Masculinity.* New York: McGraw-Hill.

———. 1984. *Ritualized Homosexuality in Melanesia.* Berkeley: University of California Press.

———, ed. 1992. *Gay Culture in America: Essays from the Field.* Boston: Beacon Press.

Herskovitz, Melville. 1937. "A Note on 'Woman Marriage' in Dahomey." *Africa* 10(3): 335–41.

Hooker, Evelyn. 1967 (1961). "The Homosexual Community." In *Sexual Deviance,* ed. John Gagnon and William Simon, 167–84. New York: Harper and Row.

Humphreys, Laud. 1979. *Tearoom Trade: Impersonal Sex in Public Places.* New York: Aldine.

Jacobs, Sue-Ellen, Wesley Thomas, and Sabine Lang, eds. 1997. *Two-Spirit People: Native American Gender Identity, Sexuality, and Spirituality.* Urbana: University of Illinois Press.

Jagose, Annamarie. 1996. *Queer Theory: An Introduction.* New York: New York University Press.

Johnson, David. 1997. "The Kids of Fairytown: Gay Male Culture on Chicago's Near North Side in the 1930s." In *Creating a Place for Ourselves: Lesbian, Gay, and Bisexual Community Histories,* ed. Brett Beemyn, 97–118. New York: Routledge.

Johnson, James H. 1967. *Urban Geography: An Introductory Analysis.* New York: Pergamon.

Katz, Jonathan Ned. 1976. *Gay American History: Lesbians and Gay Men in the U.S.A.* New York: Thomas Crowell.

———. 1983. *Gay/Lesbian Almanac: A New Documentary.* New York: Harper and Row.

———. 1990. "The Invention of Heterosexuality." *Socialist Review* 20(1): 7–34.

———. 1995. *The Invention of Heterosexuality.* New York: Plume.

Kelly, Raymond. 1976. "Witchcraft and Sexual Relations: An Exploration of the Social and Semantic Implications of the Structure of Belief." In *Man and Woman in the New Guinea Highlands,* ed. Paula Brown and Georgeda Buchbinder, 36–53. Washington, D.C.: American Anthropological Association.

Kennedy, Elizabeth Lapovsky, and Madeline D. Davis. 1993. *Boots of Leather, Slippers of Gold: The History of a Lesbian Community.* New York: Routledge.

Kinsey, Alfred, Wardell B. Pomeroy, and Clyde E. Martin. 1948. *Sexual Behavior in the Human Male.* Philadelphia: W.B. Saunders Company.

Kinsey, Alfred, Wardell B. Pomeroy, Clyde E. Martin, and Paul H. Gebhard. 1953. *Sexual Behavior in the Human Female.* Philadelphia: W. B. Saunders Company.

Kreiger, Susan. 1983. *The Mirror Dance: Identity in a Women's Community.* Philadelphia: Temple University Press.

Langum, David. 1994. *Crossing Over the Line: Legislating Morality and the Mann Act.* Chicago: University of Chicago Press.

Lee, John Allan. 1978. *Getting Sex: A New Approach, More Sex, Less Guilt.* Don Mills, Ont.: Musson Book Co.

Lewin, Ellen, and William L. Leap. 1999. *Final Report of the Commission on Lesbian, Gay, Bisexual, and Transgender Issues in Anthropology.* Arlington: American Anthropological Association.

Levine, Martin P. 1979. *Gay Men: The Sociology of Male Homosexuality.* New York: Harper.

Lewin, Ellen. 1993. *Lesbian Mothers: Accounts of Gender in American Culture.* Ithaca: Cornell University Press.

Leznoff, Maurice, and William A. Westley. 1967 (1956). "The Homosexual Community." In *Sexual Deviance,* ed. John Gagnon and William Simon, 184–96. New York: Harper and Row.

Marshall, Donald S., and Robert C. Suggs, eds. 1971. *Human Sexual Behavior: Variations in the Ethnographic Spectrum.* New York: Basic Books.

McIntosh, Mary. 1968. "The Homosexual Role." *Social Problems* 16(2): 182–92.

McMurtrie, Douglas. 1914. "A Legend of Lesbian Love among North American Indians." *Urologic and Cutaneous Review* (April): 192–93.

Mumford, Kevin. 1996. "Homosex Changes: Race, Cultural Geography, and the Emergence of the Gay. *American Quarterly* 48(3): 395–414.

———. 1997. *Interzones: Black/White Sex Districts in Chicago and New York in the Early Twentieth Century.* New York: Columbia University Press.

Murray, Stephen O. 1979. "The Institutional Elaboration of a Quasi-Ethnic Community." *International Review of Modern Sociology* 9(2): 155–75.

Nardi, Peter, and Beth Schneider, eds. 1998a. *Social Perspectives in Lesbian and Gay Studies.* New York: Routledge.

———. eds. 1998b. "Kinsey: A Fiftieth-Anniversary Symposium." *Sexualities* 1(1): 83–106.

Newton, Esther. 1972. *Mother Camp: Female Impersonators in America*. Englewood Cliffs: Prentice-Hall.

———. 1993. *Cherry Grove, Fire Island: Sixty Years in America's First Gay and Lesbian Town*. Boston: Beacon Press.

———. 2000. *Margaret Mead Made Me Gay: Personal Essays, Public Ideas*. Durham: Duke University Press.

Odem, Mary. 1995. *Delinquent Daughters: Protecting and Policing Adolescent Female Sexuality in the United States, 1885–1920*. Chapel Hill: University of North Carolina Press.

Ortner, Sherry B., and Harriet Whitehead, eds. 1981. *Sexual Meanings: The Cultural Construction of Gender and Sexuality*. New York: Cambridge University Press.

Padgug, Robert. 1979. "Sexual Matters: On Conceptualizing Sexuality in History." *Radical History Review* 20 (Spring–Summer): 3–23.

Park, Robert E., Ernest W. Burgess, and Roderick McKenzie. 1967 (1925). *The City*. Chicago: University of Chicago Press.

Peiss, Kathy. 1986. *Cheap Amusements: Working Women and Leisure in Turn-of-the-Century New York*. Philadelphia: Temple University Press.

Peiss, Kathy, and Christina Simmons (with Robert A. Padgug), eds. 1989. *Passion and Power: Sexuality in History*. Philadelphia: Temple University Press.

Plummer, Kenneth. 1975. *Sexual Stigma: An Interactionist Account*. New York: Routledge.

———. ed. 1981. *The Making of the Modern Homosexual*. London: Hutchinson.

———. ed. 1992. *Modern Homosexualities: Fragments of Lesbian and Gay Experience*. New York: Routledge.

Polanyi, Karl, Conrad Arensberg, and Henry Pearson. 1971 (1957). *Trade and Market in the Early Empires: Economies in History and Theory*. Chicago: Gateway.

Ponse, Barbara. 1978. *Identities in the Lesbian World: The Social construction of Self*. Westport: Greenwood Press.

Read, Kenneth E. 1980. *Other Voices: The Style of a Male Homosexual Tavern*. Novato, Calif.: Chandler and Sharp.

Reckless, Walter C. 1969 (1933). *Vice in Chicago*. Montclair: Patterson Smith.

Reinharz, Shulamit. 1995. "The Chicago School of Sociology and the Founding of the Graduate Program in Sociology at Brandeis University: A Case Study in Cultural Diffusion." In *A Second Chicago School? The Development of a Postwar American Sociology*, ed. Gary Allan Fine, 273–321. Chicago: University of Chicago Press.

Reiss, Albert. 1967 (1961). "The Social Integration of Peers and Queers." In *Sexual Deviance*, ed. John Gagnon and William Simon, 197–227. New York: Harper and Row.

Reiter, Rayna R., ed. 1975. *Toward an Anthropology of Women*. New York: Monthly Review Press.

Robinson, Paul. 1976. *The Modernization of Sex*. New York: Harper and Row.

Rosaldo, Michelle Zimbalist, and Lousie Lamphere, eds. 1974. *Women, Culture, and Society*. Stanford: Stanford University Press.

Roscoe, Will. 1991. *The Zuni Man-Woman.* Albuquerque: University of New Mexico Press.

Rubin, Gayle S. 1984. "Thinking Sex." In *Pleasure and Danger: Exploring Female Sexuality,* ed. Carole S. Vance, 267–319. New York: Routledge.

———. 1994. "The Valley of the Kings: Leathermen in San Francisco, 1960–1990." Ph.D. diss. University of Michigan.

——— (with Judith Butler). 1995. "Sexual Traffic." *differences* 6(2–3): 62–99.

———. 1997. "Elegy for the Valley of the Kings: AIDS and the Leather Community in San Francisco, 1981–1996." In *In Changing Times: Gay Men and Lesbians Encounter HIV/AIDS,* ed. Martin Levine, Peter Nardi, and John Gagnon, 101–44. Chicago: University of Chicago Press.

———. 1998. "The Miracle Mile: South of Market and Gay Male Leather in San Francisco 1962–1996." In *Reclaiming San Francisco: History, Politics, Culture,* ed. James Brook, Chris Carlsson, and Nancy Peters, 247–72. San Francisco: City Lights Books.

———. 2000. "Sites, Settlements, and Urban Sex: Archaeology and the Study of Gay Leathermen in San Francisco 1955–1995." In *Archaeologies of Sexuality,* ed. Robert Schmidt and Barbara Voss, 62–88. New York: Routledge.

Sahlins, Marshall. 1972. *Stone Age Economics.* Chicago: Aldine-Atherton.

Schneider, Beth, and Peter Nardi, eds. 1999. "John H. Gagnon and William Simon's *Sexual Conduct: The Social Sources of Human Sexuality.*" *Sexualities* 2(1): 113–33.

Simon, William. 1999. "*Sexual Conduct* in Retrospective Perspective." *Sexualities* 2(1): 126–33.

Simon, William, and John Gagnon. 1969 (1967). "Homosexuality: The Formulation of a Sociological Perspective." In *The Same Sex: An Appraisal of Homosexuality,* ed. Ralph Weltge, 14–24. Philadelphia: Pilgrim Press.

Snitow, Ann, Christine Stansell, and Sharon Thompson, eds. 1983. *Powers of Desire: The Politics of Sexuality.* New York: Monthly Review Press.

Sonenschein, David. 1966. "Homosexuality as a Subject of Anthropological Inquiry." *Anthropological Quarterly* 2:73–82.

Stein, Arlene, and Kenneth Plummer. 1996. "'I Can't Even Think Straight': 'Queer' Theory and the Missing Sexual Revolution in Sociology." In *Queer Theory/Sociology,* ed. Steven Seidman, 129–44. Cambridge: Blackwell.

Thomas, W. I. 1907. *Sex and Society: Studies in the Social Psychology of Sex.* Chicago: University of Chicago Press.

Thomas, W. I., and Florian Znaniecki. 1918–20. *The Polish Peasant in Europe and America: Monograph of an Immigrant Group.* Chicago: University of Chicago Press.

Thompson, E. P. 1963. *The Making of the English Working Class.* New York: Vintage Books.

———. 1993 (1967). "Time, Work Discipline, and Industrial Capitalism." In *Customs in Common: Studies in Traditional Popular Culture,* 141–62. New York: New Press.

Turner, William B. 2000. *A Genealogy of Queer Theory*. Philadelphia: Temple University Press.

Vance, Carole S., ed. 1984. *Pleasure and Danger: Exploring Female Sexuality*. New York: Routledge.

———. 1989a. "Social Construction Theory: Problems in the History of Sexuality." In *Homosexuality, Which Homosexuality?* ed. D. Altman, C. Vance et al., 13–34. London: GMP Publishers.

———. 1989b. "The War on Culture." *Art in America* (Dec.): 39–45.

———. 1990a. "Misunderstanding Obscenity." *Art in America* (May): 49–55.

———. 1990b. "Negotiating Sex and Gender in the Attorney General's Commission on Pornography." In *Uncertain Terms: Negotiating Gender in American Culture*, ed. Faye Ginsburg and Anna L. Tsing, 118–34. Boston: Beacon Press.

———. 1990c. "Reagan's Revenge: Restructuring the NEA." *Art in America* (Nov.): 49–55.

———. 1990d. "The Pleasures of Looking: The Attorney General's Commission on Pornography vs. Visual Images." In *The Critical Image: Essays in Contemporary Photography*, ed. Carole Squiers, 38–58. Seattle: Bay Press.

———. 1991. "Anthropology Rediscovers Sexuality: A Theoretical Comment." *Social Science and Medicine* 33(8): 875–84.

Vice Commission of Chicago. 1911. *The Social Evil in Chicago: A Study of Existing Conditions*. Chicago: Gunthorp-Warren Printing.

Vicinus, Martha. 1982. "Sexuality and Power: A Review of Current Work in the History of Sexuality." *Feminist Studies* 8(1): 133–56.

———. 1992. "'They Wonder to which Sex I Belong': The Historical Roots of the Modern Lesbian Identity." *Feminist Studies* 18(3): 467–97.

Walkowitz, Judith R. 1980a. *Prostitution and Victorian Society*. New York: Cambridge University Press.

———. 1980b. "The Politics of Prostitution." *Signs* 6(1): 123–35.

———. 1982. "Male Vice and Feminist Virtue: Feminism and the Politics of Prostitution in Nineteenth-Century Britain." *History Workshop Journal* 13 (Spring): 21–40.

———. 1992. *City of Dreadful Delight: Narratives of Sexual Danger in Late-Victorian London*. Chicago: University of Chicago Press.

Walkowitz, Judith, and Daniel Walkowitz. 1973. "We Are Not Beasts of the Field: Prostitution and the Poor in Plymouth and Southampton under the Contagious Diseases Acts." *Feminist Studies* 1(3–4): 73–106.

Weatherford, Jack McIver. 1986. *Porn Row*. New York: Arbor House.

Weeks, Jeffrey. 1977. *Coming Out: Homosexual Politics in Britain, from the Nineteenth Century to the Present*. London: Quartet.

———. 1981. *Sex, Politics, and Society: The Regulation of Sexuality since 1800*. London: Longman.

———. 1985. *Sexuality and Its Discontents*. New York: Routledge.

———. 1986. *Sexuality*. London: Tavistock.

————. 1991. *Against Nature: Essays on History, Sexuality, and Identity.* London: Rivers Oram Press.

————. 1998. "The 'Homosexual Role' after Thirty Years: An Appreciation of the Work of Mary McIntosh." *Sexualities* 1(2): 131–52.

————. 2000. *Making Sexual History.* Cambridge: Blackwell.

Weston, Kath. 1991. *Families We Choose: Lesbians, Gays, Kinship.* New York: Columbia University Press.

————. 1993. "Lesbian/Gay Studies in the House of Anthropology." *Annual Review of Anthropology* 22:339–67.

————. 1998. *Long Slow Burn: Sexuality and Social Science.* New York: Routledge.

Whitehead, Harriet. 1981. "The Bow and the Burden Strap: A New Look at Institutionalized Homosexuality in Native North America." In *Sexual Meanings: The Cultural Construction of Gender and Sexuality,* ed. Sherry B. Ortner and Harriet Whitehead, 80–115. New York: Cambridge University Press.

Williams, F. E. 1936. *Papuans of the Trans-Fly.* New York: Oxford University Press.

Williams, Walter. 1986. *The Spirit and the Flesh: Sexual Diversity in American Indian Culture.* Boston: Beacon Press.

Winkler, John J. 1990. *The Constraints of Desire: The Anthropology of Sex and Gender in Ancient Greece.* New York: Routledge.

Wolf, Deborah Goleman. 1979. *The Lesbian Community.* Berkeley: University of California Press.

Zorbaugh, Harvey Warren. 1976 (1929). *The Gold Coast and the Slum: A Sociological Study of Chicago's Near North Side.* Chicago: University of Chicago Press.

TWO

Reading Sexualities across Cultures: Anthropology and Theories of Sexuality

Evelyn Blackwood

In this essay, I will explore theories of sexuality that were propounded in the 1970s and 1980s to explain women's sexuality. I focus on this period because it was formative for studies of sexuality both in feminist theory and in the anthropology of homosexuality. In these disciplines, two dominant models appeared at that time in the study of sexuality, one coming from the radical feminists and one from the masculinist, or mainstream, study of homosexuality.[1] Radical feminists asserted that sexuality was a male-defined institution, whereas masculinist scholars developed their models based on men's sexual practices. I will explore the assumptions and limitations of these models and then examine how ethnographic studies of female same-sex practices responded to and complicated them. This historical review reveals some of the early contentions and possibilities offered by ethnographic studies of female same-sex practices. It closes at the turn of lesbian and gay studies to postmodern and queer theories, a shift in theory that embraced a different set of questions about the self, agency, sexuality, and identity.

Two problems need to be noted immediately regarding terminology. First, part of my effort here is to explore the relevance of anthropological evidence and theories to the early debates on sexuality. As such, I draw from anthropological studies of indigenous, colonized, and postcolonial cultures, excluding works on the dominant white cultures of Europe and North America. Although such a move may be problematic in a globalized world where the divisions between the West and the rest have disappeared, it is not meant to suggest the boundedness of these culture areas but to expand the conversation beyond works by and about European and American lesbians that dominated feminist studies at the time. Studies about female same-sex relations in cultures other than dominant white cultures provided critical evidence to counter models of sexuality proposed in both radical feminist and masculinist studies.[2]

Second, in the period discussed in this essay, the term *lesbian* was used to describe same-sex practices between women. Using "lesbian" as a global signifier is problematic, however, because it imposes a Eurocentric term, which connotes a fixed sexual identity, on practices and relationships that may have very different meanings and expectations in other cultures. In terms of sexuality, it assumes an essential linkage among practices whose connections may be tenuous at best. Used as a signifier of non-normative gender practices such as butch or tomboy, it subsumes under the rubric of sexuality, and thus makes invisible, a wide range of genders and gender transgressions (Cromwell 1999). The term *lesbian* falls far short of expressing the diversities of female gender and sexual identities, yet it has historical significance in the West as the only term that identifies female as opposed to male homosexuality. Thus, although I want to stress the importance of the term *lesbian* as a signifier of women's same-sex eroticism, I will use "female same-sex relations" in this discussion as a more inclusive term.

Sexuality as a Form of Oppression by Men

One of the early second-wave feminist perspectives in the United States coalesced in the 1970s under the term *radical feminist*. Like other feminists, radical feminists argued against the idea that women's sexuality was the natural product of biologically given drives, articulating instead a powerful theory of the social construction of sexuality. But unlike others, radical feminists argued that sexuality was defined by patriarchal institutions and as such was oppressive to women. According to this perspective, women's sexuality was the result of a long period of history in which men had power over women and thus defined and controlled their sexuality.[3] Through their laws, customs, and other institutions, radical feminists maintained, men had appropriated women's sexuality (Shulman 1980). For Janeway, the polar split in Western sexuality between woman as Eve and woman as Mary was not a product of "female being" but of "masculine emotions at work in a male-dominated society" (1980:575). Women learn this model, she asserted, as a means of survival, but it does not originate with women. In patriarchal societies, so the argument went, sexuality was a tool used by men to dominate and oppress women through their sexual objectification (Ferguson 1984). The term *patriarchy* was used to identify all societies that were controlled by men.

Radical feminists disagreed on whether the long period of patriarchy was a historical product or transhistorical phenomenon, but they generally agreed that men defined female sexuality (Lerner 1986). Their project became one of erasing men's sexual inscriptions from women's bodies and psyches and eradicating men's sexual control over women. The "new feminist analysis" urged women to take control of their own sexuality (Shulman 1980).

In one of the early and formative anthropological works in the study of sexuality, Rubin (1975) offered a historical analysis of women's sexual oppression, arguing that oppression arises in systems of kinship in which women are exchanged in marriage. Drawing on Lévi-Strauss (as well as Marx and Freud), she suggested that this system of exchange gave men rights in women that women did not have in themselves, ensuring heterosexual unions by creating an obligatory heterosexuality. Arguing against Lévi-Strauss's assertion that the principle of exchange (originating in the incest taboo) constitutes the origin of culture, Rubin located women's oppression in culture and history. Many scholars outside anthropology, however, took Rubin's argument as explanation of the origin of a universal and transhistorical repression of women's sexuality by men and men's institutions, using it to substantiate the radical feminist view.

Drawing on her reading of anthropology and the work of radical feminists, Adrienne Rich (1980) reinforced the idea of the transhistorical nature of women's sexual oppression. She argued provocatively that heterosexuality is a political institution that disempowers women. Using Gough's (1975) analysis of sexual inequality in "archaic states" and capitalist nations, Rich made the challenging assertion that men "in archaic and contemporary cultures" enforce not just inequality but heterosexuality as well (1980:638). Citing a wide range of practices, including arranged and child marriages, brideprice, foot-binding, purdah (the segregation of women from men typical of some Islamic societies), veiling, the chastity belt, clitoridectomies, and female infanticide, she highlighted the cultural constraints and sanctions that "historically, have enforced or insured the coupling of women with men" (1980:636). "Whatever its origins," Rich stated, "the enforcement of heterosexuality for women" was "a means of assuring male right of physical, economical and emotional access" (647). Through a selective appropriation of anthropological materials across cultures and time, Rich implied that women's history was the history of compulsory heterosexuality.

Rich made a convincing case for what she called "compulsory heterosexuality," and the concept has become central in many subsequent feminist analyses of women's sexuality. The debate that took place after publication of her article, however, was not about her analysis of compulsory heterosexuality but about her concept of the "lesbian continuum" and lesbianism as an act of resistance. Ferguson criticized Rich for employing a transhistorical discourse but was more concerned that Rich had portrayed compulsory heterosexuality as "the key mechanism underlying and perpetuating male dominance" (1981:170). She argued that lesbian identity was a historical development, insisting that Rich's use of that term to define women's relations in other cultures was incorrect. As to Rich's suggestion of the universality of compulsory heterosexuality, Ferguson agreed that "lesbian and male-male attractions are indeed suppressed cross-culturally" (170), leaving in place a blanket of compulsory heterosexuality worldwide. Zita's (1981) analysis was more explicit in connecting compulsory heterosexuality with patriarchy rather than all cultures while again lamenting the way Rich lumped all resistance to patriarchy into the lesbian continuum.[4] Neither the historical specificity nor applicability of compulsory heterosexuality across cultures was adequately questioned.

By the late 1970s and early 1980s, the debates over women's sexuality led to the "sex wars," a term referring to the ideological struggle in the feminist movement over pornography and censorship. Radical feminists, whose view of sexuality as dangerous led to an attack on pornography, were countered by feminists who emphasized the potentially liberating aspects and pleasures of sexuality (Ferguson 1984; Philipson 1984). Both sides, however, seemed to uphold the view that society had long been in the business of suppressing sexuality, supporting in their own ways the need to reclaim sexuality from men's hands.

The radical feminist notion of patriarchy and compulsory heterosexuality as an unchanging, transhistorical force was deeply entrenched by the early 1980s (Philipson 1984). In response, Amber Hollibaugh and Cherríe Moraga complained that the discussion of "our sex lives has dead-ended into silence within the feminist movement" (1983:395). That silence was due to what they saw as a narrow-minded focus on women's sexual oppression and suffering at the hands of men. When most feminists talk about sexuality, Hollibaugh and Moraga maintained, they are talking not about desire but about the dynamics of oppressor/oppressed. From this perspective, sex, reproduction, and marriage all amounted to the same thing—oppression and obligation. Sexuality became equivalent to "marriage," and marriage was an institution that forced women to be heterosexual (Hollibaugh and Moraga 1983).

As a radical feminist model, the concept of compulsory heterosexuality provided a limited vision of sexuality that was always already oppressive. Compulsory heterosexuality, taken at its baldest, assumes that women are forced through the dictates of male-imposed culture to be pawns in a sex and marriage system not of their own making and not for their benefit. Having misunderstood the historical production of such a system, radical feminists implied that women were not agents but passive victims or property in the cultural drama of patriarchy. Although little attention was paid to sexuality in societies outside Europe and North America, a feminist view of third-world women primarily as victims (critiqued by Mohanty 1984) had as its subtext the claim that these women were shackled to their marriage beds. In that scenario, women were carried silently and complicitously to their bridal beds, the objects of men's marriage and alliance schemes. Compulsory heterosexuality assumed that the control of women was so absolute and so pervasive that women could not participate in the active creation or production of culturally legitimated sexual practices. This view effectively denied the possibility of pleasure in heterosexual relations.

The corollary to the concept of compulsory heterosexuality, that nonheterosexual forms of sexuality constituted resistance to patriarchy, was equally problematic. Rich suggested that lesbianism, where it existed, constituted a form of resistance to heterosexuality, the "breaking of a taboo" (Rich 1980, see also Clarke 1981). According to Rich's romantic and eloquent view of lesbian resistance, "Women in every culture and throughout history *have* undertaken the task of independent, non-heterosexual, woman-connected existence, to the extent made possible by their context. . . . They have undertaken it even though few women have been in an economic position to resist marriage altogether; and even though attacks against unmarried women have ranged from aspersion and mockery to deliberate gynocide" (635, emphasis in the original). Many feminists, accepting Rich's view, came to valorize nonheterosexual forms of sexuality as forms of resistance, achieved at great risk, to compulsory heterosexuality.

Beyond Patriarchy and Oppression

Drawing on feminist theories concerning the social construction of sexuality, anthropological studies of female same-sex practices complicated the radical feminist model of sexuality. In particular, these studies helped to rework the notion of compulsory heterosexuality and its corollary, lesbian resistance. In contrast to the radical feminist model, work on female same-sex sexualities in other cultures provided solid evidence of women's active construction of sexuality.

The corollary to compulsory heterosexuality, the idea that lesbianism constituted a form of resistance, was also refined by anthropological studies of female sexuality. Many feminists of the time, such as Rich, were unaware of the range of women's sexualities and so were unable to imagine that women's same-sex erotic practices could exist except as resistance to compulsory heterosexuality. To be sure, a number of anthropological cases supported the idea that lesbianism in certain patriarchal cultures was a form of resistance, but even in these cases other factors were found to be relevant to the creation of lesbian relations.

One important case study that underscored the resistance model was that of the Chinese sisterhoods in Quangdon Province.[5] These sisterhoods were formed by women who never married, choosing instead to join together in lifelong associations that provided economic, emotional, and intimate bonds (Sankar 1986). Women who refused the heterosexual marriages arranged for them went through a ritual in which they formalized their status as unmarried. Many had independent incomes from their work in the silk factories of the province. Although a variety of different types of sisterhoods were formed, women members usually pooled their incomes and established a pension fund to cover illnesses, retirement, and funeral rites (Sankar 1986). Joining a sisterhood constituted a refusal to be exchanged in marriage, a refusal to live a life dependent on and obligated to husbands or fathers. Outsiders and family alike interpreted these women's actions as a rejection of men and heterosexuality in favor of strong friendships and erotic bonds with other women.

Another notable case in Kenya was also attributed to the resistance model. Lesbian relations for wealthy Mombasa women made sense, according to

Shepherd, if understood as "the desire to escape the economic conventions of [heterosexual] marriage" (1987:268). Because these women lived in a patriarchal society, Shepherd argued that "being a lesbian brings freedom from the extreme constraint normally placed upon high-ranking women in Muslim societies" (257). Both Sankar's and Shepherd's studies foregrounded resistance as a way to understand women's same-sex relations.

The concept of resistance has the value of attributing agency to women, but it is a negative agency, a reaction to an oppressive condition rather than a power to create sexual relations. Other anthropological studies showed that not all same-sex relations between women were acts of resistance against patriarchal domination. Resistant acts are by definition trangressions against dominant norms and acceptable definitions of sexuality. The anthropological record provided several cases in which women who engaged in same-sex practices did not experience their relations as breaking taboos or going beyond the bounds of acceptable sexual behavior.

In rural Lesotho, South Africa, "mummy-baby" relations were an institutionalized friendship between older and younger adolescent girls who exchanged gifts and intimate affections (Gay 1986). For adolescent girls who became "mummies" and babies to each other, the partnership was an element of the romantic drama of growing up and learning the pleasures and responsibilities of relationships. Mummies could have several babies but a baby could only have one mummy. Older girls sometimes had boyfriends who became part of the relationship. According to Gay, most of the girls later had boyfriends and married heterosexually but were not under pressure from local people to end their same-sex friendships. Gay observed that "these relationships point to the normality of adolescent homosexuality" (1986:111). She also mentioned an older tradition of bond friendship among rural women that might have provided a normalizing frame for schoolgirl friendships.[6]

According to Evans-Pritchard (1970), married Azande women formed intimate bond friendships with other women, including co-wives. These friendships were solemnized through a ceremony called *bagburu,* a public statement that the women were partners and would give each other preference in trading and other social needs. Such relationships broadened women's social and trade networks (Blackwood 1986). Evans-Pritchard noted that husbands were concerned that wives might be erotically involved but were told by senior women not to interfere in women's business. In this case women did not refuse heterosexuality or the constraints of marriage. Rather, they built strong networks of relationships with women, and erotic attachments played a part in those relationships.

Cases of gender transgression were also cited as markers of "lesbian" resistance. Passing "women" (females who passed as men and lived with women) in Europe have generally been interpreted as rejecting their own oppressive gender and claiming men's privileges (Crompton 1981; Katz 1976; Wheelwright 1989, but see Cromwell 1999).[7] But not all such cases fit that model. For many Native American cultures, female two-spirits (formerly called "berdache") lived their lives as social men. Within these cultures the practice was understood as a legitimate response to spiritual visions or dreams (Blackwood 1984b; Medicine 1983; see also Grahn 1986; Midnight Sun 1988). These men occupied established gender categories, suggesting that their gender was not interpreted as resistance to dominant cultural norms but the fulfillment of a spiritual desire.[8]

These studies exposed the limitations of the concept of "compulsory heterosexuality" by demonstrating that women in a number of societies worldwide engaged in legitimate forms of nonheterosexual erotic practice.[9] The studies raised questions about the usefulness of the trope of resistance to explain women's same-sex erotic relationships. In these societies women's erotic practices were not seen as "deviant" expressions of desire (outside the bounds of proper culture) or resistance to heterosexual institutions but were understood as expressions of desire within the context of women's social lives and relations. Anthropological accounts of adolescent female same-sex play, sex practice in initiation schools, same-sex relations between heterosexually married women, and intimate friendships between older and younger women or co-wives provided solid evidence that women engage in noncompulsory and nonoppressive forms of sexual practices. The accounts reflected women's agency in sexuality, showing that they actively construct and rework sexual meanings and desires.[10]

Although the historical and cultural contexts differ widely in these cases, in each instance sexual or gender practices were constructed as legitimate and valued social relationships. Heterosexual marriage may be the norm in all societies and often constitutes the only avenue to adulthood, but sexuality does not equal marriage, nor does marriage deny women's construction of (or participation in) other sexual practices, heterosexual and otherwise. Once marriage and heterosexual institutions are dislodged as fundamental categories of sexuality, it becomes possible to imagine women's sexualities beyond the limits imposed by patriarchal cultures.[11] It is not *marriage* or *heterosexuality* that is oppressive to women but particular systems in which masculinity and masculine desire are constructed as valuable and powerful. Women's sexuality, however, is constructed as limited or necessarily constrained.

Masculinist Models in the Anthropology of Homosexuality

While some radical feminists decried sexuality as oppressive and valorized the lesbian resistor, the masculinist approach to sexuality lumbered along apparently unaware of the debates raging next door. Sexologists were busily normalizing, naturalizing, and legitimizing heterosexual intercourse, the double standard, and male sexuality.[12] Other masculinist scholars turned their attention to homosexuality across cultures. The vast majority of evidence reported pertained to male homosexuality; very little data was included on lesbian practices. Some of the first American researchers who surveyed cross-cultural data on homosexuality argued that lesbianism was cross-culturally less well developed, less common, and less visible than men's homosexuality (Ford and Beach 1951; Gebhard 1970). That view set the tone for the formative years in the anthropology of "homosexuality" that began to take shape in the 1970s following the rise of the gay rights movement.

Anthropological studies of homosexuality in the 1970s and 1980s sought to uncover the variety of homosexual practices worldwide. This evidence was at first used to dismantle deviance theories of homosexuality still popular in the 1970s. By providing examples of cultures in which same-sex acts were accepted, it was hoped that attitudes toward homosexuals in the West would change. Cases of homosexual behavior in other cultures historically were sometimes cited as evidence of "our" gay ancestors, a view that imagined deep connections between Western gay identity and other forms of homosexual practice. Several ethnographic studies of male homosexuality conducted during this period made significant contributions to the study of sexuality.[13]

Although this period could also be called the beginnings of lesbian and gay studies in anthropology, I identify it as the "anthropology of homosexuality" to reflect the belief of some of its protagonists that there was a coherent and identifiable domain of homosexuality across time and cultures, like religion or the domestic, about which broad generalizations could be made. "Homosexuality" was the common (and problematic) term applied during that period to all forms of same-sex eroticism and transgender behavior.[14] Several works in the 1980s, which are the focus of my review, provided a catalog of homosexual practices and were then used to develop general theories of homosexuality. Two problematic assumptions underlined this work: Male homosexuality could stand in as the norm for all homosexual practices, and homosexual practices share a commonality of meaning.

In an important attempt to theorize homosexuality cross-culturally, Carrier (1980) used a wide range of cases of primarily male homosexual behavior to pinpoint some of the sociocultural factors connected with its expression. Carrier suggested, for instance, that homosexual behavior increases in the absence of the other sex, which results variously from the value placed on women's virginity; segregation of men in initiatory camps; men's migration; and polygyny (marriage to more than one woman). He noted that some cultures accommodate what he called cross-gender behavior (more recently labeled "transgender behavior"), whereas others disapprove of it. His discussion rested heavily on cases of male cross-gender behavior; cases of female cross-gender behavior were nearly absent.[15]

Several male scholars sought to develop a reliable typology of homosexual practices that could then be used to identify and catalog specific cases. Such a typology, it was hoped, would help explain why and under what conditions homosexual relations appeared. Although the terms varied, three general categories were devised to identify and describe homosexual practices: gender-differentiated relations (partners of differing genders); transgenerational relations (also age-differentiated or age-structured relations); and egalitarian relations (modern gay or partners who occupy the same status category) (see, for example, Adam 1986; Greenberg 1988; and Herdt 1988). Greenberg, a sociologist, in 1988 added a class-differentiated type to account for homosexual relations between members of different classes. His massive work *The Construction of Homosexuality* relied heavily on anthropological data on male homosexuality. Herdt (1988) included a role-specialized category that included shamans, who are thought to have spiritual sanction to engage in homosexual acts. According to these scholars, the typologies were meant to be inclusive of both men's and women's homosexual practices.

Following Ford and Beach's lead, each of these works presented detailed cases of male homosexuality cross-culturally but very few cases of female homosexuality. The typologies and conclusions that they drew were based on men's homosexual practices cross-culturally. Data on female sexuality rarely entered into the analysis, even in cases where women fit into the typologies that masculinist scholars constructed. For instance, Greenberg's (1988) discussion of age-differentiated relationships failed to mention relationships between mummies and babies in Lesotho (Gay 1986), between older married and younger unmarried women in Carriacou in the Caribbean (Blackwood 1986), or woman-marriage in Africa. The recurrent phrases that females "were also known to" (engage in whatever is being discussed) or that "no examples of females are known" are typical of these writings (e.g., Herdt 1988). Following sexologists' model of sexuality in which men's sexuality was the norm, these scholars assumed that models based on male homosexuality would be generalizable to (or inclusive of) female homosexuality.

The scholars then sought to make comparisons between male and female homosexuality. Carrier, for instance, stated that "male homosexual behavior generally appears to be more regulated . . . than female homosexual behavior" and that "females [are] less likely *than males* to engage in homosexual activity" (1980:118, emphasis added). Echoing the masculinist mantra of female invisibility, Greenberg asserted that "we know *far less* about lesbianism than about male homosexuality" (1988:19, emphasis added) and that lesbianism "is less common and less tolerated" (74). Comparing the differences in types of relationships in which men and women engage, Greenberg concluded that women in "kinship-based" societies tend *more often than men* to have "egalitarian" lesbian relations, "possibly because women are not socialized to compete for status with other women, or to dominate" (73, emphasis added). Regarding the societies he labeled "early civilizations," he concluded that lack of independence made lesbian relations less possible (183), an assertion apparently based on the lack of evidence of lesbian relations in comparison to men.

In another example of the comparative mode, Adam stated that his category of age-structured homosexuality had "few parallels among women" (1986:20), citing examples of youthful homosexuality in bachelorhood and that between older and younger men (in Melanesia, Greece, and Africa). Although he mentioned the report of sexual relations between Azande co-wives first published by Evans-Pritchard (1970), he noted that their relationships "did not parallel the male form" of "warrior homosexuality" of Azande men (1986:24). Adam mentioned the occurrence of sex between female cross-cousins in Australian groups but did so in the context of a discussion of age-graded relations, which were not relevant to these cross-cousin relations.

These scholars used male homosexuality as the standard by which to understand homosexuality, in effect creating a universalizing narrative of men's sexuality that conflated male and female homosexuality. By cataloging the ways in which women were the same or different than men in their homosexual practices, the writers oriented data on female homosexuality around male homosexuality. Consequently, masculinist attempts to theorize about female homosexuality provided a limited perspective on practices that were inadequately explored and analyzed.

The second basic assumption underlying the masculinist model of homosexuality, that homosexual practices share a commonality of meaning, led to an emphasis on genital sexual activity as the link among all expressions of alternative sex and gender practices. Because they tended to assume certain acts between men were always homosexual, most masculinist writers included under the rubric of "homosexuality" everything from Greek man-boy relations, to Native American "berdaches," to semen practices among the Sambia of Papua New Guinea. Practices as diverse in meaning and context as the ritual oral insemination of young Sambian boys by Sambian men and the mentoring/sexual relationship between elite Greek men and adolescent boys resided together in the category of age-differentiated homosexuality. In masculinist studies of homosexuality, the sex act was the determining element. Although arguing generally for the social construction of these practices, their focus on sexuality and desire distanced their theories from the cultural contexts that gave rise to particular sexual practices.[16] With their focus on sexuality and sex acts, masculinist theories gave little attention to gender in the construction of men's homosexuality. Questions concerning the relation of masculine gender ideology and male privilege to particular forms of male homosexuality were never addressed.

Like women in mainstream anthropology texts before the rise of feminist anthropology, female same-sex practices were nearly invisible in the masculinist catalogs of homosexuality in the 1980s. So complete was the invisibility of female same-sex practices in these works—and in gay studies in general—that the editors of *Hidden from History* felt confident in asserting that "the data for women are still far too sketchy to allow for even preliminary generalizations" about lesbians in non-Western societies (Chauncey, Duberman, and Vicinus 1989:10).[17] There were, however, a substantial number of works already available concerning female same-sex practices and transgender relations, works that exploded the myth of invisibility and argued for a feminist analysis of female homosexuality.

Culture and Female Same-Sex Relations

To counter the biases of masculinist studies of homosexuality, cultural studies of female same-sex practices in the 1980s focused on women's experiences and lives. Early feminist scholars took the masculinist model to task for assuming that lesbianism must be the mirror image of male homosexuality. Mary McIntosh, in her formative work on homosexuality, pointed out that "the assumption always is that we can use the same theories and concepts for female homosexuality and that, for simplicity, we can just talk about men and assume it applies to women" (1981:45). For her part, Rich was emphatic in her rejection of any correspondence between homosexuality as experienced by women and that experienced by men: "Any theory . . . that treats lesbian existence . . . as the mirror image of either heterosexual or male homosexual relations is profoundly weakened thereby, whatever its other contributions" (1980:632).

Anthropological work on female-sexuality provided evidence that raised questions about the relevance of male models to women's sexuality. In contrast to masculinist studies of sexuality that viewed women's sexuality from the standpoint of men, ethnographic studies of female same-sex practices highlighted the importance of analyses of women's, as distinct from men's, sexualities. Because gender enables and structures differential practices for women and men, ideologies of men's and women's sexualities would be, if not contrastive, certainly not identical. The factors that were significant in the construction of male same-sex practices might not pertain to female same-sex practices (Blackwood 1986).

The study of "ritualized homosexuality" in Papua New Guinea provided strong support for this argument. The semen practices that Herdt (1981) documented for Sambian men appeared to have no correlate among women. These practices are explicitly linked to the ritual development of masculinity in young boys. Girls, being viewed as having inherent femininity and reproductive competence, have no such need to be given their femininity ritually (Herdt 1981). A similar example came from the Chinese sisterhoods of Quangdon Province. The oppressive conditions of marriage for women in China, which gave rise in Quangdon Province to the marriage resistance and sisterhoods mentioned earlier (see also Sankar 1986 and Topley 1975), had no parallel among Chinese men, who were entitled to control wives and family property.

In both cases, the absence of a mirror image to men's or women's homosexual practices underscored the way cultural gender ideologies construct sexual practices. For the Sambia of Papua New Guinea, a cultural practice rooted in an ideology of gender antagonism and the efficacy of fluids legitimated particular sexual behaviors between men and boys. In China, patriarchal institutions vested with control of women produced public resistance by women to oppressive marital and economic conditions. The different constraints imposed on women and men affect the construction of sexual roles, behaviors, meanings, and desires. Thus, these cases indicated that models of sexuality based on male sexual practices could not stand in for women's sexualities. Gender had to be taken into account in understanding sexuality.

Where masculinist researchers represented lesbianism as "rare" and women as less sexually active in relation to men, ethnographic studies of female same-sex practices revealed previously overlooked information concerning female transgender practices and same-sex relations between women. Based on a survey of primarily English-language anthropological and historical texts (Blackwood 1984a), the evidence of female transgender and same-sex practices greatly exceeded previous estimates by American researchers.[18] Ford and Beach's (1951) often-cited survey of the Human Relations Area Files placed the number of societies with homosexual behavior at seventy-six, with only seventeen accounts of lesbianism. My survey, however, identified reports of female same-sex practices in ninety-five societies, including sexual practices between differently gendered females, such as two-spirit individuals and their partners, which were at that time considered instances of homosexuality. Neither of these estimates is definitive, particularly given the number of methodological problems associated with studies of sexuality, but the huge disparity in evidence raised questions about the reliability of assertions concerning the "absence" or rarity of "lesbianism."

The few examples of female homosexuality that were typically presented in masculinist studies of homosexuality included erotic acts among women in Greek literature; in harems (without, however, recognizing the wide range of cultures included in the sample); and between Azande co-wives of central Africa. Other ethnographic reports of female same-sex practices that went largely unnoticed consisted of an account of erotic same-sex dances celebrating first menstruation and marriage rites in the Solomon Islands (Blackwood 1935); an intriguing note that lesbian relations were common among adult women in Malekula and the Big Nambas in Melanesia (Deacon 1934); and reports of erotic ritual practices and cross-cousin affairs among Australian aboriginal women (Kaberry 1939; Roheim 1933). Although these reports were brief, they provided provocative hints of forms of female sexuality beyond heterosexuality. Other well-documented anthropological reports concerning indigenous, colonized, and postcolonial cultures included Schaeffer's (1965) biography of a Kutenai "female berdache" (a Native American female two-spirit of the nineteenth century) and Hart's

(1968) article on *lakin-on,* the transgender females/butches and their women partners in the Negros Islands of the Philippines.[19]

In contrast to the masculinist emphasis on the commonalities of homosexual practices, anthropological work on female-female sexuality developed within the larger issues of gender and culture. Drawing their inspiration from feminist anthropology, these writers asked questions about the relationship of gender hierarchies or gender ideologies to the construction of sexuality. Not surprisingly, one of the early questions concerned the role of gender hierarchy in the suppression of lesbianism. Gayle Rubin provided one of the first formulations of this relationship, asserting that where men have greater control over women than vice versa "homosexuality in women would be subject to more suppression than in men" (1975:183). In contrast, Sankar (1986) argued that men in the patriarchal society of Quangdon Province tacitly condoned lesbianism as long as it did not threaten the reproduction of the patrilineage. Her analysis, however, suggested that sisterhoods were the exception in Chinese society because they were the product of a fairly localized economic system (silk production) in which women earned sufficient income to be independent. Left unanswered was the question of women's sexual oppression in Chinese society as a whole.

Further analysis of cases of female same-sex relations suggested another formulation of the relation between female same-sex practices, social hierarchies, and gender ideologies. Same-sex practices in societies highly stratified by class and gender were either nonexistent (unreported) or limited to clandestine relations (such as in harems) or marginalized groups (such as the Chinese sisterhoods). In these societies, nonheterosexual relations for women were neither publicly tolerated nor legitimated. Evidence from foraging and horticultural groups suggested that egalitarian gender ideologies correlated with the presence of institutionalized or culturally sanctioned female same-sex practices, such as among the !Kung of South Africa, the indigenous people of Australia, and certain native North American groups (Blackwood 1986).

While masculinist studies of homosexuality developed typologies based on sexual acts to bring clarity to their wide-ranging data, this approach was problematic from the perspective of feminist anthropology. Feminist anthropology provided a model for analysis that took into account relations of power and their meaning within particular cultural contexts. Applying these insights to studies of sexuality meant prioritizing the cultural context and meaning of sexual relations for those involved in them over the fact of particular sexual acts.[20] Studies of female same-sex relations paid particular attention to the way constructions of gender and sexuality shaped women's same-sex practices as well as to the meaning of particular same-sex relationships. Writers sought to go beyond the psychological and biological explanations of earlier decades, arguing instead that women's relationships were embedded in and constituted wider social relations of kinship (indigenous Australians), exchange and trade networks (Azande co-wives, mummies and babies, and Chinese sisterhoods), and ritual (native North Americans). In many cases these relationships coexisted with heterosexual marriage (Blackwood 1986; Gay 1986).

Rather than lumping together all instances of certain types of homosexual acts regardless of cultural meaning or context, a preliminary framework for women's same-sex relations was proposed based on their articulation within larger social processes. This framework distinguished between types of relations that pertained only to the immediate social context (informal) and those that were part of a network or social structure extending beyond the relationship (formal) (Blackwood 1986). Although rather limited, this framework underscored the idea that sexual relations are embedded within social systems and gain their meanings from the social context.

Most writers presented rich, local studies of lesbian relations attuned to the nuances of the particular culture (without, however, looking at the larger colonial or postcolonial processes). These studies helped to complicate the relationship between culture and women's sexuality, pointing to a number of factors that shaped the construction and/or presence of particular sexualities and genders, including marriage and kinship norms, gender polarity, control of fertility and sexuality, social stratification, and economics. The studies made visible the extent and embeddedness of female transgender and same-sex practices in broader social structures.

Ethnographic studies of female same-sex relations brought new material to another important debate in studies of sexuality, the relation between gender and sexed bodies. Shepherd (1986) argued that lesbians in Mombasa did not change their gender, concluding that biological sex is a much more important determinant of gender than behavior in the Swahili sex/gender system.[21] According to Shepherd, men are men and women are women; engaging in same-sex practices does not change that designation. Other work on female transgender practices, however, helped unsettle a model that linked sexed bodies with gender. Evidence from studies of two-spirit people was used to suggest that gender and sexed bodies are separable because people can inhabit a gender not usually assigned to their particular bodies (Blackwood 1984b; Midnight Sun 1988).

This work also helped to illuminate the social construction of categories that were frequently asserted to be "natural," such as the family, the domestic domain, and sexuality. The diversity in forms of women's sexuality underscored the bias of the Euro-American folk model that claimed only one form of "normal" sexuality. More important, the cases of long-term, same-sex relations in other cultures, such as that noted by Evans-Pritchard for Azande women, problematized the privileging of heterosexuality as the model and basic grid for family, kinship, and sexuality. Where theories of kinship and family tended to emphasize women's roles as reproducers and mothers, this evidence broadened the view of their lives to include a range of social relations not defined by domestic caretaking (for example, mummies and babies and Chinese sisterhoods). It even disputed the "naturalness" of heterosexual marriage with evidence of female-bodied persons who created families with their female spouses (e.g., Native American female two-spirits) or who took the father role (woman-marriage in some African societies).

Masculinist studies of homosexuality provided a limited model of sexuality in which male sexuality was the norm and point of origin for all conversations about women's sexualities. Marked by inattention to women, it assumed to speak for the whole while only including half. Ethnographic studies of female same-sex relations revealed some of the problems with this universalizing narrative as it turned its focus on women and systems of gender. Preferring to situate women's sexuality within cultural systems of meaning and power rather than within a comparative model of sexual acts, these studies foregrounded the importance of the broader cultural context to an understanding of sexuality.

Conclusion

In sum, anthropological evidence from ethnographic studies of female same-sex relations and transgender practices offered new insights to some of the early models of sexuality proposed by radical feminist and masculinist scholars.[22] It complicated the radical feminist assertion that sexuality was an oppressive, male-defined institution. The evidence spoke to the plurality of women's sexual practices even while revealing some of the constraints of oppressive gender ideologies. It provided evidence that "lesbianism" could not be characterized simply as a form of resistance, deviance, or means to overthrow the patriarchy, because in many cultures it was deeply embedded in the social fabric. It underscored women's agency in the construction of sexual meaning, showing that women actively produced their own sexuality, whether in adolescent sexual play or in sisterhoods and intimate friendships. Finally, ethnographic research on female same-sex practices underscored feminist assertions about the relation of gender to sexuality.

In contrast to masculinist studies of homosexuality, studies of female same-sex relations highlighted the importance of studying women's, as distinct from men's, sexual practices. These studies sought to understand the conditions that produced difference in men's and women's experiences and understanding of sexuality. They demanded attention to (and analysis of) gender systems and female bodies and for the first time made visible not only the extent of female same-sex relations and transgender practices worldwide but also their relation to larger social processes.

Notes

Parts of this essay were published in somewhat different form in two essays written collaboratively with Saskia E. Wieringa in our coedited book *Female Desires: Same-Sex Relations and Transgender Practices across Cultures* (New York: Columbia University Press, 1999). I thank Saskia and Columbia University Press for allowing me to rework this material and publish it separately here. I am deeply grateful to Mina Davis Caulfield, my mentor and teacher at San Francisco State University, who, in the early 1980s, encouraged my research on lesbians by stating that it was an important topic to undertake. I am also grateful to other scholars who have encouraged me along the way, including John DeCecco, Bonnie Zimmerman, Ellen Lewin, and William Leap. My work has benefited greatly from the perceptive comments, thoughtful proddings, and unfailing support of Saskia E. Wieringa.

1. I use the term *masculinist* to refer to those whose object of study is the unmarked "universal" man and whose work assumes to speak for humanity while referencing only half of the human race (men). This perspective has been an enduring object of criticism in feminist theory. Rather than just calling it mainstream scholarship, I think it is important that its peculiarly myopic vision of the world be marked by the bias it takes, the study of men, hence masculinism.

2. For a critique of Western feminist views and their misappropriation of third-world women's lives, see Grewal and Kaplan, eds. (1994), Mohanty (1984), and Rosaldo (1980).

3. Relevant works include Barry (1979), Brownmiller (1975), Daly (1978), Dworkin (1974), Griffin (1978), MacKinnon (1979), and Millett (1969).

4. The universality of compulsory heterosexuality continues to be a powerful concept in feminist studies. As Vicinus states, "All societies that I know of have

denied, controlled, or muted the public expression of active female sexuality," suggesting a general suppression of female sexuality historically (1993:434).

5. The older, Anglicized spelling of the name of this province was Kwangtung.

6. According to M'pho Nthunya (1997, see also Kendall [1999]), married women formed bond friendships called *motsoalle*. She thought the custom died out sometime during the 1950s.

7. More recent work critiques the assumption that these "passing women" are lesbians who resist patriarchal dictates. Cromwell (1999) argues that the great majority of these "women" were transgendered individuals.

8. See Blackwood (1997) and Jacobs, Thomas, and Lang, eds. (1997) for more recent analysis of two-spirit females and the problem of fixed categories.

9. For a more detailed account of specific cases, see also Blackwood (2000b). Some of the original sources include Gregor (1977), Mead (1928), Roheim (1933), and Shostak (1981).

10. Although these cases only concern same-sex practices, it should be clear that they have implications for heterosexual relations as well. I have suggested that women's erotic friendships indicate a cultural ideology of women's agency in sexuality more generally (Blackwood 2000a).

11. Foucault's work (1978) was a key text producing a "history" of sexuality, which, however, left unaddressed a number of questions concerning women's sexual history.

12. For feminist critiques of sexology, see Jackson (1984) and Vance (1983) among others.

13. Some of these studies include Fry (1986), Herdt (1981), and Taylor (1986).

14. See Elliston (1995) and Weston (1993) for further discussion of the problems of definition and terminology in this field.

15. At least two detailed cases on transgendered females had already been published in scholarly works at that time. Relevant material can be found in Devereux's (1937) account of Mohave *hwame* and Hart's (1968) account of *lakin-on* in the Philippines.

16. See also Elliston's (1995) critique of the concept of "ritualized homosexuality."

17. This invisibility persists in some mainstream anthropology publications. Although lesbian and gay studies is now well recognized as a field of study in anthropology, the entry on "homosexuality" in Blackwell's *The Dictionary of Anthropology* (Barfield, ed. 1997) contains no mention of female homosexuality.

18. Karsch-Haak (1911) was an important German-language source on cross-cultural lesbian practices, but most American researchers did not consult his work.

19. Important early works on U.S. women of color that informed the debates on Western sexualities included Hull, Scott, and Smith, eds. (1981), Moraga and Anzaldúa, eds. (1981), and Smith, ed. (1983).

20. For further discussion of problems associated with the masculinist typology of homosexuality, see Elliston (1993).

21. A later article questioned Shepherd's assertions about gender in Mombasa, ar-

guing that "some homosexual men and women do transgress gender categories and thus pose a threat to elite male hegemony" (Porter 1995:135).

22. For essays on and analyses of female same-sex practices in Asia, Africa, Latin America, and native North America, see Blackwood and Wieringa, eds. (1999).

References Cited

Adam, Barry. 1986. "Age, Structure, and Sexuality: Reflections on the Anthropological Evidence on Homosexual Relations." In *The Many Faces of Homosexuality: Anthropological Approaches to Homosexual Behavior,* ed. Evelyn Blackwood, 19–33. New York: Harrington Park Press.

Barfield, Thomas, ed. 1997. *The Dictionary of Anthropology.* Malden: Blackwell Publishers.

Barry, Kathleen. 1979. *Female Sexual Slavery.* Englewood Cliffs: Prentice-Hall.

Blackwood, Beatrice. 1935. *Both Sides of Buka Passage.* New York: Oxford University Press.

Blackwood, Evelyn. 1984a. "Cross-Cultural Dimensions of Lesbian Relations." Unpublished master's thesis. San Francisco State University.

———. 1984b. "Sexuality and Gender in Certain Native American Tribes: The Case of Cross-Gender Females." *Signs* 10:27–42.

———. 1986. "Breaking the Mirror: The Construction of Lesbianism and the Anthropological Discourse on Homosexuality." In *The Many Faces of Homosexuality: Anthropological Approaches to Homosexual Behavior,* ed. Blackwood, 1–17. New York: Harrington Park Press.

———. 1997. "Native American Genders and Sexualities: Beyond Anthropological Models and Misrepresentations." In *Two-Spirit People: Native American Gender Identity, Sexuality and Spirituality,* ed. Sue-Ellen Jacobs, Wesley Thomas, and Sabine Lang, 284–94. Urbana: University of Illinois Press.

———. 2000a. "Culture and Women's Sexualities." *Journal of Social Issues* 56(2): 223–38.

———. 2000b. "Indigenous Cultures." In *Lesbian Histories and Cultures: An Encyclopedia,* ed. Bonnie Zimmerman, 392–97. New York: Garland.

Blackwood, Evelyn, and Saskia E. Wieringa, eds. 1999. *Female Desires: Same-Sex Relations and Transgender Practices across Cultures.* New York: Columbia University Press.

Brownmiller, Susan. 1975. *Against Our Will: Men, Women, and Rape.* New York: Simon and Schuster.

Carrier, J. M. 1980. "Homosexual Behavior in Cross-Cultural Perspective." In *Homosexual Behavior: A Modern Reappraisal,* ed. Judd Marmor, 100–122. New York: Basic Books.

Chauncey, George, Jr., Martin Duberman, and Martha Vicinus. 1989. Introduction. In *Hidden from History: Reclaiming the Gay and Lesbian Past,* ed. Duberman, Vicinus, and Chauncey, 1–13. New York: Penguin.

Clarke, Cheryl. 1981. "Lesbianism: An Act of Resistance." In *This Bridge Called*

My Back: Writings by Radical Women of Color, ed. Cherríe Moraga and Gloria Anzaldúa, 128–37. Watertown, Mass.: Persephone Press.

Crompton, Louis. 1981. "The Myth of Lesbian Immunity: Capital Laws from 1270 to 1791." *Journal of Homosexuality* 6(1–2): 11–25.

Cromwell, Jason. 1999. *Transmen and FTMs: Identities, Bodies, Genders, and Sexualities.* Urbana: University of Illinois Press.

Daly, Mary. 1978. *Gyn/Ecology: The Metaethics of Radical Feminism.* Boston: Beacon Press.

Deacon, A. Bernard. 1934. *Malekula: A Vanishing People in the New Hebrides,* ed. Camilla Wedgewood. London: Routledge and Sons.

Devereux, George. 1937. "Homosexuality among the Mohave Indians." *Human Biology* 9(4): 498–597.

Dworkin, Andrea. 1974. *Woman Hating.* New York: Plume.

Elliston, Deborah. 1993. Review of *Oceanic Homosexualities. Journal of the History of Sexuality* 4(2): 319–21.

———. 1995. "Erotic Anthropology: 'Ritualized Homosexuality' in Melanesia and Beyond." *American Ethnologist* 22(4): 848–67.

Evans-Pritchard, E. E. 1970. "Sexual Inversion among the Azande." *American Anthropologist* 72(6): 1428–34.

Ferguson, Ann. 1981. "Patriarchy, Sexual Identity and the Sexual Revolution." *Signs* 7(1): 158–72.

———. 1984. "Sex War: The Debate between Radical and Libertarian Feminists." *Signs* 10(1): 106–12.

Ford, C. S., and F. A. Beach. 1951. *Patterns of Sexual Behavior.* New York: Harper and Bros.

Foucault, Michel. 1978. *The History of Sexuality,* vol. 1: *An Introduction.* Trans. Robert Hurley. New York: Pantheon.

Fry, Peter. 1986. "Male Homosexuality and Spirit Possession in Brazil." In *The Many Faces of Homosexuality: Anthropological Approaches to Homosexual Behavior,* ed. Evelyn Blackwood, 137–53. New York: Harrington Park Press.

Gay, Judith. 1986. "'Mummies and Babies' and Friends and Lovers in Lesotho." In *The Many Faces of Homosexuality: Anthropological Approaches to Homosexual Behavior,* ed. Evelyn Blackwood, 97–116. New York: Harrington Park Press.

Gebhard, Paul. 1971. "Human Sexual Behavior: A Summary Statement." In *Human Sexual Behavior: Variations in the Ethnographic Spectrum,* ed. Donald S. Marshall and Robert C. Suggs, 206–17. New York: Basic Books.

Gough, Kathleen. 1975. "The Origin of the Family." In *Toward an Anthropology of Women,* ed. Rayna R. Reiter, 51–76. New York: Monthly Review Press.

Grahn, Judy. 1986. "Strange Country This: Lesbianism and North American Indian Tribes." *Journal of Homosexuality* 12(3–4): 43–57.

Greenberg, D. F. 1988. *The Construction of Homosexuality.* Chicago: University of Chicago Press.

Gregor, Thomas. 1977. *Mehinaku: The Drama of Daily Life in a Brazilian Indian Village.* Chicago: University of Chicago Press.

Grewal, Inderpal, and Caren Kaplan, eds. 1994. *Scattered Hegemonies: Postmodernity and Transnational Feminist Practices*. Minneapolis: University of Minnesota Press.

Griffin, Susan. 1978. *Woman and Nature: The Roaring Inside Her.* New York: Harper and Row.

Hart, Donn V. 1968. "Homosexuality and Transvestism in the Philippines." *Behavior Science Notes* 3(4): 211–48.

Herdt, Gilbert. 1981. *Guardians of the Flutes: Idioms of Masculinity.* New York: McGraw-Hill.

———. 1988. "Cross-Cultural Forms of Homosexuality and the Concept 'Gay.'" *Psychiatric Annals* 18(1): 37–39.

Hollibaugh, Amber, and Cherríe Moraga. 1983. "What We're Rolling around in Bed With: Sexual Silences in Feminism." In *Powers of Desire: The Politics of Sexuality,* ed. Ann Snitow, Christine Stansell, and Sharon Thompson, 394–405. New York: Monthly Review Press.

Hull, Gloria, Patricia Bell Scott, and Barbara Smith, eds. 1981. *All the Women Are White, All the Blacks Are Men, but Some of Us Are Brave: Black Women's Studies.* New York: Feminist Press.

Jackson, Margaret. 1984. "Sex Research and the Construction of Sexuality: A Tool of Male Supremacy?" *Women's Studies International Forum* 7(1): 43–51.

Jacobs, Sue-Ellen, Wesley Thomas, and Sabine Lang, eds. 1997. *Two-Spirit People: Native American Gender Identity, Sexuality, and Spirituality.* Urbana: University of Illinois Press.

Janeway, Elizabeth. 1980. "Who Is Sylvia? On the Loss of Sexual Paradigms." *Signs* 5(4): 573–89.

Kaberry, Phyllis. 1939. *Aboriginal Woman, Sacred and Profane.* London: Routledge and Sons.

Karsch-Haack, Ferdinand. 1911. *Das Gleichgeschlechtiche Leben der Naturvölker.* Munich: Reinhardt.

Katz, Jonathan Ned. 1976. *Gay American History: Lesbians and Gay Men in the U.S.A.* New York: Crowell.

Kendall. 1999. "Women in Lesotho and the (Western) Construction of Homophobia." In *Female Desires: Same-Sex Relations and Transgender Practices across Cultures,* ed. Evelyn Blackwood and Saskia E. Wieringa, 157–78. New York: Columbia University Press.

Lerner, Gerda. 1986. *The Creation of Patriarchy.* New York: Oxford University Press.

MacKinnon, Catherine. 1979. *Sexual Harassment of Working Women: A Case of Sex Discrimination.* New Haven: Yale University Press.

McIntosh, Mary. 1981. "The Homosexual Role Revisited." In *The Making of the Modern Homosexual,* ed. Kenneth Plummer, 30–49. Totowa: Barnes and Noble.

Mead, Margaret. 1928. *Coming of Age in Samoa.* New York: William Morrow.

Medicine, Beatrice. 1983. "'Warrior Women': Sex Role Alternatives for Plains Indian Women." In *The Hidden Half: Studies of Plains Indian Women,* ed. Patricia Albers and Bea Medicine, 267–80. New York: University Press of America.

Midnight Sun. 1988. "Sex/Gender Systems in Native North America." In *Living the Spirit: A Gay American Indian Anthology,* ed. Gay American Indians and Will Roscoe, 32–47. New York: St. Martin's Press.

Millett, Kate. 1969. *Sexual Politics.* New York: Ballantine.

Mohanty, Chandra. 1984. "Under Western Eyes: Feminist Scholarship and Colonial Discourse." *Boundary 2* 12(3)/13(1): 333–58.

Moraga, Cherrie, and Gloria Anzaldua, eds. 1981. *This Bridge Called My Back: Writings by Radical Women of Color.* Watertown, Mass.: Persephone Press.

Nthunya, M'pho M'atsepo. 1997. *Singing away the Hunger: Stories of a Life in Lesotho,* ed. K. Limakatso Kendall. Bloomington: University of Indiana Press.

Philipson, Ilene. 1984. "The Repression of History and Gender: A Critical Perspective on the Feminist Sexuality Debate." *Signs* 10(1): 113–18.

Porter, Mary. 1995. "Talking at the Margins: Kenyan Discourses on Homosexuality." In *Beyond the Lavender Lexicon: Authenticity, Imagination, and Appropriation in Lesbian and Gay Languages,* ed. William L. Leap, 133–53. Newark: Gordon and Breach.

Rich, Adrienne. 1980. "Compulsory Heterosexuality and Lesbian Existence." *Signs* 5(4): 631–60.

Roheim, Geza. 1933. "Women and Their Life in Central Australia." *Journal of the Royal Anthropological Institute of Great Britain and Ireland* 63: 207–65.

Rosaldo, Michelle Z. 1980. "The Use and Abuse of Anthropology: Reflections on Feminism and Cross-Cultural Understanding." *Signs* 5(3): 389–417.

Rubin, Gayle. 1975. "The Traffic in Women: Notes on the Political Economy of Sex." In *Toward an Anthropology of Women,* ed. Rayna R. Reiter, 157–210. New York: Monthly Review Press.

Sankar, Andrea. 1986. "Sisters and Brothers, Lovers and Enemies: Marriage Resistance in Southern Kwangtung." In *The Many Faces of Homosexuality: Anthropological Approaches to Homosexual Behavior,* ed. Evelyn Blackwood, 69–81. New York: Harrington Park Press.

Schaeffer, Claude E. 1965. "The Kutenai Female Berdache: Courier, Guide, Prophetess, and Warrior." *Ethnohistory* 12 (3):193–236.

Shepherd, Gill. 1987. "Rank, Gender, and Homosexuality: Mombasa as a Key to Understanding Sexual Options. In *The Cultural Construction of Sexuality,* ed. Pat Caplan, 240–70. New York: Tavistock.

Shostak, Marjorie. 1981. *Nisa: The Life and Words of a !Kung Woman.* Cambridge: Harvard University Press.

Shulman, Alix Kate. "Sex and Power: Sexual Bases of Radical Feminism." *Signs* 5(4): 590–604.

Smith, Barbara, ed. 1983. *Home Girls: A Black Feminist Anthology.* New York: Kitchen Table, Women of Color Press.

Taylor, Clark L. 1986. "Mexican Male Homosexual Interactions in Public Context." In *The Many Faces of Homosexuality: Anthropological Approaches to Homosexual Behavior,* ed. Evelyn Blackwood, 117–36. New York: Harrington Park Press.

Topley, Marjorie. 1975. "Marriage Resistance in Rural Kwangtung." In *Women in*

Chinese Society, ed. Margery Wolf and Roxane Witke, 57–88. Stanford: Stanford University Press.

Vance, Carole. 1983. "Gender Systems, Ideology and Sex Research." In *Powers of Desire: The Politics of Sexuality,* ed. Ann Snitow, Christine Stansell, and Sharon Thompson, 371–84. New York: Monthly Review Press.

Vicinus, Martha. 1993. "They Wonder to which Sex I Belong: The Historical Roots of the Modern Lesbian Identity." In *The Lesbian and Gay Studies Reader,* ed. Henry Abelove, Michèle Barale, and David M. Halperin, 432–52. New York: Routledge.

Weston, Kath. 1993. "Lesbian/Gay Studies in the House of Anthropology." *Annual Review of Anthropology* 22: 339–67.

Wheelwright, Julie. 1989. *Amazons and Military Maids: Women Who Dressed as Men in Pursuit of Life, Liberty, and Happiness.* London: Pandora.

Zita, Jacqueline. 1981. "Historical Amnesia and the Lesbian Continuum." *Signs* 7(1): 172–87.

THREE

"These Natives Can Speak for Themselves": The Development of Gay and Lesbian Community Studies in Anthropology

Elizabeth Lapovsky Kennedy

Since the late 1970s my research has drawn freely from the disciplines of anthropology and history and the fields of women's studies, American studies, and oral history. This is true to such an extent that I feel hard-pressed to define which discipline or field plays a dominant role in my research and writing. At different points in my career I have claimed one as the prominent influence, only to change my mind as time passes. This eclecticism has been possible because I have had the luxury of being located solely in interdisciplinary departments—American studies and women's studies. They have allowed me to delineate my questions and methods according to what I felt needed to be known as a member of a social movement for justice rather than to what disciplines have designated as legitimate and required for promotion.[1] Until recently, I thought that made me an outsider to anthropology despite my doctorate in social anthropology. My critical reflections for this essay led me to understand, however, that interdisciplinary proclivities characterize a good portion of gay and lesbian scholarship in anthropology.[2] I will argue that studies of gay and lesbian communities and culture have been profoundly interdisciplinary since the late 1970s, encompassing strong connections among anthropology, history, and feminist scholarship.[3]

In 1978, when I started research for *Boots of Leather, Slippers of Gold: The History of a Lesbian Community* (Kennedy and Davis 1993), the territory was uncharted and risky. Anthropology did not offer sustained support and nurturance. Kenneth Read aptly summarizes the state of anthropological research on lesbians and gays in 1980: "When one attempts to unravel this tangled skein, one thread stands out: namely, that anthropological research on homosexual behavior has been, and, to a large extent, still is consigned to the dark recesses of the discipline's closet" (192). Since the early twentieth century anthropology has included small pockets of research on topics related to homosexuality, for example Margaret Mead's discussions of the flexibility of gender and sexuality or the writing on individuals who in the past were called "berdache" and now are called "two-spirit people."[4] In addition, in 1972 Esther Newton's substantial monograph *Mother Camp: Female Impersonators in America* was published, mapping out many contemporary concerns in its complex analysis of class and gender in gay culture.[5] But all these studies were invisible because they were isolated without a meaningful context. The dominant paradigm for conceptualizing homosexuality was heterosexist. It stigmatized homosexuals, considering them either as sick, sinners, or criminals and therefore not a serious topic for study outside of the medical or legal professions.

The movements for gay and lesbian rights and liberation changed that situation. Ample documentation exists about the ways gays and lesbians began to organize on campuses and in professional organizations for their jobs and to pursue their research interests. Here I will discuss the movement's much subtler impact on knowledge: its historicizing of homosexuality. In his introduction to *Gay American History* Katz writes:

> In recent years the liberation movements of lesbians and gay men have politicized, given historical dimension to, and radically altered the traditional concept of homosexuality. . . . From a sense of our homosexuality as a personal and devastating fate, a private, secret shame, we moved with often dizzying speed to the consciousness of ourselves as members of an oppressed social group. . . . In our lives and in our hearts, we experienced the change from one historical form of homosexuality to another. We experienced homosexuality as historical. (1976:1–2)

The gay and lesbian liberation movements and the feminist movement, and the transformations they wrought, raised provocative historical questions about the conditions that led to the formation of communities and the rise of movements of resistance.[6] Unquestionably, this context helped generate and validate my interest in lesbian history. And it appears to have done the same for other scholars. A significant strand of gay and lesbian research by anthropologists has been historically oriented since the mid-1970s. Gayle Rubin's first written work on lesbians was an introduction to the re-publication of *A Woman Appeared to Me* by Renee Vivien in 1976, a novel originally published in 1904. Rubin is explicit about the importance of looking at early-twentieth-century lesbian life to better understand the present: "Lesbians, suffering from the dual disqualification of being gay and female, have been repeatedly dispossessed of their history. The generation of lesbians who emerged out of the women's movement in the late 1960s had to discover their immediate predecessors of the 1950s, who had already undertaken the task of retrieving earlier ancestors from scanty archives" (iii).

Rubin's essay presents Vivien as perhaps one of the first women with gay consciousness and pride and suggests the context that made that possible. Similarly, Esther Newton's "The Mythic Mannish Woman: Radclyffe Hall and the New Woman," published in 1984 and her first major work after *Mother Camp,* has a historical focus. She reclaims the "mannish" woman in the early twentieth century from feminist disrepute by exploring how she signified sexual interest in women at a time when that was not accepted. She also reflects on the meaning of the mannish woman for butches and bulldaggers in the contemporary world.[7]

New developments in the discipline of history, particularly social and feminist history that encouraged study of the daily lives of ordinary people, were very useful to gay and lesbian scholars. It was not, however, a two-way exchange. Gay and lesbian research was not welcome in history departments. Nevertheless, this did not silence the movement's concern with historical questions. Grass-roots gay and lesbian history projects sprang up in cities across North America, including San Francisco, Washington, Boston, Philadelphia, and Los Angeles. The projects pursued serious historical research and had little connection to universities, although some graduate students and faculty were involved. John D'Emilio, for instance, was a graduate student and active in New York City research groups. Gayle Rubin, also a graduate student, was a member of the San Francisco Gay and Lesbian History Project. I, already a faculty member, founded the Buffalo Women's Oral History Project with Madeline Davis.[8] Most members of grass-roots lesbian history projects, however, were not academics. Jonathan Katz and Allan Bérubé published ground-breaking historical studies while remaining outside the academy, and Joan Nestle, Deb Edel, and Judith Schwarz of the Lesbian Herstory Archives founded and maintained archives.[9]

Not being based primarily in the academy, the grass-roots history movement could easily be eclectic and look everywhere for helpful sources. It created an interdisciplinary framework for gay and lesbian community studies. In an effort to reclaim the silenced voices of preceding generations of lesbians and gays, such projects enthusiastically employed the methods of oral history that traditional history departments viewed with suspicion. In addition, meticulous researchers considered what the early sexologists' case studies could offer contemporary research. They found the first psychologists, particularly Evelyn Hooker and Mary McIntosh in the 1950s and 1960s, to conceptualize homosexuality as something other than a sickness or maladjustment and to understand gay urban social life as a culture that fostered self-acceptance and health.[10] These grass-roots projects also clarified how during the 1960s the deviance school in sociology, as exemplified in the work of Howard Becker and Erving Goffman, lay the groundwork for research that focused on the way society structured deviance rather than on deviants themselves.[11] They uncovered actual studies of gay urban culture in sociology by Edwin Schur, Martin Hoffman, Nancy Achilles, and Ethel Sawyer.[12] Of course, they also found the scattered work of anthropologists.[13]

By the mid-1980s, the academy began to acknowledge the new historical scholarship on gays and lesbians, which created possibilities for the social sciences to study homosexuality. The process of legitimation was helped by the writings of such recognized scholars as Michel Foucault.[14] The value of historical approaches to homosexuality for most social science fields was multiple. Historical approaches freed studies of sexuality from the control of models derived from the medical profession, particularly from the assumptions that sex is solely a biological instinct or drive and that sexual variation manifests disease. They also provided conceptual tools for understanding changing forms of homosexuality in the West as well as variations in sexual expression due to culture and concomitantly problematized the idea of a fixed gay identity. Most important, they allowed scholars to address changing forms of resistance and persecution and explore the relationship between lesbian and gay communities and culture and the rise of gay and lesbian movements.

For a while, I was so immersed in these historical questions that I thought I was becoming a historian until Ellen DuBois, one of my history colleagues, bluntly disabused me of the idea by suggesting, quite reasonably, that I did history like an anthropologist. Indeed, it is my training as an anthropologist that led me to use oral history to study the history of Buffalo lesbian communities even if the field of anthropology itself was unable to support and nurture my work. In what ways was anthropology important in the writing of *Boots of Leather,* the first full-length book on the history of lesbian communities? Three characteristics of anthropology are particularly helpful for gay and lesbian community studies. First, anthropologists pay attention to social fact. Second, anthropology assumes an order behind what on the surface appears to be incoherent and strange behavior and symbols, and that meaning is revealed as one learns the cultural system from the "native's" point of view. Third, anthropology affirms that social communities have complicated dynamics and are worth detailed study.

First, anthropology's valuing of cultural and social facts allowed me to trust my judgment and pursue a study of butch-fem communities despite an inhospitable climate for such research.[15] Gayle Rubin has emphasized the importance of attention to social facts: "A radical theory of sex must build rich descriptions of sexuality as it exists in society and history" (1984:275). She argues, "It is difficult to develop a pluralistic sexual ethics without a concept of benign sexual variation. Variation is a fundamental property of all life, from the simplest biological organism to the most complex human social formations. Yet sexuality is supposed to conform to a single standard. One of the most tenacious ideas about sex is that there is one best way to do it, and that everyone should do it that way" (283). Rubin suggests that empirical sex research as developed by Alfred Kinsey and furthered in the work of John Gagnon and William Simon is one of the few traditions that brings curiosity rather than judgment to the study of sex.

Although anthropology did not develop an open, nonjudgmental approach to the study of sex, the tradition of a curious respect for variation is at the heart of anthropology and was certainly impressed upon students. I was trained by Meyer Fortes, and it was well known that when his students returned from the field he would ask questions such as, "How would the 'natives' blow their noses?" The speed with which a student answered, and the concreteness of the reply (perhaps even including a physical imitation), was the basis on which he judged the student's potential to become a decent ethnographer.[16]

It was unquestionably respect for the details of culture that interested me in attempting a nonjudgmental analysis of butch-fem communities. It strikes me as no accident that anthropologists were among the first to study gendered homosexuality, as evidenced by Newton (1972) and Read (1980). These studies pay careful attention to the variety of expressions of butch and fem, of queen and butch, and aim to elucidate their meanings in the context of a specific culture.[17] Their detail leaves a rich record for reference and reanalysis.

The assumption that seemingly unrelated social behavior and meanings have underlying order that needs to be learned from natives is the second useful characteristic of anthropology. Kenneth Read is quite eloquent in his analogies between fieldwork in New Guinea and in The Columbia, a tavern in a northwest city:

> Somewhat surprisingly, given my aesthetic distaste for the tavern, I have often found myself leaving companions in other bars with the remark: "I'm going to *my* tavern." The possessiveness is similar to the way in which anthropologists often refer to an exotic population as "my people." The proprietary implications underscores an investment in time and energy that represents a significant component of one's professional life, but they point to something else as well: to the slow and frequently difficult acquisition of a contextual familiarity with the details of the life observed, a process similar in many ways to learning a second language. There is a unique satisfaction, generating a feeling of identification, when eventually, you perceive the cues, the grammar and syntax of what you are watching, and become sufficiently sure to experiment with the idioms. (1980:70)

I know that learning "the native's" view piqued my interest in studying the Buffalo lesbian communities. When graduate students told me about the attractive and dignified older women who were in bars and did not speak to younger women, my immediate response was that these elder bar lesbians probably had their own rules that we needed to learn. Sure enough, as students learned the relevant customs they were able, slowly, to enter the older women's social lives, chatting and playing pool. Students were amazed that a distinct culture could be right there—in their own bars.[18]

The third very useful aspect of anthropology was its long tradition of ethnographic study of small communities and its more recent attempts to place these community studies within the hierarchical relationships of imperialism.[19] *Boots of Leather* above all explores the development of communities of resistance and the impact of such communities on the creation of culture. Anthropological analyses of the conditions that lead to more unified or more segmented communities, and to more permeable and fixed borders and boundaries, were relevant. Most important, my own "initiatory" fieldwork with the Waunan, a Native American people in the Choco forest of Colombia, challenged me to understand their cultural autonomy in the context of the domination of conquest and four hundred years of cultural interaction among African-Columbians, Mestizos, and Native Americans. Analyses of the impact of colonialism on small communities by third-world and Marxist anthropologists provided frameworks for conceptualizing working-class lesbian communities as autonomous yet part of a dominant heterosexual system.[20]

Respect for social fact, distinct cultural systems, and community studies did not, of themselves, overcome homophobia or heterosexism. Anthropology was and is ridden with homophobic skewing of social facts and homophobic interpretations. The gay and lesbian liberation movements and the feminist movements were essential in providing frameworks for raising less-biased questions about gays and lesbians and women. I am arguing that the methods and approaches of anthropology were very helpful once groups such as the Anthropological Research Group on Homosexuality (ARGOH) and Society of Lesbian and Gay Anthropologists (SOLGA) challenged and contained homophobia.[21]

As important as the intersections of anthropology and history have been for my work and that of other anthropologists in gay and lesbian community studies, feminism has been equally formative. That seems to be true not only for scholars like myself who are located in women's studies but also for those located in history and anthropology. Without feminist perspectives, contemporary gay and lesbian community studies would be significantly different, giving less, if any, attention to gender and/or lesbians. Lesbians were not a visible part of the gay anthropology that emerged in the 1980s, as demonstrated strikingly by Read's absolute lack of attention to lesbians in *Other Voices*. Yet feminist scholarship did more than argue for the inclusion of women. It advocated making women's experience central and asking questions from that location. By doing so, feminist scholars developed frameworks for analyzing the social construction of gender and gender hierarchy and for studying everyday life and intimacy, all essential elements for contemporary anthropological studies of gay and lesbian communities.

Despite the centrality of feminist scholarship to my work, having devoted my life since the 1970s to building women's studies and fostering a revolution in knowledge about women and gender, I am painfully aware of its limitations. Just as scholars who identify as anthropologists need to turn to feminist scholarship, I had to turn to anthropology and history, a further testament to the need for interdisciplinarity in early gay and lesbian community studies.

At times while working on *Boots of Leather*, feminism caused me more difficulties than even anthropology. The relationship of lesbians to feminism has not been easy. In its inception in the early 1970s, feminist anthropology did not encourage research on lesbians or gay men (Lewin and Leap, ed. 1996:viii). When I started work on *Boots of Leather,* feminist scholars in all disciplines had marginalized the study of butch and fem. Madeline Davis and I could not receive a serious hearing in feminist contexts; moreover, we often were met with extreme hostility. Butch and fem communities were sexual communities, and, as Gayle Rubin (1984) has argued, feminism is not necessarily the most helpful framework for analyzing sex. In addition, our research was on working-class communities, which required complex understandings of gender and class hierarchies that feminism had not yet developed.

Nevertheless, *Boots of Leather* is anchored deeply in feminist scholarship. It generates research questions from the perspective of women's/lesbians' experiences. To do so, it places lesbians in the context of gay history while it creates a separate lesbian history. It argues that patriarchy/male supremacy affects lesbians in ways that make their culture and history profoundly different from, as well as similar to, that of gay men. Feminism has had similar affects on other anthropologists, which has led some scholars to include lesbians as well as gay men in their research or to support women who focus exclusively on women's experience. In the 1990s, Esther Newton's and Kath Weston's monographs fully included women as well as men, and Ellen Lewin's *Lesbian Mothers* (1993), like my own work, focuses exclusively on women. Newton provides an ideal model of including women in every aspect of her study of Cherry Grove while also devoting separate chapters to the specific issues they face. In generating research questions from women's experiences, this body of literature not only looks at the details of women's lives but also raises questions about the control of their sexuality.[22]

I chose the phrase "these natives can speak for themselves" for the title of this essay because it encapsulates the complex questions of voice in modern anthropological research. Who has the right to speak for whom? These issues became prominent for gays and lesbians in events surrounding a panel on "AIDS and the Social Imaginary" at the 1992 American Anthropological Association meetings. The panel included no members from the AIDS and Anthropology Research Group and no members from SOLGA.[23] In response, SOLGA activists had T-shirts imprinted with the slogan "these natives can speak for themselves," and the incident became one element of a broader campaign to improve the status of lesbians and gays in anthropology. This book is part of that fight against systemic marginalization because it offers a history of research by, for, and/or about gays, lesbians, bisexuals, and transgenders in anthropology. Community studies have been central in making public gay and lesbian voices because they are usually based on gay and lesbian words, perspectives, and interpretations. Equally important, the authors shape the pasts and futures of lesbian and gay research as well as cultural and social anthropology, a major site of community studies.

The interdisciplinary linkages among history, anthropology, and feminism in lesbian and gay community studies in North America do not prevent gay, lesbian, bisexual, and transgender anthropologists from setting their own research agendas. Rather, this history leads me to delineate four major research areas that anthropologists are particularly well suited to consider.

First, I propose there be an effort to bring into dialogue anthropological work on gays and lesbians that has been influenced by historical studies and work influenced by medical and psychological anthropology. The gap between these approaches is quite substantial. Usually that means very different understandings of identity, community, and coming out. In general, one could characterize the difference between these approaches as what Eve Kosofsky Sedgwick calls "minoritizing" and "universalizing" views of homosexuality. The former refers to those who see homosexuality as important "primarily for a small, distinct, relatively fixed homosexual minority," and the latter to those who see it as "an issue of continuing, determinative importance in the lives of people across the spectrum of sexualities" (1990:1–2). Anthropology as a discipline is uniquely well suited to address different perspectives because it is familiar with the comparative method and considers data from all over the world. It also has a tradition of including cultural as well as physical anthropologists and medical anthropology, which often combines the two.

I first became aware of the chasm separating my colleagues and the frameworks they used for research when John D'Emilio's *Making Trouble* was reviewed negatively by the *SOLGA Newsletter* (Paloma 1993). I was shocked that the reviewer dismissed D'Emilio, whose work had so positively influenced my thinking, as ideological. The reviewer had no understanding of D'Emilio's project to understand the way sexual identities are socially constructed in different historical periods.

For research to go forward and not be trapped by dogmatism, dialogue between these two different tendencies in anthropology should be encouraged. Are there constant attributes of homosexuality? Is it correct to identify a third-gender cross-culturally? Or is it more useful to focus on the multiple varieties of sexual behavior and sexual persecution? What are the variations in human sexuality? Do they follow regular patterns? During the conference "Gay and Lesbian History: Defining the Field" at the CUNY Graduate School in 1995, Will Roscoe and I, anthropologists, took opposing views on these questions. Rather than ignore these differences, we need to scrutinize them.

Second, as part of these dialogues, gay, lesbian, bisexual, and transgendered research needs to continue problematizing the concepts of identity and community. Refining the interconnections between identity and community is central to future gay and lesbian studies. In what ways is community integral to the construction of gay and lesbian identity and in what ways is it an imagined construction that fosters a repressive master narrative?[24] We need new ways of thinking about these topics, ways that escape the enlightenment polarities of individual and society. Further exploration of the ways sexual identity is mutually constituted by race, class, and gender might be useful for this task. Research that explores regional, geographical, and ethnic variations in identities and communities, aiming to account for similarities and differences, also seems promising. In addition, research about identities such as bisexual or transgender that blur fixed categories and challenge neat community boundaries can potentially offer new perspectives about the relationship between sexual identity and community.[25] Because of its past commitment to study of community and its recent commitment to deconstructing fixed identity, anthropology is well suited to this challenge.

Third, with the unnatural toll that AIDS has taken on gay communities, and with the natural aging of the gay and lesbian population, there is more and more reason to record life stories. Anthropology can begin to take a lead in this area of work by problematizing stories, showing the multiplicity of identity, and suggesting how life stories connect to communities. When I first started conducting oral histories about lesbian communities, my primary concern was with recording social facts and being able to turn an oral history into a historical document. As I used the method and read more widely, however, I realized that the question of how memory is constructed is equally important.[26] These are concerns that dovetail nicely with contemporary anthropologists' concern about representation and reflexivity and with feminism's concern about the construction of the other. During the 1990s, the concerns of feminism, anthropology, and history came together nicely and in new ways, continuing to make disciplinary boundaries hard to draw.

Fourth, anthropology has pioneered the documentation and analysis of camp and gendered cultures, an area of research that transformed dramatically in the 1990s. Cultural critics have introduced theories of performativity while transgendered and transsexual people have raised new perspectives from their life experiences on the ways gender is inscribed on the body. These new directions raise exciting questions for anthropologists. Connections with cultural criticism promise to characterize a segment of contemporary gay and lesbian anthropological work in the way that connections with history characterized the late 1970s and 1980s.[27]

Despite anthropology's expertise in the ethnography of small communities, anthropologists studying gay and lesbian communities have been drawn to, and needed, other disciplines and fields, especially history and women's studies, in order to achieve satisfactory conceptual frameworks. It has not been a one-way street, however, because many historians have found anthropological methods useful for studying gay and lesbian community and culture. This interdisciplinary tendency is likely to be strengthened by the further development of the field of gay, lesbian, bisexual, and transgender studies. These developments do not necessarily undermine the integrity of the discipline of anthropology.

My proposed research agenda locates anthropologists at the center of studies of sexualities in general and homosexualities in particular and argues the importance of anthropologists' contributions. Those who discuss these issues—identity, community, sexual possibility, memory, and the performance of gender—and dare to bridge different intellectual orientations will strengthen their own research as well as their influence on the direction of research in the American Anthropological Association. They might also be of use to the lesbian, gay, bisexual and transgendered people and communities organizing to expand their liberties and survive the attacks of a growing anti-gay movement.

Notes

This is a revised version of a paper originally presented on a panel on "Anthropology and Homosexuality: A Critical Retrospective" at the American Anthropological Association meetings in San Francisco on November 20, 1996. Thanks to Ellen Lewin for inviting me to participate in this panel and to my Buffalo writing group for their feedback on an early draft of this essay—Betsy Cromley, Rosemary Feal, Carol Zemel, Carolyn Korsmeyer, and Claire Kahane. Special thanks to Susan Cahn for carefully reading the manuscript and making useful suggestions.

1. In my experience, interdisciplinarity is rarely supported. The University of Buffalo regularly challenged the integrity of its American studies department, with the latest assault coming in 1996 and 1997. The attacks always required an elaborate defense and justification that were draining and undermining. Unfortunately, the responses did not have the cumulative effect of moving the university toward becoming a more hospitable place for interdisciplinary scholarship and teaching. They merely

bought time until the next round of criticism. When I left in 1998 it appeared that the university had managed to decimate the existing American studies department and intended to build a new program, the shape of which had yet to be determined.

2. There are several excellent recent reviews of the history of lesbian and gay research in anthropology, such as Weston (1991a) and Lewin and Leap (1996:1–28). "These Natives Can Speak for Themselves" draws upon these essays and is intended as a complement to them.

3. The importance of this interconnection between history and anthropology can be seen from the fact that two of the four major historical studies of gay and/or lesbian communities since the 1980s are written by scholars who have Ph.D.'s in history and two by scholars with Ph.D.'s in anthropology (Chauncey 1994; D'Emilio 1983; Kennedy and Davis 1993; Newton 1993). Another major historical study, but not of communities, is Faderman (1991), which also highlights the importance of interdisciplinary work to gay and lesbian studies. Faderman is in literature, not in history. All five of these researchers have been deeply influenced by feminism.

Similarly, for the panel "Classic Debates in Lesbian and Gay History: Gender and the Homosexual Role" at a conference on "Gay and Lesbian History: Defining the Field" at the CUNY Graduate School in October 1995, only two of the five panelists had degrees in history. Randolph Trumbach, a historian who was the organizer and chair of the panel, also made an opening presentation. George Chauncey was the other historian; Will Roscoe and I were the two anthropologists; and Martha Vicinus, a literary scholar, was the fifth participant.

4. For discussion of the importance of Mead's work to contemporary understanding of the social construction of sexuality, see Weeks (1989). Similarly, many contemporary works draw on earlier anthropological studies of "berdache" (Gay American Indians, comps., and Roscoe, ed. 1988; Jacobs, Thomas, and Lang, eds. 1997).

5. When I think of how isolated I felt studying lesbian community history in 1978 and then think of Newton's work fifteen years earlier, I shudder. What imagination and self-reliance was required to research and write *Mother Camp* with virtually no movement support.

6. Bravmann (1997) discusses the ways history has been an important part of gay popular culture and therefore politics and suggests that the narratives of gay liberation are really versions of the narrative of modernization already entrenched in history.

7. In contrast, Read's ethnography (1980), although interesting, lacks a historical framework. The absence highlights what such a framework offered to anthropologists. Read sets bar communities outside history and ignores any connections between bars and gay and lesbian social movements. Rather, he explicitly indicates a dichotomy between bar patrons and movement activists, implying that this division was always there. Lacking a historical framework for questions about communities of resistance, he cannot explore or explain changing forms of bar life. His book focuses on entirely different issues. Drawing on literature and psychology, he creates an existential framework that analyzes gay alienation.

8. I am not sure if Esther Newton was a member of any of these grass-roots groups,

but I know that she had some connection through her research at the Lesbian History Archives.

9. This account of grass-roots history projects comes from my own experience; for another account see D'Emilio (1992).

10. D'Emilio (1983:140–44) offers a good discussion of changing intellectual currents during the 1960s, although he does not discuss Mary McIntosh, Nancy Achilles, or Ethel Sawyer. For mention of the place of McIntosh, see Weeks (1991:4, 16); for mention of Achilles and Sawyer, see Kennedy and Davis (1993:20).

11. Esther Newton (1970 [1972]) had already discovered Goffman in the 1960s.

12. I have searched my memory to try to recall how I first learned of the work of Nancy Achilles and Ethel Sawyer, both of whom were useful to Davis and I for the historical context they provided our research. I think it was through word of mouth at some conference attended by grass-roots historians. I certainly do not remember finding it in a bibliographic search or in someone else's footnotes.

13. Although the questions were primarily historical, they did not eschew a comparative perspective. Katz (1978) includes a long section, "First Americans, Gay Americans." He was introduced to this material through Harry Hay, who influenced several anthropologists as well. See Jacobs (1997:24).

14. It is worth noting that Foucault (1990 [1978]), Katz (1978), and Weeks (1977) all developed these ideas about changing forms of sexual identity and expression in history at about the same time and without reading one another.

15. Feminism at the time negatively judged butch-fem roles and was ideologically committed to erasing them from lesbian history (Nestle 1987). History and anthropology were so mired in anti-gay and anti-lesbian approaches that they could not possibly consider butch-fem communities as worthy of study.

16. I relish the thought of what it would have been like had Fortes asked how Waunan make love or copulate. Such questions were highly unlikely at the time.

17. Although L. L. Langness mentions Newton's book in the preface, Read (1980) does not refer to Newton in his analysis. This is particularly striking because the connections between her analysis and his are deep. Most likely, male supremacy made women's research and writing irrelevant to male anthropologists. In addition, at the time Read did his work, gay men and lesbians were so separated from one another that they did not discuss work. In 1980 panels on gays and lesbian research in twentieth-century North America were still not a part of AAA meetings.

Paul Kutsche has documented the separateness of men and women in his reporting of the history of SOLGA from 1984 to 1986. In addition, he attributes Newton's writing of *Mother Camp* as occurring five to ten years later than the pioneering research of Joe Carrier, Clark Taylor, and Steve Murray on male homosexuality in Latin America and Kenneth Read in New Guinea. "Influential publications by lesbian anthropologists, like Ester Newton's *Mother Camp* [sic] and Carole Vance's *Pleasure and Danger* [sic]," Kutsche states, "came out five to ten years later" (1993:25)." That is true of Vance's work but not of Newton's, which was researched during the 1960s and published in 1972. Kutsche adds that he is writing away from home and his files, and it is therefore understandable that he was not able to check publication dates.

What is interesting is that his memory did not include Newton as a pioneer, an omission that confirms my view that gay male anthropologists did not know and appreciate Newton's work until relatively recently.

18. This combination of attention to social fact and the search for underlying social meaning continues to help me in my current work, creating the life story of Julia Boyer Reinstein. In "'But We Would Never Talk about It'" (Kennedy 1996), I follow her lead and explore the way she and her social group structured discretion. The research revealed that being out can mean very different things in different periods and that being discrete, in some cultures and time periods, is not necessarily oppressive.

19. Feminism in the 1970s had difficulty with complex discussions of power. For the most part, it limited its concern to power in gender relations.

20. Dell Hymes (1969) offers a sample of the kinds of sources that originally helped me think about the way small communities are caught in the relations of imperialism. Of course today the sources are myriad.

21. For documentation of the actions of SOLGA and its parent group ARGOH against homophobia in the AAA, see Lewin and Leap, ed. (1996:vii–x) and Kutsche (1993).

22. To the best of my knowledge, no male anthropologists have included lesbians fully in research on gay communities and culture, but many have begun to read feminist scholarship and use its analytical tools, as for instance William Leap's discussion of gender throughout *Word's Out* (1996).

23. The panel had no gay activist members and, for that matter, no people actively engaged in community groups fighting AIDS. Once SOLGA became aware of the situation, it proposed some speakers, but they were turned down by the event's organizers on the grounds that the panel was already full. Thus the research and teaching of many gay and lesbian anthropologists on AIDS, as well as their struggle against the devastation of AIDS, was made irrelevant and invisible. I was not at the San Francisco meetings and therefore could not attend the panel, although it shaped my term as SOLGA co-chair, which started immediately afterward. SOLGA made its primary concern education about how the AAA had treated the subject of gays and lesbians and AIDS, and the connections between the two, in the late 1980s and early 1990s before the Commission on Lesbian and Gay Issues in Anthropology. The American Anthropological Association has a long history of political organizing by groups—notably women and African Americans—that aim to address the exclusion of their voices and perspectives. Gays and lesbians are one of the more recent groups.

24. Read, as early as 1980, questions the usefulness of homosexual community studies. He argues that the concept of community is only useful for political activists trying to build community for effective action. But for the majority of "homosexuals" community is not meaningful. They are not associated with a community on the basis of sexuality anymore than heterosexuals are. In his study of a bar, The Columbia, he focuses on a common style that people share. Weston (1996a) deepens this approach by dedicating *Families We Choose* (1991b) to a young woman whose lesbian community failed her. Weston's work is informed by a theoretical orientation that questions the usefulness of the concept of community: Community

studies tend to reify and simplify identity and reinforce master narratives of dominant groups. In contrast, Newton's work on Cherry Grove (1993) and my work on
Buffalo working-class lesbians reveal the importance of community in shaping lesbian and gay identity and culture. In *Boots of Leather,* for example, we document
the impact of community on the construction of butch and fem identities. Many
butches did not polarize masculinity and femininity until they entered the bar community, and for many fems it was the permanency of bar communities that made it
easier for them to claim an identity as lesbian as well as fem.

25. I am grateful to Jessica Nathanson for educating me on this topic through her
dissertation proposal.

26. Helpful sources for understanding contemporary issues in oral history include
Frisch (1990), Gluck and Patai, eds. (1991), Kennedy (1997), and Portelli (1991).

27. Both Newton's and Weston's work on gendered sexuality have drawn on cultural criticism (Newton 1996; Weston 1996b).

References Cited

Bravmann, Scott. 1997. *Queer Fictions of the Past: History, Culture and Difference.*
    New York: Cambridge University Press.
Chauncey, George. 1994. *Gay New York: Gender, Urban culture, and the Making of
    the Gay Male World, 1890–1940.* New York: Basic Books.
D'Emilio, John. 1983. *Sexual Politics, Sexual Communities: The Making of a Ho-
    mosexual Minority in the United States, 1940–1970.* Chicago: University of Chi-
    cago Press.
————. 1992. "Not a Simple Matter: Gay History and Gay Historians." In D'Emilio,
    Making Trouble: Essays on Gay History, Politics, and the University, 138–47. New
    York: Routledge.
Faderman, Lillian. 1991. *Odd Girls and Twilight Lovers: A History of Lesbian Life
    in Twentieth-Century America.* New York: Columbia University Press.
Foucault, Michel. 1990 (1978). *The History of Sexuality,* vol. 1: *An Introduction.*
    Trans. Robert Hardy. New York: Pantheon.
Frisch, Michael. 1990. *A Shared Authority: Essays on the Craft and Meaning of Oral
    and Public History.* Albany: State University of New York Press.
Gay American Indians, comps., and Will Roscoe, ed. *Living the Spirit: A Gay Amer-
    ican Indian Anthology.* New York: St. Martin's, 1988.
Gluck, Sherna Berger, and Daphne Patai, eds. 1991. *Women's Words: The Feminist
    Practice of Oral History.* New York: Routledge.
Hymes, Dell, ed. 1969. *Reinventing Anthropology.* New York: Pantheon.
Jacobs, Sue-Ellen. 1997. "Is the 'North American Berdache' Merely a Phantom in
    the Imagination of Western Social Scientists?" In *Two-Spirit People: Native Amer-
    ican Gender Identity, Sexuality and Spirituality,* ed. Sue-Ellen Jacobs, Wesley
    Thomas, and Sabine Lang, 21–43. Urbana: University of Illinois Press.
————, Wesley Thomas, and Sabine Lang, eds. 1997. *Two-Spirit People: Native*

American Gender Identity, Sexuality and Spirituality. Urbana: University of Illinois Press.

Katz, Jonathan. 1976. *Gay American History: Lesbians and Gay Men in the U.S.A.* New York: Thomas Y. Crowell.

Kennedy, Elizabeth Lapovsky. 1996. "'But We Would Never Talk about It': The Structures of Lesbian Discretion in South Dakota, 1928–1933." In *Inventing Lesbian Cultures in America,* ed. Ellen Lewin, 15–39. Boston: Beacon Press.

———. 1997. "Telling Tales: Oral History and the Construction of Pre-Stonewall Lesbian History." In *A Queer World: The Center for Lesbian and Gay Studies Reader,* ed. Martin Duberman, 181–90. New York: New York University Press.

Kennedy, Elizabeth Lapovsky, and Madeline Davis. 1993. *Boots of Leather, Slippers of Gold: The History of a Lesbian Community.* New York: Routledge.

Kutsch, Paul. 1993. "One View of Our History from 1984–1987." *Society of Lesbian and Gay Anthropologists Newsletter* 15 (3): 24–27.

Leap, William L. 1996. *Word's Out: Gay Men's English.* Minneapolis: University of Minnesota Press.

Lewin, Ellen. 1993. *Lesbian Mothers: Accounts of Gender in American Culture.* Ithaca: Cornell University Press.

——— and William Leap, eds. 1996. *Out in the Field: Reflections of Lesbian and Gay Anthropologists.* Urbana: University of Illinois Press.

Newton, Esther. 1979 (1972). *Mother Camp: Female Impersonators in America.* Chicago: University of Chicago Press.

———. 1984. "The Mythic Mannish Lesbian: Radclyffe Hall and the New Woman." *Signs* 9(4): 557–75.

———. 1993. *Cherry Grove, Fire Island: Sixty Years in America's First Gay and Lesbian Town.* Boston: Beacon Press.

———. 1996. "'Dick(less) Tracy' and the Homecoming Queen: Lesbian Power and Representation in Gay Male Cherry Grove." In *Inventing Lesbian Cultures in America,* ed. Ellen Lewin, 161–93. Boston: Beacon Press.

Nestle, Joan. 1987. "Butch-Femme Relationships: Sexual Courage in the 1950s." In Nestle, *A Restricted Country,* 100–109. Ithaca: Firebrand.

Paloma, Luis. 1993. Review of *Making Trouble: Essays on Gay History Politics and the University. Society of Lesbian and Gay Anthropologists Newsletter* 14(1): 38.

Portelli, Alessandro. 1991. *The Death of Luigi Trastulli: Form and Meaning in Oral History.* Albany: State University of New York Press.

Read, Kenneth E. 1980. *Other Voices: The Style of a Male Homosexual Tavern.* Novato, Calif.: Chandler and Sharp Publishers.

Rubin, Gayle. 1976. "Introduction." In Renee Vivien, *A Woman Appeared to Me,* iii–xxix. Trans. Jeannette H. Foster. Reno: Naiad Press.

———. 1984. "Thinking Sex: Notes for a Radical Theory of the Politics of Sexuality." In *Pleasure and Danger: Exploring Female Sexuality,* ed. Carole S. Vance, 267–319. New York: Routledge.

Sedgwick, Eve Kosofsky. 1990. *Epistemology of the Closet.* Berkeley: University of California Press.

Weeks, Jeffrey. 1977. *Coming Out: Homosexual Politics in Britain from the Nineteenth Century to the Present.* London: Quartet.

———. 1989. *Sexuality.* New York: Routledge.

———. 1991. *Against Nature: Essays on History, Sexuality and Identity.* London: Rivers Oram Press.

Weston, Kath. 1991a. "Lesbian/Gay Studies in the House of Anthropology." *Annual Review of Anthropology* 22: 339–67.

———. 1991b. *Families We Choose: Lesbians, Gays, Kinship.* New York: Columbia University Press.

———. 1996a. "Requiem for a Street Fighter." In *Inventing Lesbian Cultures in America,* ed. Ellen Lewin, 131–41. Boston: Beacon Press.

———. 1996b. *Render Me, Gender Me: Lesbians Talk Sex, Class, Color, Nation, Studmuffins. . . .* New York: Columbia University Press.

FOUR

Another Unhappy Marriage? Feminist Anthropology and Lesbian/Gay Studies

Ellen Lewin

The anthropological study of homosexuality, the new creature that we have taken to calling "lesbian/gay studies" and has only recently begun to have an official place in the wider discipline, is the progeny of a disparate, sometimes antagonistic, set of ancestors. Like the marriages examined in anthropological studies of kinship, the conjugal bond between its parents was inspired more by political considerations than by love. The marriage between the lesbian and gay male anthropological traditions that produced the new field is primarily one of convenience. The family quarrels that have punctuated this unlikely union grow out of distinct approaches to causality and meaning that have the depth of cultural difference. Like an intercultural or "mixed marriage," lesbian/gay studies in anthropology have moments of domestic bliss that alternate with bitter combat. While the predominantly gay male side of this marriage favors an approach rooted in a focus on sexual behavior, the predominantly lesbian side has drawn its inspiration from feminist anthropology's concern with gender.

Thus, lesbian/gay studies in anthropology emerged from (at least) two rather different, and at times antagonistic, fields, often but not always separated by the gender of both subjects and objects. And while we propose in this volume that lesbian/gay anthropology can be usefully understood as a distinct subfield in its own right, it is also true that the division between work that focuses on sexual behavior and work that focuses on gendered identities has continued to characterize the direction taken by more recent scholarship.

One family line is descended from the comparative study of sexual behavior, the chronicling of the varied faces of (usually male) same-sex eroticism, or what Kath Weston has aptly called, in some of its most descriptive incarnations, the "ethnocartography" of homosexuality. These works provided a vital antidote to naturalized assumptions about heterosexuality and confronted anthropologists' tendency to assume the universality of some sort of generic heterosexuality. They also tended to naturalize homosexual behavior as a sort of freestanding category that could be unproblematically found in any cultural context.

The other line finds its ancestry in feminist anthropology, realized in an early concern with the cross-cultural study of sexual variation among women but eventually moving toward a politically inflected understanding of gender. These inquiries were often animated more by questions about identity under conditions of male and heterosexual dominance (that is, with gender and power as key analytical domains) than with scrutiny of homosexual behavior itself. A fascination with the possible parameters of women's resistance to patriarchal domination often fueled examination of something understood to constitute lesbianism.[1]

The Patriline: Anthropologies of Homosexual Behavior

The direct forebear of this field is probably to be located among those few cross-cultural surveys of sexuality and sexual practices that acknowledged the existence of homosexuality when the topic was still considered far too embarrassing to be raised in polite—not to mention academic—company. This genealogy begins with the Kinsey studies of male and female sexual behavior and continues in the work of Ford and Beach (1951) and Marshall and Suggs (1971) as reviewed by Gayle Rubin in chapter 1 of this volume.

Emerging from these roots were a number of path-breaking (if not "seminal") ethnographies that forced anthropology to reconsider its tendency to place sexuality in the realm of the natural and use that assumption as the foundation for naturalizing two other domains we now view as cultural—kinship and gender. Gilbert Herdt's work in New Guinea (1981) was, of course, particularly influential in this regard, notably in the success he achieved in teasing apart behavior and identity, but other works by Joseph Carrier (1976, 1992), Walter Williams (1986), and Stephen Murray (1979, 1987), among others, stand out as significant players in this emerging field.

The aforementioned works examine different ethnographic areas and document distinct cultural phenomena, but they share a core concern with sexual behavior as the *sine qua non* of homosexuality. That is, how we know what we are looking for can be determined by what it takes to find men (and perhaps women) engaging in sexual behavior together. Under what conditions that actually occurs, what specific behaviors are displayed, what the identities of the players turn out to be, and how they are regarded in their cultures all are open to investigation. These works challenge the researchers' own experience of homosexuality by demonstrating both that homosexual behavior existed in other cultures and that its place in other cultures cannot be assumed to resemble the degraded status of "perversion" that it holds in twentieth-century North American and European societies.

In other words, by holding a particular behavioral phenomenon (homosexual behavior) constant, these works offer an explicit critique of Western homophobia. Like Margaret Mead's investigation of Samoan adolescence (1928), they point out that a presumably biological condition may take a very different form and be differently evaluated in a different cultural context. Noticeably absent, at the same time, is an interrogation of the homosexual behaviors themselves; while their meanings are shown to vary, their physical substance is assumed to be transparent. Homosexuality, and thus sexuality in general (sometimes characterized more broadly as "desire"), are naturalized and made concrete, assumed to be no less essential to human life than adolescence as a developmental stage. Most of these works focused on male-male sexuality, although some related contributions by female scholars such as Evelyn Blackwood (1984, 1986a, 1986b) searched for and documented cross-cultural evidence of homosexual behavior among women.

As things have played themselves out, the more or less gay male wing of the field has excelled at documenting the variations in erotic behavior and attendant social arrangements that the ethnographic record can supply. These works have some important strengths, particularly as they seek to make direct applications to the battle against the AIDS/HIV epidemic. Dwayne Turner's *Risky Sex* (1997), for example, draws on notions of sex as biologically motivated behavior to question inflexible oppositions between notions of safe and unsafe sex as these are deployed in AIDS-prevention campaigns. Sexual pleasure, according to Turner, resists rational decision making. Culture enters the process insofar as it "provides the setting for sexual encounters, impacts the meaning of specific acts, and provides sexual constraints upon (but also allows for) sexual expression" (122). For cultural reasons, Turner argues, some activities are more pleasurable than others, but once the biological drive for sexual pleasure has been activated, more fundamental, precultural forces shape their realization. In this view, questions of identity or ambiguities of affiliation have no relevance; gay men are defined according to a range of sexual behaviors in which they engage. Their categorization is self-evident.

Other recent works on gay male sexuality share basic assumptions with Turner. The essays in William Leap's *Public Sex/Gay Space,* to draw on just one exemplary work, offer a rich variety of cross-cultural examples of how gay men manage constructions of public and private to find suitable venues for sexual expression. In his introduction to the volume, Leap explains, "Rather than assuming that the participants in public sex are (in some essentialized sense) 'gay' men, this collection explores the *identities* and *other self-descriptions* of the men who participate in sex-with-other-men at these [public] sites, the overlap between sexual experiences and gender-identity, and the connections between sexual practices, ethnic/racial identity, class position and claims to privilege" (1999:3).

The essays that follow scrutinize notions of public and private in ways that challenge early feminist thinking, using observations or narratives of sexual interactions themselves as the starting point for the analysis. Gender enters into the discussion insofar as male-male erotic connections disrupt conventional expectations for masculinity but not with respect to the concerns with hierarchy and status that are at the heart of feminist understandings of gender. Although hardly apolitical in a world that largely condemns homosexual practices, the approach promotes a very different political sensibility than that rooted in a concern with gender.

The essays thus draw on a concept which Gilbert Herdt has called "sexual lifeways," by which he refers to "the specific erotic ideas and emotions, categories and roles, that constitute individual development within a particular sexual culture. These lifeways can be broken down into component forms, most of them gendered according to whether one is male or female or third gender" (1997: 20). The starting point for Herdt, and for most of the scholars who work in this tradition, is the individual sexual act; discussions of gender contextualize or locate the acts that form the basic content of homosexuality or of any other type of sexual behavior.

Central to this body of work is an interrogation of the interactions between specific sexual behaviors and cultural contexts that they may alter or that may alter them. Are these behaviors understood in particular cultural settings to be normal but to violate generally accepted standards of conduct in others? Does their performance vary according to the extent to which they are stigmatized or honored? Do other cultural categories—such as age, social status, or race—interrupt or amplify their meanings? How do these behaviors collaborate with or contradict individual or group formation of identity? How do broader cultural themes shape experiences of pleasure or desire?

A focus on sexual behavior has also characterized much of the work of gay and lesbian anthropologists who have joined the recent move toward reflexive personal narrative. Ralph Bolton (1995), writing about erotic encounters in the field, has argued that no other form of data collection about sexual behaviors and preferences can substitute for direct personal experience. Similarly, Evelyn Blackwood's account of her love affair in the field (1995) also hinges on the assumption that same-sexual activities in distant cultural settings are transparently comparable to such relationships at home.

But not all studies that consider sexual interactions between males consistently privilege behavior over gender. In Don Kulick's *Travesti* (1998), a study of transgendered prostitutes in Brazil, intersecting issues of gender and identity are at the heart of the analysis. In sharp contrast to the discourse of transgendered persons in the United States, Kulick's narrators seek to maximize their femininity but do not perceive themselves to be "women." Rather, they understand gender to be the product of particular sexual practices and thus to be the outcome of desire. Persons who penetrate are defined as "men," while *travestis* and women are both recipients of penetration. In this system, gender and biological sex need not correspond; biological sex is conceived of as fixed, defined by the presence of either a penis or a vagina. Gender results from behavior and hence is not fixed, although it is resolutely binary. Kulick's work makes sense of the wider system of Brazilian gender, placing *travestis* at its heart: "Whereas the northern Euro-American gender system is based on anatomical sex, the gender system that structures travestis' perceptions and actions is based on *sexuality*. . . . [T]he determinative criterion in the identification of males and females is not so much the genitals as it is the role those genitals perform in sexual encounters" (227, emphasis in the original). Gender, for *travestis,* is understood to be a product or result of sexual desire.

Similarly, Michael Tan's exploration (1995) of the various identities that compose the behavioral category of men who have sex with men (MSMs) in the Philippines foregrounds complex intersections between identity and class, potentially undermining AIDS management efforts that depend on reaching persons engaged in risky sexual activities. In the Filipino context, there are several distinct MSM subcultures, although the extent to which their members self-identify as homosexual varies considerably. Male sex workers, known as "call boys," provide sexual services to both male and female clients but generally view themselves as straight and are often heterosexually married. A second group, known as *parloristas* because they tend to work in beauty parlors, or *bakla,* a Filipino word that labels one as effeminate or combining characteristics of male and female, are also distinctly lower class. A third group, typically from middle-class or higher economic strata, self-identifies as "gay," a term that has class as well as sexual connotations. This group, however, like the *bakla,* subscribe to binary gender-based definitions of sexuality, seeing appropriate sexual partners as those whose gender presentation is distinctly different. In particular, sex between two *bakla* is condemned as "lesbianism" or a "clash of cymbals"; not unexpectedly, *bakla* express a preference for sex with a "straight man." Tan shows how both *bakla* and gay sexual sensibilities depend on, and in fact reinforce, gender constructions more generally deployed in Filipino culture rather than constituting a distinct cultural domain. That this pattern presents a challenge to HIV/AIDS prevention programs is not surprising. It also reverses the circumstances described by Kulick for Brazilian *travestis;* in the Filipino case, gender determines sexual desire in a manner that mirrors the system governing heterosexual behavior.

It should be clear from these examples that the emphasis on behavior that has been characteristic of the mainly gay male side of this marriage is by no means monolithic. Behavior often eludes analysis unless identity is also considered, and analyses of behavior may lead to novel readings of gender identity. At the same time, however, sexuality in its most physical aspect tends to be naturalized in this approach in that it is assumed to be a universal and uniquely driven dimension of human existence.

The Matriline: Anthropologies of Lesbian/Gay Identities

While studies of homosexuality were taking the path I have outlined, many forerunners of the anthropology of lesbianism were busy elsewhere. Largely galvanized by the emergence of second-wave feminism in the early 1970s, significant early contributions to this new field were driven by questions about basic categories and units of analysis that had long been taken for granted in anthropology, kinship being a case in point, although they followed on earlier efforts to document the varied lives of women across cultures and sought to render visible what had mostly been invisible. These scholars drew on a political understanding of the differential status of women and men. Their ability to understand particular patterns of sexual preference among women was firmly grounded in recognition of gender as, at least partly, a system that organizes responses to sexual inequality. In other words, these anthropologists situated lesbianism (and male homosexuality) within a larger consideration of gender, always mindful of the fact that lesbians were also women and that gay males were men.

Rather than being an autonomous category, sexual behavior emerges in these works as understandable only in relation to relations of power that shape and are shaped by systems of gender. These scholars understand same-sex desire and behavior as different phenomena, depending upon the gender of the actors, embedded in the system of meanings that surrounds gender in particular cultural contexts. To mention just a couple of possible interpretations, a preference for same-sex partners for women might suggest either conscious or implicit resistance to domination by men. For men, homosexual choices might reveal a celebration of egalitarian relationships. For both men and women, same-sex preferences have material and social consequences, whether we consider the harmful effects of economic discrimination, threats to physical safety, and cultural erasure or whether we look at the distinct opportunities presented by gay/lesbian social networks and by freedom from the strictures of conventional social expectations. These conditions can be considered whether we regard homosexuality to be a naturally occurring sexual variation or whether we understand it to be a nexus of interpretations that surfaces under particular cultural conditions—whether we start, that is, from an essentialist or constructionist position.

Strikingly, considering anthropology's long-standing preference for work that highlights the distant and exotic other, several key works that set the tone in this area dealt with lesbians (and sometimes gay men as well) in American cultural milieux. Inspired in part by a desire to respond to the androcentrism that permeated gay studies and by the urgency of the struggle for lesbian/gay rights that had erupted around them, but probably driven most powerfully by their commitment to feminist politics, these scholars considered homosexuality as they encountered it in their own surroundings. Their choice of field-site, of course, obviated some of the problems of definition that confronted investigators who approached homosexuality as a cross-cultural phenomenon, although somewhat ironically it also often led to their work being regarded as not really anthropology.

The perspective all these contributors, particularly Kath Weston (1991, 1993, 1998), Liz Kennedy (1993), Esther Newton (1979 [1972], 1993), and Ellen Lewin (1993), also was fundamentally shaped by their immersion in the emerging subfield of the anthropology of gender. Sexual behavior itself was less directly a focus of concern in their works than was a consideration of how the social and cultural consequences of such behavior might realign gendered meanings, particularly insofar as such systems had generally been assumed to be produced by a heterosexuality that had rarely been problematized. These works understood homosexuality, particularly lesbianism, as sexualities that emerged in particular gendered surroundings not as genders themselves or as behavior that could be understood without reference to gender or that transcends cultural boundaries.

Kath Weston's *Families We Choose* (1991) is one of the core texts of this emerging subfield. Her study of how lesbians and gay men in San Francisco conceptualize kinship testifies to the durable significance of biological kinship in the lives of women and men whose position in these families has been undermined (at least hypothetically) by their homosexuality. At the same time, Weston's narrators detail a system they call "families we choose" or "gay families," which organizes kinshiplike relations with friends. Both of these systems depend on shared understandings of what kinship is supposed to be about in American culture, particularly in terms of expectations of enduring solidarity and loyalty that are stable, presumably because they are not chosen. But because gay men and lesbians may be rejected by their "blood families," gay and lesbian understandings of relatedness reveal biological kinship to be as contingent as relations between friends. "Chosen families," in contrast, can be depended upon unconditionally and thus paradoxically embody the qualities conventionally associated with biological kin.

Weston's work evocatively describes the lives of contemporary lesbians and gay men and their use of American cultural elements in their construction of community and shifts our gaze back to the mainstream. Kinship—in the biological sense—is revealed to be less than unconditional, not only for gays and lesbians but also for other people. Relationships with friends, and lovers as well, emerge as having a potential for enduring solidarity to the same extent as bonds forged by blood. Fundamental understandings of the foundations of kinship in American culture are rethought but not only for those at the margins.

In a somewhat different vein, Elizabeth Kennedy and Madeline Davis's ethnohistorical account of working-class, lesbian, bar-centered culture in Buffalo, New York, (1993) also draws on feminist concerns with women's status. At the center of this work is a concern with the politicization of lesbian identity and its development in relation to the particular historical, economic, and racial context in which it was situated. The working-class Buffalo lesbians who hung out in a series of bars during the 1930s, 1940s, and 1950s were resisting invisibility, creating circumstances under which they could act on their desires, and laying the groundwork for the eventual formation of gay rights and feminist movements. Although desire, in some senses, is the engine that fueled the existence of the bars, Kennedy and Davis focus on the political consequences of the bonds forged in these institutional settings, largely excluding direct discussion of erotic practices they may also have fostered.

Similarly, Esther Newton's ethnohistory of Cherry Grove (1993), a predominantly gay male resort community outside New York City, situates gay and lesbian identities in a particular locality and historical tradition. The community has been dominated by gay men throughout its history, and their particular sexual sensibilities and behaviors shaped local culture, often making virtual outsiders of lesbians. On the one hand, Newton documents the centrality of the Meat Rack, the location of outdoor (male) sexual activity, as a key element of the community's cohesion and identity. On the other hand, however, she shows how women have been able to establish themselves in the community; eventually appropriate some of its emblematic ritual expressions, particularly drag performance; and adapt these to correspond to their own definitions of identity and community. Further, despite the centrality of specific sexual symbols as foundational marks of community, life in the Grove has always been modified and stratified according to indicators of gender, race, and class as they emerge under particular historical conditions. Here, male sexual behavior is a sign of identity as well as a symbol of community membership and cohesion. Female sexual behavior is implied in this system but need not be specified or observable. The actual content of sexual behaviors in either case bears only oblique significance to the wider project of community formation and persistence.

Newton's earlier work *Mother Camp* (1979 [1972]) also takes up matters of identity with far greater specificity than it documents particular sexual behaviors. Sexual behavior, in fact, is only implied in this classic ethnography of the culture of female impersonators. At issue is the problem of identity, a question of how professional drag queens organize their understandings of gender in relation to themselves and the larger world. Newton analyzes the multilayered symbols deployed in drag performance, connecting its seeming contradictions to the stigma gay men—both performers and audience—experience in American life.

In my *Lesbian Mothers: Accounts of Gender in American Culture* (Lewin 1993), sexual behavior itself is an implied but not actually necessary component of women's identities. The fact that shapes these mothers' experiences and choices is not a particular definitional sexual desire or outcome but a label that is applied to or chosen by the women. In this context, being a lesbian is particularly significant because it is popularly understood to contradict being a mother; the two identities are cultural oxymorons. How lesbian mothers make sense of these contradictions and work with them to craft manageable identities is the subject of the book. Motherhood, I have found, tends to overwhelm and supersede lesbianism as the source of expressed individual identity, a process in which behavior is either irrelevant or simply assumed to have specific characteristcs.

While these emphases on identity have long been characteristic of lesbian anthropology, a growing body of scholarship by and about gay men also builds on these foundations. For example, William Hawkeswood (1996) tells little in his vivid ethnographic study of gay black men in Harlem about specific erotic practices and preferences that make the men he studied "gay." Rather, he provides a complex understanding of the intersection between sexuality and race, particularly in relation to the varied meanings the men attach to notions of family. In this community, family, on the one hand, refers to the members of each person's gay social network, a constellation in which relationships are defined according to categories of fictive kinship. On the other hand, however, the men also use the language of family to refer to the extended ties of biological kinship that constitute each individual's roots. Although the terms are deployed somewhat differently in different contexts and situations, they are also conceptually linked and produce, in large part, the experience of being gay for men who grew up and have remained in Harlem and for whom being black is as central to personal identity as being gay.

These approaches to identity have mainly appeared in work that focuses on American culture, but they also make their way into some new feminist work on lesbianism in other cultural milieux. Jennifer Robertson's study (1998) of the Japanese all-woman musical theater group Takarazuka interrogates the fanatical devotion of female fans to the performers as a kind of proto-lesbian phenomenon. Performers who play men's roles in Takarazuka's productions, the *otokoyaku,* represent both the rigid separateness of the genders and a subversive possibility for women to invade men's privileged domains. They are both perfect men—almost better than the originals—and not-men. The theater's popularity is comprehensible only in the context of Japanese assumptions about gender. Butch performances that captivate so many women in Takarazuka's audience may have sexual elements, but they are never simply about desire. Robertson's analysis offers a vision of a kind of lesbianism that does not require a specific sexual realization. It is, instead, the direct product of the broader system of gender asymmetry that dominates Japanese life.

At the same time, however, these analyses do not necessarily neglect the behavioral domain. Some studies of female homosexuality have explicitly considered sexual behavior, often with an eye toward destabilizing assumptions about the cross-cultural applicability of Western sexual identity labels. Gloria Wekker (1999), for example, has written about the phenomenon of intimate same-sex relationships that women in Suriname call *mati work*. These bonds have little to do with women's self-identification because most women are involved in what Wekker calls a "dual sexual system" that includes both opposite-gendered and same-gendered arenas and does not shape identity. Nevertheless, Wekker's account also makes clear that homosexual and heterosexual relationships are neither interchangeable nor reducible to free-floating desire. Whether women are exclusively heterosexual or whether they are involved with both men and women, their relationships with men have an explicitly transactional character conceptualized as bringing money and motherhood:

> [But] in their relationships with women, mati deploy money in a much less direct way. Although female lovers do exchange money and help each other cope financially, this aspect of the relationship is embedded in a rich flow of reciprocal obligations, which include the sharing of everyday concerns, the raising of children, nurturing, emotional support, and sexual pleasure. Money, as an exchange object for sex, thus plays an independent and outspoken role in relationships with men, but it is part of a more elaborate, a "thicker" stream of exchanges and reciprocal obligations in relationships with women. In fact, the term *work* in mati work implies that there are mutual obligations involved between the two female partners. (Wekker 1999:127)

What is noteworthy about Wekker's analysis is her understanding of the sexual behaviors that constitute mati work in the context of a wider system of gendered inequality. She is thereby able to avoid situating the phenomenon as naturally occurring sexual desire and intrinsically resistant to cultural interpretation. Mati work is about much more than raw sexual impulse, and Wekker's feminist perspective allows her to reveal this.

The predominantly lesbian side of the union, then, has used insights gleaned from feminist anthropology to forge an approach to sexuality that foregrounds identity and places correspondingly less emphasis on who does what with whom. In a sense, this approach naturalizes sexual behavior no less than the gay male approach, in that sexual behavior is simply assumed to happen and therefore seems to need little specification.

Can This Marriage Be Saved?

Do the divergent histories of these two lineages doom them to antagonism? What sort of counseling might allow them to reconcile and perhaps even to go about reproducing—that is, generating—a new field that would incorporate characteristics of each parent? Can this (seemingly arranged) marriage be saved?

Some might suggest that a resolution lies in a move toward the sort of queer perspective that has come to characterize recent work on lesbian and gay, as well as bisexual and transgendered, topics in disciplines other than anthropology, particularly in the humanities. Queer theory, and the queer sensibility on which it depends, seems to promise a unifying identity for our otherwise multiply initialed selves that allows us to subvert all manner of academic conventions and devise approaches that are more thoroughly transgressive of mainstream categories. Queer theory not only encourages a destabilization of dichotomous thinking but it also answers that destabilization with a playfulness that appeals to people's naughty sides. Established knowledge about identity and politics offers few guideposts for negotiating this new terrain (or so it seems), and as we dive into the intricacies of performance that are central preoccupations in queer scholarship we experience the exhilaration that comes of having encountered the cutting edge.

But observations have already been made in other disciplines that the emergence of queer studies, particularly in the humanities, has come at the cost of an increasingly hostile stand-off between feminist and queer perspectives. Drawing on the metaphor of marriage, philosopher Jacqueline Zita (1994) has pointed out that queer studies rest on a sense of inventiveness that obscures the importance of feminist theory as a progenitrix of the field. In their rush to declare "queerness" a unifying identity that may even supersede ethnicity, Zita argues, scholars have not only ignored feminist contributions to the field but have also used the performative framework to subsume gender under sexuality. In the process they have obscured the social and political foundations of both. The disembodied projections that emerge from this analytic style mainly validate queer studies in the increasingly apolitical opportunity structure of the academy, evaporating the activist origins of both fields and (probably not coincidentally) inflating the careers of its leading practitioners.

Responding to some of the same stimuli, sociologist Suzanna Walters (1996) has deplored the denigration of feminism she sees as integral to the emergence of the queer sensibility that has attached to the growing gay visibility evident in culture and the academy. Walters notes that queer perspectives draw momentum from a vilification of feminist theory as old-fashioned, conformist, anti-sexual, and beholden to mainstream assumptions. She argues persuasively that queer theorists, by discarding the emphasis on gender and power that was the motive force of feminism, also effect the disappearance of a distinct lesbian reality and cannot help but erase politics from their interpretations.

Walters's wariness seems particularly relevant to the intersection between anthropologies of sexual behavior and anthropologies of lesbian/gay identity. The tendency of the mainly lesbian wing of the field to foreground the ramifications of lesbian (or gay) identity and to delve little into detailed explorations of sexual practices can easily be read as the result of puritanical impulses. And the emphasis placed on sexual specifics by the mainly gay male wing of the field is likely to appear obsessive or self-indulgent to a reader who finds such behavior irrelevant to issues of gender asymmetry she considers important.

Given this history, I would argue that attempts to theorize lesbian/gay anthropology from a queer perspective will lead to even more intense polarization. In particular, such attempts are likely to reemphasize the extent to which the sexual behavior, largely gay male wing of the field has erased its own feminist forebears. It seems, instead, that some useful directions might be suggested by efforts to bring the divergent approaches discussed here into some sort of conversation. Can we make a conscious choice to put the behaviorally based approaches typical of male-centered work into a perspective that fully considers the political ramifications of gender that feminist anthropology has emphasized? Can those who have studied the complex identities shaped by sexual preferences begin to consider whether those preferences themselves need to be scrutinized and described more thoroughly?

Overlooked in the focus on the disparity between the patrilines and matrilines that spawned lesbian/gay anthropology is a source of convergence that can form the basis for a renewed common venture. Despite specific, seemingly gender-based differences in vision, lesbian and gay anthropologies share a tendency to assume the transparency of either behavior or identity, drawing on familiar concepts to imagine meanings even in distinct cultural contexts. These are the understandings that need to be problematized and disrupted if anthropological approaches to the diverse domain called homosexuality are to make a worthwhile contribution. In the case of (predominantly) gay male anthropology, the content of behavior is assumed to be isomorphic with something the analyst and the reader can readily imagine. For (predominantly) lesbian anthropology, the process of identity formation, and its relation as an element of protest against gender inequality, is similarly implicit. In other words, in neither case does cultural analysis overcome assumptions about the importance of fundamental human drives, whether these consist of particular sexual behaviors or of the need to form identities based on such behaviors.

The relationship between these two largely disparate traditions is certainly more aptly characterized as one of marriage rather than blood. It is a marriage that is strategically chosen, as are marriages in many of the cultures anthropologists study, to mediate between opposing political factions and lay the foundation for peaceful coexistence. That is, the continuing disenfranchisement of both lesbian and gay anthropologists and the continuing marginality of research on gay and lesbian topics have generated considerable pressure to constitute ourselves as a unified interest group that can advocate both for lesbian/gay research and for the rights of lesbian and gay anthropologists in the profession. These pressures have made organization as a unified subdiscipline a pressing political priority.[2] But they have not bridged some of the differences that continue to epitomize its two branches.

Must the solution, then, to our marital woes be a kind of intellectual bisexuality or perhaps cross-dressing? To put ourselves into each other's worlds, if not each other's heads, must we be willing to experiment with sexual identity, to undermine definitions we have long believed in, and perhaps to submit ourselves to the uncertainties of crossing gender boundaries? We might be able to achieve this if we are willing to accept that a feminist-inspired focus on gender can be injected into these studies. Such a focus might lead not only to an infusion of feminist energy into more of the anthropology of gay men but also make it possible for anthropologists of lesbianism to profit from work done on men. Perhaps the most promising and provocative of these approaches are those that seek to connect sex and gender in innovative ways, whether such analyses locate gender as a product of sex or sex as a product of gender.

Like marital conflicts, not all of the disparities between lesbian and gay approaches in anthropology can ever be resolved. And like domestic disputes that can only be addressed by an agreement to disagree—I won't complain about the laundry if you promise to do the dishes—our differences speak eloquently to the reality of gender as a fact of life. But they also demonstrate fundamental differences in women's and men's perceptions of the importance of "sex" as a behavior and of the fundamental definitions of what sex is. As Marilyn Frye has observed, "sex" is an inappropriate term for "whatever it is that lesbians do," because lesbians have difficulty specifying their erotic activities in terms of a model that speaks of "sexual acts" or that asks how many "times" one has "had sex" (1991:3). Frye argues that the notion that sex is an event draws on a phallic ideal that may describe heterosexual intercourse but has little to do with the more fluid experience that typifies lesbian sexuality. One might also add that the notion that sex is something that occurs in discrete episodes may also apply more accurately to gay male sex.

I can't claim to have a simple solution to offer to the problem at hand. Like most domestic conflict, finding the truth of what happened—who said and did what—is an unlikely outcome to any investigation. Continued cohabitation may require both parties to become reconciled to an existence that neither meets their needs nor conforms to their notions of reality. A final decision to stay together may emerge more from an awareness of the hazards that come with separation than from unambiguous assurance that continued union will have clear benefits. Accommodation may come from elaborating separation, acknowledging that union will continue, but not at the price of reconfiguring worldviews. Our intellectual foundation lies in the heritage of feminist anthropology and studies of gender that gives our field its character. Any effort to erase these origins in favor of a sexier, younger, and queerer spouse will surely be met with swift vengeance from an anthropological "First Wives Club."

Notes

An earlier version of this essay was presented at the American Anthropological Association meetings invited session on "Anthropology and Homosexuality: A Critical Retrospective" in San Francisco on November 23, 1996.

1. Feminist theorist Adrienne Rich (1980) contributed to these positions as she proposed that virtually all forms of female cooperation and subversion of male suprem-

acy be considered part of a "lesbian continuum" that did not necessarily involve or require explicitly sexual behavior. Rich's nonsexual definition of lesbianism followed earlier radical feminist formulations, most notably the classic statement that appeared in the Radicalesbians' manifesto "The Woman-Identified Woman" (1973) as well as the influential historical work of Carroll Smith-Rosenberg (1975) on intimate female friendships in the nineteenth century. See also Rothblum and Brehony, eds. (1993) for a more recent effort to apply the nineteenth-century notion of "Boston marriages" to contemporary lesbian relationships.

2. See the Introduction for a discussion of the gay rights movement in general, and the Society of Lesbian and Gay Anthropologists in particular, as they have influenced the emergence of lesbian/gay anthropology.

References Cited

Blackwood, Evelyn. 1984. "Sexuality and Gender in Certain Native American Tribes: The Case of Cross-Gender Females." *Signs* 10(1): 27–42.

———, ed. 1986a. *Anthropology and Homosexual Behavior.* New York: Haworth Press.

———. 1986b. "Breaking the Mirror: The Construction of Lesbianism and the Anthropological Discourse on Homosexuality." In *Anthropology and Homosexual Behavior,* ed. Evelyn Blackwood, 1–17. New York: Haworth Press.

———. 1995. "Falling the Love in An-Other Lesbian: Reflections on Identity in Fieldwork." In *Taboo: Sex, Identity and Erotic Subjectivity in Anthropological Fieldwork,* ed. Don Kulick and Margaret Willson, 51–75. New York: Routledge.

Bolton, Ralph. 1995. "Tricks, Friends, and Lovers: Erotic Encounters in the Field." In *Taboo: Sexual, Identity and Erotic Subjectivity in Anthropological Fieldwork,* ed. Don Kulick and Margaret Willson, 140–67. New York: Routledge.

Carrier, Joseph M. 1976. "Cultural Factors Affecting Urban Mexican Male Homosexual Behavior." *Archives of Sexual Behavior* 5(2): 103–24.

———. 1992. "Miguel: Sexual Life History of a Gay Mexican American." In *Gay Culture in America: Essays from the Field,* ed. Gilbert Herdt, 202–24. Boston: Beacon Press.

Ford, Clellan S., and Frank A. Beach. 1951. *Patterns of Sexual Behavior.* New York: Harper and Row.

Frye, Marilyn. 1991. "Lesbian 'Sex.'" In *An Intimate Wilderness: Lesbian Writers on Sexuality,* ed. Judith Barrington, 1–9. Portland: Eighth Mountain Press.

Hawkeswood, William G. 1996. *One of the Children: Gay Black Men in Harlem.* Berkeley: University of California Press.

Herdt, Gilbert. 1981. *Guardians of the Flutes: Idioms of Masculinity.* New York: McGraw Hill.

———. 1997. *Same Sex, Different Cultures: Exploring Lesbian and Gay Lives.* Boulder: Westview Press.

Kennedy, Elizabeth Lapovsky, and Madeline D. Davis. 1993. *Boots of Leather, Slippers of Gold: The History of a Lesbian Community.* New York: Routledge.

Kulick, Don. 1998. *Travesti: Sex, Gender and Culture among Brazilian Transgendered Prostitutes.* Chicago: University of Chicago Press.

Leap, William L. 1999. Introduction. In *Public Sex/Gay Space,* ed. William L. Leap, 1–21. New York: Columbia University Press.

Lewin, Ellen. 1993. *Lesbian Mothers: Accounts of Gender in American Culture.* Ithaca: Cornell University Press.

Marshall, Donald S., and Robert C. Suggs, eds. 1971. *Human Sexual Behavior.* New York: Basic Books.

Mead, Margaret. 1928. *The Coming of Age in Samoa: A Psychological Study of Primitive Youth for Western Civilization.* New York: William Morrow.

Murray, Stephen O. 1979. "The Institution of a Quasi-Ethnic Community." *International Review of Modern Sociology* 9(2): 155–75.

———, ed. 1987. *Male Homosexuality in Central and South America.* New York: Gay Academic Union.

Newton, Esther. 1979 (1972). *Mother Camp: Female Impersonators in America.* Chicago: University of Chicago Press.

———. 1993. *Cherry Grove, Fire Island: Sixty Years in America's First Gay and Lesbian Town.* Boston: Beacon Press.

Radicalesbians. 1973. "The Woman-Identified Woman." In *Radical Feminism,* ed. Anne Koedt, Ellen Levine, and Anita Rapone, 240–45. New York: Quadrangle Books.

Rich, Adrienne. 1980. "Compulsory Heterosexuality and Lesbian Existence." *Signs* 5(4): 631–60.

Robertson, Jennifer. 1998. *Takarazuka: Sexual Politics and Popular Culture in Modern Japan.* Berkeley: University of California Press.

Rothblum, Esther D., and Kathleen A. Brehony, eds. 1993. *Boston Marriages: Romantic but Asexual Relationships among Contemporary Lesbians.* Amherst: University of Massachusetts Press.

Smith-Rosenberg, Carroll. 1975. "The Female World of Love and Ritual: Relations between Women in Nineteenth-Century America." *Signs* 1(1): 1–29.

Tan, Michael L. 1995. "From *Bakla* to Gay: Shifting Gender Identities and Sexual Behaviors in the Philippines." In *Conceiving Sexuality: Approaches to Sex Research in a Postmodern World,* ed. Richard G. Parker and John H. Gagnon, 85–96. New York: Routledge.

Turner, Dwayne C. 1997. *Risky Sex: Gay Men and HIV Prevention.* New York: Columbia University Press.

Walters, Suzanna D. 1996. "From Here to Queer: Radical Feminism, Postmodernism, and the Lesbian Menace (or, Why Can't a Woman Be More Like a Fag?)." *Signs* 21(4): 830–69.

Wekker, Gloria. 1999. "What's Identity Got to Do with It? Rethinking Identity in Light of the *Mati* Work in Suriname." In *Female Desires: Same-Sex Relations and Transgender Practices across Cultures,* ed. Evelyn Blackwood and Saskia E. Wieringa, 119–38. New York: Columbia University Press.

Weston, Kath. 1991. *Families We Choose: Lesbians, Gays, Kinship.* New York: Columbia University Press.

———. 1993. Lesbian/Gay Studies in the House of Anthropology. *Annual Review of Anthropology* 22: 339–367.

———. 1998. "The Virtual Anthropologist." In *Long Slow Burn: Sexuality and Social Science.* New York: Routledge, 189–211.

Williams, Walter L. 1986. *The Spirit and the Flesh: Sexual Diversity in the American Indian Culture.* Boston: Beacon Press.

Zita, Jacquelyn N. 1994. "Gay and Lesbian Studies: Yet Another Unhappy Marriage?" In *Tilting the Tower: Lesbians, Teaching, Queer Subjects,* ed. Linda Garber, 258–76. New York: Routledge.

FIVE

Studying Lesbian and Gay Languages: Vocabulary, Text-making, and Beyond

William L. Leap

Studying the language (more properly, languages) of lesbian and gay experience is a relatively new component of lesbian and gay anthropology and equally so of language and gender studies and of anthropology as a whole.[1] Research and publication in this area has grown rapidly since the late 1980s, yielding studies of sentence and paragraph structures, specialized vocabulary, narrative styles, and turn-taking strategies as well as uses of silence and other forms of nonverbal communication—all as deployed in the everyday lives of lesbians and gay men in English-speaking North Atlantic domains. During the late 1990s, researchers began to explore the languages of same-sex desires, practices, and identities attested in linguistic settings other than English. Some of these studies began to examine the "diffusion" of "gay English" into locations associated with other linguistic traditions and to describe the mechanisms (tourism, economic displacement, and broadcast and other public media) through which such diffusion unfolds. They also drew attention to the conflicts between gay English and indigenous languages of same-sex desire and to the effects that those conflicts have on indigenous constructions of same-sex desires.

In part, these developments reflect the more general "turn to language" that has become prominent in cultural and social anthropology since the 1970s. But interests in language also reflect interests in gaining access to components of lesbian/gay experience that are not always accessible through other sources of data. In that sense, lesbian/gay-centered language research not only raises interesting anthropological questions in its own right but also complements, and in some ways enhances, the work unfolding elsewhere in lesbian/gay studies as a whole.

This chapter begins by tracing the emergence of lesbian/gay language studies and identifying some of the considerations that prompted the emergence of this inquiry and others that hindered its emergence. I will then consider what has been learned from these studies, focusing particularly on three concerns: (1) what lesbian and gay language research reveals about the experience of same-sex desires, identities, and practices in late-modernity; (2) how text-making and textual products provide representation for those desires, identities, and practices; and (3) how studies of text lead to broader questions about social and historical dimensions of lesbian and gay life in North Atlantic domains and other locales.

Discovering Lesbian and Gay Languages

In 1966, while discussing the particular contributions that ethnography and physical anthropology could bring to the study of homosexuality, anthropologist David Sonenschein observed, "The linguist may contribute studies of the general verbal behavior of homosexuals and make ethnolinguistic analysis of their 'special languages'—the formation, maintenance, change, and function of the terms. Some work using vocabulary tests has been done (Slater and Slater 1947), but a cultural approach in terms of both unit studies and general analyses is needed" (78–79).

Sonenschein was writing before Stonewall and before lesbian and gay presence began to claim greater public visibility in the United States and other North Atlantic locales. His comments largely describe work that could (and should) be done but had yet to be undertaken in anthropology. As he noted, "This paper is presented more as a simple plea for research and as a departure point for discussion" (73).

It seems doubtful that Sonenschein's "simple plea" actually had much effect on practitioners in linguistics or other anthropological subfields. But his observation that the "verbal behavior" of homosexuals constituted a "special language" worthy of scholarly attention in its own right was an important one. More important, the equation of "special language" with special *terminology* reflected an interest in vocabulary that became the primary subject matter for lesbian and gay linguists in the following years.

Before Sonenschein's time, linguists had paid very little attention to the linguistic dimensions of homosexuality. Some scholars, writing about gender-crossing or third-gender categories in tribal societies, referenced the terminology through which individuals marked and publicly proclaimed their membership in such categories and through which others marked and proclaimed that membership for them.[2] But comments about labels were usually quite brief and often anecdotal; they were not presented as primary points within the analysis. Moreover, the distant, exotic locations of these speech communities ensured that homosexual persons in those settings were assigned the status of other and that their expressions of same-sex desires and identities confirmed Western expectations about the sexual wantonness of "primitive" societies and thereby reinforced in these formulations the Western equation of heterosexuality and civilization.[3]

Beginning in the late 1960s, detailed studies of vocabulary and lexical usage (Conrad and More 1976; Farrell 1972; Lakoff 1975; [Stanley] 1970; Warren 1974) made valuable contributions to lesbian/gay scholarship by drawing attention to contexts of lexical usage, the benefits of expressing lesbian/gay meanings through coded language, and the symbolic values such coding proclaimed. For example, Ron Farrell's discussion of what he termed the "argot of [male] homosexual culture" begins with brief but intriguing remarks about the value of [gay] language for ethnographic fieldwork in gay social settings. Farrell then lists the sexually and socially explicit terminology he collected through questionnaires and other ethnographic means. The sheer detail of the lexicon, the diversity of (sexual and other) topics that its references address, and the unfamiliarity of the words and meanings to most heterosexuals and some homosexual men as well (Conrad and Moore 1976) provide convincing evidence that same-sex desire was socially constructed and not merely a by-product of individualized sexual pathology.

It was unfortunate that Farrell and other scholars did not say more about the cultural implications of their lexical materials or about the social settings and other details of context that were relevant to usage. But the minimal commentary reflected the relatively undeveloped state of lesbian/gay "theory" and the keen interest in description that were characteristic of lesbian/gay studies of the period.[4] These circumstances make all the more remarkable the appearance of *Mother Camp* (1972), Esther Newton's book-length exploration of exaggeration, parody, masquerade, and other characteristics of drag performance and drag-queen identities. Newton has never claimed that what she did in this project was linguistic research. Yet just as her work laid the foundation for Judith Butler's later theorizing (1990) of gendered performativity and queer theory's fascination with camp, Newton's attention to the communicative properties of drag (what some would now call its semiotics) anticipated the attention that several of us would give to the linguistics of lesbian and gay performativity during the 1990s.

Beyond the Lavender Lexicon

By the end of the 1970s, sociolinguistic theory had moved into the foreground of linguistics, as had interest in language and gender.[5] Accordingly, context-free studies of lesbian/gay vocabulary began to be eclipsed by newer interests in connecting language and context, the effects of social location on verbal performance, and other aspects of the ethnography of communication.[6] Julia Penelope [Stanley] (1975, 1982, 1986) used themes from linguistic pragmatics as the starting point for exploring women-oppressive (and ultimately the lesbian-oppressive) messages conveyed by agentless passives and other seemingly neutral syntactic structures in English. Delph (1978) examined nonverbal dimensions of gay men's linguistic skills and used examples from his ethnographic fieldwork to show how nonverbal communication becomes essential to gay men's negotiations of public sexual encounters.

Other studies of gay men's situated language use from this period included Stephen Murray's (1979) description of linguistic dueling at an all-gay dinner party; Deborah Tannen's (1984) description of gay and straight turn-taking at a Thanksgiving dinner; and Kenneth Read's (1980) and Joseph Goodwin's (1989) descriptions of the centrality of language for cultural and social practices in gay bars.[7] Each study showed how gay men use linguistic skills, broadly defined, to support their claims to gay subjectivity. Moreover, Murray's comparisons of the verbal dueling at a gay dinner party and "playin' the dozens" on inner-city street corners showed that lesbian and gay linguistic research could benefit from comparisons outside of same-sex specific settings and could contribute data to such comparisons as well.

Discussions of lesbian and gay language issues also began to emerge apart from linguistics and linguistic anthropology during the 1980s. Speech and communication studies provided the focus for the essays in Chesebro (1981), for example. Individual chapters in that edited collection examined the disruptive effects that such terms as *homosexual, gay,* and *lesbian* bring to everyday conversation; the linguistic presentations of lesbian and gay identity, gay masculinity, and gay fantasy; and the linguistic rhetoric invoked by gay liberation. All were issues suitable for study by ethnographers of language, although it took another ten years before anthropological linguists began to do so. The cross-disciplinary synthesis—ethnography, linguistics, and folklore studies—that Joseph Goodwin attempted in *More Man Than You'll Ever Be* (1989) was a substantial first step in that direction.

An additional set of scholarly interests began to influence lesbian-oriented linguistics during the 1980s. Robin Lakoff and Julia Penelope had drawn attention to the heterosexist and misogynist themes within American English grammar and discourse. In the 1980s, British feminist linguists such as Dale Spender (1980) and Deborah Cameron (1985), along with French feminist philosophers, also focused attention on the male-affirming, female-erasing biases that permeated formal and informal speech. The forms of linguistic erasure and oppression these studies identified were not lesbian-specific.[8] Their comments, however, certainly implied that lesbian language was the ideal site for exploring the ties between language and patriarchy and the unresolvable contradictions which, according to these arguments, "women's language" unavoidably contained. Studies that investigated linkages between women's language and women's social power began to appear during the 1980s. Aside from the work of Julia Penelope (1990) and Birch Moonwomon (1986), however, patriarchy and resistance had yet to become a central theme in lesbian-centered linguistic anthropology.

The 1990s and Beyond

During the 1990s, a fluorescence of interest occurred in studies of lesbian/gay languages, much as had been the case in all areas of lesbian/gay studies. Sessions on lesbian and gay languages were included in scientific programs of the American Anthropological Association, the Linguistics Society of America, and the International Association for Applied Linguistics. Organizers of the Berkeley Women and Language Conference, recognizing that lesbian/gay language researchers faced difficulties in access similar to those experienced by feminist linguists during the 1970s and 1980s, actively encouraged presentations on lesbian and gay language at each of their meetings (Moonwomon 1986). Moreover, the International Gender and Language Association, formed in the spring of 2000, included a specialist in queer linguistics on its steering committee.

One international conference is devoted exclusively to the discussion of lesbian, gay, bisexual, and transgendered language themes: the now-annual Lavender Languages and Linguistics Conference at American University. Conference activities provide colleagues with opportunities to discuss their findings, and in doing so they confirm the importance of such inquiry and the academic legitimacy of such exchange. Such support is not always available through traditional systems of rewards in linguistics, anthropology, and gender studies.[9]

Three major collections of papers on lesbian and gay language themes also appeared during the 1990s (Leap, ed. 1995; Livia and Hall, eds. 1997; and Ringer, ed. 1994). So did book-length monographs exploring gay men's English (Leap 1996b); language and transgender politics (Wilchins 1997); and the erasure of lesbians' presence (and women's presence generally) in spoken and written English (Penelope 1990). Lesbian- and gay-oriented essays have also been included in other collections exploring the connections among language, gender, identity, and power (Bucholtz, Liang, and Sutton, eds. 1999; Hall and Bucholtz, eds. 1995; Perry, Turner, and Sterk, eds. 1992). Birch Moonwomon's search for defining characteristics of lesbian narrative (1995), Zwicky's "three questions for lavender linguists" (1997), and other essays in collections demonstrated that lesbian and gay language research could address serious questions in linguistics as well as in gender theory, as did Rudolf Gaudio's analysis of the distinctively "gay" features of gay men's pronunciation of English (1994). Other papers on lesbian/gay language themes also began to receive publication in professional journals during this time.

In addition, although not intended to be publications in linguistics in the strict sense of that term, textual materials and language-centered research contributed richly to the data-gathering and theorizing in Kennedy and Davis's ethnohistorical study of the Buffalo lesbian community (1993; see also Davis and Kennedy 1990); Lewin's explorations of lesbian motherhood (1993) and lesbian and gay commitment ceremonies (1998); Sears's study of gay adolescence in the American South (1991); Newton's retracing of community history of Cherry Grove, Fire Island (1993); and Herdt's interpretations of sexual cultures in the United States and New Guinea (Herdt 1992; Herdt and Boxer 1993; Herdt and Stoller 1990).

Other discussions of the languages of same-sex related identities outside U.S. settings appeared during the 1990s through the work of researchers such as Rudolf Gaudo on Hausa *>yan daudu* (1997); Don Kulick on Brazilian *travesti* (1997, 1998a); Kira Hall on *hijra* in urban and rural India (1997); Stephen Murray on Latin America (1995a); Peter Jackson on "lady boys" and *tom dee* in urban Thailand (1989); Gary Simes on urban Australia (1992); Martin Manalansan on Filipino diaspora (1995); and Gerrit Oliver on South Africa (1994). Anticipating interests to come, *World Englishes: The Journal of English as an International Language* published a set of papers exploring "Linguistic Creativity in LGBT Discourse" (Frenck, ed. 1998), all of which were presented at the Fifth Lavender Languages Conference in 1997. An interest group devoted to lesbian and gay language studies is also being formed in conjunction with the International Conferences on World Englishes.

Finally, there are signs that lesbian/gay language research is not just a passing fad but likely to continue within the next generation of language scholars. "Queer" representation on the International Language and Gender Association (ILGA) steering committee is especially important in that regard, as is the small but growing number of doctoral dissertations that give central focus to lesbian/gay language issues and related themes. Some graduate programs in linguistics and anthropology in the United States, Great Britain, Germany, and Australia are now recruiting master's and Ph.D. students interested in lesbian and gay language/culture studies. Applicants—and their mentors—are hopeful that such specializations will not come up against the barriers to publication and employment so widely attested in earlier times.

Situating Discovery within Their Contexts of Support

To a great extent, the developments described in the preceding section reflect a more general coming-of-age of lesbian and gay politics in the United States and elsewhere as well as more aggressive lesbian and gay claims to public visibility. Although these claims to location have met with resistance in some areas of academe, linguistics and anthropology included, they have also led to more extensive opportunities for lesbian and gay scholarship.

Within linguistics, an important event was the creation of OUTIL, the "out in linguistics" list-serve long maintained by Arnold Zwicky and now by his colleagues at the University of Delaware. OUTIL has made it easier for lesbian and gay linguists to organize get-togethers at national and regional meetings, exchange comments on research issues, and keep in touch in other ways. OUTIL also facilitates planning for lesbian and gay language-oriented sessions at meetings, proposed publications, and advertised conference sessions and other events of interest to lesbian and gay language scholars. Moreover, OUTIL provides a network of connections for newcomers to lesbian and gay linguistics.[10] Within anthropology, an equally important step was the transformation of the Anthropological Research Group on Homosexuality (ARGOH) into the Society of Lesbian and Gay Anthropologists (SOLGA).[11] As part of its efforts to formalize anthropological interests in the study of lesbian and gay cultures, SOLGA sponsored the first session on "lavender languages" to be included in the American Anthropological Association's scientific program at its 1993 meetings in Chicago. *Beyond the Lavender Lexicon* (Leap, ed. 1995) was one of the results of that session.

Also supporting the emergence of lesbian and gay language research in the 1990s was the emergence of queer theory in lesbian and gay studies. That emergence brought renewed interest to questions of representation, textuality, and performativity. One of queer theory's earliest goals was to destabilize the more conservative, heterosexualized discussions of sexuality and gender that were part of traditional Western social science. The attention to marginality and erasure, to the limitations of labels and the hegemonic significance of categories, and to the interface of sexuality, gender, and power overlapped with questions that engaged lesbian and gay language research— or, more accurately stated, questions it *needed* to engage.

Many lesbian and gay language scholars now incorporate references to the queerness of research subjects within research plans and publications. Very few of these scholars, however, offer analyses of linguistic practices that differ in any substantial ways from the work done under lesbian/gay paradigms. As I explain later, interest in queer theory has, however, prompted researchers to begin examining masculinist and heterosexist biases in lesbian and gay (especially gay) text-making; the performative effects that "talking lesbian/gay" versus "talking straight" bring to the speech event; the further diversification of such contrasts across boundaries of race and class; and other connections among language use, social location, and speech setting. Essays in volumes edited by Livia and Hall (1997) and Bucholtz, Liang, and Sutton (1999) demonstrate how some researchers are addressing these themes through lesbian/gay–centered language inquiry.[12]

What have we learned, and where does this knowledge take us?[13] So far in this chapter I have reviewed the growth of interest in lesbian/gay languages research since 1970 and discussed some of the contextual features, inside and outside academe, which have supported that growth and at times worked against it as well. Next, I will examine what lesbian/gay language research has to say—and still leaves unsaid—about the relationships linking language, politics, and same-sex identities and desires.

The Subject Matter Is *Language*

Is lesbian and gay linguistic text-making best described as *language* or *dialect, variety* or *secret code, sociolect* or *argot?* Even more to the point, does the choice of label matter?

During the 1970s, when studies of lesbian and gay linguistics were just beginning to appear, much of the research focused on details of usage. Discussions of linguistic "status" were qualified accordingly. Hence, although Joseph Hayes (1976:260, passim) referred to gayspeak as a language he also defined it in terms of "'insider jokes, play on words, exaggeration in speech, . . . part 'camp,' part adaptation to the need for secrecy, part defensiveness, yet at the same time a kind of assertiveness." These features speak to an exaggerated linguistic performance, something any speaker can master once having learned the correct techniques of linguistic minstrelsy. The linguistic knowledge at issue has little to do with the rules of sentence construction, story-telling, or conversational turn-taking that often dominate scholarly understandings of linguistic knowledge. Such features provide background for expressions of linguistic exaggeration but are not necessarily gay under this argument. Hayes, at least, never addressed such features as elements of gayspeak in this discussion.

Similarly, Julia Penelope [Stanley] focused her discussion of a "vocabulary common to the homosexual subculture" (1970:45) around "homosexual slang." This usage established from the outset that she was discussing a subset of some more inclusive sociolinguistic tradition and drawing parallels to the relationship between "homosexual subculture" and the larger, cultural mainstream. Accordingly, sentence construction and text-making processes did not need to be addressed in this analysis.[14]

Writing about the "political vocabulary of homosexuality" several years later, Edmund White discussed gay-relevant "private language" through which gay men could confirm shared identities in public places and then "name everything anew [and] appropriate experiences in terms that made sense only to the few" (1980:245). He then reflected on changes in linguistic usages that would emerge "now that homosexuals have no need for indirection, now that their suffering has been eased and their place in society adumbrated if not secured" (245). Once again, references to "language" are really references to the functional dimensions of language use rather than to its structural details. What is unexplored is the linguistic knowledge upon which naming, appropriation, and (borrowing White's term) effective social adumbration ultimately depend.

Now that the subject matter of lesbian and gay linguistics has moved beyond lexicon, camp, and concealment, and the complexities of sentence construction, narration, and conversation have become primary topics for research, the status of lesbian/gay linguistic practices has become even more problematic. Contributors to *Queerly Phrased* (Livia and Hall, eds. 1997) refer to lesbian/gay speech, talk, or discourse, terms that allude to linguistic uniqueness without citing its location within one (or more) domains of linguistic competence and performance. In the same collection, Robin Queen suggests that "lesbian language consists of the interaction between several *stylistic tropes* and their conventionalized social meanings" (1997:233, emphasis added). Such remarks ensure that studies of what Queen terms lesbian *language* will address the dialogic relations between audience and speaker as well as the linguistic features through the dialogic relations become marked within speech events.

In the introductory notes to her essay in Livia and Hall's collection, Birch Moonwomon broadens the research agenda in lesbian (and gay) linguistics, bringing sharper focus to the claims to language that research, conducted in these terms, can now command:

> It may be the case that careful quantitative study of lesbian speech will show that some phonological or other linguistic forms have a greater probability of showing up in lesbian talk than in heterosexual women's talk, and if this is the case, it will be good for us to know it. . . . But I have come to think that language use among lesbians, at least across ethnicities and social classes of English speaking American lesbians, is particularly lesbian in that interlocutors assume shared knowledge about many extradiscursive matters touching on both gender and social-sexual orientation. These areas of knowledge partly inform and are partly constituted by societal discourses (not confined to any specific set of situated linguistic discourses). (1997 [1986]:202–3)

Later in the same paragraph Moonwomon observes, "We are heard as lesbians, at least by ourselves; the authentic lesbian voice is characterized not by intonational peculiarities or, for the most part, by use of special lexicon, but by implication, inference and presupposition that reveal a speaker's stance within the territories of various societal discourses" (202–3).

Similar interests in uniqueness and distinctiveness of lesbian and gay linguistic skills (compared to the language skills of heterosexual persons as well as to different language skills among lesbians and gay men) has prompted me to refer to lesbian and gay *languages* in my research and writing and to define my research interests in language-centered terms. The usage is, in part, political. As I argued in *Word's Out* (1996:1–11), How can there be gay discourse—or gay cultures for that matter—without there being gay language? Moreover, such terms as *dialect, sociolect, argot,* and *register* imply that the linguistic practices in question are subordinated to some larger, more inclusive, linguistic authority (e.g., the standard language or other hetero-normative code). Read in terms of lesbian/gay experience, dialect, sociolect, argot, and register are not liberatory frameworks but reinvent the demands of conformity symbolized by "the closet" and bring those demands to the foreground of linguistic description. In contrast, *language*-centered research starts by asking the extent to which lesbian/gay linguistic practices replicate more conventional linguistic norms and by drawing attention to shared (linguistic and extra-linguistic) knowledge and other features that allow speakers and audience to find distinctiveness in lesbian/gay text-making.

Language-centered research also overlaps with other, equally interesting, themes in lesbian/gay studies. How do would-be speakers, for example, gain access to these linguistic skills when regulatory structures of mainstream society actively conspire to conceal lesbian/gay presence, devalue it, and otherwise make its details inaccessible? How is it that some lesbians and gay men do *not* become proficient in lesbian or gay-related text-making and other domains of lesbian or gay culture, whereas others who are not lesbian or gay-identified become quite skilled in that regard? Such questions draw attention to issues of opportunity, inequality, and privilege that need careful analysis in lesbian/gay contexts. Political scientists, historians, and ethnographers are at work to that end, and language-centered research has much to bring to the inquiry. Studies of dialect, sociolect, argot, and register, in contrast, begin the discussion having predetermined the extent of a speaker's access to relevant linguistic resources and other features of the speaker's social location.

And It's Not Just *Gay* Language

If, as I argued in *Word's Out,* some American gay men are not speakers of "gay men's English" in any form (and some who speak gay men's English are neither gay nor male), then the phrase suggests connections between speaker, gender, and sexual orientation that are much less neatly focused and much more socially complex than they might first appear. Indeed, the term *gay* in this phrasing denotes a particular kind of gendered/linguistic subjectivity not necessarily mediated by bodily form, erotic desire, or object choice but constructed (and reproduced) through the act of "talking gay" within particular social and historical moments. To paraphrase Moonwomon, "We are heard as [gay men], at least by ourselves; the authentic [gay] voice is characterized not by intonational peculiarities or . . . by the use of special lexicon, but by implication, inference and presupposition that reveal a speaker's stance within the territories of various societal discourses." Under these circumstances, "gay language" cannot be assumed to be a generic, inclusive reference. Discussions of gay language (or even gay English) must be closely associated with discussions of the stances, territories, and discourses that speakers employ to question establish gay identification.

Also under these circumstances, using the phrase *gay language* (or *gay English*) to refer to the language skills of lesbians and gay men becomes even more misleading because "lesbian" and "gay" represent yet more contrastive stances, territories, and discourses. References to "lesbian/gay language" and/or "lesbian/gay English" become equally problematic for the same reasons. The conjoined wording, marked as such by the ubiquitous lesbian/gay bar (de Lauretis 1991:iv), implies that speakers of this "language" share a commonality of subjectivity and social stance that are not attested in real-life experience. The conjoined usage could be justified, perhaps, by basing claims to a shared sexual/gendered identity on the fact of same-sex desire. But even that leaves unaddressed the ever-present risk that lesbian linguistic experiences, under such combined reference, will become silenced and not subordinated by a more inclusive gay/male norm. To include a discussion of bisexual languages (or the languages of transgendered persons) under a more totalizing "gay," "lesbian/gay," or even, as I have done in this essay, "lesbian and gay" linguistic label makes the politics of reference even more complex. The implied similarities in forms of desire and other domains of lived experience are entirely fictional. Erasure of bi-presence and trans-gendered presence under this all-inclusive label leaves the fictional status of these similarities uncontested and recasts bi- and transgendered subjectivi-ties as special cases of lesbian/gay linguistic experience. More recent work has begun to demonstrate the uniqueness of bisexual and transgendered text-making and the particular forms of linguistic knowledge on which such text-making depends.[15] Such projects are reminders that bi-languages and trans-languages require discussion on their own terms rather than as adjuncts or afterthoughts to a primarily lesbian/gay–oriented linguistic analysis.

Lavender Language, Queer Linguistics

American University's Lavender Languages Conferences confront the di-versity of interests associated with lesbian, gay, bisexual, and transgendered language research. Each time the conference planning committee begins to finalize the event's program it uses the term *lavender languages* deliberate-ly to cover participants' interests. As Judy Grahn has explained (1984:3–17), long-standing Western connections concern the color purple, forms of mys-tical power, and alternative and disruptive sexualities. In that sense, the word *lavender* underscores connections between current experiences of same-sex identifications and desires and their culture histories.[16] "Lavender" offers a more compact statement than does the full listing of relevant speaker sexu-al stances within the conference advertising and is less awkward stylistical-ly than a cryptic abbreviation like LGBT.

Another, and intellectually more powerful, suggestion to this end has emerged in the proposal (e.g., Barrett 1997; Kulick 1999) that queer theory should provide the framework for exploring diverse connections among lin-guistic performance and same-sex subjectivities, that the inquiry itself should be called "queer linguistics," and that its subject matter be termed "queer lan-guage." The attractiveness of a queer linguistics, and the appeal of queer lan-guage research, builds on the idea that the category *queer* unifies what are otherwise distinctive forms of sexual/gendered subjectivity. Barrett (1997), for example, suggests that queer linguistics encourages researchers to move away from "speech community" as a starting point for linguistic inquiry and build inquiry around what Mary Louise Pratt terms a "linguistics of contact."[17]

Studying queer language in terms of contacts "across social differentia-tion" is quite consistent with the idea that queerness itself is "multiple, unstable and regulatory" and that one of the goals of queer theory is "to render [all forms of identity, including queerness] permanently open and contestable as to its meaning and political role" (Seidman 1996:12). Moreover, under this framework the social relationships that characterize a speech community become the products of inquiry rather than its starting point. That is because social relationships in queer theory are products of social performance, not their foundation.

Although I applaud the suggestion that we trace speech community as performative and not prediscursive, I remain suspicious of the suggestion that queer become a cover term that unifies otherwise distinct lesbian versus gay versus bisexual versus transgendered versus other socially unconventional sexuality/gender-related language use. Queerness is not limited only to diverse forms of sexual and gendered subjectivity. Its references to marginality and instability extends outside sex/gender–based domains of sexual same-sex desire and across any number of claims to difference in social location. In that unity lies the significance of queerness as a research focus and queer theory as a mode of inquiry. Research guided by this frame of reference can lead us to discover the dynamics of language use as they interface not only with sexuality and gender but also with claims to race, ethnicity, nationalism, and class—and as sexuality, gender, race, ethnicity, nationalism, and class intersect with each other. These are important research tasks, particularly for anthropologists and linguists whose work confronts the contradictions and cultural consequences of post-Fordian capitalism. As important as those tasks may be, however, the particulars of lesbian, gay, bisexual, and/or transgendered textmaking are likely to be downplayed in such inquiry in favor of larger, more inclusive, questions about language, subjectivity, and inequality.

To be effective, queer linguistics has to find ways to keep lesbian, gay, bisexual, and transgendered "subjects" in subject position as broader explorations also unfold. There are ways to do that. Spaces of queerness, for example, continue to be one of the enduring concerns of queer theory (e.g., the margin, borderland, and frontier and how greatly sexuality, gender, racialized status, ethnic background, class position and other such features influence the production and reproduction of those spaces).[18] In many instances—and paralleling the research agenda outlined in Gayatri Spivak's eloquent essay "Can the Subaltern Speak?" (1988)—voices from the margin, borderland, and frontier offer insights that can help theory-building destabilize conventional definitions of social place and upstage the claims to normative power with which place is often associated.

Unfortunately, language-centered perspectives on voice and text had not, as of the fall of 2001, become prominent in these studies of spatial queerness. Linguistic research, however, can be of great value to the spatial project. It provides documentation for marginal voices and marginality in voice as well as textual descriptions of borderland experience and life across the frontier and also clarifies the workings of heteronormative authority against which sites of queerness (and queer subjectivities) are forged. Brown (2000), Higgins (1999), and Leap (in press) suggest some of the insights that can emerge from such inquiry.

Whether the linguistic skills underlying spatial queerness resemble those enabling claims to lesbian, gay, or other gender-localized subjectivity remains to be seen. The existence of such resemblances cannot be accepted uncritically. Marginality is a familiar stance to some gay men, but there are others who occupy positions far away from the borderland and closely embedded within the mainstream. Given what we already know about the complex connections among language, gender, and social location, we can expect different "sites of queerness" occupied by lesbians and gay men (and the associated claims to lesbian and gay subjectivities which emerge from those sites) to be expressed in distinctive ways through linguistic performance, even when the topics under discussion appear to be the same.

Creating "Authentic" Lesbian and Gay Languages in a Globalizing World

One of the exciting dimensions of current work with lesbian and gay languages has been the effort to explore textual authenticity. At issue is the object brought under close scrutiny through the use of "gaydar" (Leap 1996:49–66) that seemingly undefinable social skill (Painter 1981, esp. 68–70) that allegedly allows lesbians and gay men to identify each other in heterosexually dominated social contexts. Stated more formally, authenticity refers to the textual properties that confirm a speaker's (or listener's) lesbian or gay identity, locate the text messages within larger domains of lesbian or gay experience, and otherwise provide participants in speech events with assurances of lesbian or gay "presence" within those settings.

Authenticity is, in large part, a theory of text reception in that listeners often make associations between text and gendered meanings even when speakers do not intend that they do so. Authenticity also overlaps with speaker intentionality because speakers make adjustments to text construction to ensure that listeners will take notice of a text's lesbian or gay themes.

Earlier work along these lines assumed authenticity to be largely a matter of referential semantics. Lesbian or gay language was lesbian or gay because the topic of discussion addressed lesbian or gay themes (e.g., my "coming out" story or how I met my current girlfriend/boyfriend) or because words and phrases used in the discussion provided explicit, if often coded, references to those themes. The early interest in compiling word lists and dictionaries was closely aligned with those concerns.[19]

Equally prominent in earlier work on authenticity were assumptions that lesbian or gay-explicit messages could be marked through intonation, gesture, and other features of verbal style. Those claims overlapped with widely accepted cultural stereotypes about lesbian and gay language use and with growing interest in the prominence of camp in lesbian and gay cultures. Researchers, however, rarely explored tone of voice issues in lesbian and gay text during this period, perhaps because "real-life" examples of spoken text were more difficult to collect during the pre-Stonewall years than were samples of lavender vocabulary.

Today's discussions of lesbian and gay linguistic authenticity build on richer awareness about sexual and gendered textuality and much greater access to linguistic materials. Findings from this research are contradictory and unsurprisingly do not agree. Birch Moonwomon (1995) holds that there are no linguistic features unique to lesbian text. Instead, she continues, the "lesbian" authenticity of a text derives from the textual incorporation of issues relevant to lesbian social discourse. In this argument, authenticity is marked semiotically, but not necessarily linguistically, within text structure. In contrast, I have argued (Leap 1996a:21–23) that certain features of co-construction in gay men's text-making are not attested in lesbian text or in the textual products of heterosexual men. Don Kulick (2000) sees no evidence to support that claim and suggests (quite appropriately) that terms such as *co-construction* should be used with much greater precision than has been the practice in previous years.

Admittedly, such debates over the authenticity of lesbian and gay texts, and over the properties that establish textual uniqueness in that regard, may appear to be at distance from real-world conditions. Yet these debates are not as detached as they might appear. However authenticity is defined, the criteria in question are culturally constructed and situated within the particulars of social and historical location. What constitutes authentic gay men's

English in Washington, D.C., may have nothing to do with "authentic" gay English relevant to London, England, Cape Town, South Africa, or Sydney, Australia. Differences in vocabulary, metaphor, and trope contribute to these contrasts, as do sociolinguistic connections between language and sexual cultures, for example, the prominence of *polari* in the London gay underground (Cox and Fay 1994; Lucas 1997); the use of coded women's names as gay-related nouns and verbs in Cape Town's *moffie-tal* (Oliver 1994); and the prominent attention given to sodomy and the sodomite throughout Australian colonial history (Simes 1992:43).

Even more complex—but even less studied—are the contrasts in linguistic authenticity that distinguish lesbian and gay English (and other North Atlantic–based linguistic expressions of same-sex desires) from the verbal traditions of cross-gender/third-gender identities found in areas outside North Atlantic control. Some sources offer general discussions of identity labeling and related terminology (e.g., Besnier 1994; Blackwood 1984; Devereaux 1937; Jacobs 1968; Williams 1986), but narratives and other textual data collected from members of these sex/gender categories are lacking for almost every area of the non-Western world.[20]

The limited presence of these linguistic data is due, in part, to colonial governments' efforts to eliminate the categories and their participants from the social fabric and to efforts by colonized people to retain traditions by moving them underground or through other forms of resistance. Either way, languages associated with cross-gender/third-gender identities and practices in these settings became restricted, private, and even more highly valued, and outsider access to such languages has become all the more difficult to obtain.[21]

Intensifying the absence of textual data, and complicating efforts to collect it, is the increasing globalization of North Atlantic sexual cultures and with that the worldwide spread of the languages of North Atlantic lesbian and gay experience. Stephen Murray (1995b) refers to this as "the international diffusion of *gay*" because one indicator of globalization has been the introduction of "lesbian," "gay," and other terms for North Atlantic–based, same-sex identity into local linguistic usage, either in addition to (or as a replacement for) indigenous categories of same-sex identity and desire. This diffusion is enabled by the movement of people through tourism, migration, and diaspora and the movement of ideas and images through the media in addition to the ever-expanding connectedness of telecommunication networks and the Internet.

In South Africa, such diffusion has resulted in conflicting claims to gender identity, and the messages in conflict here extend far beyond the fact of lexical choice.[22] *Moffie,* one of the options, is an Afrikaner term deeply implanted in South African history. It identifies an effeminate male but makes no statement about his sexual practices or object-choice preferences. It also identifies an alignment of gender with Afrikaner culture and thus an oppositional stance relative to the details of North Atlantic gender/culture summarized under the term *gay.* The details moved into the foreground under British colonial rule and have become even more prominent as European gay men have begun to transform South Africa into a gay playground.

Black South African cultural traditions have their own references for same-sex male identities that highlight the cross-dressing, gender-crossing practices expected from men who claim identity in these terms. One of these categories—*isi tabane*—is widely identified as Zulu in its linguistic origin but is rapidly becoming used by speakers of Xhosa and other South African indigenous language traditions as a way of describing a particular claim to male same-sex identities and desires without resorting to Afrikaans or English terminology. Non-indigenous terms move back into the foreground, however, when male-identified men began to refer to urban bar culture, to the politics of sexual liberation, or to HIV illnesses. These terminological shifts occur even if the language of discussion is otherwise indigenous. No indigenous term for female gender-crossing has emerged to this end, and women-identified women in Xhosa townships use "lesbian" or "friend" as terms of female sexual sameness.

Claims to lesbian or gay authenticity become complex and polyvocal, whether in South African settings such as these or in the Thai-language versions of the letters in Peter Jackson's collection (Jackson 1989); the negotiations of "gay" versus "maricon" versus "cochon" versus "machismo" in urban Nicaragua (Lancaster 1992:235–78) or elsewhere in Spanish-speaking Latin America (Murray 1995b); and the reinvention of Filipino *bakla* as a more valued alternative to "gay" within the contexts of the Filipino diaspora (Manalansan 1995 and chapter 9 of this volume). Moreover, none of these claims are stable, and lesbian and gay authenticity itself becomes subject to negotiation and refinement as part of the text-making process. In such instances (and perhaps in North Atlantic–centered, language-related lesbian and gay research as well) it may be best not to ask whether the text is authentically lesbian or gay but to ponder in what sense or for what reasons lesbian or gay authenticity has become a component of text design and feature of the language use the text contains.

Conclusion

This chapter has reviewed some of the concerns informing current discussions of lesbian and gay languages. My focus has been largely academic, and I have not said much about direction in the lesbian/gay language research taking place in public service, human rights, or advocacy, largely because published descriptions of such projects are not widely available. That is especially unfortunate, given that so many who are involved in lesbian and gay language studies are also deeply involved in achieving social justice for sexual minorities. It would be very useful to see how scholar/activists see linguistic inquiry being relevant to those goals.

In the meantime, however, the vitality of lesbian and gay-oriented language research lies in basic linguistic/social description, and anthropological linguists' long-standing interests in ethnography of communication are especially well suited for such research tasks. In this sense, it may be surprising that so little work on these themes has emerged from anthropological contexts in recent years. Limitations of subject matter is not the problem. Many facets of lesbian and gay language(s) have yet to be examined, and many questions about lesbian and gay language have yet to be answered. If anything, it is anthropology's long-standing discomfort with explicit discussions of the sexual/gendered margin that imposes limits on such inquiry. Upstaging that discomfort becomes an important part of efforts to help anthropology "come out," and language-centered research, for reasons outlined in this chapter, has much to contribute to those ends.

Notes

This essay has grown out of a talk-piece on lavender language research that Kira Hall and I presented at a session on "Directions in Lesbian and Gay Anthropology" at the annual meetings of the AAA in 1996. In addition to Kira's helpful suggestions to the argument, my thanks to Mary Wiesmantel, Louise Lamphere, and colleagues at American University for helping shape this essay into its current form and to Ellen Lewin who gave a careful and critical line-by-line edit to each of its several drafts.

1. I explain below why *language* is preferable to *variety, code, speaking style, register,* or *dialect* in discussions of lesbian/gay communication. I also explain below why this essay focuses on lesbian/gay languages and does not address the importance of language for bisexual and transgendered experience.

2. Devereaux's citation of terminology in his writings on Mo[j]ave homosexuality (1937, passim) is especially rich in this regard. See also the references to labels and other vocabulary cited in Sue-Ellen Jacobs's now-classic review of the early literature on "berdache" (1968).

3. Herdt (1991a, 1991b) explores how studies of homosexuality in primitive societies reinforced other, more inclusive assumptions about the contrasts between "primitive society" and "civilization."

4. Moreover, what little theory there was in lesbian/gay studies was dominated by psychological perspectives. Cultural perspectives had yet to gain prominence in this conversation.

5. Most of that work was dominated by studies of the language use of white, heterosexual women and studies conducted by women from the same backgrounds.

6. In some ways, Newton's *Mother Camp* also anticipated these developments.

7. Although feminist linguists paid close attention to language-based oppression of women during this period, site-specific studies of lesbian language use were not so widely attested. Male interests still dominated linguistics in the 1970s, and discussions of women's languages were struggling to establish their place within the discipline. Relationships between language use and speaker sexuality (or that of the researcher) were of secondary concern, viewed in the light of this larger struggle for feminist legitimacy within the academe.

8. Some scholars argued, however, that a lesbian subjectivity was the only stance through which resistance to heterosexism could truly be affected.

9. Although it seems fair to say that lesbian/gay language studies have become deeply rooted within linguistics, anthropology, and other academic disciplines, the picture is not entirely upbeat and progressive. The career success of several scholars notwithstanding, linguists and anthropologists specializing in lesbian/gay language studies generally find it difficult to secure academic employment on the basis of that expertise alone. No Department of Linguistics or Department of Anthropology has (to my knowledge) listed lesbian and gay language studies as an area of scholarly expertise considered valuable for a new faculty hire. The Sexuality Program of the Social Science Research Council gives favorable consideration to lesbian- and gay-oriented language research, as does the Wenner-Gren Foundation for Anthropological Research. But language has never been a priority for either of these organizations. And while U.S. government-based funding agencies are willing to review proposals for lesbian/gay-oriented research projects, their support for such projects continues to be minimal.

These considerations may not pose problems for senior scholars, but they do put the research activities and other career development efforts of graduate students and junior scholars in U.S.-based academic settings at particular disadvantage. Much remains to be done before lesbian/gay linguistics—and lesbian/gay linguists—can claim to have achieved a secure foothold within academe. Understandably, some lesbian and gay doctoral students—including some who are otherwise quite open about their sexuality—have decided against writing their dissertations on lesbian/gay language and culture themes in the hope that more conventional dissertation research will make them more employable (Leap et al. 1999). Others are looking outside of academe in the hope of finding a market for the critical perspectives on lesbian and gay experiences that language-centered research provides. Clatts (1999), Clatts, Davis, and Sothern (1994), Treichler (1987), and other work on AIDS-related text-making have provided inspiration to that end.

10. The "out-in-linguistics" list-serve's focus has remained primary social, and discussions of lesbian/gay language research are minor topics of message exchange. That pattern reflects the fact that although many lesbian/gay persons are in linguistics, very few of them are actually involved in lesbian/gay language research.

11. Issues prompting the name change and other components of the ARGOH-SOLGA reorganization, including ARGOH's misogyny, are examined in the Introduction of this volume.

12. *Word's Out* (Leap 1996b) has been criticized—and rightly so I think—for its failure to interrogate these issues and for its treatment of "gay identity" as a homogeneous social stance. My more recent work, particularly *Gay City* (in press) responds to these issues directly.

13. Unavoidably, the issues and discussion in this section reflect my own interests and biases. Readers will want to consult sources such as Atkins (1998:xxix–li), Frenck (1998), Kulick (2000), and Livia and Hall (1997) to see how other researchers have synthesized these themes.

14. In subsequent essays (1975, 1977, 1978, 1990) Penelope pays careful attention to intersections of syntax and power.

15. Examples include Christa Craven's in-depth analysis of bi-conversation (1998), Jason Cromwell's description of transgendered "protective language" (1995), Riki Anne Wilchins's (transgendered) reactions to *"sex!* as a verb" (1997), and Don Kulick's reflections on the conversations of Brazilian *travesti* and their boyfriends (1997).

16. Unfortunately, these connections are lost on those unfamiliar with the historical message or who do not understand the aggregate to which the term refers. The misunderstanding is especially acute when heterosexual newspaper reporters attempt to write informed stories about the conference's mission and its program.

17. Mary Louise Pratt explains, a linguistics of contact "decenter[s] community, that place[s] at its centre the operation of language across lines of social differentiation, a linguistics that focus[es] on node and zone of contact between dominant and dominated groups, between persons of different and multiple identities, that focus[es] on how speakers constitute each other relationally and in difference, how they exact difference in language" (1987:60, cited in Barrett 1997:191–92).

18. Important sources include Beemyn, ed. (1997), Betsky (1997), Ingram, Bouthillette, and Retter, eds. (1997), Raffo, ed. (1997), and Whittle, ed. (1994).

19. The focus of these studies was usually gay men's vocabulary. Very rarely did research explore the vocabulary specific to lesbians.

20. An important exception here is Peter Jackson's *Male Homosexuality in Thailand* (1989), his translation into English of letters sent to a Thai newspaper columnist known for giving advice on homosexual matters. The letters provide detailed

insight into the complexities of male same-sex experience in Thailand. How greatly the translation process may have reframed the narrative details, and the particulars of sexuality, presented in the book cannot be judged. Jackson's more recent work continues to elaborate on these themes (Jackson and Sullivan, eds. 1999).

21. Language/gender research projects like that of Navajo anthropologist Wesley Thomas (1997) or Filipino American anthropologist Martin Manalansan (1995 and ch. 9 of this volume) provide glimpses into the rich details of these languages and point out how superficially outsiders described language/gender relationships in these settings in earlier research.

22. These comments on South African terminology and identities come from my ongoing field research, but the tensions are amply documented in the life-story reflections presented in Gevisser and Cameron, ed. (1994).

References Cited

Atkins, Dawn. 1998. Introduction. In *Looking Queer,* ed. Atkins, xxix–li. New York: Haworth Press.

Barrett, Rusty. 1997. "The 'Homo-Genius' Speech Community." In *Queerly Phrased: Language, Gender, and Sexuality,* ed. Anna Livia and Kira Hall, 181–201. New York: Oxford University Press.

Beemyn, Brett, ed. 1997. *Creating a Place for Ourselves: Lesbian, Gay and Bisexual Community Histories.* New York: Routledge.

Besnier, Niko. 1994. "Polynesian Gender Liminality through Time and Space." In *Third Sex, Third Gender: Beyond Sexual Dimorphism in Culture and History,* ed. Gilbert Herdt, 285–328. New York: Zone Books.

Betsky, Aaron. 1997. "Introduction: Some Queer Constructs." In *Queer Space: Architecture and Same-Sex Desire,* 2–15. New York: William Morrow.

Blackwood, Evelyn. 1984. "Sexuality and Gender in Certain Native American Tribes: The Case of Cross-dressing Females." *Signs* 10(1): 27–42.

Brown, Michael P. 2000. *Closet Space: Geographies of Metaphor from the Body to the Globe.* New York: Routledge.

Bucholtz, Mary, Anita Liang, and Laurel Sutton, eds. 1999. *Reinventing Identities.* New York: Cambridge University Press.

Butler, Judith. 1990. *Gender Trouble: Feminism and the Subversion of Identity.* New York: Routledge.

Cameron, Deborah. 1985. *Feminism and Linguistic Theory.* New York: St. Martin's Press.

Chesebro, James W., ed. 1981. *Gayspeak: Gay Male and Lesbian Communication.* New York: Pilgrim Press.

Clatts, Michael. 1999. "Ethnographic Observations of Men Who Have Sex with Men in Public." In *Public Sex/Gay Space,* ed. William Leap, 141–56. New York: Columbia University Press.

———, W. R. Davis, and J. L. Sothern. 1994. "At the Cross-roads of HIV Infec-

tion: A Demographic and Behavioral Profile of Street Youth in New York City."
In *Symposium on Drug Abuse, Sexual Risk and AIDS: Prevention Research 1995–2000.* Flagstaff: Northern Arizona University.

Conrad, James R., and William W. Moore. 1976. "Lexical Codes and Sub-Cultures: Some Questions." *Anthropological Linguistics* 18: 22–26.

Cox, Leslie J., and Richard J. Fay. 1994. "Gayspeak, the Linguistic Fringe: Bona Polari, Camp Queerspeak, and Beyond." In *The Margins of the City: Gay Men's Urban Lives,* ed. Stephen Whittle, 103–28. Brookfield Vt.: Ashgate.

Craven, Christa. 1998. "Bi-Lingualism: Queering Community and Identity in Bi Women's Discourse." Presented at the Lavender Languages and Linguistics Conference, American University, Washington, D.C.

Cromwell, Jason. 1995. "Talking about without Talking about: The Use of Protective Language among Transvestites and Transsexuals." In *Beyond the Lavender Lexicon: Authenticity, Imagination, and Appropriation in Lesbian and Gay Languages,* ed. William Leap, 267–96. Newark: Gordon and Breach.

Davis, Madeline, and Elizabeth Lapovsky Kennedy. 1990. "Oral History and the Study of Sexuality in the Lesbian Community: Buffalo, New York, 1940–1960." In *Unequal Sisters,* ed. Ellen DuBois and Vicki Ruiz, 387–99. New York: Routledge.

de Lauretis, Teresa. 1991. "Queer Theory: Lesbian and Gay Sexualities: An Introduction." *differences* 5(2): iii–xviii.

Delph, Edward William. 1978. *The Silent Community: Public Homosexual Encounters.* Beverly Hills: Sage.

Devereaux, George. 1937. "Homosexuality among the Mohave Indians." *Human Biology* 9(4): 498–597.

Farrell, Ronald A. 1972. "The Argot of the Homosexual Subculture." *Anthropological Linguistics* 14(3): 97–109.

Frenck, Susan. 1998. "Symposium on Linguistic Creativity in LGBT Discourse: Introduction." *World Englishes* 17(2): 187–90.

———, ed. 1998. "Symposium on Linguistic Creativity in LGBT Discourse." *World Englishes* 17(2): 187–262.

Gaudio, Rudolf P. 1994. "Sounding Gay: Pitch Properties in the Speech of Gay and Straight Men." *American Speech* 69(1): 30–57.

———. 1997. "Not Talking Straight in Hausa." In *Queerly Phrased: Language, Gender, and Sexuality,* ed. Anna Livia and Kira Hall, 416–29. New York: Oxford University Press.

Gevisser, Mark, and Edwin Cameron, eds. 1994. *Defiant Desire: Gay and Lesbian Lives in South Africa.* Johannesburg: Ravan Press.

Goodwin, Joseph P. 1989. *More Man Than You'll Ever Be: Gay Folklore and Acculturation in Middle America.* Bloomington: Indiana University Press.

Grahn, Judy. 1984. *Another Mother Tongue: Gay Words, Gay Worlds.* Boston: Beacon Press.

Hall, Kira. 1995. "Hijra/Hijirin: Language and Gender Identity." Ph.D. diss., University of California, Berkeley.

————.1997. "'Go Suck Your Husband's Sugarcane': Hijras and the Use of Sexual Insult." In *Queerly Phrased: Language, Gender, and Sexuality,* ed. Anna Livia and Kira Hall, 430–60. New York: Oxford University Press.

————, and Mary Bucholtz, eds. 1995. *Gender Articulated: Language and the Socially Constructed Self.* New York: Routledge.

Hayes, Joseph. 1976. "Gayspeak." *Quarterly Journal of Speech* 62: 256–66.

Herdt, Gilbert. 1991a. "Representations of Homosexuality in Traditional Societies: An Essay on Cultural Ontology and Historical Comparison, Part 1." *Journal of the History of Sexuality* 1(3): 481–504.

————. 1991b. "Representations of Homosexuality in Traditional Societies: An Essay on Cultural Ontology and Historical Comparison, Part 2." *Journal of the History of Sexuality* 2(1): 603–32.

————. 1992. "'Coming Out' as a Rite of Passage: A Chicago Study." In *Gay Culture in America: Essays from the Field,* ed. Herdt, 29–67. Boston: Beacon Press.

————, and Robert J. Stoller. 1990. *Intimate Communications: Erotics and the Study of Culture.* New York: Columbia University Press.

————, and Andrew Boxer. 1993. *Children of Horizons.* Boston: Beacon Press.

Higgins, Ross. 1997. "A Sense of Belonging: Pre-liberation Space, Symbolics, and Leadership in Gay Montreal." Ph.D. diss., McGill University.

Ingram, Gordon Brett, Anne-Marie Bouthillette, and Yolanda Retter, eds. 1997. *Queers in Space: Communities, Public Places, Sites of Resistance.* Seattle: Bay Press.

Jackson, Peter A. 1989. *Male Homosexuality in Thailand.* Amsterdam: Global Academic Publishers.

————, and Gerard Sullivan, eds. 1999. *Lady Boys, Tom Boys, Rent Boys: Male and Female Homosexualities in Contemporary Thailand.* Binghamton: Harrington Park Press.

Jacobs, Sue-Ellen. 1968. "Berdache: A Brief Review of the Literature." *Colorado Anthropologist* 1(2): 25–40.

Kennedy, Elizabeth Lapovsky, and Madeline Davis. 1993. *Boots of Leather, Slippers of Gold: The History of a Lesbian Community.* New York: Routledge.

Kulick, Don. 1997. A Man in the House: The Boyfriends of Brazilian Travesti Prostitutes." In *Queer Transexions of Race, Nation, and Gender,* ed. Philip Brian Harper et al., 133–60. Durham: Duke University Press.

————. 1998. *Travesti: Sex, Gender and Culture among Brazilian Prostitutes.* Chicago: University of Chicago Press.

————. 1999. "Transgender and Language: A Review of the Literature and Suggestions for the Future." *GLQ* 5(4): 605–22.

————. 2000. "Gay and Lesbian Language." *Annual Review of Anthropology* 29: 243–85.

Lakoff, Robin. 1975. *Language and Women's Place.* New York: Harper and Row.

Lancaster, Roger. 1992. *Life Is Hard: Machismo, Danger and the Intimacy of Power in Nicaragua.* Berkeley: University of California Press.

Leap, William L., ed. 1995. *Beyond the Lavender Lexicon: Authenticity, Imagina-*

tion, and Appropriation in Lesbian and Gay Languages. Newark: Gordon and Breach.

———. 1996a. "Studying Gay English: How I Got Here from There." In *Out in the Field: Reflections of Lesbian and Gay Anthropologists,* ed. Ellen Lewin and William Leap, 128–46. Urbana: University of Illinois Press.

———. 1996b. *Word's Out: Gay Men's English.* Minneapolis: University of Minnesota Press.

———, et al. 1999. *Final Report: Commission on Lesbian, Gay, Bisexual, and Transgendered Issues in Anthropology.* Arlington: American Anthropological Association.

———. In press. *Gay City.* Minneapolis: University of Minnesota Press.

Lewin, Ellen. 1993. *Lesbian Mothers: Accounts of Gender in American Culture.* Ithaca: Cornell University Press.

———. 1998. *Recognizing Ourselves: Ceremonies of Lesbian and Gay Commitment.* New York: Columbia University Press.

Livia, Anna, and Kira Hall. 1997. "'It's a Girl!': Bringing Performativity Back to Linguistics." In *Queerly Phrased: Language, Gender, and Sexuality,* ed. Livia and Hall, 2–19. New York: Oxford University Press.

———, eds. 1997. *Queerly Phrased: Language, Gender and Sexuality.* New York: Oxford University Press.

Lucas, Ian. 1997. "The Color of His Eyes: Polari and the Sisters of Perpetual Indulgence." In *Queerly Phrased: Language, Gender, and Sexuality,* ed. Anna Livia and Kira Hall, 85–94. New York: Oxford University Press.

Manalansan, Martin. 1995. "'Performing' the Filipino Gay Experience in America: Linguistic Strategies in a Transnational Context." In *Beyond the Lavender Lexicon: Authenticity, Imagination, and Appropriation in Lesbian and Gay Languages,* ed. William L. Leap, 249–66. Newark: Gordon and Breach.

Moonwomon, Birch. 1986. "Toward the Study of Lesbian Speech." In *Proceedings of the First Berkeley Women and Languages Conference, 1985,* ed. Sue Bremner, Noelle Caskey, and Birch Moonwomon, 96–107. Berkeley: Berkeley Women and Language Group, University of California.

———. 1995. "Lesbian Discourse, Lesbian Knowledge." In *Beyond the Lavender Lexicon: Authenticity, Imagination, and Appropriation in Lesbian and Gay Languages,* ed. William L. Leap, 45–64. Newark: Gordon and Breach.

———. 1997. "Toward the Study of Lesbian Speech." In *Queerly Phrased: Language, Gender, and Sexuality,* ed. Anna Livia and Kira Hall, 233–56. New York: Oxford University Press.

Murray, Stephen O. 1979. "The Art of Gay Insulting." *Anthropological Linguistics* 21(5): 211–20.

———. 1995a. *Latin American Male Homosexualities.* Albuquerque: University of New Mexico Press.

———. 1995b. "Stigma Transformation and Relexification in the International Diffusion of Gay." In *Beyond the Lavender Lexicon: Authenticity, Imagination, and*

Appropriation in Lesbian and Gay Languages, ed. William L. Leap, 297–318. Newark: Gordon and Breach.

Murray, Stephen O., and Wayne Dynes. 1995. "Hispanic Homosexuals: A Spanish Lexicon." In *Latin American Male Homosexualities,* ed. Stephen O. Murray, 181–91. Albuquerque: University of New Mexico Press.

Newton, Esther. 1972. *Mother Camp: Female Impersonators in America.* Chicago: University of Chicago Press.

———. 1993. *Cherry Grove, Fire Island: Sixty Years in America's First Gay and Lesbian Town.* Boston: Beacon Press.

Oliver, Gerrit. 1994. "From ADA to ZELDA: Notes on Gays and Language in South Africa." In *Defiant Desire: Gay and Lesbian Lives in South Africa,* ed. Mark Gevisser and Edwin Cameron, 219–24. Johanesberg: Raven Press.

Painter, Dorothy S. 1981. "Recognition among Lesbians in Straight Settings." In *Gayspeak: Gay Male and Lesbian Communication,* ed. James W. Cheesebro, 68–79. New York City: Pilgrim Press.

Penelope, Julia [Stanley]. 1970. "Homosexual Slang." *American Speech* 45(1–2): 45–59.

———. 1975. "Passive Motivation." *Foundations of Language* 3(1): 25–39.

———. 1977. "Gender Marking in American English: Usage and Reference." In *Sexism and Language,* ed. Alleen Pace Nilsen et al., 43–74. Urbana: National Council of Teachers of English.

———. 1978. "Sexist Grammar." *College English* (March): 800–811.

———. 1982. "Topicalization: The Rhetorical Strategies It Serves and the Interpretive Strategies It Imposes." *Linguistics* 20(4): 683–95.

———. 1986. "Heteropatriarchal Semantics: Just Two Kinds of People in the World." *Lesbian Ethics* (Fall): 58–80.

———. 1990. *Speaking Freely: Unlearning the Lies of the Fathers' Tongues.* New York: Teachers College Press.

Perry, Linda A. M., Lynn H. Turner, and Helen M. Sterk, eds. 1992. *Constructing and Reconstructing Gender.* Albany: SUNY Press.

Pratt, Mary Louise. 1987. "Linguistic Utopias." In *The Linguistics of Writing: Arguments between Language and Literature,* ed. Nigel Fabb et al., 48–66. Manchester: Manchester University Press.

Queen, Robin. 1997. "'I Don't Speak Spritch': Locating Lesbian Language." In *Queerly Phrased: Language, Gender, and Sexuality,* ed. Anna Livia and Kira Hall, 233–56. New York: Oxford University Press.

Raffo, Susan, ed. 1997. *Queerly Classed.* Boston: South End Press.

Read, Kenneth E. 1980. *Other Voices: The Style of a Male Homosexual Tavern.* Novato, Calif.: Chandler and Sharp Publishers.

Ringer, R. Jeffrey, ed. 1994. *Queer Words, Queer Images: Communication and the Construction of Homosexuality.* New York: New York University Press.

Sears, James T. 1991. *Growing Up Gay in the South.* New York: Harrington Park Press.

Seidman, Steven. 1996. Introduction. In *Queer Theory/Sociology,* ed. Seidman, 1–29. Cambridge: Blackwell.

Simes, Gary. 1992. "The Language of Homosexuality in Australia." In *Gay Perspectives: Essays in Australian Gay Culture,* ed. Robert Aldrich and Garry Wotherspoon, 31–58. Sydney: Department of Economic History, University of Sydney.

Slater, E., and P. Slater. 1947. "A Study in the Assessment of Homosexual Traits." *British Journal of Medical Psychology* 21(1): 61–74.

Sonenschein, David. 1966. "Homosexuality as a Subject of Anthropological Inquiry." *Anthropological Quarterly* 39(2): 73–82.

Spender, Dale. 1980. *Man Made Language.* London: Pandora Press.

Spivak, Gayatri. 1988. "Can the Subaltern Speak?" In *Marxism and the Interpretation of Culture,* ed. Cary Nelson and Larry Grossberg, 271–313. Urbana: University of Illinois Press.

Tannen, Deborah. 1984. *Conversational Style: Analyzing Talk among Friends.* Norwood: Ablex.

———. 1986. *That's Not What I Meant! How Conversational Style Makes or Breaks Relationships.* New York City: William Morrow.

Thomas, Wesley. 1997. "Navajo Cultural Constructions of Gender and Sexuality." In *Two-Spirit People: Native American Gender Identity, Sexuality, and Spirituality,* ed. Sue-Ellen Jacobs, Wesley Thomas, and Sabine Lang, 156–73. Urbana: University of Illinois Press.

Treichler, Paula. 1987. "AIDS, Homophobia, and Biomedical Discourse: An Epidemic of Signification." In *AIDS: Cultural Analysis/Cultural Activism,* ed. Douglas Crimp, 31–70. Cambridge: MIT Press.

Warren, Carol A. B. 1974. *Identity and Community in the Gay World.* New York: John Wiley and Sons.

White, Edmund. 1980. "The Political Vocabulary of Homosexuality." In *The State of the Language,* ed. Leonard Michaels and Christopher Ricks, 235–46. Berkeley: University of California Press.

Whittle, Stephen, ed. 1994. *The Margins of the City: Gay Men's Urban Lives.* Brookfield Vt.: Ashgate.

Wilchins, Riki Anne. 1997. *Read My Lips.* Ithaca: Firebrand Books.

Williams, Walter L. 1986. *The Spirit and the Flesh: Sexual Diversity in the American Indian Culture.* Boston: Beacon Press.

Zwicky, Arnold M. 1997. "Two Lavender Issues for Linguists." In *Queerly Phrased: Language, Gender, and Sexuality,* ed. Anna Livia and Kira Hall, 21–34. New York: Oxford University Press.

SIX

The Iceman Cometh: Queering the Archaeological Past

Robert A. Schmidt

Anthropological archaeologists have long fancied their work as down to earth in several senses. According to the epistemology proposed by C. F. Hawkes (1954) in his well-known Ladder of Inference, the nature of archaeological evidence constrains the inferences that can be made from that evidence. The constraints are understood to be progressive. Those aspects of behavior most directly tied to material culture evidence (e.g., technology and economy, the lower rungs of the ladder) are deemed more reliably knowable than more distant aspects such as social structure (the higher rungs of the ladder). Ideology—still more distant from the evidence—is even further from our grasp. Thus archaeologists have resisted making inferences about aspects of social and cultural life that soar too far from the quotidian physicality of material culture evidence or cannot be tied convincingly to that evidence.

Due in part to this purported epistemological insecurity, sexuality and sexual behaviors have not, with some limited exceptions, been regarded as legitimate objects of knowledge in the discipline of archaeology until the twenty-first century. This attitude toward sexuality in general has been especially true for homosexuality and other forms or patterns of sexual behavior considered in several senses as marginal (Voss and Schmidt 2000). In this chapter, I will address the origins of this attitude in the discipline and discuss a prominent example of archaeological resistance to the interrogation of sexuality: the case of the Tyrolean "Ice Man" nicknamed Ötzi. Uncovering this reluctance to interrogate sexuality, sex, and gender in general, and homosexuality in particular, reveals a hitherto unsuspected consequence that ought to concern archaeologists: Some portion of the variation in the archaeological record has been masked and/or misinterpreted through avoidance of any consideration of sexuality as a social phenomenon. As with other social phenomena, however, sexuality both structures and is structured by every human society. It is a mutable and contingent element of human societies, both in ideological and behavioral aspects.[1]

I will then outline how and why homosexuality may be considered relevant to archaeological investigations of past societies and demonstrate that relevance by outlining several more recent archaeological case studies that make homosexuality a central analytical focus. In describing these examples I discuss some of the ways in which inferences about homosexual behavior in past societies may be supported. I also suggest that incorporating contributions from queer studies into archaeological practice will enable archaeologists to provide information about varieties of sexuality, and about sex and gender systems more generally, which would be unavailable through historical or ethnographic sources.

Archaeology and Sexuality

In addition to the epistemological assertion that material culture evidence cannot by its nature inform us about sexuality or sexual behaviors in the past, a further, more general impediment has existed to the legitimatization of sexuality as an object of knowledge in archaeology. This impediment is composed of an amorphous, all-too-familiar set of mid-twentieth-century, Euro-American assumptions about the nature of sexuality and, to employ Gayle Rubin's (1975) concept, of sex/gender systems generally. Implicitly accepted by most archaeologists, these assumptions include the notion that sexuality is fundamentally a binary, male-female phenomenon both diachronically and cross-culturally; that a limited but unavoidable range of implications for sexual and gender relations necessarily flow from the male-female binary; that the bulk of sexual behavior in every society is heterosexual and at least potentially procreative; and that sexual behaviors that do not fit into this model are by definition exceptions or deviations from norms and thus inherently marginal and unimportant.

It can come as no surprise that archaeologists informed by these assumptions would presume that cross-cultural differences among patterns of sexuality in various societies must be minimal and must lead to only one archaeologically visible conclusion: reproduction. The corollary to these beliefs has been the view that sexuality and sex/gender systems are trivial topics in archaeological contexts and that nonreproductive sexualities must be subjects of negligible interest (Voss and Schmidt 2000).

During the last half of the twentieth century, several theoretical movements arose and gained prominence within the discipline of archaeology. They strongly influenced both the practice of archaeology and the goals toward which archaeologists have understood themselves to be striving. Although the movements I will briefly discuss each has had the potential to support investigations of sexuality as an explicit and relevant social variable, none substantially challenged negative attitudes toward sexuality. It is only with the more recent infusion of queer theoretical perspectives into archaeology that investigations of sexuality within archaeological contexts have arisen as a perceptible trend.

In the 1960s, a powerful critique arose of the way archaeology had previously been envisioned and conducted. The energetic new critics characterized that tradition as the "culture-historical" approach because of its focus on the identification and description of cultural sequences through time. Louis Binford (1962) and other proponents of what was then described as "New Archaeology" and later also known as "processual archaeology" championed an approach wherein archaeologists were encouraged to adopt a more explicitly "scientific" rather than historical model of knowledge production. Rather than attempting to produce historical descriptions and accounts of past cultures, the processual ideal was to create hypotheses that would be tested against data recovered from the archaeological record. From that, generalized laws of human social behavior could be adduced.

In the beginning, Binford and his colleagues were extraordinarily optimistic about the potential of the new approach for revealing novel and exciting understandings of the past that would far exceed what had been produced before. Instead of further refining chronologies, their ambition was to be social scientists in a profound sense. Processualists wanted to understand fundamental social processes and trace changes in those processes through time. The initial optimism regarding the practicality of achieving these ideals began to wane, however, as Binford and others began to recognize the difficulties inherent in connecting archaeological data with human behavior and social processes (a set of issues they called "middle range theory"). By the 1980s, Binford's optimism had transmuted into extreme pessimism over the feasibility of deepening archaeological interpretation in a rigorous scientific fashion.

Nevertheless, the processualist enterprise unleashed enormous energy that led many archaeologists to explore, often fruitfully, a variety of new theoretical, methodological, and topical paths. These new directions did not include investigations of sexuality, even though in hindsight we can identify several developments in the discipline at this period that would have facilitated such investigations. For example, a vogue in the 1970s for using "systems theory" to model interactions between social subsystems or components provided an opening to explore sexuality, a possibility certainly suggested by Rubin's (1975) coinage of the term *sex/gender system*. But use of such potential openings had to await further developments.

Beginning in the 1980s and continuing into the 1990s, a reaction to what was seen as the excesses of positivist and empiricist impulses within processual archaeology began to be articulated by writers such as Ian Hodder (1982) and Michael Shanks and Christopher Tilley (1992). That postprocessual critique rejected "narrow scientism" as a way to validate archaeological interpretation (Hodder 1991:xiv). In its place, postprocessualists advocated a search for cultural meanings within specific contexts.

The search is necessary because *all* the material culture whose remains archaeologists use as evidence has a symbolic dimension; relationships between things and people are variably affected, depending upon contingent, historically changing, conditions. Thus meanings that archaeologists infer from material culture evidence cannot be drawn from, or employed to support the existence of, universal laws of human behavior as processualists attempted to do. We can only hope to create robust interpretations of the archaeological record by examining contexts within which the meaningful relationships between people and things arose and changed. In contrast to the New Archaeologists, postprocessualists returned to a view of archaeology as a primarily historical rather than social-scientific discipline.

With the clarity of hindsight, the programmatic focus of postprocessualists upon specificities within societies would seem to have provided an excellent opportunity for archaeological investigations of sexuality, particularly sexual minorities. The opportunity seems even more obvious when one considers the contemporary development of document-based histories of sexuality and homosexuality (e.g., Boswell 1994; Brown 1989; Chauncey 1989, 1994; Davidson 1987; Foucault 1978; Halperin 1989, 1990; Ng 1989; Padgug 1989; Ringrose 1994; Trumbach 1989; van der Meer 1994; Weeks 1997, 1981, 1985, 1991; Winkler 1990). Most of these historical studies were based to a greater or lesser extent upon a social-constructionist perspective.[2] With its emphasis upon resistance to scientifically based, cross-cultural definitions of human behavior and its stress upon the crucial importance of historical context, the social-constructionist perspective bears a strong resemblance and affinity to postprocessualist attitudes and concerns. Thus the absence (with the exception of the work of Yates [1993]) of investigations of sexuality within the postprocessualist movement seems even more surprising than within processualism.

With the emergence of feminist-inspired investigations of gender issues in archaeology after the appearance of the ground-breaking essay "Archaeology and the Study of Gender" (Conkey and Spector 1984), some postprocessualists assumed for many years that gender was another specificity whose exploration could be included under the rubric of postprocessualism (e.g., Hodder 1991:168–72). Yet not all feminist archaeologists welcomed inclusion under the postprocessualist umbrella (e.g., Engelstad 1991). As the gender archaeology project grew significantly through the 1990s while the contentious New Archaeology–postprocessualist debate decreased in salience, it became clear that gender or feminist-inspired archaeology had emerged as an essentially separate venture.

Feminist archaeology has successfully challenged androcentric assumptions about past societies and highlighted much of the variability related to gender in prehistoric societies (Joyce and Claasen 1997). It did not until the late 1990s, however, support or produce archaeological studies of sexuality. While other concerns may at first have led feminist archaeologists in directions away from sexuality, the primary obstacle has been a failure to challenge the universality of the male-female binary paradigm.[3] This binary paradigm has profound implications for the archaeological understanding of emic social categories. It constitutes a place where queer theory, with its critique of the ontological basis of all sex and gender categories, offers an important contribution to archaeological theory.

Most archaeologists, feminist or otherwise, would accept that gender categories are socially and culturally constructed and would distinguish these from sex categories based upon the "natural" biological categories of male and female. But as queer theorists such as Butler (1990, 1993) and others have pointed out, if both gender (the "cultural" category) and sex (the "biological" category) are each composed of precisely two discrete categories, male and female, then sex and gender inevitably collapse into one another. In fact, gender reduces to sex, for, as Roscoe puts it, in this hierarchical relationship, "anatomy has primacy over gender, and gender is not an ontologically distinct category but merely a reiteration of sex" (1994:345).

Although at times clearly uncomfortable with the implications of this collapsing of sex and gender, feminist archaeologists who accepted the binary paradigm have been unable to resolve this difficulty. Queer theory presents a convenient remedy by recognizing that both social and biological categories are constructed (Dowson 2000). Because all categories are inherently arbitrary, the analytical categories that researchers employ must be defined with care and with an eye to their strengths and limitations.

That insight is congruent with attitudes fundamental to the practice of archaeology. Archaeologists must guard against the imposition of inappropriate etic categories on data from the archaeological record, perhaps even more vigilantly than their sociocultural colleagues, for, unlike them, archaeologists cannot interrogate or interact directly with their subjects.

As Herdt (1994b) points outs, sex and gender categories seem so "natural" and "inevitable" that it is no surprise that they should constitute a major bastion of archaeological unreflexivity. The penalty for this has been the masking of an unknown amount of sex/gender variation in prehistory under the smothering blanket of universally imposed, twentieth-century sex/gender categories. This penalty has been unwittingly paid by many archaeologists previously unconcerned with sex or gender as well as by feminists caught within the binary sex/gender paradigm. For feminists and nonfeminists alike, the queer theory critique of sex and gender categories provides alternatives to collapsing male and female gender categories into male and female biological sex categories.

Archaeology and a Multiple Sex/Gender Paradigm

Queer studies can provide archaeology with more than just the deconstruction of categories. A "third sex/third gender" paradigm (or, to use an alternative term I prefer, a "multiple sex/gender" paradigm) offers archaeologists a theoretical perspective within which emic sex/gender categories may be modeled and tested against data. In contrast to the binary paradigm, a multiple sex/gender paradigm implicitly acknowledges that the number of sex and/or gender categories constituting the sex/gender system of any society cannot be assumed before analysis. Nor is there any requirement specifying the nature of categorical boundaries. In addition to discrete, nonoverlapping sets, categorical variation may be continuous, such that categories grade into one another. Instead of a condition of universal, unvarying sets within a given society—where, once fixed, it would be inconceivable to modify terms of membership—categorical membership may be context-dependent to a greater or lesser degree.

The multiple sex/gender approach that I advocate, as with much of the best feminist-inspired archaeological work, can be viewed as something of an amalgam of the central concerns of both the processualist and postprocessualist enterprises. On the one hand, the multiple sex/gender paradigm entails initial skepticism regarding the composition of a given sex/gender system. As a consequence of that skepticism, an archaeologist must model or test various hypotheses to account for the data. This constitutes both an attitude and an activity that the New Archaeology made central to the construction of archaeological explanation. On the other hand, the goal of the multiple sex/gender approach is to understand the historically specific conditions pertaining to a given archaeological context, conditions that may not be readily universalized. That is congruent with the postprocessualist stress upon the particularities of context as opposed to the processualist search for laws of human behavior.

Non-binary sex/gender distinctions have been recognized in a number of cross-cultural contexts. In many Native American societies, including the Navajo, Mohave, Zuni, and others, emically recognized third- and fourth-gender roles have been documented ethnographically and/or ethnohistorically (Jacobs, Thomas, and Lang, eds. 1997; Roscoe 1987, 1991, 1994, 1998; Williams 1986). Similar categories have been described in Siberian cultures (Balzer 1996; Schmidt 2000). Membership in particular gender categories may shift over an individual's lifetime and for many differing, socially sanctioned reasons, including personal inclination or preference, social influences, and spiritual or religious prescriptions deriving from varying experiences, including dreams or trances (Roscoe 1994). Shifting sex/gender categorical affiliations might vary more or less predictably with age (i.e., position in the life-cycle). Infants, the elderly, or spirits of the deceased may be understood to occupy sex/gender classes distinct from those of most adults (Lesick 1997). Various interventions by adults may be seen as critical influences in the development of full acceptance for, and participation in, one of several adult sex/gender categories that each society recognizes.

No such distinction can be fully acknowledged and understood within the framework of the exclusive binary paradigm within which most archaeologists continue to operate. Yet many of these distinctions may have material culture correlates that are potentially recognizable in the archaeological record. Currently, it is difficult to assess just how much variation in the archaeological record may be linked to previously unsuspected social factors, although the extent of the masking could be considerable in some contexts. It may be best to assess this issue along two lines, including reexaminations of previously excavated data and formulation of research questions sensitive to issues regarding sex/gender systems.

Another reason to reexamine data is the fact that sex and gender may crosscut many, if not most, other major social variables. Failing to take aspects of the sex/gender system of a society into account may have caused misinterpretation of data previously assumed to be sexless or genderless. Thus, previous archaeological interpretations of data related to these other social phenomena may well alter after reviews that incorporate sex and gender.

In this connection, I return briefly to the assertion that the behavior and categories constituting sex/gender systems, including but not limited to sexuality, are too epistemologically insecure for archaeologists to waste time pursuing. The problem with that assertion is that archaeologists have no qualms about investigating social phenomena that occupy roughly the same rung of Hawke's Ladder of Inference, including phenomena such as status and ranking. Such study is commonly accepted throughout the discipline, and work in this area can be the basis for accruing high status and esteem (Margaret Conkey personal communication, 1996). If gender and sexuality are indeed roughly equivalent in their epistemological security, then the argument for dismissing archaeological investigations of sex/gender systems lacks merit.

Stone Age Homosexuality? The Case of Ötzi the Iceman

The 1991 discovery high in the Alps of an ancient, uniquely mummified corpse subsequently known as the Tyrolean Ice Man, the Man from Hauslabjoch, Similaun [Glacier] Man, or simply Ötzi, created a sensation among archaeologists and in the general press (Sjovald 1992; Spindler 1994). Both scholarly and public interest continued throughout the 1990s (Hess et al. 1998). As soon as Ötzi's antiquity of more than five thousand years was suspected, the issue of ownership arose between Italy and Austria, near whose mutual border the corpse was discovered. Resolving the political contest over national ownership eventually required involvement at the highest levels of government (Sjovald 1992; Spindler 1994).

Within a year of discovery, the corpse became the subject of another controversy as remarkable press reports circulated in Europe and North America. Both the general press (Spindler 1994) and the gay press alleged that "there was semen in Ötzi's anal canal . . . Ötzi is the first known homosexual man" (Wockner and Frings 1992:4). Thus the case of Ötzi constitutes one of the most prominent, and probably the best publicized, examples of an archaeological discovery that has become a site of contestation about homosexuality.

In his book *The Man in the Ice,* which has been called "the 'official' interim account of the find" (Barfield 1994:10), Konrad Spindler, head of the international team assembled to study the Iceman, makes clear his profound distaste for having to address the "host of rumours" and "[h]alf-truths and untruths [that] are spread as established facts" (Spindler 1994:173–74), which, he says, are the inevitable consequences of any spectacular find. Nevertheless, he was unable to ignore an account in the "reputable German weekly *Der Spiegel* (No. 10, 1993)," reporting "the rumour that 'sperm was found in Ötzi's anus,' a story said to have appeared in gay periodicals" (174).

To support his insistence that the claim is a "complete fabrication," Spindler provides two arguments. First, no examinations had yet been made of "the preserved soft tissue of the pelvis, nor were samples taken." Moreover, the rectum had yet to be identified in the computer tomograph of the body's internal organs, "greatly shrunken as they were through dehydration" (Spindler 1994:174). The second argument, which, we are told, makes the fabricated nature of reports of semen "particularly obvious," is that "the anal region of the corpse, through to the bony pelvic area, was destroyed by the first recovery team and their pneumatic chisel" (174).

But what, precisely, does the "destruction of the anal region" mean? Was every bit of the possibly relevant tissue removed from the corpse, or was it not recovered? Because the rectum and the associated internal organs have not yet been identified, it would seem premature for Spindler to come to this conclusion. Unfortunately, although color reproductions of rear-view photographs of the corpse in Spindler's volume as well as in other sources do indeed display damage to the left buttock and thigh, the extent of damage remains ambiguous and cannot unequivocally resolve the question of whether any relevant rectal tissue remains intact. Subsequent investigations have indicated that the epithelial and muscle tissue "generally suffered from conspicuous disintegration" and were "transformed into masses of amorphous to crystalline material, so-called 'white grave wax' or adipocere" (Hess et al. 1998:526–27), which would interfere with if not prevent identification of the relevant soft tissue of the rectal area.

Thus it seems clear that no evidence now exists that would either support—or definitively refute—the claim that Ötzi was the passive partner in homosexual anal intercourse not long before his demise some five thousand years ago. The lack of evidence can—at least in part—be attributed to the fact that researchers who have custody of the corpse have not addressed the question. Moreover, Spindler's published rhetoric suggests that he might actively resist conducting the sorts of tests that would either affirm or deny the presence of semen in the anal canal (Taylor 1996:15–16).

The controversy over the anal canal of the five-thousand-year-old corpse, and its relevance to contemporary political debates over the legitimacy of alternative sexual behaviors and sexual identities, involves stakes that include both economic and political dimensions. Exploiting his remarkable celebrity and fame, a substantial souvenir business sprang up around Ötzi (Spindler 1994:267–68), a business that many worried would be threatened by his identification as a homosexual (Wockner and Frings 1992). Local politicians in Austria and Italy, who had delighted in associating themselves with the well-known figure from prehistory (one even claimed that Ötzi had decided to vote for him for mayor [Spindler 1994:268]) grew markedly cooler to the Iceman after claims about his homosexuality appeared (Wockner and Frings 1992).

What lessons does the case of Ötzi hold for the conduct of archaeology? Although one may sympathize with archaeologists who feel understandable frustration that their work may be so frequently misunderstood and misconstrued by an impatient and unsophisticated press and public, it is a mistake to adopt in response the position that "scientific experts" should be the only legitimate voices in discussions of archaeological evidence. One need not read far between the lines of his book to gain a strong impression that Spindler believes that a scientific elite should "own" the Iceman or at least dispense or control all substantive discourse about him.

Such a perspective distances archaeologists from the public, whose support of archaeology is increasingly critical in the contemporary climate of shrinking budgets and sites in danger of destruction from economic development and looting. It also denies archaeologists the chance to learn from groups that may have valuable insights to offer. Within American archaeological circles, feminist challenges to such scientific elitist views have been articulated since the mid-1980s (e.g., Wylie 1992), and challenges from Native American groups gained increasing prominence with the implementation in 1990 of the Native American Graves Protection and Repatriation Act (NAGPRA) (Thomas 2000).

Although it may be highly unlikely that corroborating evidence will ever be found that would support the claim that Ötzi had anal sex not long before his demise, and it is appropriate to reject inaccurate claims that such evidence has already been obtained, it is assuredly *not* appropriate to dismiss the possibility that such evidence might exist. Yet this is just the attitude that Spindler argumentatively projects. There would be no need to reject a search for such evidence out of hand were not Spindler personally invested in rejecting the possibility of Ötzi being associated with homosexuality but simultaneously convinced that no evidence likely existed to support the claim of anal intercourse. Why not welcome, or at least not stand in the way of, research that one believes would support one's position?

Spindler and most archaeologists have seen the past through a form of heterosexual tunnel vision. This blindness has led the vast majority of archaeologists to promulgate and disseminate versions of a past inhabited only by normative males and females, "normative" being read as "heterosexual." Although the particulars of the Ötzi case may never produce evidence to unequivocally demonstrate the existence of homosexual behavior five thousand years ago in the Alps, the controversy has opened a Pandora's box of erotic, sexual, and gender possibilities in the archaeological imagining of the past. Whatever sexual behaviors he may or may not have engaged in, Ötzi has been good to think about for those who prefer not to unnecessarily constrain interpretations of the past.

Incorporating the full range of variability of sex/gender systems into theoretical frameworks and research strategies will benefit archaelogy through the inclusion of a sensitivity to sexual and erotic relations. I do not advocate that archaeologists acquiesce to the demands of social or political movements that find the appropriation of archaeological evidence or interpretations convenient to advancing their agendas. On the contrary, archaeologists should acknowledge that their interpretations have generally, if often unintentionally, reinforced a contemporary conservative social and political agenda regarding sex, gender, and sexuality. By refusing to permit or legitimize research into issues of sexuality, Spindler has been a participant (even if an unintentional one) in an agenda that seeks to deny any place for nonreproductive sexual behaviors in prehistory. In addition to acknowledging that state of affairs, the remedy will consist of being ready to entertain and test explanations perhaps not limited to normative notions about sex, gender, and sexuality.

Was Ötzi homosexual or heterosexual? Or, to use the phrase independently suggested by several colleagues, in one of his last moments did the Iceman cometh? As has become clear from a plethora of scholarship over the last generation (Davidson 1987; Foucault 1978; Padgug 1989; Weeks 1989, 1985, 1991), we must move beyond that essentializing, overly simplistic way of framing (homo)sexual relations and/or identity to be able to more richly imagine how sets of social relations regarding sex, gender, and sexuality were articulated in prehistoric societies.

Homosexuality as a Relevant Social Variable for Interpretations of the Past

I have outlined challenges to assumptions about sex/gender systems in societies archaeologists study and proposed a multiple sex/gender paradigm as a new theoretical tool for modeling the complexities of sex/gender systems. Using the example of Ötzi, I have also identified and discussed some of the problems associated with resistance to any consideration of homosexuality or homosexual behavior as factors in the archaeological past. I will continue by sketching several examples of more recent archaeological research that take seriously the proposal that homosexuality or homosexual behavior were meaningful elements in the constitution of past societies. These examples illustrate how investigations of homosexuality can broaden an understanding of social relations in the past. All but two examples are associated with a book (Schmidt and Voss, eds. 2000) whose explicit purpose is to demonstrate to the discipline of archaeology the utility of considering sexuality as a legitimate object of knowledge.

Before I take up these individual examples, it is important to begin with the recognition that variation in sex/gender systems (which the binary or dimorphic sex/gender paradigm is inadequate to explain) should not be understood or envisioned as an amorphous haze of potentiality within a given sex/gender system. Rather, the sex/gender system of any given society at a particular historical moment is composed of and structured by patterns of relationships. For example, many classic ethnographies outline impressively complex marriage patterns with remarkable implications for social organization (e.g., Leach 1952). And we know from work such as that of Herdt

(1994a) that patterns of sexual interactions external to marriage can also be considered as very important from both emic and etic perspectives.

The point to stress here is that sexual relations, like other forms of social relations, tend to be patterned. Because archaeological evidence is generally a composite or accumulation of materials associated with many episodes of behavior, with some exceptions it is *patterns* rather than individual instances of behavior that are potentially visible in the archaeological record (Matthews 1995). Thus it will be *patterns of sexual relations* that compose one set of sources for archaeological evidence. That is not to ignore the fact that exceptional individuals and circumstances exist and are potentially instructive, each in its own right. It is, rather, recognition of the nature of most archaeological evidence and allied with the intention to make a virtue of the inherent limitations of archaeological evidence.

Interpretation is impoverished when the search for patterns ends with, or goes no further than, identification of a single normative pattern. Identification of the patterns of sexual relations in which minority subsets of a given population engage may ultimately prove more interesting and illuminating than research that focuses only upon a dominant type or norm (Matthews 1995).

Archaeological Examples

The first archaeological example, which is the earliest I will discuss and the only one that ought to be credited as being explicitly associated with the postprocessualist enterprise, concerns the work of Tim Yates (1993). Of course, Yates is hardly the first archaeologist ever to mention sexuality or homosexuality, but his is the first work I know that does more than argue for the antiquity of the practice of homosexuality or whose analysis of the social utility of sexuality goes deeper than simply relating it to religious or cosmological belief systems (e.g., Kauffmann Doig 1979). Rather, Yates employs homosexuality as an element in a more probing analysis.

Yates's subject is a remarkable body of prehistoric rock art, most dating from the Bronze Age, in the county of Bohuslän on the western coast of Sweden between the city of Gothenburg and the Norwegian border. Thousands of individual sites, each with at least one individual panel of art but with many containing more than one panel, are scattered across the landscape of this district. The designs incised and pecked onto the rocks can be grouped into six major categories. Yates's analysis focuses upon the second most common "representational" category: human figures. For these, Yates correlates the presence or absence of an erect phallus with various other features, some anatomical (e.g., exaggerated hands and/or fingers, exaggerated calf muscles, and long hair) and some related to clothing (horned hats) and other types of artifacts, most of which are forms of arms (e.g., swords, spears, scabbards, and axes). Given the thematic prominence of figures associated with ideals of aggressive masculinity, Yates asks, what class or classes of human are represented by the other types of anthropomorphic design?

For various reasons, Yates argues that the evidence does not support the argument that nonphallic figures must be female. The best evidence usually cited to support this interpretation, which Yates questions, has been the so-called marriage scenes, wherein two figures appear to be embracing and a line between them at the waist appears to be an erect phallus. Given the assumption that sexual activity is represented by these depictions, the standard interpretation has been that one figure must be male and the other female.

Yates draws upon Lacan, Deleuze, and Guattari as well as the work of Herdt (1994a) to argue that the anthropomorphic figures depicted in the rock art of Bohuslän may not be interpretable in terms of a binary ontology of sexuality. Instead, he suggests that figures that have been traditionally interpreted as representing marriage or heterosexual intercourse between male and female may in fact represent two males. Further, the contemporary notions of assigned, fixed, and immutable sexual identities may well be inapplicable in prehistoric social contexts in which the rock art served specific social purposes. Yates problematizes the rock art representations of aggressive masculinity by suggesting that such manifestations were not an inherent part of the "male" body in Bronze Age society. Rather, he suggests that bodies may have required supplementation of attachable or detachable parts (such as exaggerated calves) to achieve full male expression.

Yates concludes by arguing that systems of meaning coexisted in the past (for example, a discourse of chiefly elites and a discourse of the body, which were intimately linked but independent of one another) so that contemporary monolithic interpretations of past behavior miss the variability that must have been present. By implication (Yates states some but not all of the following explicitly), some or all of the "marriage scenes" in the rock art of Bohuslän may have nothing at all do with the expression of sexuality. Some or all may depict male-male sexual expression within a particular context of meaning, such as a transfer of masculinity from warrior to youth in a fashion analogous to that of the Sambia. Or, perhaps some or all of the "marriage scenes" represent heterosexual unions. The task for archaeologists is to be flexible enough to be able to imagine the intersecting subtleties of meaning with which people in the past imbued their lives as we do now.

The second archaeological case study also derives from an analysis of representation. Rosemary Joyce (1992, 1993; see also Gillespie and Joyce 1997) has previously employed representational analyses to define and describe discourses regarding the articulation of gender in prehispanic Maya societies. In a fascinating, more recent work (2000), she explores suggestions of a visual and textual discourse that celebrated the male body as an object of a male gaze, a celebration at some points realized in sexual relations between males and also realized in the sexual desire of women for the aestheticized male body.

In Maya representations painted upon ceramic vessels and upon the interior walls of buildings, male bodies are exposed by elaborate costuming that leaves arms, legs, and chests uncovered. Male figures wear loincloths with long ends that hang and draw attention to genitalia as much as conceal them. The little clothing that is worn consists primarily of body adornment such as cuffs and anklets, ornamented helmets or headdresses, massive belts, pendants, and ear ornaments. The muscular bodies shown in these performances are highly idealized and presented in timeless young adulthood.

The male bodies commonly appear in groups engaged in all-male pursuits that demand physical strength and skill. The multifigure compositions engage their male subjects in visual hierarchies directed at male viewers within the scene. In other words, in these scenes male bodies are being viewed by noble male lords. Moreover, contemporary understandings of the uses of the polychrome vessels that provide the most abundant corpus of all-male, multifigure scenes suggest that the vessels were produced for patrons who were noblemen. Thus the internal visual relationships depicted in these scenes reflexively invoke the objectification of male bodies as subjects of the gaze of the owners of these elaborate objects.

Joyce infers sexualization of these aestheticized male bodies from several lines of evidence, including colonial period ethnohistorical reports; analyses of Classic Maya texts, linguistic analyses of contemporary Maya words, and (from a marginalized aspect) some Classic Maya art—representations of the erect penis. The existence of a "phallic cult" in late-Classic and Postclassic Maya society was distasteful to, but nonetheless acknowledged by, early-twentieth-century students of the Maya. Phallic representations occur in architectural and cave contexts that Joyce suggests were locations of all-male socialization. One practice associated with such sites included ritual blood-letting from the erect penis. Another theme depicted in some all-male group contexts is masturbation, a form of sexual activity explicitly depicted in Classic Maya images and for which colonial Yucatec Maya vocabularies provide a diverse lexicon.

Joyce concludes with the observation that contemporary Euro-American attitudes toward male-male sexual activities have blinded researchers to the possibility that eroticization of the male body need not be associated with the implications some would read from this. Specifically, homosexuality need not immutably refer to a masculine act of domination in relationship to an effeminate act of subordination. She suggests sensitivity to alternative implications, nuance, and ambiguity in readings of Maya sexuality.

The third case study uses evidence from an excavation of a nineteenth-century women's "factory" or prison in the Australian state of Tasmania. Of British birth, the inmates of factories had been convicted of various felonies and transported to Australia to serve their sentences. Eleanor Casella (2000a, 2000b) has used archaeological evidence in conjunction with documentary evidence to argue that women incarcerated in the Ross Female Factory used various strategies to adjust their lives to the wholly new circumstances in which they found themselves and resist the disciplinary programs intended to reform their behavior.

One strategy of adjustment and resistance was to establish a sexual economy that challenged penal discipline. Casella suggests that one way for inmates to regain some control of their sexualized bodies was to establish and conduct lesbian relationships. She supplements various documentary sources that describe and condemn these relationships with archaeological evidence suggesting that women inmates, through relationships with each other, were able to negotiate the privations of prison life with greater success than documentary sources indicate. Despite their incarceration, some managed to acquire access to contraband materials such as alcohol and tobacco. In fact, there appears to have been a thriving black-market trade of illicit goods in the factory. Documents written by male prison officials indicate that some inmates regularly gave illicit gifts to others in order to cement and maintain lesbian sexual relationships. Thus the internal sexual economy would have been reflected in the material culture economy of the prison and possibly in the archaeological deposits related to the prison.

Casella tested this hypothesis with excavations of different areas of the factory site. With regard to the recovery of remains of illicit objects (e.g., bottles for alcoholic beverages and tobacco pipes), she found that the solitary-cells area of the prison had considerably more illicit materials than the crime-class area, in terms of both relative frequency and minimum number of vessel (MNV) counts. That is surprising given the much higher occupation density of the latter than the former as well as the greater degree of isolation and deprivation that prison authorities intended occupants of the solitary cells to experience. Casella suggests that occupants of the solitary cells, who were typically the most recalcitrant recidivists, were at the apex of the prison's sexual economy. They were also at the center of networks of resistance, resistance that was an opportunity to reject the passivity and modesty of the ideal femininity of the period. Through networks of the sexual economy, inmates could increase their colonial survival knowledge and skills and find emotional solace and sexual satisfaction.

Thus women who were in these circumstances had many reasons to establish and maintain the sort of sexual economy that led to the pattern of illicit artifact deposition Casella found. Her work adds a new dimension to the understanding of female convict incarceration in nineteenth-century Australia, a material dimension that sole reliance upon documentary evidence could not hope to establish. Her work both confirms and expands our appreciation of the role of sexual economies within prison environments.

As with Casella's work, the fourth case study addresses differential uses of space in archaeological sites. Elizabeth Prine (2000) has used spatial analysis to create an archaeological window of visibility for two-spirit ("berdache") identities during the prehistoric and protohistoric periods among the Hidatsa. The Hidatsa were horticulturalists who lived in villages along the Missouri River in what is now North Dakota from the fifteenth through the nineteenth centuries. For a number of reasons the Hidatsa are among the Native American groups who have been most extensively ethnographically documented.

As with many native North American people, the Hidatsa recognized a third gender category of personhood. Their name for members of this category was *miati*. The miati were distinguished in a number of ways from Hidatsa male and female genders. Miati were male-bodied persons who in adolescence chose to adopt or embody the miati role, which was fraught with religious significance because the miati were the most active class of persons who conducted ceremonies. Euro-American observers tended to focus on the fact that miati wore feminine attire and seemed disposed to have sexual relationships with males. Prine has undertaken the challenge of trying to identify archaeological evidence relating to the miati members of Hidatsa society. What material culture signature might miati leave in the archaeological record?

One answer refers to the uses of social and architectural space in Hidatsa villages that would tend to be associated with miati as distinct from male and female genders. The Hidatsa lived for much of the year in large, dome-shaped, earthen homes that were supported by timbers. One of the principal ritual tasks of the miati was related to architectural production. They were responsible for erecting posts for religious ceremonies as well as for erecting posts for the earth-lodge homes of the tribe.

In a survey of records of twenty-three earth lodges excavated at two confirmed Hidatsa sites, twenty-two conform to classic earth-lodge design characteristics, including a set of single supporting posts arranged in circular fashion beyond the main support posts of the lodge. The exception had a set of double rather than single secondary posts. This is significant for several reasons. There appears to be solid evidence that the Hidatsa were quite conservative with regard to material culture. According to ethnographic information, however, the miati were reputed to be innovative in the arena of ritual. The use of doubled posts suggests that the lodge could have been that of a miati household.

Another line of evidence supports this interpretation. Consisting of a miati plus husband and adopted children, miati households tended to be smaller than the ordinary matrilocal Hidatsa household. "Double Post" (the name Prine assigns to this exceptional dwelling) was by far the smallest Hidatsa house of the twenty-three excavated and had a maximum diameter of only thirty-four feet. The next-largest lodges were forty-two feet in diameter (the overall average house diameter being 43.7 feet). The size differential between the Double Post earth lodge and all the other lodges is statistically significant and should not be attributed to chance. With these and several other lines of evidence supporting this interpretation, Prine concludes that although she cannot definitively state that Double Post was a miati household, the evidence in favor of that explanation is very strong.

The fifth case study approaches the problem of the archaeological identification of two-spirits from different angles in a different social context. Sandra Hollimon (1991, 1996) has previously investigated issues of gender and sexuality among the Chumash of southern California, a Native American group noted for its pre-contact social complexity as demonstrated by the emergence of specialist groups. One specialist group in Chumash society was the 'aqi, or two-spirit undertakers. That social category inextricably links gender, labor, and sexuality in its definition. The 'aqi were distinct from two-spirit roles found in many other Native American groups, but there were also similarities, including a pattern of sexual expression that was nonprocreative, such as homosexuality. At the time of European contact, the 'aqi composed a guild of undertakers. Hollimon (1997) has suggested that because the Chumash understood 'aqi to be nonprocreative they were then qualified to be mortuary practitioners. Their nonprocreative social roles meant that the symbolic pollution of a corpse could not harm them. The point is reiterated by ambiguities in some documentary sources that seem to indicate that both male-bodied persons and women beyond child-bearing years—both nonprocreative social roles—could become 'aqi.

Having proposed guidelines by which two-spirit individuals might be identified in archaeological mortuary contexts, Hollimon (2000) has made tentative identifications of two separate two-spirit Chumash burials. Both males were about eighteen years of age and had severe spinal arthritis, which was very unusual for contemporaneous males but not for females (males tended to develop arthritis in other joints of the body). Hollimon hypothesizes that these individuals had placed severe strain upon their backs through the repeated heavy use of digging sticks, either for harvesting tubers or digging graves. Moreover, the two individuals were buried with a complete tool kit of 'aqi undertakers, something that was true for no other males in this mortuary context. We know from contact-period records that the two uses, food-gathering and grave-digging, had to be kept completely separate by the use of separate sets of tools despite the fact that tools for both uses appear to be identical.

Because of such cases, where meanings and associations of artifacts may vary due to circumstances that are not obvious, archaeologists must continually question the meanings they assign to material culture evidence. To make the argument that a particular archaeological artifact was associated with the undertakers' guild, and thus that the individual associated with that artifact was an undertaker, it is desirable to bring additional lines of evidence to bear. In the case of the two tentatively identified 'aqi individuals, Hollimon has been able to marshal two separate lines of evidence. The first is the pattern of associated mortuary goods; no other males in her mortuary context were buried with the full set of undertaker's guild tools. The second is the differential patterns in the development of arthritis between the sexes. The two young male 'aqi candidates had developed arthritic pathologies consistent with the heavy use of digging sticks. Together, the two lines of evidence strengthen the argument that the individuals were members of the 'aqi guild.

Given most societies' tendency toward conservatism in religious and cosmological belief systems, Hollimon (2000) has proposed that the 'aqi undertakers of the Chumash may have considerably predated the development of other craft specializations among the Chumash by hundreds or even thousands of years. Provocatively, she further suggests that the undertakers' guild may even have served as a template for the development of the other craft specializations that arose in the centuries before contact.

The work of Elizabeth Perry (Perry and Joyce 2001) examines constructions of both gender and sexuality in Pueblo communities in the North American Southwest region, focusing especially upon a period starting around 1275 A.D. This was a time of widespread social change when the classic pueblo sites in the Four Corners region of New Mexico, Colorado, Utah, and Arizona were abandoned and new sites to the south and east were founded in the Rio Grande valley and elsewhere throughout the Southwest. The widespread social change of the period was characterized by extraordinary shifts in community structure, social organization, and ritual practice. These shifts produced new forms of knowledge, performance, behavior, material culture, and architecture. Ritual systems such as Katsina religion facilitated these changes and may further have integrated people within and across regions.

Perry and Rosemary Joyce cite work suggesting that the emergence of plaza architecture at this time may have had profound implications for redrawing gender divisions within pueblo societies. Drawing explicitly upon the work of Judith Butler, they point out that reiterative performances of domestic as well as ceremonial activities, centered within the public plaza, may have helped create highly dualistic male and female gender roles in these societies, as ethnographers have noted. Moreover, they suggest that one can reasonably expect that any highly dualistic gender system will simultaneously produce gender transgressive performances. At historic Zuni, the status of the *lhamana* (trans-gendered person) was tied up both in the performance of gender-specific domestic labor and in the ceremonial performance of Kolhamana, the trans-gendered Katsina. Perry proposes that, if Katsina religion did indeed crystalize during and following the end of the thirteenth century (or at least if the public performative aspects of the religion were formalized at that time), then the historically documented social status of the lhamana may also have roots in this period as well. Following Hollimon, Perry and Joyce also suggest that it may be possible archaeologically to identify individuals who occupied the role of lhamana or related roles through evidence of differing mortuary treatment as well as differential labor stresses on sexed skeletons, and they offer a candidate skeleton for such identification from a site in northeastern Arizona. Perry and Joyce's work offers opportunity to consider how homosexuality, as a single performative ingredient of trans-gendered identity, may have participated in pueblo sex and gender systems as an important element.

The final archaeological example is based upon my own work (Schmidt 2000) from the northern European Mesolithic ("Middle Stone Age") period ca. 5000–4000 B.C. Like their Paleolithic ancestors, Mesolithic people were hunter-gatherers, and their descendants of the Neolithic period were, by definition, farmers and pastoralists. Scholars of the last generation have come to have an increasing appreciation for the sophistication of the hunter-gatherer life-style of Mesolithic people. From this has come a willingness to entertain the possibility that social and cultural complexity was not an artifact of the agricultural subsistence mode, and necessarily associated with it, but may have arisen in some hunter-gatherer societies before the introduction or invention of food production techniques (Price and Brown 1985; Zvelebil, ed. 1986).

One of the most important European Mesolithic sites is Oleny Ostrov in Karelia in western Russia. With 177 individuals identified, Oleny Ostrov is one of the largest Mesolithic cemeteries yet discovered. Excavated in the 1930s, the scale of the cemetery and its "evident social wealth betokened by the abundant mortuary artifacts" (Jacobs 1995:369) led Russian researchers to an interpretation consistent with Marxist orthodoxy of the period. Oleny Ostrov must have been the product of the Engelsian "'Late Clan' stage typical of very early farmers and animal herders" (369). The startlingly early dates for the site produced through later radiocarbon dating confirmed what the complete absence of ceramics at the site had earlier suggested: The cemetery at Oleny Ostrov preceded the penetration of Neolithic technologies into Karelia by thousands of years (Jacobs 1995; O'Shea and Zvelebil 1984).

In 1984 O'Shea and Zvelebil reanalyzed the site in light of the new dating. They suggested that the society that produced the cemetery of Oleny Ostrov was larger and more internally differentiated than previously believed, with a complex system of social differentiation that included both horizontal and vertical ranking. It also participated in an extensive regional exchange network that moved exotic goods and raw materials over considerable distances. The authors argued that the climax of forager occupation in the Boreal Zone, characterized by a maximum density of population and maximum social complexity, occurred during late Mesolithic times. More recent hunter-fisher-gatherer occupations continuing to the twentieth century represent only a pale reflection of this peak. O'Shea and Zvelebil suggest that it has been our inability to imagine such a socially complex hunter-gatherer society that has limited our ability to recognize the evidence that points to such complexity. It must be pointed out, however, that in a reanalysis a decade later Jacobs (1995) argued that O'Shea and Zvelebil may have overstated the case for social complexity at the site.

Two females and two males from the Oleny Ostrov cemetery population deserve particular attention due to their unusual mortuary treatment. In contrast to all other graves at the site, the four are interred in a nearly vertical or standing position, and three of the four possessed grave assemblages of the highest wealth level (O'Shea and Zvelebil 1984:19). With some minor reservations on the part of one interpreter of the site, the suggestion that these individuals were shamans seems to be relatively uncontroversial (Jacobs 1995). Zvelebil (1993, 1997, 1998) in particular makes that argument in the context of proposing that there was a generalized conservative continuity of religious and cosmological systems of representation, meaning, and belief throughout northern Eurasia for many thousands of years, from the middle Mesolithic period to the present. Because of this continuity, he asserts, nineteenth- and twentieth-century ethnographic information from Siberia can be relevant to northern European Mesolithic societies. If he is right, it would be reasonable to infer the presence of Mesolithic shamans—or comparable ritual specialists—at Oleny Ostrov.

One of the best-known generalizations regarding Eurasian shamans is that many have been known to engage in behaviors that transgress sexual and gender categorical boundaries (Balzer 1996; Jacobs and Cromwell 1992). That has certainly been true of many ethnographically documented Siberian shamans from a number of different groups. In fact, the role of the shaman is frequently understood to consist of balancing and mediating spiritual energies, which often requires "the harnessing of both male and female sexual potential" (Balzer 1996:164). If Zvelebil's argument for symbolic and ideological continuity across thousands of years throughout northern Eurasia has merit, then it is reasonable to infer that the cosmological role of the shaman may have remained little changed since the Mesolithic period. If that leap is made, moreover, we may further infer that the patterns of sexual behavior of these Mesolithic people, including shamans and their sexual partners, may have resembled the patterns of sexual behavior of ethnographically described northern Eurasian people, including contemporary shamans and their sexual partners. Thus it is reasonable to argue that homosexual relations were a part of the sexual repertoire of northern Eurasian Mesolithic people six to seven millennia in the past.[4]

Inference is the inescapable stitching of every explanatory garment that archaeologists use to clothe the past. The inferences I have employed rely on the use of both ethnographic analogy and the direct historical approach. In using ethnographic analogy, the greater the number of similarities that can be demonstrated between recent and past societies the more secure is the analogical link supporting inferences about the past society. With the direct historical approach, similarities between past and present are assumed to derive from a direct historical connection, which, of course, grows fainter as the link is stretched across greater periods of time. The chain of inferences connecting Siberian and Mesolithic shamans draws on both approaches to archaeological inference and is relatively straightforward and well-grounded, although the direct historical connection must be regarded as a more tenuous line of evidence than the others due to the timespan. The fact that someone like Zvelebil, who despite his other virtues would not claim to be on the leading edge of issues of sexuality in archaeology, refers to Mesolithic shamans as "third gender" individuals (1998) demonstrates that this chain of inferences is not as controversial as it once might have been. One is left to wonder why has no one made these connections before. Given the controversy about the sexuality of the Iceman, it is ironic indeed that the archaeological argument about the sexual lives of Mesolithic shamans supports the inference that homosexuality, as a stable element in a pattern of social relations, predates by some two millennia the time of the Iceman.

Implications

The preceding illustrations of the practicability of queering the past demonstrate clearly that homosexuality in particular and sexuality in general have a place in archaeological practice and interpretation. Just as gender archaeologists have made a strong case since the mid-1980s for the importance of including gender as a factor in archaeological social analyses, the examples I have discussed will, along with work to come, add sexuality and homosexuality to the same list.

Contrary to the suppositions of many archaeologists, we do not need a "smoking pen" writing about and explicitly describing sexual expression in the past to be able to make inferences about sexuality in the past. As with other objects of knowledge, variation in patterns of sexuality can be inferred from a number of approaches.

Yates and Joyce demonstrate that analyses of representation can lead to nuanced and flexible interpretations of homosocial and homosexual relations. Casella and Prine—and to a lesser extent, Joyce—showcase some of the ways in which spatial and architectural analyses can identify subgroups and provide information about them that would otherwise be unavailable. Hollimon, Perry, and Schmidt combine direct historical approach and ethnographic analogy to argue for considerable antiquity for differing patterns of homosexual relations in the respective temporal and geographic locales of their work.

One of the goals of an archaeology of homosexuality will be to uncover evidence about variation in homosexual expression that only archaeology can contribute. Matthews (1994, 1995) argues that the postprocessual approaches that arose in archaeology during the 1980s and 1990s enabled consideration of variability between different subcultures in every society instead of focusing solely upon norms. All of these approaches rely upon at least one prerequisite—to find something, one must first be willing and motivated to look for it. The time has finally come to look for homosexuality in the past through the use of archaeological evidence.

As various archaeologies of homosexuality are developed, archaeologists will have to grapple with some of the same issues that feminist archaeologists have encountered successfully, such as the tendency toward an "invisibility" of women in the past (Conkey and Spector 1984; Gero and Conkey, eds. 1991). Note, for example, that of the archaeological case studies I have briefly described, Yates, Joyce, Hollimon, and Prine investigate male/male patterns of sexuality, Perry and Schmidt address same-sex patterns of sexuality for both males and females, and Casella is the only researcher who focuses her analysis on female/female sexuality. As archaeologists expand their investigations into the patterns of sexual relations in many societies in the past, that imbalance must not remain unchallenged.

When looking for evidence of relatively low-frequency patterns of behavior, which may be a fair description of homosexuality in many but certainly not all contexts, it must be obvious that documentary evidence, where it exists, can prove very helpful. That principle is exemplified in Casella's work. While text-based evidence can clearly be of enormous assistance in some cases, archaeologists must examine that evidence as critically as they examine all other lines of evidence. Perhaps text-based evidence should be even more suspect than material culture evidence because authors of texts necessarily write from limited perspectives on any issue and can even deliberately falsify positions, something that happens less frequently with nontextual archaeological evidence. This principle, too, is exemplified in Casella's work. But as several of the examples indicate, homosexuality can credibly be investigated archaeologically, even without primary documentary resources. In many ways that is the most surprising, as well as hopeful, conclusion that one can draw from the work described here.

Archaeological Contributions to Queer Studies

The bulk of this chapter has focused on the benefits that archaeology can derive from what I have called "queering the past." Along with the incorporation of insights from queer studies into archaeological theory and practice, archaeologists will be able to offer contributions of their own in return. One benefit consists of the potential expansion of knowledge regarding sex/gender systems to include societies about which we would know nothing absent archaeological investigations. This has both synchronic and diachronic aspects. The first will consist of greater understanding of particular sex/gender systems in specific sociohistorical periods and circumstances. The second will offer the chance to trace changes in sex/gender systems. Such analyses may aid in the understanding of how changes in sex/gender systems came about in the past and have potential relevance to contemporary political struggles.

Another benefit archaeology may offer to queer studies parallels the contributions that historical archaeologists have already been making to historical studies of more recent periods. Even in periods and situations where abundant documentary resources are available, there are many classes and groups of people who are not given voice (for various reasons). By examining the material culture traces that such groups leave behind, historical archaeologists have significantly added to the understanding of the contributions of such people. Historical archaeologists have demonstrated, for example, that enslaved African American populations in the American South retained African lifeways and resisted oppression to an extent that could not be appreciated from documentary evidence alone (Ferguson 1992). As Casella's work with women in the nineteenth-century Australian penal system illustrates, we can further expect that historical archaeologists will shed light upon undocumented or under-documented aspects of sex/gender systems in recent periods.

Conclusion

The voices of archaeology can be relevant to contemporary political activism because the future is built from the past. Archaeologists need not and should not shrink from such relevance. Increasing knowledge of past variability correspondingly increases the palette of possibilities from which we choose our futures. The more that archaeologists can expand society's understanding of the myriad ways people have found to be human, the richer all our futures may become.

But it can work both ways. As society's capability to imagine more diverse futures grows, so may a corresponding appreciation by archaeologists for the variability of the past increase. In other words, respect for contemporary social variability by archaeologists may open their eyes to new visions of the past. Surely it is an outcome that the discipline of anthropological archaeology can embrace.

Notes

1. By focusing upon the fact that sexuality has been avoided in archaeology, I do not mean to reify any particular analytical formulation of the category "sexuality" itself. Rather, I recognize that just as manifestations of sexuality vary, so must the category "sexuality" itself vary. Thus the analytical tools archaeologists use to understand these social phenomena must be flexible. For example, consider how the contemporary understanding of sexuality must bend to incorporate social phenomena that marry sexuality with religious or spiritual expression (as in temple "prostitution"). Moreover, as with any other concept, the category "homosexuality" itself has been identified with a shifting melange of culturally and historically contingent meanings (Katz 1995).

2. This is even true of the work of Boswell (1989, 1994) despite his arguments against what he saw as over-extensions of the social-constructionist approach.

3. For a discussion of the emergence of archaeological studies of sexuality from feminist archaeologies, see Voss (2000). This is not to say that there have not been laudable acknowledgments by gender archaeologists that gender must not be assumed to be a binary phenomenon (Gilchrist 1994:6; Whelan 1991). Nevertheless, this recognition has only begun to be pursued and extended by a few gender archaeologists. Moreover, the pursuit of this aspect of the variability of gender has often been tied to investigations of sexuality.

4. In saying this, I wish to reiterate that describing what was happening in the Mesolithic with the word *homosexuality* or the phrase *homosexual relations* should not

be understood to imply a simplistic equation with the meanings of those words when applied to various twentieth- and twenty-first-century contexts or contexts from other times and places.

References Cited

Balzer, Marjorie Mandelstam. 1996. "Sacred Genders in Siberia: Shamans, Bear Festivals, and Androgyny." In *Gender reversals and gender cultures: Anthropological and historical perspectives,* ed. Sabrina Petra Ramet, 164–82. New York: Routledge.

Barfield, Lawrence. 1994. "The Iceman Reviewed." *Antiquity* 68(258): 10–26.

Binford, Lewis R. 1962. "Archaeology as Anthropology." *American Antiquity* 28(2): 217–25.

Boswell, John. 1989. "Revolutions, Universals, and Sexual Categories." In *Hidden from History: Reclaiming the Gay and Lesbian Past,* ed. Martin Duberman, Martha Vicinus, and George Chauncey, Jr., 17–36. New York: Meridian.

———. 1994. *Same-Sex Unions in Premodern Europe.* New York: Villard.

Brown, Judith. 1989. "Lesbian Sexuality in Medieval and Early Modern Europe." In *Hidden from History: Reclaiming the Gay and Lesbian Past,* ed. Martin Duberman, Martha Vicinus, and George Chauncey, Jr., 67–75. New York: Meridian.

Butler, Judith. 1990. *Gender Trouble: Feminism and the Subversion of Identity.* New York: Routledge.

———. 1993. *Bodies That Matter: On the Discursive Limits of "Sex."* New York: Routledge.

Casella, Eleanor. 2000a. "Bulldaggers and Gentle Ladies: Archaeological Approaches to Female Homosexuality in Convict-Era Australia." In *Archaeologies of Sexuality,* ed. Robert Schmidt and Barbara Voss, 143–59. New York: Routledge.

———. 2000b. "Doing Trade: A Sexual Economy of Nineteenth-Century Australian Female Convict Prisons." *World Archaeology* 32(2): 209–21.

Chauncey, George. 1989. "Christian Brotherhood of Sexual Perversion? Homosexual Identities and the Construction of Sexual Boundaries in the World War I Era." In *Hidden from History: Reclaiming the Gay and Lesbian Past,* ed. Martin Duberman, Martha Vicinus, and George Chauncey, Jr., 294–317. New York: Meridian.

———. 1994. *Gay New York: Gender, Urban Culture, and the Making of the Gay Male World, 1890–1940.* New York: Basic Books.

Conkey, Margaret W., and Janet D. Spector. 1984. "Archaeology and the Study of Gender." In *Advances in Archaeological Method and Theory,* ed. Michael B. Schiffer, 1–38. New York: Academic Press.

Davidson, Arnold I. 1987. "Sex and the Emergence of Sexuality." *Critical Inquiry* 14(1): 16–48.

Dowson, Thomas A. 2000. "Why Queer Archaeology? An Introduction." *World Archaeology* 32(2): 161–65.

Engelstad, Ericka. 1991. "Images of Power and Contradiction: Feminist Theory and Post-Processual Archaeology." *Antiquity* 65(248): 502–14.

Ferguson, Leland. 1992. *Uncommon Ground: Archaeology and Early African America, 1650–1800.* Washington: Smithsonian Institution Press.

Foucault, Michel. 1978. *The History of Sexuality,* vol. 1: *An Introduction.* New York: Vintage Books.

Gero, Joan M., and Margaret W. Conkey, eds. 1991. *Engendering Archaeology: Women and Prehistory.* New York: Oxford University Press.

Gilchrist, Roberta. 1994. *Gender and Material Culture: The Archaeology of Religious Women.* New York: Routledge.

Gillespie, Susan D., and Rosemary A. Joyce. 1997. "Gendered Goods: The Symbolism of Maya Hierarchical Exchange Relations." In *Women in Prehistory: North America and Mesoamerica,* ed. Cheryl Claassen and Rosemary A. Joyce, 189–207. Philadelphia: University of Pennsylvania Press.

Halperin, David M. 1989. "Sex before Sexuality: Pederasty, Power and Politics in Classical Athens." In *Hidden from History: Reclaiming the Gay and Lesbian Past,* ed. Martin Duberman, Martha Vicinus, and George Chauncey, Jr., 37–53. New York: Meridian.

———. 1990. *One Hundred Years of Homosexuality and Other Essays on Greek Love.* New York: Routledge.

Hawkes, C. F. 1954. "Archaeological Theory and Method: Some Suggestions from the Old World." *American Anthropologist* 56(2): 155–68.

Herdt, Gilbert. 1994a. *Guardians of the Flutes: Idioms of Masculinity.* Chicago: University of Chicago Press.

———. 1994b. "Introduction: Third Sexes and Third Genders." In *Third Sex, Third Gender: Beyond Sexual Dimorphism in Culture and History,* ed. Herdt, 21–81. New York: Zone Books.

Hess, M. W., G. Klima, K. Pfaller, K.H. Kunzel, and O. Gaber. 1998. "Histological Investigations of the Tyrolean Ice Man." *American Journal of Physical Anthropology* 106(4): 521–32.

Hodder, Ian. 1982. *Symbols in Action.* New York: Cambridge University Press.

———. 1991. *Reading the Past: Current Approaches to Interpretation in Archaeology.* New York: Cambridge University Press.

Hollimon, Sandra E. 1991. "Health Consequences of Division of Labor among the Chumash Indians of Southern California." In *The Archaeology of Gender: Proceedings of the Twenty-second Annual Conference of the Archaeological Association of the University of Calgary,* ed. Dale Walde and Noreen D. Willows, 462–69. Calgary: University of Calgary Archaeological Association.

———. 1996. "Gender in the Archaeological Record of the Santa Barbara Channel Area." *Proceedings of the Society for California Archaeology* 9: 205–8.

———. 1997. "The Third Gender in Native California: Two-Spirit Undertakers among the Chumash and Their Neighbors." In *Women in Prehistory: North America and Mesoamerica,* ed. Cheryl Claasen and Rosemary A. Joyce, 173–88. Philadelphia: University of Pennsylvania Press.

————. 2000. "Archaeology of the *'Aqi:* Gender and Sexuality in Prehistoric Chumash Society." In *Archaeologies of Sexuality,* ed. Robert Schmidt and Barbara Voss, 179–96. New York: Routledge.

Jacobs, Ken. 1995. "Returning to Oleni'ostrov: Social, Economic, and Skeletal Dimensions of a Boreal Forest Mesolithic Cemetery." *Journal of Anthropological Archaeology* 14(4): 359–403.

Jacobs, Sue-Ellen, and J. Cromwell. 1992. "Visions and Revisions of Reality: Reflections on Sex, Sexuality, Gender and Gender Variance." *Journal of Homosexuality* 23(4): 43–69.

————, Wesley Thomas, and Sabine Lang, eds. 1997. *Two-Spirit People: Native American Gender Identity, Sexuality, and Spirituality.* Urbana: University of Illinois Press.

Joyce, Rosemary A. 1992. "Images of Gender and Labor Organization in Classic Maya Society." In *Exploring Gender through Archaeology: Selected Papers from the 1991 Boone Conference,* ed. Cheryl Claassen, 63–70. Madison: Prehistory Press.

————. 1993. "Women's Work: Images of Production and Reproduction in Pre-Hispanic Southern Central America." *Current Anthropology* 34(3): 255–74.

————. 2000. "A Precolumbian Gaze: Male Sexuality among the Ancient Maya." In *Archaeologies of Sexuality,* ed. Robert Schmidt and Barbara Voss, 263–83. New York: Routledge.

————, and Cheryl Claasen. 1997. "Women in the Ancient Americas: Archaeologists, Gender, and the Making of Prehistory." In *Women in Prehistory: North America and Mesoamerica,* ed. Cheryl Claassen and Rosemary A. Joyce, 1–14. Philadelphia: University of Pennsylvania Press.

Katz, Jonathan Ned. 1995. *The Invention of Heterosexuality.* New York: Dutton.

Kauffmann Doig, F. 1979. *Sexual Behavior in Ancient Peru.* Lima: Kompaktos.

Leach, E. R. 1952. "The Structural Implications of Matrilateral Cross-Cousin Marriage." *Journal of the Royal Anthropological Institute* 81: 23–53.

Lesick, Kurtis S. 1997. "Re-Engendering Gender: Some Theoretical and Methodological Concerns on a Burgeoning Archaeological Pursuit." In *Invisible People and Processes: Writing Gender and Childhood into European Archaeology,* ed. Jenny Moore and Eleanor Scott, 31–41. New York: Leicester University Press.

Matthews, Keith. 1994. "An Archaeology of Homosexuality? Perspectives from the Classical World." In *TRAC 94: Proceedings of the Fourth Annual Theoretical Roman Archaeology Conference Held at the Department of Archaeology, University of Durham, 19th and 20th March 1994,* ed. S. Cottam, D. Dungworth, S. Scott, and J. Taylor, 118–32. Oxford: Oxbow Books.

————. 1995. "Archaeological Data, Subcultures, and Social Dynamics." *Antiquity* 69(264): 586–94.

Ng, Vivien W. 1989. "Homosexuality and the State in Late Imperial China." In *Hidden from History: Reclaiming the Gay and Lesbian Past,* ed. Martin Duberman, Martha Vicinus, and George Chauncey, 76–89. New York: Meridian.

O'Shea, John, and Marek Zvelebil. 1984. "Oleneostrovski Mogilnik: Reconstructing the Social and Economic Organization of Prehistoric Foragers in Northern Russia." *Journal of Anthropological Archaeology* 3(1): 1–40.

Padgug, Robert. 1989. "Sexual Matters: Rethinking Sexuality in History." In *Hidden from History: Reclaiming the Gay and Lesbian Past,* ed. Martin Duberman, Martha Vicinus, and George Chauncey, Jr., 54–64. New York: Meridian.

Perry, Elizabeth M., and Rosemary A. Joyce. 2001. "Providing a Past for 'Bodies That Matter': Judith Butler's Impact on the Archaeology of Gender." *International Journal of Sexuality and Gender Studies* 6(1–2): 63–76.

Price, T. Douglas, and James A. Brown. 1985. *Prehistoric Hunter-Gatherers: The Emergence of Cultural Complexity.* Orlando: Academic Press.

Prine, Elizabeth. 2000. "Searching for Third Genders: Towards a Prehistory of Domestic Space in Middle Missouri Villages." In *Archaeologies of Sexuality,* ed. Robert Schmidt and Barbara Voss, 197–219. New York: Routledge.

Ringrose, Kathryn M. 1994. "Living in the Shadows: Eunuchs and Gender in Byzantium." In *Third Sex, Third Gender: Beyond Sexual Dimorphism in Culture and History,* ed. Gilbert Herdt, 85–109. New York: Zone Books.

Roscoe, Will. 1987. "A Bibliography of Berdache and Alternative Gender Roles among North American Indians." *Journal of Homosexuality* 14(3–4): 81–171.

———. 1991. *The Zuni Man-Woman.* Albuquerque: University of New Mexico Press.

———. 1994. "How to Become a Berdache: Toward a Unified Analysis of Gender Diversity." In *Third Sex, Third Gender: Beyond Sexual Dimorphism in Culture and History,* ed. Gilbert Herdt, 329–72. New York: Zone Books.

———. 1998. *Changing Ones: Third and Fourth Genders in Native North America.* New York: St. Martin's Press.

Rubin, Gayle. 1975. "The Traffic in Women: Notes on the 'Political Economy' of Sex." In *Toward an Anthropology of Women,* ed. Rayna R. Reiter, 157–210. New York: Monthly Review Press.

Schmidt, Robert. 2000. "Shamans and Northern Cosmology: The Direct Historical Approach to Mesolithic Sexuality." In *Archaeologies of Sexuality,* ed. Robert Schmidt and Barbara Voss, 220–35. New York: Routledge.

———, and Barbara Voss, eds. 2000. *Archaeologies of Sexuality.* New York: Routledge.

Shanks, Michael, and Christopher Tilley. 1992. *Re-Constructing Archaeology: Theory and Practice.* New York: Routledge.

Sjovold, Torstein. 1992. "The Stone Age Iceman from the Alps: The Find and the Current Status of Investigation." *Evolutionary Anthropology* 1(4): 117–24.

Spindler, Konrad. 1994. *The Man in the Ice: The Discovery of a Five-Thousand-Year-Old Body Reveals the Secrets of the Stone Age.* New York: Harmony Books.

Taylor, Timothy. 1996. *The Prehistory of Sex: Four Million Years of Human Sexual Culture.* New York: Bantam Books.

Thomas, David Hurst. 2000. *Skull Wars: Kennewick Man, Archaeology, and the Battle for Native Amercian Identity.* New York: Basic Books.

Trumbach, Randolph. 1989. "The Birth of the Queen: Sodomy and the Emergence of Gender Equality in Modern Culture, 1660–1750." In *Hidden from History: Reclaiming the Gay and Lesbian Past,* ed. Martin Duberman, Martha Vicinus, and George Chauncey, Jr., 129–40. New York: Meridian.

van der Meer, Theo. 1994. "Sodomy and the Pursuit of a Third Sex in the Early Modern Period." In *Third Sex, Third Gender: Beyond Sexual Dimorphism in Culture and History,* ed. Gilbert Herdt, 137–212. New York: Zone Books.

Voss, Barbara L. 2000. "Feminisms, Queer Theories, and the Archaeological Study of Past Sexualities." *World Archaeology* 32(2): 180–92.

———, and Robert Schmidt. 2000. "Archaeologies of Sexuality: An Introduction." In *Archaeologies of Sexuality,* ed. Schmidt and Voss. New York: Routledge.

Weeks, Jeffrey. 1977. *Coming Out: Homosexual Politics in Britain, from the Nineteenth Century to the Present.* London: Quartet Books.

———. 1981. *Sex, Politics and Society: The Regulation of Sexuality since 1800.* London: Longman.

———. 1985. *Sexuality and Its Discontents: Meanings, Myths, and Modern Sexualities.* New York: Routledge.

———. 1991. *Against Nature: Essays on History, Sexuality and Identity.* London: Rivers Oram Press.

Whelan, Mary K. 1991. "Gender and Historical Archaeology: Eastern Dakota Patterns in the Nineteenth Century." *Historical Archaeology* 25(4): 17–32.

Williams, Walter L. 1986. *The Spirit and the Flesh: Sexual Diversity in American Indian Culture.* Boston: Beacon Press.

Winkler, John J. 1990. *The Constraints of Desire: The Anthropology of Sex and Gender in Ancient Greece.* New York: Routledge.

Wockner, Rex, and Bliss Frings. 1992. "AC/DC in 3500 BC?" *Bay Area Reporter,* Sept. 3, 4.

Wylie, Alison. 1992. "The Interplay of Evidential Constraints and Political Interests: Recent Archaeological Research on Gender." *American Antiquity* 57(1): 15–35.

Yates, Tim. 1993. "Frameworks for an Archaeology of the Body." In *Interpretive Archaeology,* ed. Christopher Tilley, 31–72. Providence: Berg.

Zvelebil, Marek, ed. 1986. *Hunters in Transition: Mesolithic Societies of Temperate Eurasia and their Transition to Farming.* New York: Cambridge University Press.

———. 1993. "Concepts of Time and 'Presencing' the Mesolithic." *Archaeological Review from Cambridge* 12(2): 51–70.

———. 1997. "Hunter-Gatherer Ritual Landscapes: Spatial Organisation, Social Structure and Ideology among Hunter-gatherers of Northern Europe and Western Siberia." *Analecta Praehistoria Leidensia* 29: 33–50.

———. 1998. "Hunter-Gatherer Ritual Landscapes: Questions of Time, Space and Representation." Presented at a meeting of the European Association of Archaeologists, Gothenburg.

SEVEN

Bareback Sex, Risk, and Eroticism: Anthropological Themes (Re-)Surfacing in the Post-AIDS Era

Benjamin Junge

Sometimes bodily orifices seem to represent points of entry to social units.
   —Mary Douglas

Gay men have always been driven to risk and transgressive acts.
   —Eric Rofes

Most of us still can't talk honestly about why getting fucked is so powerful.
   —Richard Elovich

The impetus for this essay comes from an experience I had in the spring of 1999. Perusing a Web-site known as "Xtreme Sex," I encountered a series of narrativized sexual fantasies of "bareback sex," loosely defined as anal intercourse in which condoms are intentionally disregarded. During its operative period, Xtreme Sex aimed to facilitate, through posted introductions and personal narratives, fantasy and sexual liaisons between HIV-positive men and between men of discordant serostatus.[1] The following excerpt, whose author and intended function are uncertain, comes from a longer narrative:

He liked to fuck hard, and soon was really slamming it to me. I don't know how long it was, but it seemed he was going to fuck me to death before he muttered about being about to come. He reared back, and then slowly pulled his hard cock from my asshole, intending to shoot on my back. Quick as a flash, I whipped my right arm behind me, grasped his cock, and worked the head and part of the shaft back in my hole. He let out a moan, and fell forward onto me, driving his cock deep inside. Even though he was moaning and thrashing on top of me, I could still feel his dirty load splatter inside me when he shot. I knew he was infecting me, and I was so turned on by it that I too shot my own load into the sheets under me. I seroconverted a couple of weeks later.

When I encountered this text, I found myself uncomfortable and yet fixated. Is this real? I wondered. Did this really happen or is it "just a fantasy"? How might the numerous cultural taboos inscribed in this narrative (for example, intentional and eroticized disregard for disease prevention) engage the mind and body of an adult gay male? Why would a gay man eroticize exposure to a deadly virus? My understanding that it *could* be understood as erotic derived not only from my familiarity with heated debates around barebacking in the popular gay press but also, more disturbingly, from the unwitting realization that I found something erotic in this chilling text (although at the time I couldn't have said what)—erotic despite my background in HIV epidemiology and my self-important identity as one who always uses condoms. Then it occurred to me that my understanding of sexual risk—a variation of which was being eroticized in this narrative—derives primarily from my professional background in public health and from years of trying to "use a condom every time" (as the safer-sex slogan goes) in my personal life.

Themes and Methodology

Despite representations in the popular gay press and public health literature as peripheral and of primary relevance and interest to gay men, debates in the United States about bareback sex speak to a wide range of anthropological interests in unconventional male and female sexuality. This essay aims to highlight those interests through critical analysis of understandings of risk, often implicit, which have pervaded popular debates surrounding bareback sex. Although these debates have brought to the fore issues specific to the so-called post-AIDS era of protease inhibitors (for example, how to re-frame HIV prevention in light of increased survival rates due to the new treatments), what has made bareback sex powerful is its symbolic connection to deeper, unresolved, and inadequately studied questions about unconventional sexuality. Particularly at issue are questions about how moral valence is generated and assigned to aspects of social and erotic experience through discussion and practice within queer communities themselves rather than through the imposition of heteronormatively framed moralities by "mainstream" society. By focusing on the ways public health constructions of risk have been drawn upon—by and about queers—to articulate moral judgments about social and erotic life, I aim to shed light on the processes by which we generate our own moralities.

Since the early 1980s, anthropological inquiry into unconventional sexuality has emerged principally in the context of research about HIV and AIDS. Although HIV and AIDS have helped to legitimate sexuality research in unprecedented degree and scope, they have also tended to privilege inquiries into aspects of sexuality linked to risky sexual behaviors, thereby reinforcing a subtle yet pervasive association between non-normative sexuality and disease. Studies carried out in the context of HIV and AIDS research have, moreover, tended to sidetrack anthropological attention to aspects of sexuality not directly related to questions of public health, for example, questions about intergenerational cultural differences and about the origins of eroticism and the dynamics of sexual fantasy.[2]

Earlier, I drew on personal experience to posit a link between discourse and feeling, a connection between scientific understandings of risk, safer-sex ideology, processes of stigmatization, and embodied sexual desire. In this analysis, I will use debates about bareback sex as a lens to consider a broader analysis of the complex interplay between public health constructions of risk (enacted in the ideas and practices of "safer sex") and the plurality of queer male subjectivities inhabiting the post-AIDS era. My intention is neither to defend nor criticize the practice of bareback sex or those individuals who identify as "barebackers." Rather, I take the position that an ethical stance cannot be formulated until the densely constituted discourses of barebacking have been deconstructed.

Following a brief introductory discussion of the linguistic instability of the category "barebacking," I will describe the historical emergence of barebacking as a recognized and named social phenomenon. Next, I will engage three themes—"Risk and Public Health," "Rights, Responsibilities, and Group Identities," and "Risk and Pleasure"—which begin to map links between scientific and popular understandings of risk on the one hand and individual sexual subjectivity on the other. Then I will examine themes evoked in the debates about bareback sex that resonate for lesbian and gay anthropology, both in terms of research already carried out and important work for the future.[3]

The analysis that follows draws from three types of discourse: debates about barebacking in the popular gay press; representations of risk in public health research and practice; and representations of bareback sex via forms of computer-mediated communication, particularly personal ads at barebacking Web-sites. I will also draw from a series of interviews carried out in the spring of 1999 with "Jason," a forty-one-year-old, HIV-positive gay man and self-identified barebacker who lives in San Francisco.[4] Empirical data notwithstanding, this analysis does not intend to prove anything but rather to develop ideas and arguments based on my own subjective interpretations.

Defining Bareback Sex

Although the practice of condomless anal sex no doubt predates the U.S. AIDS epidemic, its fusion with willful intention and linkage to a recognized sexual identity are fairly recent. The precise origins of the term *bareback sex* are not entirely clear.[5] The notion of a barebacker—construed as a type of person rather than simply a person who engages in a type of behavior—emerged sometime around 1995. Nonetheless, there continues to be substantial variability in the precise meanings and usages of the term *barebacking,* indicative of the unstable contested nature of the values and practices under discussion.

In popular and scientific media, semantic variation has played out along at least six distinct conceptual axes. First, although barebacking has generally been taken to refer specifically to anal intercourse (Crain 1997; Gendin 1999; Kirby 1999; Peyser, Roberts, and Stout 1997; Scarce 1999; Sheon and Plant 1997), it has occasionally been used to signify any form of sex (presumably penetrative) occurring without condoms (Gauthier and Forsyth 1999). Second, agreeing that barebacking refers to anal sex specifically, there is the question of intentionality. Is barebacking *any* anal sex without condoms or only anal sex where condoms are willfully and explicitly disregarded?[6]

Third, the willful intention that the term generally implies can be taken to further indicate consensus among participating sex partners. Although a sexual episode in which two partners make a conscious, premeditated decision not to use condoms can be classified as barebacking relatively unproblematically, a scenario in which one participant has made an explicit decision not to use condoms but the other partner's avoidance of condoms may not be premeditated (but rather situationally emergent) is more difficult to classify. This conundrum beckons a subtle distinction between how men engaging in condomless anal sex might view themselves versus how other people may view them. A related distinction concerns the difference between etic labeling schemes (e.g., the labels developed by an epidemiologist to conduct a survey) and emic labels used by the subjects of investigation themselves (in this case, queer men in the United States). One could decide to disregard the issue of consensus in a definition of barebacking—thus rendering the scenario involving intentionality unqualifiable as barebacking even though the participating individuals themselves might label their encounter "bareback sex."[7]

A fourth area of variability in how bareback sex is defined concerns the inchoate distinction between action and identity, that is, between bareback*ing* and bareback*ers*. References to bareback sex, as commonly articulated by public health researchers, emphasize the practice itself, whereas others highlight the social/sexual identities of the individuals who engage in the practice. Fifth, there is the question of serostatus of the individuals who bareback. Some HIV-positive gay men profess barebacking to include condomless anal sex only with other HIV-positives (e.g., Folger 1999).[8] However, the much-publicized presence of computer-mediated communication media (e.g., Web-sites, chat rooms, and e-mail discussion lists/list-servs) that facilitate sexual liaison between men who are HIV positive and those who are HIV negative suggests conceptual models of barebacking that imply discordant serostatus. Sixth and finally, much popular literature on barebacking fails to examine the distinction between fantasy and practice. In other words, does eroticization of exposure to HIV alone make one a barebacker or does one have to expose oneself in actual sexual practice to qualify?[9]

Given the definitional variability I have described, "bareback sex"—whether invoked as an analytic category to describe particular behaviors or as a label used by some queer men to describe themselves and their actions—should be understood as an emergent, semantically unstable, and contested construction of sex and sexual identity. Here, I will use an operative definition that attempts to balance behavioral specificity with contextual relativity in the interest of a fruitful analysis. Specifically, I take "bareback sex" to refer to condomless anal sex that is willfully intended.[10] Accordingly, for heuristic purposes I take the word *barebackers* to mean queer men who engage in bareback sex. In this configuration, I purposefully leave open questions of participants' serostatus, consensus, and distinctions between fantasy and actual practice.

HIV, Condoms, and Anal Sex: Epidemiology and Popular Debates

The debates surrounding bareback sex find origins in the early and mid-1990s when public health research noted a resurgence of self-reported condomless anal sex among urban men who have sex with men (MSM).[11] From virtually hundreds of studies, psychological, behavioral, and demographic correlates of condomless sex were profiled. First, condomless anal sex has been linked to generational issues in the context of a "maturing" epidemic. Gay men in their late thirties and forties—men who had witnessed firsthand the devastation of AIDS through the loss of friends and lovers— have had their own set of issues, whether making sense of their survival, cumulative frustration with the sensation-inhibiting effects of condoms, and feelings of imperviousness to HIV based on years of sexual activity without HIV seroconversion. A subsequent cohort of queer men (into which I situate myself) came of age subsequent to the installation of safer sex as the guiding principle of HIV prevention. To these men, condoms were normative and the prospect of sex without them was unthinkable. In the middle years of the 1990s yet another distinct cohort emerged: young gay men who had little or no personal experience with AIDS and associated disease risk with cohorts of older gay men rather than with a specific risky behavior in which any man might engage.[12]

During the mid-1990s a variety of new, antiretroviral treatment options became available, initially through clinical trials and then directly through healthcare providers. The new class of therapies, known as protease inhibitors and typically administered in multidrug combination, demonstrated potential to dramatically reduce viral load and increase CD4 cell counts among both asymptomatic HIV-positives and individuals who had full-blown AIDS. Despite formidable economic barriers to the new drugs for poor or uninsured individuals, as well as commonly reported adverse reactions to (and subsequent discontinuation of) the therapies, the potential for a fundamentally new conceptualization of AIDS and HIV risk was evident. Rather than a death sentence, HIV infection could be perceived as a chronic, medically manageable, disease. The substantial declines in AIDS mortality among MSM in the United States, as reported by the Centers for Disease Control and Prevention during the years following the advent of protease inhibitors, were well publicized in both scientific and popular literature.[13]

Concern over the possibility that awareness of the new drug therapies might negatively influence condom use during anal sex led to a slew of attitude and behavior surveys, which, with admittedly divergent findings, tended to suggest that awareness of the new treatments might be contributing to increases in risky sexual practices (including condomless anal sex).[14]

When reports of increased rates of condomless anal sex were made public, a variety of opinions on causes and appropriate responses were expressed in the popular gay press. The image of the reckless, selfish, sex fanatic fed up with years of unsatisfying "latex sex" was epitomized in the words of the late writer and pornographic film star Scott O'Hara, who wrote in 1995: "I'm tired of using condoms, and . . . I don't feel the need to encourage negatives to stay negative" (quoted in Scarce 1999:55). As discussions of this "mentality" occupied the national and local gay press and captured the analytic attention of social scientists reconsidering the utility of "traditional" HIV-prevention strategies, local battles were fought over how (and whether) to regulate increasingly visible sex in gay spaces such as bars, bath houses, and public cruising areas. The experiences of New York City in 1995 are particularly significant.

Throughout 1995, members of the AIDS Prevention Action League (APAL), founded and carried on by a group of New York queer academics and journalists, found themselves engaged in a series of heated arguments with public health program planners and gay community organizers participating in an organization called Gay and Lesbian HIV Prevention Activists (GALHPA), which held that "any sex club that condoned behavior riskier than voyeurism and mutual masturbation should be shut" (Crain 1997:29). The division structuring this debate has turned out to be archetypal. GALHPA located its concern with the publicly visible resurgence of condomless anal sex and proposed the installation of "health monitors" in gay sex venues (Scarce 1999:54). APAL countered with an accusation of "sex panic."[15] Monitoring sexual practices—even in the name of public health—was thus construed by APAL as a technique of social control harnessed as one component of a broader crackdown on New York's gay milieu.[16]

In the mid-1990s a slew of highly influential books were published, each in its own way stimulating a debate that was by now national and extended far beyond the disciplinary confines of academia. Gabriel Rotello (Crain 1997) argued that the "condom code"—the "traditional" HIV-prevention strategy of "safe sex *every time*"—has proved inadequate in stemming the epidemic tide among gay men. Citing the statistical risk posed to the overall population of sexually active gay men by even a small group of individuals who repeatedly engage in condomless anal sex, Rotello argues that an individualistic approach to sexual behavior change is inadequate. Rather, HIV prevention must take place within an ecological framework, aiming to change behavior at the level of community.

While constructing his argument along substantially different lines, Michelangelo Signorile (1997) concluded that gay cultural norms regarding sexuality need to change—or be changed—to reduce the number of sexual partners gay men pursue.[17] Walt Odets (1995) emphasized the "mangled identity" gay men possess due to silence and media panic over anal sex, an analysis that casts bareback sex in pathological terms (i.e., as a symptom of a problematic socialization). Odets's analysis was also among the first to challenge the putative universal success of safer-sex condom promotion.[18]

In the spring of 1997 (soon after publication of Rotello's and Odets's books), members of APAL and Dangerous Bedfellows formed a new group, Sex Panic, to promote discussion and direct action aimed at individuals and institutions upholding the "regimes of the normal" (Michael Warner, as quoted in Crain 1997:27)—that is, discourses of normalcy and deviancy underlying the "crackdown" on gay public spaces in New York City.[19] By that point, Web-sites, list-servs, and chat rooms that facilitated discussion of barebacking and arrangements for actual sexual liaisons were being established regularly. Increasingly, self-labeled barebackers were participating in gay- or HIV-oriented conferences or writing editorials to appear in the popular gay press or on the Web, stating frustration with condoms (often to extremely hostile reception) and declaring the experience of "raw" sex to be "transformational."[20] Thus were engendered far-reaching and at times vitriolic debates about the ethical and public health dimensions to barebacking as well as ideological divisions akin to those between Sex Panic and GALPHA in New York City. These debates continue as of this writing.[21]

Risk and Public Health

Risk Factors, Behaviors, and Groups

Public health research and program planning is grounded in the notion of a risk factor, that is, an individual trait that has been shown in empirical research to be associated with some negative (and presumably health-related) outcome. The association is by definition statistical.[22] In and of itself, that conveys limited information regarding the nature of the linkage between the trait (the independent variable) and the outcome (the dependent variable). Through a variety of statistical techniques, causal risk factors are inferred and targeted for intervention in the interest of reducing the incidence of a negative outcome. Populations in which a given risk factor and its associated outcomes are unusually prevalent are conceived of as risk groups whose members are high-risk or at-risk individuals. Risk factors can be behavioral (e.g., smoking in relation to lung cancer) or demographic (e.g., male gender in relation to prostate cancer). Because demographic and other types of risk factors are not readily modifiable, however, most public health programs target behavioral factors (or risk behaviors).

Risk Reduction, Rationality, and Safer-Sex Ideology

The emphasis in public health research and practice on reducing the prevalence of risk behaviors within at-risk populations is predicated on the presumption that reduction of morbidity and mortality is an inherently rational endeavor. It is rational for public health practitioners to undertake the promotion of risk reduction and for at-risk populations to enact behavioral risk reduction at an individual level.[23]

In the mid-1980s, when the link between condomless anal sex and HIV infection become widely known, a new rationale was inscribed into discourse. The chief mechanism for its inscription was a set of ideas known as "safer sex," forged contentiously by community organizers, activists, epidemiologists, and public policymakers. The "doctrine" of safer sex privileged the notion of protection, that is, reducing HIV risk by making existing sexual practices (e.g., anal sex) safer rather than eliminating them altogether.

Thus, a valued element of 1970s' gay sexual liberation—the pursuit of sexual relations without shame or confined to monogamous coupling—could be preserved. If gay men would use condoms whenever they had anal (or, for that matter, oral) sex, HIV risk would decrease sufficiently to stem the tide of the epidemic.

Safer-sex ideology facilitates a distinct form of rationality. Condom usage is rational first and foremost because it provides self-protection and will (ostensibly) reduce disease and suffering within a broader population. From this perspective, "Unsafe sexual behaviour, especially fucking without a condom, is seen as a basic (irrational) drive which the (rational) will is constantly striving to control. . . . Safer sex is seen as a necessary but unpleasant course of action which is dictated by prudence rather than desire" (Pollack 1988).

Within the safer-sex framework, to eschew condoms during anal sex emerges as irrational behavior. Safer sex thus imposes an intensely cognitive framework (presuming, for example, that gay men carefully weigh the pros and cons of all known options with respect to a sexual practice and means of protection) on a set of behaviors not necessarily driven by cognitive reasoning. Safer sex, moreover, leaves unexamined the reasons why some men would continue to engage in risky sex or renders those reasons pathologic. As a consequence of that stance, HIV-prevention programs in the United States have typically been grounded in a no-tolerance position regarding condomless anal sex.[24]

MSM as a Risk Group

In the case of HIV infection among MSM, the risk behavior most strongly associated with seroconversion is receptive anal intercourse in the absence of condoms. MSM are conceived collectively as a risk group because condomless anal sex is known to be prevalent within this population. In its pure form, that construction is intrinsically abstract because it has no direct linkage to individual experience. Its problematic aspects, spilling into popular discourses, are numerous. First, in the construction of MSM as a risk group, the line is blurred between being *at risk* and being *high risk* (i.e., posing risk). Thus, in an essentializing conceptualization without empirical grounding, "instead of being understood as a group at high risk of contracting HIV, gay men are widely regarded as constituting a high risk to other people" (Watney 1989:19). That discursive sleight-of-hand potentially stigmatizes MSM and other populations at risk of contracting HIV infection. In addition, it turns a blind eye to broader factors facilitating HIV risk. In this configuration, MSM are intrinsically risky and therefore, by extension, responsible for their own HIV infections. In addition, because MSM are risky they are also dangerous and to be avoided. Attention focuses on *"who* is risky, rather than *what* is risky" (Clatts 1995:245, emphasis in the original). As Clatts and Mutchler (1989:19–20) have observed, "AIDS and the 'dangerous and anti-social other'. . . fix our attention on a relatively small range of possible vectors of this disease . . . and direct our attention away from other possible factors of [its] aetiology and spread."

This insight points to the need for anthropologists engaged in questions of sexuality to interrogate more closely their use of risk-group categories to delineate study populations. A critical sensibility in this regard lends itself to explicit distinction between imposed labels and felt identities and awareness of ideological valuations conveyed in the use of analytic terms.

It is difficult to locate precisely the sites of cultural production and re-production for discourses in which the public health notion of risk group is thus distorted. Clearly, prevention programs—informed by epidemiologic research and terminology—seem likely. HIV-prevention research has been conditioned by concepts of homosexuality that attribute a broad range of patho-psychological and behavioral traits to individuals who possess same-sex desire and/or engage in sexual encounters with members of the same sex. In many empirical surveys, for example, one still finds the categories "heterosexual," "bisexual," and "homosexual" to describe the trait referred to as "sexual orientation." These monikers, although linked to certain sexual practices, ultimately decontextualize sexuality. They take "sexual activity and sexual identity out of time and place. The use of these categories makes it impossible to identify and map changes in concepts of self over the course of an individual's life span, or to locate an ever-emergent self within social, cultural, and economic institutions that are themselves dynamic in character" (Clatts 1995:246).

A related domain of discursive production is that of scientific journals. Calling for a "critical epistemology," Farmer (1998) has focused particularly on how publication of AIDS research in peer-reviewed scholarly journals provides a site of discursive production wherein choices in lexical representation may reinforce stigmatizing or essentializing conceptualizations of certain populations.[25]

Barebackers as a Risk Group

In the case of debates about bareback sex, public health discourse is clearly influential. The preexisting construction of MSM as a high-risk group (produced and reproduced in ongoing health research and program planning as well as scientific and popular media representations) appears to have been projected onto a perception of men who bareback. In this cultural configuration—articulated in both the public health arena and popular gay media—barebackers are not just a risk group but high-risk individuals, and "risk" is semantically grounded in the notion of a threat to an imagined broader population. The threat, so the discursive logic goes, is a consequence of an individual decision to engage in an inherently irrational behavior. The decision is immoral as well because of its putative consequences for the health of more innocent individuals.

Individuals who knowingly fail to reduce their own behavioral risk are cast as irrational and dangerous. That sentiment is evident in a letter to *POZ Magazine*: "I do not recall any article in *POZ* that angered me more than 'They Shoot Barebackers, Don't They?' . . . Valenzuela's irresponsible and reprehensible behavior does not warrant the sobriquet *sacrificial lamb*. . . . It feels better to get fucked up the ass without protection, exposing your partner to HIV? Valenzuela's logic . . . goes beyond rationalization. This is a dangerous narcissist who does not want to accept his responsibility for people he may have infected" (Anonymous 1999b:29).

Here, Valenzuela is "dangerous" because he engages in a behavior that he knows may facilitate HIV transmission. He betrays both individual self-protection and his responsibility to protect his sexual partners (and, by extension, the broader population). The castigatory, authorial voice in the excerpt is consistent with Goffman's assertion that stigmatization casts more than the original trait deemed reprehensible in a negative light and becomes embedded in a larger discourse of danger and risk. Thus, stigmatizers "construct a stigma-theory, an ideology to explain [the stigmatized's] inferiority and account for the danger he represents, sometimes rationalizing an animosity based on other differences. . . . We tend to impute a wide range of imperfections on the basis of the original one" (Goffman 1963:5).

Valenzuela's disregard for condoms is the "master status" that overpowers whatever other social attributes he might have (Brown 1997) and renders him subject to a totalizing rejection as a "dangerous narcissist." Conversely, once the label "barebacker" has been pejoratively invoked it signals the presence of other pathological and dangerous traits that deserve animosity. A similar sentiment has been posted to a Web-site devoted to discussion and arrangement of gay sexual encounters: "It's not simply that barebacking might cause one or both participants to become infected with HIV, changing a life or two forever. Barebacking purposefully increases the number of vectors of infection, thus increasing the chance that other men, men who likely have no desire to become infected, will become infected with a deadly virus. That's immoral" (Fall n.d.).

Sensationalistic demonization aside, the excerpt accomplishes an impressive feat. Despite the fact that it is predicated on faulty calculus, it summons up an obsessive, nearly hysterical, panic. The calculus is faulty first because barebacking is a practice and therefore cannot "purposefully" or agentically do anything (only people can). Thus, person and practice are discursively merged. The logic is also faulty because it privileges what is likely a small (or in any event undetermined) proportion of self-identified barebackers and lumps them together with HIV-positive barebackers who seek sex strictly with other seropositives.[26] The latter group thus assumes guilt by association.

Rights, Responsibilities, and Stigma

Safer Sex: Ethics and Contradiction

Rights and responsibilities are closely related to discursive categories facilitated via epidemiologic constructions of risk. The individual right to pursue preferred sexual practices is at odds with the responsibility not to contribute to some larger social harm. The ideological lightning rod on which the tension between these two poles has played out has been the issue of condom usage. As ethicist Ronald Bayer has pointed out, the rhetoric of safer sex has always been "grounded in the concepts of universal vulnerability to HIV and the universal importance of safe sexual practices" (1996:154). In that configuration, one should assume that all sexual partners are HIV positive and therefore seek protection by using a condom consistently. Safer sex has therefore emphasized self-protection over disclosure of HIV status to sexual partners.

Unfortunately, that way of conceiving risk and protection glosses over many of the complex psychosocial dynamics that influence sexual decision making among queer men. First, safer sex has tended to blur the different issues that HIV-positives and HIV-negatives face (Bayer 1996:1541). To assume, for example, that one's partner is HIV positive may be compelling to a seronegative individual but carries less sway for another seropositive. Moreover, the conventionally framed notion of universal condom usage inadequately addresses issues of trust, intimacy, and negotiation as they play out in sexual episodes between primary and casual sexual partners.

In a sense, safer sex privileges an individual's right to have sex with whomever he wants so long as the responsibility to use condoms is upheld. That configuration, however, leaves open the question of disclosure. If, for example, two men—one HIV positive, the other negative—meet for the first time and subsequently engage in anal intercourse using a condom, is the seropositive man ethically obliged to disclose his HIV status? That unresolved question of social and ethical responsibility constitutes a central tension in safer-sex ideology. It has been debated explicitly in scientific and popular gay media by prevention specialists, AIDS activists, and gay writers alike (e.g., Cornelius Baker, as reported in Kirby [1999:45]; Rotello 1995; and Signorile 1995 [as cited in Bayer 1996:1541]).[27]

Barebackers' Rights, Responsibilities, and Group Identities

The rhetoric of rights and responsibilities has been central to debates about bareback sex. Men who identify as barebackers have asserted their right to sexual practice on their own terms. As one HIV-positive subscriber to a popular barebacking e-mail list-serv posted, "Since most of us are already poz, we just want to live out our lives in peace having the sex we enjoy . . . mostly with each other. We feel that it is our right, given our limited time on this earth" (Anonymous 1999c).

I do not presume that the sentiments expressed in this statement are representative of those held by the majority of self-identified barebackers. Rather, I find it compelling because its sentiments reveal particularly salient contours of ongoing debates. First, there is the assertion that most barebackers are HIV positive and therefore need not concern themselves with fear of infection. That position is at odds with a viewpoint forwarded by individuals such as Gabriel Rotello, who would find the "mostly" in "mostly with each other" to be highly problematic. For Rotello, it is the possibility of even a small handful of HIV-negative individuals engaging (knowingly or not) in condomless anal sex with seropositives that risks fanning the flames of the ongoing epidemic.

Also contained in the posting is the notion that HIV-positive individuals have less time to live and are therefore particularly entitled—indeed, have a right—to seek pleasure so long as no one is harmed. This perspective follows Mary Douglas's theorization of how individuals respond to stigma: "What the individualist wants from the cultural project is to be left free to pursue his own activities, uncriticized and uncontrolled by others. The theory that contagion enters by very specific routes gives him the cue for saying that he is in control of his own life. He argues rationally that he is in control of those routes, at least as much as he wants to be" (1994:118).

What is being expressed is the notion that barebacking is not unsafe with respect to HIV infection. In other words, those who are already HIV positive no longer need to worry about HIV risk during episodes of condomless anal sex with other seropositives. Although a comprehensive review of the scientific literature on issues of reinfection (i.e., with new viral sub-strains) is beyond the scope of this essay, the evidence for negative HIV-related consequences for viral exposure subsequent to initial infection is as yet inconclusive. Should that change (i.e., should multiple exposures to HIV following initial infection be proven to be deleterious), barebackers' ability to write off this concern will be substantially diminished.[28]

The rhetoric of responsibility has been often invoked in popular criticisms of barebacking—the practice and the individuals who engage in it. One way this has played out concerns the responsibility of HIV-positive individuals not to expose others to the virus. That formulation is simplistic because it ignores the issue of consent; two sex partners might mutually negotiate a decision not to use condoms. Perhaps it is more accurate to state that this particular rhetoric of responsibility supersedes the possibility of consent. Even though two adult men might decide to forego condoms during anal sex, their decision is somehow intrinsically irresponsible and violates society's expectations of seropositive gay men. Sexually active gay men—more specifically, self-identified barebackers—have articulated conceptualizations of responsibility in addition to rights.[29]

The excerpt also speaks to the production of a collective identity (the entitled and defensive "we" in the text) emergent in public assertions by barebackers, often in response to attempted stigmatization. That is consistent with Goffman's assertion that individuals stigmatized on the basis of the same trait may be disposed to formal, explicitly acknowledged, group formation, although a stable organizational capacity for the emergent group is unlikely due to the lack of commonality with respect to other traits. "A good portion of those who fall within a given stigma category may well refer to the total membership by the term 'group' or an equivalent, such as 'we,' or 'our people.' Those outside the category may similarly designate those within it in group terms. However, often in such cases the full membership will not be a part of a single group, in the strictest sense; they will neither have a capacity for collective action, nor a stable and embracing pattern of mutual interaction" (Goffman 1963:23).

Stigma can, however, result in the formation of groups that have formal and sustainable organizational structures and "native" leaders who serve as representatives to other groups (Goffman 1963:27). In such instances, group activities facilitate the production of a group ideology. "Often," Goffman observes, "those with a particular stigma sponsor a publication of some kind which gives voice to shared feelings, consolidating and stabilizing for the reader his sense of the realness of 'his' group and his attachment to it. Here the ideology of the members is formulated—their complaints, their aspiration, their politics. The names of well-known friends and enemies of the 'group' are cited, along with information to confirm the goodness or the badness of these people" (25).

Rather than a publication, bareback sex ideologies are formulated principally via modes of computer-mediated communication that represent a safe milieu for discussing hot topics. Through Web-sites, chat rooms, and e-mail list-servs, an ideology is indeed formed, and "friends and enemies of the 'group'" are clarified.[30] For an individual who has only recently adopted an identity as a barebacker, there is a preexisting ideology that no doubt conditions the subsequent development of that identity.

Risk and Pleasure

In describing the psychological dynamics of bareback sex at the individual level, Elovich posits that "flirting with risk becomes part of the erotic charge" (1999:89). The notion that some conceptualized or realized exposure to HIV is an erotic turn-on permeates debates about bareback sex. Individuals who find some positive value in this notion are described in popular debates as "dangerous," "stupid," and "incomprehensible." Meanwhile, images that seem to eroticize HIV seroconversion proliferate on bareback sex Web-sites and e-mail list-servs.

Several questions soon emerge, however, regarding the meanings of this alleged eroticization of exposure. What precisely is being eroticized? What scenario or prospective outcome stimulates sexual arousal? Do some negative barebackers find the idea of seroconversion (and all that it might entail) to be arousing? Do some positive barebackers find the idea of facilitating the seroconversion of a seronegative to have erotic value? How elaborate—how developed that is—are barebackers' fantasies? Is arousal achieved through fantasization of concretely framed images or from vaguely defined traces or associations? Perhaps the most important question in public health terms concerns the relationship between fantasy and practice. To what extent does bareback fantasy predict bareback practice? For example, does a preponderance of "gift-giver" and "bug-chaser" imagery on the Internet prove (or somehow reliably indicate) that intentional seroconversion is actually occurring? Finally, how is eroticized risk linked to other elements of sexual arousal (for example, physiology) during anal intercourse?

What Makes Anal Sex Desirable?

In examining the appeal of anal sex in Western societies, the Foucauldian notion that proscription, through an incitement to discourse, begets desire is useful. In the first volume of *The History of Sexuality,* Foucault (1978) forwards a framework for analyzing the relationship between attempts at social control and emergent sexual desire. Sheon and Plant (1997:4) have pointed out one well-known example from Foucault's argument that concerns efforts to control childhood masturbation in seventeenth-century Europe. In this argument, Foucault shows "how the experts' discourses on masturbation essentially created the problem they were ostensibly trying to eliminate. By teaching the children about forbidden acts, through stern lectures in the classroom or through hushed admonitions in the confession box, efforts to stop masturbation implanted the very desires they aimed to eradicate."

A similar incitement to discuss deviant sexual practices has, through religious, juridical, and medical discourse, facilitated interest in (and among some a desire for) anal sex. The incitement to discuss gay sex stems from the need to reinforce its opposite: procreative vaginal sex between a man and a woman.[31] Anal sex in particular is transgressive for the man who is penetrated because his willingness in this regard signifies rejection of normative masculinity.[32]

It is important to acknowledge aspects of erotic pleasure of anal sex not directly linked to its status as a proscribed practice. In contemporary studies (ethnographic and epidemiologic) of urban homosexual men in the United

States and Europe, anal sex has been constructed as a particularly intimate form of sexual practice.[33] It is said to symbolize "excitement, 'the real thing,' emotional love, the culmination of sexual experience and trust between two people embarking on a relationship" (Lowy and Ross 1994:477). Even outside the context of a primary relationship there exists a common sentiment among urban gay men in the United States that anal sex is somehow more "real" than other sexual practices. Thus, the motivation to engage in it has been described as "the primal urge to feel alive, to achieve the ultimate moment of self-awareness while simultaneously getting lost in the pleasure of orgasm" (Ocamb 1999).[34]

Cultural Constructions of Condomless Anal Sex

Anthropological and quantitative attitude studies have suggested a widespread perception that sexual practices involving condoms (by no means limited to anal intercourse) are less pleasurable than their condomless equivalents. Condoms are thought to inhibit physiological sensitivity and interrupt a progression perceived to be natural, from excitement to plateau to orgasm to resolution. Condoms are also thought to be ungainly and cumbersome to dispose of (Davies et al. 1993:140). Discussions in the popular gay press suggest that HIV-positive and HIV-negative men may attach different value to condomless anal sex. "I can't comment on a negative guy's decision to go raw," Stephen Gendin notes, "but for us positive men, the benefits are obvious. The physical sensation is much better. The connection feels closer and more intimate. The sharing of cum on the physical level heightens the sense of sharing on the emotional and spiritual planes" (1999:50).[35] Yet another common complaint about condoms is that they inhibit the ability to feel the semen of a sexual partner inside the rectum following orgasm. To the best of my knowledge, it is only in the context of debates about bareback sex that such a complaint can be expressed explicitly and publicly.

An additional dimension to understanding condom use and anal sex is sexual role-playing. In a study of gay male personal advertisements, for example, Leap (1996) suggests that claims to pleasure among men identifying as "bottoms" are shaped by whether condoms are expected to be used. Bottoms who responded to an advertisement specifying the need for condoms represented themselves as more entitled and focused on their own pleasure in anticipated sexual encounters than those who anticipated no condoms and were more focused on their (top) partner's pleasure. It is possible that the absence of condoms may signify a distinct understanding of entitlement to pleasure. More generally, it may also indicate that a comprehensive account should consider both pleasure received and pleasure given by the sexual subject.

Fantasizing HIV Seroconversion?

In a thorough analysis of the meanings of bareback sex, the putative eroticization of risk in the context of condomless anal sex merits deconstruction. One important line of inquiry concerns the question of intent and whether some barebackers erotically pursue seroconversion of themselves or their sexual partners. Not surprisingly, scientifically rigorous attitudinal and behavioral data addressing this specific question are virtually nonexistent. In their absence, a great deal of speculation (some based on anecdotal reports, some based on vaguely hysterical paranoia) continues to play out in popular debates. Ocamb (1999:49) has stated that "today, what was unthinkable fifteen years ago—unprotected anal intercourse and casual exposure to HIV—is no big deal. Fast-food sex is making a comeback." The implicit (and highly problematic) assumption is that condomless anal sex that results in direct exposure to HIV has become normalized. In other words, it is assumed that not using condoms equals seroconversion—a formulation flawed in at least two respects. First, it ignores the possibility that many barebackers are HIV positive and only have anal sex with other seropositives. More important, it suggests that eroticization of HIV risk automatically implies actual intent to seroconvert—or, to put it reductively, that an attitude necessarily predicts a practice.

Bareback sex may indeed involve a certain form of eroticized risk. I am unconvinced, however, that the medical and/or social consequences of HIV seroconversion have erotic value for seronegative barebackers. In the psychological literature on sociocultural factors influencing HIV-risk behaviors among queer men several researchers have concluded that HIV seroconversion, in some settings, is associated with a positive life transformation (e.g., Odets 1995). Thus, becoming HIV-infected grants one entry to a "community" that has its own resources (e.g., social support networks). It has also been posited that some HIV-negative gay men welcome seroconversion because it provides a release from the "constant pressure of worrying about becoming infected" (Ocamb 1999:50). However common such sentiments may be among queer men in the United States, I find no evidence that they are erotic sentiments. Thus, in considering what precisely might be eroticized in the context of barebacking I remain skeptical that HIV-negative barebackers have clearly defined sexual fantasies of *being* HIV positive.

It is difficult to examine on empirical grounds the hypothesis, often expressed in popular debates, that some younger HIV-negative men are seeking seroconversion through condomless sexual practices. My interview with Jason and my review of barebacking-oriented Internet venues and the popular gay press lead me to believe that such men certainly do exist. That said, it is my impression that many such individuals are not, strictly speaking, barebackers. Their avoidance of condoms is not informed by a clear understanding of the potential consequences of their actions. According to Jason, the lack of understanding is facilitated by youthful recklessness (especially in the context of group sex encounters) and perhaps by even a conscious effort to avoid (disease transmission) information that in its gravity would de-eroticize an experience:

> Jason: If some HIV-negative idiot is allowing himself to go to a bareback party with nine hundred men and let himself get fucked, which happens—I mean it does happen—I know it happens . . .
> Ben: Why do you call that person an idiot?
> Jason: You know what? I would have told you a year ago it's his constitutional right. And it still is his constitutional right. But . . . he's an idiot. I take forty-five pills a day. You know, not just my triple cocktail. I also take acyclovir because I already had herpes. I take this drug to alleviate the symptoms of my neuropathy because I'm on two drugs that are serious neuropathy-causers, two antivirals. I'm on a antifungal because I get fungus on the bottom of my feet real bad. I'm on Prozac because . . . being HIV-positive tends to devastate you whether you like it or not. Um, and testosterone, shots, twice a month. So it's not a pretty life. You burp, you fart, you have diarrhea, you feel horrible all the time, just with the medication, are just not pleasant . . . I think anybody that doesn't think it through that far . . . and is just thinking about getting that next load up their ass . . . is an idiot. . . . So I have my own value. Like I said, I still believe they have a constitutional right to do it, but it doesn't keep me from stop calling them stupid.

From Jason's perspective, the decision to "go raw" should involve a careful scrutiny of consequences. For negatives, that should include consideration of what life will be like if one seroconverts. Given the profound hassle of managing HIV disease in his own life, he finds the prospect of ignoring such consideration to be irresponsible and "idiotic."

Fantasizing Risk

Another question concerns the role of risk in sexual fantasy irrespective of actual (behavioral) intention. Sexual fantasy and erotic value are often grounded in and driven by images of transgressive or dangerous acts. In sexual fantasy, one may transgress social norms or perceptions of individual personality.[36] Fantasized violation of safer-sex guidelines (i.e., condoms for every sexual encounter), for example, takes on erotic value, or perhaps a man who perceives himself as socially passive might be turned on through the fantasy of playing an active role in sexual encounters.[37]

Using forms of computer-mediated communication (e.g., e-mail list-servs, Web-sites and chat rooms), self-identified barebackers (HIV positive and negative) regularly post messages that suggest that various forms of risk do take on erotic value in sexual fantasy. Images of semen containing HIV, for example, proliferate on the Internet, and terms such as *gift-giver* and *bug-chaser* are common. The question of how to interpret these labels emerged several times during my interview with Jason. While discussing a well-known bareback sex Web-site, for example, he speculated that the use of such symbolically charged terms in Internet-based personal ads is, among other things, a kind of marketing scheme (i.e., a way to catch people's attention): "I think the gift-giver, bug-chasers introduction thing is the . . . catcher that brings everybody in . . . I mean, where else do you see something called the 'fuck of death'?"

I am unconvinced that contemplation of the consequences of actual seroconversion has widespread erotic value. That said, an erotic fantasy regarding seroconversion appears to exist in popular conceptualizations of barebackers and in the broader arenas where these conceptualizations have been challenged:

> Jason: I sort of bought into the eroticism of seroconversion.
> Ben: Tell me about that.
> Jason: You know, I think there's a little bit of the vampire myth . . . a vampire makes another vampire by first sucking his blood and then giving back his vampiric blood to the initiate. I'm slamming my seed on an uninitiated person's butt and making them part of the pack or something . . .

Jason claims that he has never participated in seroconverting an HIV-negative (and has no interest in doing so), nonetheless he finds (or has derived) erotic charge in that prospect. On an individual level then, his erotic fantasy poses no public health risk. What I suspect is largely the same cultural model has been described in slightly different terms by Scarce: "From the science of how the virus invades—and then is incorporated into—the host cell, combining the DNA of one organism with another to make a new form of life, these men have woven a tale of romance" (1999:70). That rendering is particularly interesting because it evinces an amalgamation of biomedical and lay perceptions of risk. In other words, images of virological processes have fused with popular myths. In such a configuration, an eroticized analogy emerges in which HIV-positive barebackers are symbolically equated with vampires and invading viruses.

In attempting to make sense of what Jason has referred to as "the vampire myth," it is important to question the setting in which this fantasy plays out. Does it occupy the imagination of barebackers while they are actually engaged in sexual activities, or is it more a "background" fantasy that structures the imagery in barebacking Web-sites and individual masturbatory fantasy but rarely occupies the attention of two men while engaged in sexual experience? Whatever notions of risk permeate the sexual fantasies of barebackers, it appears unlikely that they are cognitively explicit. Barebackers do not, in other words, appear to be thinking explicitly about risk while they engage in fantasy, whether during or outside actual sexual experience. Rather, it seems that some derive an erotic charge from a vaguely articulated awareness of exposing themselves to some sort of danger.[38]

For gay men in particular, it seems likely that the inchoate notions of risk that come into play during eroticizations of condomless anal sex involve hybrids of at least two models. As Levine and Siegal (1992) have stated, "Gay men shuttle between two competing cultural constructions of HIV transmission: the public health and the folk constructions." It is also possible that in certain contexts gay men switch to one model (which does not negatively construe the practice in question) while suspending another. That is perhaps a way by which those who at some level "know better" may do very risky and potentially self-destructive things.

Epidemiologic notions of risk have spilled into popular conceptualizations, particularly through the promotion of safer-sex ideology. Gay men, however, reconfigure these public health constructs to be less static and inherently subject to situational factors. Thus, Davies et al. have posited, "Men do not carry with them a pre-specified level of risk which is with them in the same way that their eye colour or the size of their genitalia is fixed, nor even in the way that their political preference is relatively fixed. Rather, that assessment is made about a particular session with a particular partner in a particular context" (1993:59).

Safer-sex ideology thus influences but does not determine popular gay notions of risk. Nonetheless, it seems clear that public health constructions of risk do substantially (if unconsciously) inform the sexual fantasies of bare-backers, lending clarity to which behaviors are to be considered dangerous and therefore potentially erotic.

Bareback Sex and Anthropology

The relevance of bareback sex extends much further than the con-structions of risk implicit in popular debates and how they might influence sexual fantasy. Indeed, it is barebacking's resonance with unresolved ele-ments of lesbian, gay, and other non-normative sexualities that has the po-tential to allow the discussion to emerge as a site of intense (and at times vitriolic) contestation. As such, critical analysis of debates about bareback sex points to broader concerns within lesbian and gay anthropology.

In its popular debates, bareback sex has been represented as an issue of principal relevance and interest to gay men. With few exceptions, women's voices (lesbian or otherwise) have been absent from discussions of bareback-ing in the popular gay press, on the Internet, and at scientific or activist con-ferences.[39] Further, men who write or speak on bareback sex (or issues of condom usage more generally) have seldom examined its defining themes (risk and fantasy, for example) in the context of female—more specifically, lesbian—sexuality. This unproblematized "partitioning" of queer male sex-uality facilitates the inference of underlying sexual difference between gay men and lesbian women. Because this inference remains uninterrogated, it plays into existing divisions between lesbians and gays in social and politi-cal spheres. This points to the need for continued anthropological attention to both the common ground and points of divergence between queer male and female sexuality. At the same time, however, gender remains a useful lens through which to analyze bareback sex. Willful, condomless, anal sex appears to have as much to do with being a man as being a gay man, especially with the risk-taking personality traits associated with an idealized masculinity.

Implicit in debates about bareback sex is contestation over the meaning of sex in the lives of gay men, that is, how and with whom sex is supposed to be had. As such, the practices and identities of barebacking resonate with ongoing discussion of gay marriage and adoption. At times a thinly veiled valuation is evident in those debates: Men who pursue multiple sexual encounters (or, to use the pejorative label, those who are promiscuous) are morally bereft, sad creatures. Originally, promiscuity was constructed as deviant in opposition to monogamy.[40] With the advent of HIV, however, a newly pathologized promiscuity has come to function as the oppositional grounding for constructions of respectability in the context of queer coupling and family structures. The popular press's critiques of bareback sex have tended to imply a bipolar rather than multipolar array of models of sexual and emotional coupling. The happy, monogamous couple is at one end (the good end), and sex-crazed, lonely, and "at-risk" men are at the other (the bad end).

To date, a lack of systematic empirical data on the attitudes and sexual practices of self-identified barebackers has made it difficult to know what to make of the sorts of narratives as that which began this essay. Moreover, the diversity of interpretations represented in popular debates points to inadequacies in anthropological understandings of the origins and embodied experience of sexual pleasure in queer male and female subjectivities. Although diverse ethnographic studies of non-normative sexualities have appeared since the mid-1990s, I am aware of few that have focused specifically on sexual fantasy and pleasure. Fewer still attend to the complex psychic dynamics of subject-object and viewer-image characterizing fantasy and its relationship to the experience of sexual pleasure.[41]

Barebacking also raises important questions about the role of risk in sexual fantasy and the origins and implications of transgressive fantasy. The vast literature in cognitive psychology on sexual fantasy has tended to argue that gender influences fantasy in fundamental ways.[42] Men report higher frequencies of sexual fantasy and fantasies that have greater emphasis on visual content (more and greater variety). Women's fantasies, however, tend to highlight affect more explicitly, particularly feelings of commitment, tenderness, and emotionality, and have less emphasis on sexual content. The sorts of methods used to reach these conclusions (most of them have been structured or semistructured surveys) have obvious limitations and point to the contribution that in-depth ethnographic research could make.

Conclusions

In the United States, debates about bareback sex have been the sites of struggle and articulation of new identities, new perspectives on queer male sexuality, and on the ongoing complexities of HIV prevention. These debates speak to concerns about how to frame HIV prevention in an era where the threat of death may no longer function as an effective dissuader from condomless sex and where the safer-sex call to "use a condom every time" has proven too simplistic to address realities of increasingly diverse queer male subcultures. In this essay I have examined the implicit constructions of risk that inform popular debates and argued that notions of risk originating in public health epistemology and promoted in safer sex have played a key role in processes of the pleasure and stigmatization linked to bareback sex. I have also attempted to identify points of resonance with lesbian and gay anthropology. How, I inquire, does anthropology contribute to ongoing discussions of risk, sex, and HIV? Moreover, I describe how barebacking provides a lens to a variety of broader themes about queer sexuality.

Having stated what I have attempted, it is important to note what has been left out. The first issue concerns the difficulty inherent in pursuing this type of discourse analysis in the absence of empirical behavioral or ethnographic data. Without such data, for example, it is impossible to be sure of the precise prevalence of such sensationalized behaviors as intentional seroconversion. More generally, it leaves analysts unable to untangle bareback fantasy from bareback practice and therefore how sexual fantasy relates to actual behavioral risk. Systematic ethnographic research along these lines should be undertaken. Such research, however, would do well to take to heart Clatts's call for reconceptualization of sexual practices away from models that cast them as dependent variables that ignore "the broad diversity in gender roles and meanings that exist, or of the way in which both behaviour and meaning are shaped by interacting cultural, social, economic, and political factors" (1995:242).[43]

In part, I have attempted in this analysis to respond to Richard Elovich's comment (1999:87) about the difficulties of talking openly and honestly about anal sex. That observation is readily apparent in debates over bareback sex and points to how inconsistently, uncomfortably, and at times imprecisely we discuss sex and sexual pleasure. That point became all too clear as I struggled to make sense of my initial reaction to the bareback sex narrative that began this chapter. It is my hope that the strategy I have taken lends itself to the elaboration of increasingly refined approaches to the study of queer sexuality. The bareback sex debates, meanwhile, rage on.

Notes

This essay draws heavily from presentations given at scholarly meetings during 1999 and 2000 (Junge 1999a, 1999b, 2000). I am grateful to Peter Brown, Bruce Knauft, Bradd Shore, and Debra Spitulnik at Emory University's Department of Anthropology for their support and feedback. I am also much obliged for insightful comments from William L. Leap.

1. Xtreme Sex is no longer maintained but was in operation through at least the end of 1999. Although the details of its closure are unclear, a terse explanation appears at <http://rampages.onramp.net/tmike/xtremesex/xtreme.html>.

2. An obvious exception to these lacunae has been inquiry into emergent kinship structures (fictive or otherwise) within contemporary queer cultures (e.g., Weston 1991). That research is a response to attempts by religious and political conservatives in the 1980s to reclaim an imagined "tradition" of "family values," a tradition understood as threatened by emergent queer models of "chosen" families.

3. As of November 2000, very little scholarship in the social sciences and humanities had been published on barebacking. A search of MEDLINE, PsychInfo, Healthstar, and AIDSLINE using the key words *bareback, barebacking,* or *barebacker* elicited no peer-reviewed scholarship other than Gauthier and Forsyth (1999) (see, however, Junge 1999a, 1999b, and 2000 and Bolton 2000).

4. I conducted this interview as part of an examination of barebackers' use of the Internet (Junge 1999a).

5. *Newsweek* magazine (Peyser, Roberts, and Stout 1997) credits the men who first participated in America Online chat rooms devoted to condomless sex—at least as early as 1996—with producing this label. Synonymic terms such as *raw sex* have, at any rate, been in use for substantially longer.

6. Ocamb (1999:50) quotes researcher Gibson as saying that barebacking "has come to mean any unprotected anal sex." Similarly, Armstrong (1999:85) notes that "one in sixty acts of barebacking leads to infection," citing a well-known statistic describing risk of HIV infection posed by condomless anal sex regardless of whether condoms were willfully disregarded.

7. Unfortunately, some researchers who write on bareback sex have drawn elements of an emergent, unstable linguistic construction to forge a static analytic construct (e.g., Gauthier and Forsyth 1999).

8. It has also been posited that the term *barebacking* was initially used to describe condomless anal sex among HIV-positives but has subsequently diversified semantically (Ocamb 1999:50). The contention is supported anecdotally by a statement that was posted on a prominent barebacking e-mail list-serv: "No one has a patent on

barebacking. It's not 'supposed' to be only for folks of any particular status. The stats I have collected from 800+ barebackers indicate well over 45 percent of them self-identify as negative."

9. For example, Gauthier and Forsyth (1999) have examined the category of "bug-chaser" found at Internet sites designed to facilitate bareback sex. "Bug chasing," they report, "is the term used to refer to the act of barebacking when the participants include both HIV-positive and HIV-negative gay men, and the latter knowingly seek infection by the former" (86). That characterization oversteps the possibility that some bug-chasers never engage in condomless sex but eroticize it nonetheless. Such an oversight is extremely unfortunate, because it plays into alarmist outcries against barebackers without a critical examination of underlying cultural dynamics.

10. In public health and anthropological literature on HIV among men who have sex with other men, the terms *unprotected anal intercourse* (UAIC) or *unsafe sex* are often used to describe this practice. Because I find the words *unprotected* and *unsafe* somewhat problematic for their implicit emphasis on disease prevention, I will eschew such labels and employ instead more directly descriptive terms (i.e., *condomless anal sex*). For a similar perspective, see Davies et al. (1993:43).

11. In the social science and epidemiological literature, a variety of specific correlates of condomless anal sex has been posited, most of which are framed in negative or pathological terms. These include bereavement over partners who have died of AIDS (Kalichman et al. 1998); "heat of the moment" decision-making (Gold and Rosenthal 1998); alcohol and drug use (Darrow et al. 1998); sensation-seeking (Rompa, Difranceisco, and Kelly 1998); loneliness and low self-esteem (Martin and Knox 1997); psychological stress due to social oppression and rejection (Vincke and Bolton 1995); and HIV seropositivity (Van de Ven et al. 1998). In addition, several studies have indicated that condoms are less likely to be used during anal sex in primary partner relationships, which signify a symbolic construction of trust in one's partner (Bartos, Middleton, and Smith 1996), than in casual or "recreational" sex encounters (Darrow et al. 1998; Elford et al. 1998; McLean et al. 1994; Van de Ven et al. 1997, 1998).

12. See, for example, Carballo-Dieguez and Dolezal (1998); Ekstrand et al. (1998); and Valleroy et al. (1998).

13. For a study of how gay men who have long-standing HIV infections have dealt with increased projected longevity due to new medical therapies (the "Lazarus dilemma"), see Manzilla (1998).

14. The first study, published by Dilley, Woods, and McFarland (1997) and based on interviews from a cross section of San Francisco MSM, concluded that "advances in treatment are affecting the sexual decision making of some high-risk, HIV-negative gay men" (502). In a study of sexual decision-making among MSM engaged with casual partners in Sydney, Australia (Prestage et al. 1997), taking the new antiretroviral treatment was associated with an increase in condomless anal sex between 1995 and 1996. Subsequent reports indicated a perception that sex with an HIV-positive man who had an undetectable viral load was somehow "safer" than sex with someone who had a relatively high viral level (Kalichman et al. 1998). Similarly,

Hickson et al. (1998) report that a small but measurable proportion (11 percent) of their sample of British MSM in 1997 felt more likely to "take a risk with unprotected anal intercourse" given treatment advances.

Findings from studies of this sort have not, however, all supported the treatment advances–condom usage hypothesis. For example, after additional follow-up on their San Francisco sample Dilley et al. concluded that "improved antiretroviral treatment does not affect sexual decision making among the majority of men who have high risk sex with men" (1998). Similarly, Bartos et al. (1998) concluded that within their sample of Australian adult males, beliefs about the efficacy of the new treatments did not affect beliefs about condom use. Elovich (1999) has suggested a differential effect of treatment advances on the attitudes and practices depending on HIV serostatus and the failure of ongoing prevention efforts to address this differential. "While these drugs were an amazing development for men who are infected," he comments, "they did not change anything for HIV negative men. . . . This change-without-a-change for negative men has created frustrations that most prevention efforts have yet to acknowledge or address" (87).

15. "Sex panic" has been defined by historian Alan Bérubé as "a phenomenon in which society panics about some aspect of sex—prostitution, porn, etc.—and embarks on an intense assault against sexual freedom. Civil liberties are brushed aside, minority rights trampled on, and freedom of expression threatened" (quoted in Crain 1997; also see Rubin 1984).

16. This position was elaborated in a by-now infamous collection of essays edited by a group of New York University graduate students (Dangerous Bedfellows 1996).

17. Signorile (1999:51) goes so far as to call for "putting fear back into HIV prevention" in an attempt to promote condom use and a decrease in the frequency of sexual partnering.

18. The fragmented nature of contemporary gay identity in the urban milieu has also been articulated by gay activist Eric Rofes (1998).

19. I put "crackdown" in quotes here because several individuals have called into question the extent to which the rate of closure of New York City gay establishments during this period differed from earlier periods (e.g., Rotello 1999).

20. This sentiment was epitomized in a now-infamous speech given by gay pornography star, Tony Valenzuela, at a national conference around community organizing and HIV (Valenzuela 1999).

21. Attention to these issues continues to increase. In its April 1999 edition *The Advocate* profiled barebacking in its cover story (Kirby 1999). The June 1999 issue of *POZ Magazine* headlines a cover story entitled "Beyond Condoms: How to Create a Gay Men's Culture of Sexual Health" (Elovich 1999). In another issue of *POZ* Tony Valenzuela was depicted in the nude, standing next to a horse, under the title "Tony Valenzuela and the Boys Who Bareback Take You on a Ride Inside" (1999). At the same time, writers such as Rotello (1999) and Signorile (1999) continue to argue passionately for changes in gay cultural norms surrounding gay male sexuality. Although the influence of new treatments on risk perception and sexual practice

remains uncertain, reports of dramatic increases in citywide HIV and rectal gonorrhea infections have stimulated further concern about barebacking (Anonymous
1999a; Maugh 2000).

22. Typically, a trait that has at least a 95 percent probability of occurring due to
factors other than chance is considered a risk factor.

23. This logic is analogous to that posited by Talcott Parsons in a well-known essay
on the culturally sanctioned role of a sick person: "By institutional definition of the
sick role the sick person is helpless and therefore in need of help" (1951:440). Just
as the medical establishment has social license to help the sick, public health professionals have license to undertake prevention among at-risk populations.

24. Recognizing the wider range of context-dependent, cultural factors influencing sexual decision-making (and jettisoning the presumption of irrationality in cases
of condomless anal sex), program planners in Australia and New Zealand have advanced a perspective known as "negotiated safety" whereby a space is created for
queer men to openly discuss reasons for their risky behaviors (Bartos, Middleton,
and Smith 1995; Crawford et al. 1998; Worth and Ewing 1998). In the United States
that approach has proven extremely controversial because of the fear of condoning
behavior understood as irrational and immoral by facilitating its open, nonjudgmental
discussion (Elovich 1999:89). The issue is analogous to debates around syringe exchange in the United States that lambaste (erroneously) the provision of sterile sy-
ringes to injection drug-users as a way of reducing high-risk needle-sharing. Such
exchanges are described as encouraging drug use or at any rate sending the wrong
message about drug use.

25. As Farmer observes, "Why do some persons constitute 'risk groups,' while
others are 'individuals at risk'? These are not merely nosologic questions; they are
canonical ones. Why are some approaches and subjects considered appropriate for
publication in influential journals, while others are dismissed out of hand? A critical epistemology would explore the boundaries of polite and impolite discussion in
science" (266).

26. My impression that HIV-serodiscordant sex partners who bareback are a "small
proportion" of the broader population of barebackers is speculative and based on informal sources, for example, the popular gay press, a review of bareback-oriented
Web-sites, chat rooms, and list-servs, and conversations with friends. There is ur-
gent need to collect empirical data that explicitly embraces the terminology and social
labels (unstable though they are) emergent in debates about bareback sex.

27. Along these lines, Cornelius Baker, then executive director of the National Association of Persons with AIDS, has stated that people with HIV "have a moral and
ethical responsibility to disclose their status to sexual partners. So what we're doing now is dealing with the rights and responsibilities of people with HIV. We are
developing HIV survival programs with a whole track about relationships so people can learn the skills to disclose and to negotiate healthy sex that won't transmit
HIV" (Kirby 1999:95).

28. Although condomless anal sex may not have deleterious HIV-related consequences for seropositives due to reinfection, other negative outcomes are probable

because HIV is by no means the only STD transmissible via anal sex. Others include herpes, hepatitis A, gonorrhea, and anal warts. For HIV-positives, these infections can impair the immune system and thereby accelerate the progression of HIV disease. Regardless of HIV status, these conditions are painful and disruptive. It appears that gay men—both HIV positive and negative—who self-identify as barebackers are often aware of these risks and knowingly accept them. As Jason said, "There still is the element of danger. We do not know . . . I don't know whether I'm gonna get gonorrhea up my ass the next time I get fucked. . . . Or whether I'm gonna get it from fucking someone. So there's always that element of danger in there . . . I've at least done scientific processing enough for myself to be okay with this."

29. With respect to gay men, more recent research suggests varying degrees to which sexually active, HIV-positive individuals perceive a personal responsibility to protect others from infection. Wolitski et al. (1998) found two variables to be associated with high perceived personal responsibility to protect others from HIV infection: being more than thirty-five years of age and having graduated from college. In future research on bareback sex it would be interesting to gauge the prevalence of those two traits among self-identified barebackers as one analytic entree to their conceptualizations of responsibility.

30. Bolton (2000) has asserted that barebackers represent both a subculture and a "community."

31. "The appeal of queer sex, for many," Michael Warner has written (1995), "lies in its ability to violate the responsibilizing frames of good, right-thinking people."

32. As Davies et al. (1993:128) have noted, "By claiming men can be fucked, and that they can enjoy it, was to call into question the fixedness of what it meant to be 'a man.'"

33. It is worth acknowledging the existence of social science literature describing cross-cultural variation in prevalence and relative desirability of various sex practices among homosexual men. Although oral sex may be popular within one culturally specific population of homosexual men, anal sex may be the "default" elsewhere. One commonly waged critique of safer-sex ideology has been its one-size-fits-all strategy for condom promotion. In this discursive configuration, anal sex is risky and therefore to be avoided regardless of cultural context. It is to be supplanted instead by "safer" forms, such as oral sex, which HIV-prevention campaigns seek to eroticize. For specific examples of HIV-prevention campaigns that have failed to achieve the anal-to-oral switch (which suggests that African American and Latino American gay men in some settings do not want to substitute oral sex for penetrative anal sex), see Carballo-Dieguez and Dolezal (1998) and Gomez and Halkitis (1998).

34. The reference to "the pleasure of orgasm" in the preceding quotation brings up an additional aspect of the erotic value of anal sex—physiology. Although all forms of male orgasm are centered in the prostate gland, orgasm achieved through anal stimulation is experientially distinct from that achieved by penile stimulation (for example, during mutual masturbation). In other words, the physiological experience of orgasm for the receptive partner in anal sex is distinct (from orgasm achieved in other ways) regardless of cultural context.

35. Tony Valenzuela's by-now notorious description of the experience of condomless anal sex as "transformative" is a good example of that sentiment among HIV-positive men.

36. Because "active" is a culturally (rather than biologically) defined notion, an active sexual role does not necessarily refer to the penetrative role in anal sex. although in popular U.S. conceptualizations to penetrate is considered "active."

37. None of this is particularly novel and by no means specific to gay men. What seems special about the debates of bareback sex is that the possibility that a particular sexual fantasy (in which norms forged on public health grounds are violated) has been singled out and garnered the consternation of such a wide array of individuals. Implicit thus far in these debates has been the presumption that fantasy signals practice—that fantasy of transgression signifies that transgression is actually occurring. Although I do not dispute this possibility, and at any rate have no empirical data to explore the hypothesis one way or another, I am nonetheless struck at the lack of interest in the possibility (commonly articulated in psychotherapeutical contexts) that transgressive fantasy can actually be a healthy form of stress reduction.

38. Such a sentiment is by no means limited to gay men. Indeed, the notion of "feeling the most alive when closest to death" pervades the psychological literature on risk-takers (e.g., Zorpette 1999:57). Thus, psychologists have developed scales to gauge the parameters of risk-taking dispositions, for example, "sensation seeking" (Zukerman, Buchsbaum, and Murphy 1980) and "thrill seeking" (Konner 1990). Such scales have often been applied to extreme sports, such as skydiving, bungy-jumping, and the like.

39. The one notable exception of which I am aware is Ricks (1999).

40. Elsewhere (Junge 1999a) I have argued that a model of heterosexual matrimony rooted in eighteenth- and nineteenth-century religious and juridical discourses (what Foucault [1978:38] refers to as a "legitimate coupling model") has subtly informed debates about bareback sex.

41. Understandings of fantasy as a "sexual script"—that is, an assemblage of images serving to achieve a state of arousal and satisfaction—do not capture this complexity but rather impose conventional subject-object distinctions and three-dimensional space configurations on an experience often characterized by neither.

42. See, for example, Abramson and Mosher (1979), De Martino (1979), Ellis and Symons (1990), Gil (1990), Hariton and Singer (1974), Hessellund (1976), and Sorenson (1979).

43. I have left the relationship between bareback sex and recreational drugs largely unexamined. Although my rationale for doing so has been the contention that episodes of condomless anal sex fostered through the judgment-impairing effects of drugs do not really qualify as bareback sex, I am well aware that drugs (especially in the context of group sex encounters) continue to occupy a central space in ongoing debates and therefore merit closer attention.

References Cited

Abramson, Paul R., and Donald L. Mosher. 1979. "An Empirical Investigation of Experimentally Induced Masturbatory Fantasies." *Archives of Sexual Behavior* 8: 27–39.

Anonymous. 1999a. "Increases in Unsafe Sex and Rectal Gonorrhea among Men Who Have Sex with Men—San Francisco, California, 1994–1997." *Morbidity and Mortality Weekly Report* 48: 45–8.

———. 1999b. "Letter to the Editor." *POZ Magazine,* May, 29.

———. 1999c. Posting to Gay Bareback List, Bareback@egroups.com.

Armstrong, Walter. 1999. "The Marriage of Gay men and Condoms." *POZ Magazine,* June, 85.

Bartos, Michael, Douglas Ezzy, Karalyn McDonald, Darryl O'Donnel, and Richard De Visser. 1998. "Treatments, Intimacy, and Disclosure in the Sexual Practice of HIV-Infected Adults in Australia." Abstract 641/23402. Twelfth World Conference on IDS, Geneva.

———, Heather Middleton, and G. Smith. 1995. "A Context-Dependent, Cultural Model for Understanding Sexual Practice." Abstract 80. Annual conference for the Australasian Society of HIV Medicine.

———. 1996. "Gay Men in Regular Relationships and HIV Risk." Abstract Tu.D.2698. International Conference on AIDS, Vancouver.

Bayer, Ronald. 1996. "AIDS Prevention—Sexual Ethics and Responsibility." *New England Journal of Medicine* 334: 1540–42.

Bolton, Ralph. 2000. "Barebacking Culture." Presented at the annual meeting of the American Anthropological Association, San Francisco, Calif.

Brown, Peter J. 1997. "Stigma and Coping with Chronic Illness." In *Understanding and Applying Medical Anthropology,* comp. Peter J. Brown, 310. Mountain View: Mayfield.

Carballo-Dieguez, Alex, and Curtis Dolezal. 1998. "Continued Sexual Risk Behavior among HIV-Seropositive Latino Men Who Have Sex with Men." Abstract 14145. Twelfth World Conference on AIDS, Geneva.

Centers for Disease Control and Prevention. 1999. "AIDS Mortality Statistics." Website at <http://www.cdc.gov> accessed April 20, 2000.

Clatts, Michael. 1995. "Disembodied Acts: On the Perverse Use of Sexual Categories in the Study of High-Risk Behaviour." In *Culture and Sexual Risk: Anthropological Perspectives on AIDS,* ed. Han ten Brummelhuis and Gilbert Herdt, 241–55. Sydney: Gordon and Breach.

———, and Kevin M. Mutchler. 1989. "AIDS and the Dangerous Other: Metaphors of Sex and Deviance in the Representation of Disease." *Medical Anthropology* 10:105–14.

Crain, Caleb. 1997. "Pleasure Principles: Queer Theorists and Gay Journalists Wrestle over the Politics of Sex." *Lingua Franca* 7(8).

Crawford, June, Pam Rodden, Susan Kippax, and Paul Van de Ven. 1998. "Negotiated Safety and Agreements between Men in Relationships: Are All Agreements Equal?" Abstract 23105. Twelfth World Conference on AIDS, Geneva.

Dangerous Bedfellows, ed. 1996. *Policing Public Sex: Queer Politics and the Future of AIDS Activism.* Boston: South End Press.

Darrow, William, R. D. Webster, K. I. Patel, A. K. Buckley, S. P. Kurtz, R. R. Stempel, and R. A. Roark. 1998. "Client-centered Counseling and the Continuing Problem of Unprotected Anal Intercourse (UAI) among Men Who Have Sex with Men (MSM): Critical Issues." Abstract 33303. Twelfth World Conference on AIDS, Geneva.

Davies, Peter M., Ford C. I. Hickson, Peter Weatherburn, and Andrew J. Hunt. 1993. *Sex, Gay Men and AIDS.* London: Falmer Press.

De Martino, Manfred F. 1979. *Human Autoerotic Practices.* New York: Human Sciences Press.

Dilley, James, William Woods, and William M. McFarland. 1997. "Are Advances in Treatment Changing Views about High-Risk sex?" *New England Journal of Medicine* 337(7): 501–2.

———, James Sabatino, Joanna Rinaldi, Barbara Adler, and Tania Lihatsh. 1998. "Improved Antiretroviral Treatment Does Not Affect Sexual Decision-making among the Majority of Men Who Have High Risk Sex with Men." Abstract 23130. Twelfth World Conference on AIDS, Geneva.

Douglas, Mary. 1994. *Risk and Blame: Essays in Cultural Theory.* New York: Routledge.

Ekstrand, Maria, Ron Stall, Jay Paul, Dennis Osmond, and Thomas J. Coates. 1998. "Increasing Rates of Unprotected Anal Intercourse among San Francisco Gay Men Include High UAI Rates with a Partner of Unknown or Different Serostatus." Abstract 23116 (poster). Twelfth World Conference on AIDS, Geneva.

Elford, Jonathon, G. J. Bolding, M. Maguire, and L. Sherr. 1998. "Unprotected Anal Intercourse among Gay Men and Their Regular Partners in London." Abstract 23119. Twelfth World Conference on AIDS, Geneva.

Ellis, Bruce J., and Donald Symons. 1990. "Sex Differences in Sexual Fantasy: An Evolutionary Psychological Approach." *Journal of Sex Research* 27: 527–55.

Elovich, Richard. 1999. "Beyond Condoms: How to Create a Gay Men's Culture of Sexual Health." *POZ Magazine,* June, 86–91.

Fall, J. n.d. "On Morality." Web-site at <http://www.cruisingforsex.com> accessed June 20, 1999.

Farmer, Paul. 1998. "Social Inequalities and Emerging Infectious Diseases." *Emerging Infectious Diseases* 2(4): 259–69.

Folger, Keith. 1999. "Letter to the editor." *The Advocate.* May.

Foucault, Michel. 1978. *The History of Sexuality,* vol. 1: *An Introduction.* New York: Vintage Books.

Gauthier, Deann, and Craig J. Forsyth. 1999. "Bareback Sex, Bug Chasers, and the Gift of Death." *Deviant Behavior* 20: 85–100.

Gendin, Stephen. 1999. "They Shoot Barebackers, Don't They?" *POZ Magazine,* Feb., 48–51.

Gil, Vincent E. 1990. "Sexual Fantasy Experiences and Guilt among Conservative Christians: An Exploratory Study." *Journal of Sex Research* 27: 629–38.

Goffman, Erving. 1963. *Stigma: Notes on the Management of Spoiled Identity.* Englewood Cliffs: Prentice-Hall.

Gold, Ron S., and Davd A. Rosenthal. 1998. "Examining Self-Justifications for Unsafe Sex as a Technique of AIDS Education: The Importance of Personal Relevance." *International Journal of STD and AIDS* 9: 208–13.

Gomez, Cynthia A., and Perry Halkitis. 1998. "Culture Counts: Understanding the Context of Unprotected Sex for HIV-Positive Men in a Multi-Ethnic Urban Sample in the U.S." Abstract 14223. International Conference on AIDS, Vancouver.

Hariton, E. Barbara, and Jerome L. Singer. 1974. "Women's Fantasies during Sexual Intercourse: Normative and Theoretical Implications." *Journal of Consulting & Clinical Psychology* 42: 313–22.

Hessellund, Hans. 1976. "Masturbation and Sexual Fantasies in Married Couples." *Archives of Sexual Behavior* 5: 133–47.

Hickson, Ford, David S. Reid, Laurie A. Henderson, Peter Weatherburn, and P. G. Keogh. 1998. "Treatment Advances, Risk Taking, and HIV Testing History among Gay Men in the U.K." Abstract 14159. Twelfth World Conference on AIDS, Geneva.

Junge, Benjamin. 1999a. "Bareback Sex and the Internet: Computer-Mediated Communication Used by Gay Men to Arrange Condomless Anal Sex." Presented at the Lavender Languages and Linguistics Conference, American University, Washington, D.C.

———. 1999b. "Competing Discourses of the Gay Male Subject: Analyzing the Terms of the Bareback Sex Debates." Presented at the annual meeting of the American Anthropological Association, Chicago.

———. 2000. "Risk, Pleasure and Fantasy: Constructions of Gay Male Sexuality in the Bareback Sex Debates." Presented at joint meetings of the Societies of Medical Anthropology and Applied Anthropology, San Francisco.

Kalichman, Seth C., D. Nachimson, Charsey Cherry, and Ernestine Williams. 1998. "AIDS Treatment Advances and Behavioral Prevention Setbacks: Preliminary Assessment of Reduced Perceived Threat of HIV-AIDS." *Health Psychology* 17: 546–50.

Kane, Stephanie, and Theresa Mason. 1992. "IV Drug Users and 'Sex Partners': The Limits of Epidemiological Categories and the Ethnography of Risk." In *The Time of AIDS: Social Analysis, Theory and Method,* ed. Gilbert Herdt and Shirley Lindenbaum, 199–224. Newbury Park: Sage Publications, 1992.

Kirby, David. 1999. "Risky Business: Barebacking Celebrates Unprotected Sex and Raises Difficult Issues about AIDS Prevention," *The Advocate,* April 13, 40–45.

Konner, Melvin. 1990. *Why the Reckless Survive and Other Secrets of Human Nature.* New York: Viking Press.

Leap, William L. 1996. *Word's Out: Gay Men's English.* Minneapolis: University of Minnesota Press.

Levine, M., and C. Siegal. 1992. "Unprotected Sex: Understanding Gay Men's Participation." In *The Social Context of AIDS,* ed. Joan Huber and Beth E. Schneider, 47–71. Newbury Park, Calif.: Sage Publications.

Lowy, E., and M. W. Ross. 1994. "'It'll Never Happen to Me': Gay Men's Beliefs, Perceptions and Folk Constructions of Sexual Risk." *AIDS Education and Prevention* 6: 467–82.

Manzilla, M. 1998. "The Lazarus Dilemma: Shifting Dynamics of Relationships in the Age of HIV." Abstract 60925. Twelfth World Conference on AIDS, Geneva.

Martin, James I., and Jo Knox. 1997. "Self-Esteem Instability and Its Implications for HIV Prevention among Gay Men." *Health and Social Work* 22: 264–73.

Maugh, Thomas H. III. 2000. "New HIV Infections in S.F. Increase Sharply." *Los Angeles Times,* July 1, A11.

McLean, J., M. Boulton, M. Brookes, D. Lakhani, R. Fitzpatrick, J. Dawson, R. McKechnie, and G. Hart. 1994. "Regular Partners and Risky Behavior: Why Do Gay Men Have Unprotected Intercourse?" *AIDS Care* 6: 331–41.

Ocamb, K. 1999. "Beyond Barebacking: The Complacency Crisis." *Genre Magazine,* June, 49–50.

Odets, Walt. 1995. *In the Shadow of the Epidemic: Being HIV Negative in the Age of AIDS.* Durham: Duke University Press.

Parsons, Talcott. 1951. *The Social System.* Glencoe: Free Press.

Peyser, Marc, Elizabeth Roberts, and Frappa Stout. 1997. "A Deadly Dance." *Newsweek,* Sept. 29, 76–77.

Pollack, Michael. 1988. *Les homosexuels et le SIDA: Sociologie d'une épidémie.* Paris: AM Métailié.

Prestage, Garrett, Andrew Grulich, Danielle Campbell, John Kaldor, and Susan Kippax. 1997. "Unprotected Intercourse among HIV-Positive Men: The Influence of Combination Therapies." Abstract IS113. Annual meeting, Australasian Society of HIV Medicine, Adelaide.

Ricks, Ingrid. 1999. "She Said, She Said: Eleven Lesbians Sound Off on the Controversial Practice of Bareback Sex." *The Advocate,* April 13, 48–49.

Rofes, Eric. 1998. *Dry Bones Breathe: Gay Men Creating Post-AIDS Identities and Cultures.* New York: Harrington Park Press.

Rompa, David, Wayne Difranceisco, and Jeffrey Kelly. 1998. "Predictors of High-Risk Sexual Behavior in a Sample of HIV-Positive Men Who Engage in Sex with Men." Abstract 23122. International Conference on AIDS, Vancouver.

Rotello, Gabriel. 1995. "Letter to the Editor." *The Nation,* April 17, 540.

———. 1997. *Sexual Ecology: AIDS and the Destiny of Gay Men.* New York: Dutton.

———. 1999. "An Open Letter to Sex Panic." Web-site at <http://members.aol.com/ouryouth/feat3.htm> accessed April 20, 2000.

Rubin, Gayle. 1984. "Thinking Sex: Notes for a Radical Theory of the Politics of Sexuality." In *Pleasure and Danger: Exploring Female Sexuality,* ed. Carole S. Vance, 267–319. New York: Routledge.

Scarce, Michael. 1999. "A Ride on the Wild Side." *POZ Magazine,* Feb., 52–55.

Sheon, Nicolas, and Aaron Plant. 1997. "Protease Dis-inhibitors? The Gay Bareback

Phenomenon." Web-site at <http://hivinsite.ucsf.edu/social/spotlight/2098.3445
.html> accessed April 20, 2000.

Signorile, Michelangelo. 1995. "HIV-Positive and Careless." *New York Times,* Feb.
26, 4:15.

———. 1997. *Life Outside: The Signorile Report on Gay Men.* New York: Harper
Collins.

———. 1999. "Don't Fear the Fear." *The Advocate,* April 13, 51–53.

Sorenson, Robert C. 1979. "Various Aspects of Masturbation by Teenage Boys and
Girls." In *Human Autoerotic Practices,* ed. Manfred F. De Martino, 94–103. New
York: Human Sciences Press.

Valenzuela, Tony. 1999. "Let's Talk about Sex without Condoms." Web-site at <http://
www.geocities.com/~sexpanicnyc/sexsans.htm> accessed April 20, 2000.

Valleroy, Linda, Duncan A. Mackellar, Daniel Rosen, and Gina Secura. 1998. "Prev-
alence and Predictors of Unprotected Receptive Anal Intercourse for Fifteen- to
Twenty-Two-Year-Old Men Who Have Sex with Men in Seven Urban Areas,
USA." Abstract 23139. International Conference on AIDS, Vancouver.

Van de Ven, Paul, Susan Kippax, June Crawford, Judy French, Garrett Prestage, Andrew Grulich, John Kaldor, and Paul Kinder. 1997. "Sexual Practices in a Broad
Cross-Sectional Sample of Sydney Gay Men." *Australian and New Zealand Journal of Public Health* 21: 762–76.

Van de Ven, Paul, Danielle Campbell, Susan Kippax, Stephanie Knox, Garrett Prestage,
June Crawford, Paul Kinder, and David Cooper. 1998. "Gay Men Who Engage Repeatedly in Unprotected Anal Intercourse with Casual Partners: The Sydney Men
and Sexual Health Study." *International Journal of STD and AIDS* 9: 336–40.

Vincke, John, and Ralph Bolton. 1995. "Social Stress and Risky Sex among Gay
Men: An Additional Explanation for the Persistence of Unsafe Sex." In *Culture
and Sexual Risk: Anthropological Perspectives on AIDS,* ed. Han ten Brummelhuis and Gilbert Herdt, 183–203. Amsterdam: Gordon and Breach.

Warner, Michael. 1995. *Village Voice,* Jan.

Watney, Simon. 1989. "Taking Liberties: An Introduction." In *Taking Liberties: AIDS
and Cultural Politics,* ed. Erica Carter and Simon Watney, 59–68. London: Serpent's Tail.

Weston, Kath. 1991. *Families We Choose: Lesbians, Gays, Kinship.* New York: Columbia University Press.

Wolitski, R., C. A. Gomez, J. T. Parsons, T. Ambrose, and R. H. Remien. 1998. "HIV-
Seropositive Men's Perceived Responsibility for Preventing the Transmission of
HIV to Others." Abstract 23361. Twelfth World Conference on AIDS, Geneva.

Worth, H., and T. Ewing. 1998. "'Trust, Love, Condoms': An HIV Education Campaign Based on Survey Data on Men in Relationships with Men in New Zealand."
Abstract 43282. International Conference on AIDS, Vancouver.

Zorpette, Glenn. 1999. "Extreme Sports, Sensation-Seeking and the Brain." *Scientific American Presents* 10: 56–59.

Zukerman, M., M. S. Buchsbaum, and D. L. Murphy. 1980. "Sensation-Seeking and
Its Biological Correlates." *Psychological Bulletin* 88: 187–214.

EIGHT

We're "Not about Gender":
The Uses of "Transgender"

David Valentine

"I've been gay all my life, been a woman all my life," says Fiona. I am with Fiona and several other people—mostly people of color—at a support group billed as being for "HIV-positive transgender people" at New York Hospital. Apart from myself and the group leader, who like me is a gay white man in his thirties, all of those present, although born male, are feminine-identified. Few if any, however, use the category *transgender* to talk about themselves as feminine people. Indeed, like Fiona, they refer to themselves variously as women, as gay, and sometimes as fem queens.

Fiona's use of "gay" to identify herself—in the same sentence in which she identifies herself as a woman—is complicated by how the category *gay* has taken on new meanings in mainstream and national discourses about homosexuality and gender variance since the 1970s. Indeed, the labeling of the group as a transgender support group—and the fact that none of those in the group use or in some cases even understand the term—raises a range of complicated political, cultural, and theoretical issues that form the basis of this essay. In particular, I will ask what does "transgender" as a category do that categories such as "transexual," "cross-dresser," "transvestite," or "gay" are unable to achieve.

In thinking and writing about disruptions, theorists are increasingly employing the concept of transgender to fulfill several related performative roles: to indicate the constructedness of gender, to show how a binary sex/gender system is not a natural fact, and to further develop feminist observations that have unhinged gender from biological characteristics. In local and national politics in the United States it has also become both a category of identity and a term around which social and political activism is increasingly taking shape.

In this essay, however, I will claim that "transgender" presents a deeper disruption in that this category and that the varied experiences of cross-gender expressions, practices, and identities gathered under this term present a challenge to a set of theoretical relations upon which gay and lesbian anthropology (and gay and lesbian scholarship more generally) is based: the necessary theoretical (and political) separation of sexuality and gender.

The separation of gender and sexuality as different realms of human experience has been an important political and theoretical innovation (Rubin 1984). It has allowed the development of histories, ethnographies, and theories that highlight the complex relationships between gendered and sexual subjectivities and the political and cultural meanings and contexts within which such subjectivities are produced and experienced. Yet this analytic separation— in tandem with broader political shifts in the gay and lesbian community— has drawn attention away from other feminist and queer concerns about how gender and sexuality are closely intertwined. Further, the institutionalization of "gender" and "sexuality" as separable realms of experience in disciplinary organization, journals, conferences, and so on gives weight to this separation that discourages an examination of the constitution of gender and sexuality as cultural categories themselves. To put it another way, How do we decide which experiences count as gender and which as sexuality?

This is clearly a central question for queer scholars, but one that is often elided by the heuristic and political value of thinking of gender and sexuality as different entities. In this chapter, through an analysis of the terms *transgender* and *gay* as I heard them used during my fieldwork, I hope to show some of the ways in which the solidifying of such a heuristic in disciplinary terms must be seen in its historical and political context alongside a contemporary "mainstreaming" of the gay and lesbian movement in the United States (D'Emilio 1983; Vaid 1995). In particular, over the past century (especially since the 1970s) the category *gay*—in its sense of including gay men and lesbians—has been increasingly de-gendered, by which I mean that it has been increasingly defined in a broad range of discourses as a category that cannot be explained by reference to the experience of gender. It is this unmarked sense of gay that I will examine in this chapter, and it is this meaning I employ when I invoke "gay." At the same time, I will show how a (desexualized) category of "transgender" has filled the empty space left by such a de-gendering. From this analysis, I will make observations about what this means for gender and sexuality as cultural categories themselves. To rephrase the issue in terms of the opening anecdote, How can it make sense for Fiona to call herself both "gay" and "a woman" in the same breath while such an understanding of self cannot be represented in contemporary mainstream LGBT politics and theory?

Queer Dilemmas

The body of literature that has tentatively come to be named "gay and lesbian anthropology" occupies an odd space within anthropology and gay and lesbian studies more broadly. On the one hand, the fight to gain some kind of hearing in the realms of institutional and disciplinary power has been long and hard and has depended on a certain amount of strategic essentialist politics in order to open a space for the scholarship that would make them a topic of its investigation. On the other hand, anthropological and ethnohistorical accounts of homosexuality and of gay and lesbian lives (e.g., Chauncey 1994; D'Emilio 1983; Herdt, ed. 1992; Newton 1979[1972], 1993; Shokheid 1995; Weston 1991) have indicated how "same sex sexuality" or even "sexuality" itself (Elliston 1995) are both historically and culturally constructed. The deployment of the term *queer* as a blanket term to cover all sexual and gender difference has complicated the field further.[1]

Queer theorists have challenged the basis of the identity categories that name the field, and the insights of queer/gay/lesbian anthropologists have challenged the kinds of essentialisms that underlie such identity categories. These accounts, by providing historical and ethnographic data that indicate the complexities of lived experience in specific contexts, have reined in both essentialized accounts of homosexualities and the theoretical fascination with performativity as the primary theoretical tool for understanding gender and sexual difference (Morris 1995).

More recently, the social, political, and intellectual movement bearing the label *transgender* has entered the fray, demanding a place within the spaces carved out under the labels *gay* and *lebian*. In the overheated atmosphere of identity politics of the late 1990s, gay and lesbian organizations of all kinds increasingly included the *b* of bisexual and the *t* of transgender in their names and mission statements. Within anthropology, too, a recognition that transgender lives complicate gendered and sexual categories of analysis has required a rethinking of how to theorize and describe queer lives and experiences.

Although a similarity of interests around issues of discrimination, hate crimes, and civil rights is generally offered as the reason for LGBT alliances, there is also frequent insistence on the differences between the subjectivities described by gay/lesbian (and to some extent bisexual) on the one hand and transgender on the other. If gay/lesbian/bisexual people are at root defined by sexuality, then transgender, in this view, is different because it is based on variant expressions of gender.

The inclusion of "bisexual" and "transgender" in many formerly exclusive gay and lesbian spaces has also found its way into anthropology. The Society of Lesbian and Gay Anthropologists (SOLGA) voted overwhelmingly in 1997 to change its bylaws to include "bisexual" and "transgender" in them.[2] At the same time and for a variety of reasons (primarily a lack of unanimity on an alternative name) members voted down a name change that might have included those terms.[3] This happens commonly when the inclusivity of formerly gay and lesbian groups is being renegotiated. Changes to mission statements, bylaws, and the use of inclusive language have become issues in organizations as large as the National Gay and Lesbian Task Force and as local as university social groups. The names of these organizations, however, have usually remained the same. Unwillingness to highlight the inclusion of bisexuals or transgender people was not necessarily the reason for voting down the name change in the case of SOLGA, although that pattern is evident across many organizations and indicates a somewhat ambivalent attitude toward transgender (and bisexual) issues. The reason for such ambivalence is, I would argue, that transgender identities are seen to have a distinct and ontologically different source from those described by the labels *gay* and *lesbian*. As one anthropologist who responded to my queries on SOLGA's e-mail list about the vote wrote, "Transsexuals and transgendered persons are analytically and politically distinct from homosexuals and, no doubt, there are many who do not want to ratify the stereotype that homosexuality and gender nonconformity are linked (let alone unitary)."

If anthropologists are set the special task of investigating the cultural assumptions behind the social organization of categories of personhood, then it is necessary to look at the assumptions behind this statement. To do so, we need to revisit the place where gay/lesbian/bisexual experiences and transgender experiences are seen to part company: the perceived distinction that gay/lesbian/bisexual identities and experiences are located in "sexual orientation" while transgender identities and experiences are rooted in "gender identity." Although queer theorists have dissected LGBT identity categories and problematized them by reference to cultural, historical, class, and racial difference, they have avoided analyzing the thing that supposedly brings all gay, lesbian, and bisexual people together: sexual orientation. I am suggesting, in other words, that the ways in which "gender" and "sexuality" have been used as unproblematic categories need to be opened for investigation and that anthropologists need to examine the basis for their disciplinary theories of sexuality.

To this end, I draw on my ethnographic research in transcommunities in New York City and nationwide.[4] Based as I was at the Gender Identity Project (GIP) of the Lesbian and Gay Community Services Center, one of the oldest and most powerful of the national lesbian and gay community centers, my fieldwork was not simply within a "transgender community" but necessarily at the place where the negotiations of inclusion were and are happening. Moreover, this fieldwork took place over a variety of settings, from bars, clubs, drag balls, and sex work strolls to social service settings, national activist organizations, and even in the U.S. Congress. The anecdotes that follow are intended to indicate the vastly different realms in which the distinction between gay and transgender have come to be significant and the political ramifications of its use.

Lobby Day

On a morning in early May 1997 I was standing in front of the Capitol Building in Washington, D.C., with about sixty men and women of all genders. The occasion was the Second National Gender Lobby Day, an event sponsored by the Gender Public Advocacy Coalition (GenderPAC), a group devoted to "gender, affectional, and racial equality" in order to highlight transgender issues for members of Congress. Those present included transexual men and women, male cross-dressers, and others who refuse gendered identities.[5] Apart from one or two people, virtually everyone present was white. A couple of staffers from the Human Rights Campaign (HRC), a national organization dedicated to achieving lesbian and gay civil rights, were present to offer expertise and advice about lobbying.

Two months before this event it would have seemed unlikely that the HRC would be with us that morning. GenderPAC had been locked in a battle with the HRC over the wording in the Employment Non-Discrimination Act (ENDA). ENDA, an HRC project that had come very close to passage in the previous session of Congress, would prohibit discrimination against lesbians and gay men in employment. GenderPAC and others had been trying to get the HRC to include "gender expression" or "gender identity" as protected categories within ENDA.[6] The HRC, however, had stonewalled that attempt and argued against it on two points—first, that they were committed to gay and lesbian issues and that transgender issues were not within their purview, because the HRC is "not about gender."[7] The second was that inclusion of "gender identity" in ENDA would put to an end any chance the bill would have of passage.

As Vaid (1995) notes, the HRC (formerly the Human Rights Campaign Fund) has a long history in the gay and lesbian community and has actively taken what Vaid calls a "mainstreaming" approach to gay and lesbian rights, working within existing political structures to achieve such ends. Vaid also notes that such mainstreaming has been at the expense of representing non-"respectable" gay men and lesbians—drag queens, butch women, effeminate men, and the leather community—implicitly marking "gay" as white, middle class, and gender-normative. Further, the HRC's endorsement of anti-abortion New York Sen. Alfonse D'Amato in the 1998 elections could be seen partly as evidence of the distinction the HRC made between "gender" issues (abortion rights in this case) and those of "sexual orientation."[8]

By the morning of Lobby Day, however, the HRC, together with the National Gay and Lesbian Task Force (NGLTF), had persuaded GenderPAC officers that a more productive way of introducing transgender issues on the Hill would be to lobby for the inclusion of "gender identity" in the Hate Crimes Statistics Act. This had been an initial strategy of gay and lesbian lobbyists, and it had opened the way for work on more complex legislative concerns around gay and lesbian issues. Although the HRC's position still angered many activists gathered in front of the Capitol that morning, GenderPAC officers had recognized the political realities at hand, and most of those present had agreed that a focus on hate crimes would be the official theme of Lobby Day.

Now we were gathered rather nervously in front of the Capitol, somewhat unsure about how to begin. HRC staffers (offering advice but also presumably on hand to do damage control) herded us into small groups and gave last-minute pointers on lobbying. I stood talking with Riki Anne Wilchins, executive director of GenderPAC and founder of the direct action group Transexual Menace. A little way off stood an HRC staffer, a lesbian who was dressed in a double-breasted suit and tie. Riki glanced in her direction and, unable to resist the opportunity to drive home a point, said to me so the woman could hear, "And they say they're not about gender."

The Legends' Ball

A few months later, sometime in the early hours of the morning of August 18, 1997, I was at the Marc Ballroom on Union Square in New York City at the annual Legends' Ball. The drag balls made famous by Jenny Livingstone's film *Paris Is Burning* underwent some shifts in makeup and style during the 1990s, but many of the same faces are still there. The MC for the evening was Junior Labeja, who was featured in *Paris Is Burning.*

Starting in the 1960s, drag balls have been a central element of the African American and the Latina/Latino gay community. Ball houses, formed around particularly well-known or admired people—the "mothers" and "fathers" of the houses—are important sites of community, support, and kinship. I didn't see Fiona there, but she and others in the support group have participated in the ball scene at various times.

The Legends' Ball is always one of the biggest of the summer, and the place was packed. Apart from myself and some few others, the crowd was almost entirely African American or Latina/Latino. In the back where I was standing, the House of Xtravaganza was building a lavish float to push up the runway for one of the categories. As they built, Junior Labeja held forth on the ball's categories, in which people would be competing for cash and trophy prizes. He reminded the crowd that "there is different genders" and then announced a category for butches.

In the ball scene, butches can be described as "female-bodied masculine persons." On the whole, butches live in a masculine gender and take on masculine names; some may take testosterone shots if they have access to them, and some have taken fem queens who walk in the balls as girlfriends. Fem queens are, to use a similar construction, "male-bodied feminine persons," although with the relatively easy availability of female hormones and plastic surgery many have feminized their bodies with breast augmentation, electrolysis, and other cosmetic procedures. The other significant category of personhood at the balls is "butch queen": a masculine-identified gay man.

The House of Xtravaganza was now ready to "walk." Its float, a plywood and plexiglass structure, had been designed to look like a sauna and was filled with House of Xtravaganza members (almost all Latina/Latino) clad in towels. A smoke machine hidden inside gave the impression of steam, and when the Xtravaganzas opened the door at the judge's table they issued forth amid clouds of billowing smoke. The applause was deafening. Of those in the float, some were fem queens, some butches, and some butch queens.

At the Gender Identity Project, a social service agency for transgender people where I conducted much of my fieldwork and worked as a safer-sex outreach worker, fem queens and butches are seen to fall on the "transgender spectrum," a concept that gathers a wide range of gender possibilities under the collective term *transgender.* As such, they are considered as part of a newly emerging transgender community; certainly, they are seen to fall under the purview of GIP as a social service and community-building organization. The butch queens who share the makeshift sauna, though, are not. As gay men they are seen to fall outside the category *transgender.*

Yet during one of the butch categories Junior Labeja observed, "The butches are so good it's no longer gay and lesbian but lesbian and gay!" What I found remarkable about this statement, and what made me scramble for my notebook, was the fact that Junior, as with so many in the ball community, didn't use the term *transgender* but rather referred to the butches as lesbians. If my interest as an anthropologist is in studying a transgender community or transgender spectrum, what does it mean that the identity labels that those in the ball community use are not "transgender" but rather "gay" or "lesbian"? And, if butches and fem queens are seen to be included in the categories "gay and lesbian," what of GIP's distinction between them and butch queens?

The Transgender Spectrum

The transgender spectrum is essentially a literalization of the meanings of "transgender," a term that emerged in its current usage as a collective category of personhood in the early 1990s.[9] This usage—pioneered in social service and activist settings—indexes a category of personhood seen to include everyone from drag queens and male-identified butch lesbians to intersex people and post-operative transexual men and women.[10] Transgender in this collective sense arose out of activist- and community-based social service contexts in New York and San Francisco in the late 1980s and early 1990s. Central to this process was the founding of the Gender Identity Project by Barbara Warren and Riki Anne Wilchins at the Lesbian and Gay Community Services Center in New York City.[11] GIP was a response to a large number of gender-variant people who sought help through Project Connect, a substance abuse counseling program at the center, and to a perceived need for a more formal social service and community-building program for those who were increasingly being referred to as transgender. It is this sense of transgender—that of its collectivity—that is implicit in contemporary social services, activism, and academic discourses.

The importance of GIP's founding at the center in New York is not to be underestimated. Although the majority of GIP's clients are white, mainly middle-class, transexual women (Valentine n.d.), the development of a concept of transgender to include all gender-variant people of all racial, class, and cultural backgrounds is central to its mission. GIP literature reflects this: "Wherever you are on the transgender spectrum . . . Drag, CrossDresser, Cross-Gender, Femme Queen, BiGender, Transvestite, Transexual, FTM, MTF, NewWoman, NewMan . . . you are not alone!"[12] The implications of this formulation have two important outcomes of concern here. First, it allows a space for a more cohesive, relatively more powerful, political movement to arise and claim space within wider queer political structures and within queer scholarship. Second, such a use of transgender includes people who may not want to be included—or indeed may not know they are included.

Among those who may or may not see themselves as part of a transgender spectrum are many of the fem queens and butches who walk the balls. Although they may be classified as part of a transgender spectrum in a national queer political conceptualization, within the ball scene they are perceived as simply gay, alongside butch queens and fem lesbians. Some transgender activists argue that these individuals are not yet educated into the language of the new transgender movement. Indeed, some in the ball community have adopted both the identity label and the language of transgender.[13] At the same time, however, to presume that those not yet educated in the issues are not fully aware of their true identities risks the trap of "false consciousness" and assumes that there is only one way to understand, describe, or experience what may be labeled "transgender." What then are we to make of fem queens and butches who refer to themselves as gay?

On Being Gay: Class, Race, and Difference

What brings both the above ethnographic anecdotes together is the different use of specific identity labels that are often seen within queer politics and queer scholarship to be based on separate originary experiences. How is it that the HRC is able to rhetorically claim it is "not about gender" and that transgender people are not within its purview but that Junior Labeja is able to refer to what might be called transgender men (in other circumstances) as lesbians? How is it that butches and fem lesbians (both female-bodied people) and fem queens and butch queens (male-bodied people) are seen in the ball community as all being simply gay, while GIP proposes a radical distinction between fem lesbians and butch queens as gay and fem queens and butches as transgender?

I want to argue that in these two accounts, "gay" has different meanings that arise from a particular history of the term in the twentieth century and the development of the concept transgender in the 1990s. This history is marked by a separation of experiences of sexuality and gender in emerging cultural, political, and theoretical discourses and practices as well as in psychiatric diagnostic categories (Valentine 2000). But it is also a history that hides other organizations of gender and sexuality, and one that resists a class, race, and cultural analysis.

In her always quotable "Thinking Sex," Gayle Rubin notes that however much sexuality and gender are related experiences "they form the basis of two distinct arenas of social practice" (1984:308). Writing in the context of the debates between anti-pornography and sexual liberationist feminisms, Rubin seeks to "challenge the assumption that feminism is or should be the privileged site of a theory of sexuality" (307). This argument has formed the basis for a very productive analytical separation of gender and sexuality as different realms of human experience. From this perspective, a person's gender and sexuality do not necessarily have anything to do with one another.[14] Although this observation has been invaluable for separating gender from sexuality in theoretical and political terms, it also engages a central element of gay and lesbian politics since the mid-1970s:

that gay and lesbian identities are "about sexuality" and cannot be explained by reference to gender.

From another perspective, Shannon Minter has argued persuasively for a history of "gay" that has not only social and theoretical but also legal and political roots. Minter's (n.d.) argument is that gay and lesbian activists have sought to define "gay," particularly in the realm of legal precedent and legislation, as being "the same" as heterosexuality "but for" the one fact of desire (see also Vaid 1995). That is, homosexuality is seen to reside in the realm of sexuality and not gender. Minter's discussion echoes historical and ethnographic accounts of homosexuality in the United States from the turn of the twentieth century. Chauncey (1994) describes the ways in which some early-twentieth-century homosexual subjectivities were formed in opposition to medical and popular discourses that linked homosexuality to feminine gender (see also D'Emilio 1983) and the ways in which "fairies" (homosexual men who displayed feminine or effeminate characteristics) were spurned by mainly white, middle-class, gay men who developed subjectivities based on a gender-normative understanding of their same-sex desire. "Only in the 1930s, 1940s and 1950s," Chauncey observes, "did the now-conventional division of men into 'homosexuals' and 'heterosexuals,' based on the sex of their sexual partners, replace the division of men into 'fairies' and 'normal' men as the basis of their imaginary gender status as the hegemonic way of understanding sexuality. Moreover, the transition from one sexual regime to the next was an uneven process, marked by significant class and ethnic differences" (1994:13).

Accounts of the homophile movement of the 1950s—in particular of the Mattachine Society—casts further light on this process. The pressure by white, middle-class members of the newly established society on its leftist, and in some cases communist party–member, founders to abandon its radical politics was not only a response to McCarthyism (D'Emilio 1983; Katz 1976) but also to the broader theme of "mainstreaming" that Vaid identifies as a strong undercurrent in gay and lesbian politics.

As other ethnohistorical accounts show, the gender-sexuality nexus is implicitly connected to issues of class and race. In their study of working-class butch-fem communities in Buffalo, New York, Kennedy and Davis (1993) demonstrate how an insistence on a lesbian identity in the 1960s and 1970s, distinct from gendered butch-fem roles, resulted in "'the lesbian' [becoming] white and middle class." Likewise, in her study of Cherry Grove, a gay community on Fire Island near New York City, Newton describes how tensions between the more established Cherry Grove and the newer communi-

ty of The Pines was structured, at least in part, by class and gender conformity. "In the 1960s," she writes, "the 'blatant' [i.e., gender (non)-conformi-
ty] issue got entangled with the class and ethnicity of the gays and lesbians
who were going to the Grove. Ultimately, Pines property values soared; class,
ethnicity, 'blatant' all-gayness, and lower house prices all merged into the
perception that being closeted in the Pines meant higher property values"
(1994:275).

The historical unevenness of the process whereby "gay" has come to
index gender-normativity is further apparent in an autobiographical account
of Jayne County, a transexual woman and musician who writes of Atlanta
in the 1960s: "There were certain divisions in the gay world even then, but
we didn't have the words for them. Everyone was just gay as far as we were
concerned; that was the word we used. . . . It didn't matter whether you were
a very straight gay man, or a screaming street queen, or a full-time drag
queen, or a transsexual who wanted to have a sex change: you were gay"
(1995:29–30).

It is significant that County refers to "straight" gay men.[15] As the historical studies I have cited make clear, the ejection of a gendered explanation
of homosexuality—and the assertion of essentialized sexual identity—has
been a key element of much gay and lesbian scholarship, politics, and activism for decades. Lesbians, engaged in debates within feminism, have had
a more complex history of dealing with the distinction between sexuality and
gender. Indeed, the gender-normativizing push of lesbian separatism in the
1970s and 1980s insisted on a similar essentializing of the category *woman,* one that led to the exclusion of transexual women from many lesbian
organizations and events (see also Kennedy and Davis 1993).[16] As lesbian
separatism waned as the predominant form of lesbian politics in the 1990s,
however, the model of "gay," implying a "gender-appropriateness" and
"sameness," developed primarily from a gay male model. Indeed, D'Amato's
endorsement by HRC is one indicator of that process. In HRC's understanding, D'Amato's (alleged) support of gay and lesbian issues was separate from
his position on abortion. Lesbians, in this view, are understood in terms of
their sexual desires and not in terms of their experiences as mothers who
demand reproductive rights, a "gender" issue.

Consequently, in contemporary mainstream gay and lesbian politics an
assumption of "sameness" is employed not only to imply gender-appropriateness to both partners in a gay or lesbian relationship (sexual or romantic)
but also, more complexly, the sameness of the gay person to heterosexual
people. The political mobilization of sameness is a central feature of nation-

al political battles being fought on the turf of traditional "family values": kinship, marriage, and the recognition of a gay or lesbian partner as equally deserving of spousal benefits (Lewin 1993, 1998; Weston 1991). In these discourses, difference is relegated to one realm, sexuality, indexed as private in U.S. culture. By removing difference to the private space of sexuality, the difference in "gay" thus becomes invisible.[17] I am not trying to imply that such an idea is uniformly accepted or that gay men and lesbians have, by force of this argument, won the kinds of civil rights battles that are currently being waged. As debates in the gay and lesbian press over public sexuality and HIV transmission indicate, however, the gay male community in particular is ambivalent about how to negotiate the meanings of sex and the realm in which it should be practiced (Rotello 1997). Therefore, the marketing of this brand of "gay" not only erases the differently gendered person but also the person who does not "do" their sexuality, the realm of "gay," in an acceptably private way (Lewin 1998; see also Bawer, ed. 1996; Sullivan 1995).

Sameness also operates along other lines. While "gay" and "transgender" have become movements about sexuality and gender identity respectively, other elements of social difference—class, race, and cultural differences—are made invisible through the mobilization of such labels. Since the late 1960s a national gay and lesbian politics has grown alongside other shifts in the broader queer community and in U.S. culture, particularly with the increasing number of queer people of color in the United States from Asia, Africa, and South and Central America. Even as a gay male clone, the supremely masculine gay man, was hitting gay bars in the 1970s (Levine 1998), queers from outside the United States, who had their own understandings of gender and sexuality, were arriving. As Manalansan (1997) points out in his discussion of Filipino immigrants to the United States, American discourses of gender normativity as central to gay identity cannot make sense of other systems that conceptualize gender and sexuality quite differently. His fine analysis shows how the internationalization of gay rights discourse posits a teleological shift from "premodern" (implicitly non-Western) conceptions of gender-inflected homosexuality to "modern" Western gay identities where normative gender is the underpinning assumption of gay identity. He writes that this conceptualization of "gay" is only "meaningful within the context of the emergence of bourgeois civil society and the formation of the individual subject that really only occurs with capitalist and Western expansion" (488).

That the clone is essentially a white gay male figure (middle class in origin although emulating working-class styles) is significant, particularly as the beginning of the commodification of gay identities in the 1970s and

1980s required a relatively prosperous base in order to succeed (Castells 1983). As Amory has pointed out, the idea that the gay community is relatively more prosperous than the rest of society may mean that queers who are poor are not being counted (1996:155n26; see also Badgett 1998; and Maskovsky in this volume). Understandings of gender and sexuality that come from sources outside the United States are drowned out by imperatives of national strategizing and, importantly, the commodification of what it means to be gay in these contexts: gender-normative, white, and middle class.

Within non-immigrant communities of color in the United States, however, there are also challenges to the (relatively) powerful national discourses of "gay." To return to the Legends' Ball, among male-embodied persons in the ball scene—that is, people born with male genitalia—the distinction made is not between gay men and transgender women but between butch queens and fem queens. A butch queen might be described (to use County's term) as a "straight gay man." Indeed, the category of "butch queen realness" is a complex statement of gender and sexual meanings. Winners of this category are those who can pass as straight men, the implication being that gay men need to work in order to gender themselves masculine. Yet the implicit work for a fem queen in the "fem queen realness" category is in the necessity to pass as a woman in a hostile world. In the same way that butches are seen as lesbians by Junior Labeja, however, both fem queens and butch queens are seen as "gay."

The identities and experiences of ball partipants is a complex issue. Some fem queens consistently referred to their conception of self as "gay" and their gender identity as male—or at least as "not woman" (cf. Kulick 1998). As one participant told me, "I know I'm not a woman, I'm gay. I know what I am," echoing a common phrase I heard throughout my research. Yet people like Fiona also refer to themselves as "women" as well as "gay." Versed as I was at the beginning of my fieldwork in the discourses of the transgender and gay movements, I was often disconcerted by fem queens' assertions of a female name, gender presentation, and, sometimes, of womanhood, while at the same time, referring to their genitalia as the essential truth of their gender identity and sexual orientation (Newton 1979[1972]).

The apparent discrepancy between my understandings of "gay" and "transgender" disappears, however, if it is recognized that there are other ways of organizing experiences of non-normative genders and sexualities. In other words, at the balls, "everyone is gay," where "gay" *indexes any gendered or sexual difference that marks you off from heteronormativity,* a difference that can be named in a variety of ways: as gay, as transgender, as a woman, as a man, as a butch, or as some kind of queen. It is the difference *from* heteronormativity (rather than the difference *between* "gay" and "transgender") that underpins their organization of gender and sexuality.

This is a conflation of those categories of experience—gender and sexuality—that feminist and queer writers and activists have sought to separate out, but it is not a simple restatement of the traditional conflation of homosexuality with cross-gender identification. At the balls, masculine-identified homosexual men and feminine-identified women are as much a part of the category *gay* in this context as are fem queens and butches. Yet despite their unity as gay people (defined by the conjunction of their class and racial memberships and their non-normative genders or sexualities), they are precluded from representation in the contemporary mainstream understanding of either "gay" or "transgender." Indeed, they become unrepresentable in mainstream contemporary LGBT discourses precisely because national gay and lesbian politics has increasingly worked with a model of gay that implicitly foregrounds its similarity to heterosexuality while it simultaneously highlights its difference from gender variance. Transgender activists, lobbying Congress with all good intention, imagine that they represent the ball community in the same way that GIP imagines them to fall within their purview. Yet such representation rides roughshod over the categories of personhood proposed by the organization of gay at the balls. In so doing, it reiterates the structures of (relative) power whereby in demanding the state's protection, identity must be represented as being based on either gender or sexuality and is nonsensical if one claims, as does Fiona, to have been "gay all my life, been a woman all my life."

In short, the discourses employed in national gay and lesbian organizations not only exclude gender-variant people but are also formed along lines of race and class in complex and inter-related ways. This is not to say that organizations like NGLTF or the HRC do not attempt to deal with issues of race or (less frequently) class but rather that the very constitution of the category *gay* in its current usage depends upon a particular separation of certain human experiences that can be classified as gender and sexuality; that class and race are implicated in this process; and, further, that other organizational schemes of these experiences are devalued, silenced, or even seen as nonsensical.

This gender-normative understanding of gay is at the heart of the ENDA bill and has effectively further established a distinction between the categories of gender and sexuality. A strict reading of ENDA (if and when it is passed) would not necessarily extend protection to an effeminate self-identified gay man or a butch lesbian, for the HRC has explicitly rejected the inclusion of "gender expression" as a protected category. It is possible, therefore, to imagine a post-ENDA situation where an effeminate gay man could be fired with impunity not because of whom he sleeps with but because of the way he acts, that is, because he is not the same as gender-straight people—be they heterosexual or homosexual. At the heart of the HRC's—and others'—arguments that they are "not about gender" is what Vaid identifies as a central fallacy in the gay and lesbian movement, that "homosexual sexuality is merely the queer version of heterosexuality" (1995:44; see also Warner, ed. 1993).

Activists who work toward the idea of a transgender spectrum expend much energy in explaining why transgender isn't gay. But it is only because "gay" has become implicitly coded as requiring gender-appropriateness that such a movement has had to take form in the way it has. In other words, gay has developed since the mid-1970s in uneven and complex ways as a concept that means, implicitly, gender-appropriate men or women who have sex with, or desire, other gender-appropriate men or women.

A whole range of people who may identify as gay or lesbian—effeminate gay men, drag queens, fem queens, stone butches, and perhaps even leather men and women—are increasingly in danger of falling out of a categorical system that indexes gender-appropriateness, private sexuality, and ignores gender expressions and practices as elements of gay identities. The dynamic that Chauncey identifies as uneven—the establishment of gay male sexuality as distinct from feminine gender—is ongoing, as evidenced by the ethnographic accounts I have offered here. It has become even more complex, though, through the development of the category *transgender,* which seems to offer a place for those who fall out of this system. Yet those who should neatly fit into this category do not always do so and in fact insist on another interpretation of gay that demands that gender and gendered subjectivity be a part of it.

Drag in particular is a useful category to consider here. It is usually drawn upon by gender theorists as a way of indicating how gender is constructed and negotiated in performative contexts (Butler 1990). I would argue, though, that drag is more productively seen not as some kind of liminal zone between male and female or of how gender is performative, but rather as a site of disagreement and complex negotiation in the construction of what has become gay and what has become transgender.

The job at hand here is not to figure out if someone is "really" a butch lesbian or a transgender man or an effeminate gay man or a transgender woman, but rather to investigate the history and set of power relations whereby such disputes arise and such definitions are required of people—and what effects those requirements have. At least three issues of concern arise out of the data presented here: first, that the theoretical usefulness of the separation of gender and sexuality has had other, political, consequences; second, following this, those people excluded from the category *gay* have needed to develop an identity politics of "transgender"; and, third, that other organizations and understandings of gender and sexuality that escape the gay/transgender binary are devalued, silenced, or read as false consciousness in the deployment of a national gay and lesbian politics.

Clearly, the theoretical separation of gender and sexuality is useful in that it does explain and help describe the subjectivities of many gay men and lesbians as well as many transexual- and transgender-identified people. However, the ways in which this separation echoes the mainstreaming arguments of many national gay and lesbian organizations is problematic in that both discourses—political and academic—are unable to describe the subjectivities I lay out here.

On "Queer Anthropology"

The word *queer* has been increasingly used to bring together a variety of identities and also to stand in opposition, in some readings, to identity politics (e.g., Warner, ed. 1993). As with any newly emerging discourse, its meanings are contested, multiple, and shifting. In some ways, "queer" recaptures the kind of dynamic that County describes where "everyone was just gay." While it stands as a kind of unifying label, it is also sometimes used as a collective term so that "queer" and "LGBT" are interchangeable. My concern with some of the discourses of "queer," though, is that tacking a *t* or a *b* onto the list does not necessarily address the more substantive issues raised by the preceding points.

Indeed, my data suggest that rather than simply accepting "transgender" as a naturalized and unproblematic category to be incorporated under an increasingly nuanced queer spectrum, we should investigate the underlying history and assumptions whereby such a move is deemed necessary and desirable. To do that, we should examine the notion of sexual orientation or same-sex sexuality and the historical reasons that gay has come to exclude other meanings that have been, and in some communities still are, attached to this category of personhood. These reasons include political expediency, legislative imperatives, the devaluation of the feminine in U.S. society, and the development of a gay and lesbian market. Gay, in other words, is not "naturally" and simply about same-sex sexual relations between gender-normative people, but rather has been actively constructed as such and with a model of gender-normativity that excludes gender-variant people. It is formed on a model of (white, middle-class) heterosexuality and implicitly elides other organizations of gender and sexuality emerging from other communities, particularly communities of color. Most important, such a use of gay rests on a binary understanding of gender categories, perhaps the reason that transgender has had such difficulty gaining acceptance in historically resistant gay and lesbian venues. Included in these venues are gay and lesbian scholarship and queer theory, which, although welcoming transgender as a new and theoretically productive category, have yet to examine what is at stake in problematizing gay and transgender in the age of ENDA and a market for rainbow refrigerator magnets.

Having said all that, I need to return finally to how these issues impact on the realm of anthropology termed "gay and lesbian" by some, "queer" by others, or being denotated by the ever-expanding alphabet soup of LGBT.[18] The challenge lies not simply in incorporating diverse voices of people of color, non-Western people, and the economically marginal, and not simply in incorporating within scholarship people who are marginalized because of their gender expression. Rather, the categories of gender and sexuality themselves should be seen as available for investigation rather than being assumed to be natural, taken-for-granted, descriptions of clearly separable human experiences.

The anthropologist I quoted at the introduction of this essay also forwarded to me an e-mail correspondence with a person who supported his understanding of the analytical and political differences between transgender and gay identities. The writer argued that "a man dressed in a women's dress is less threatening [to a straight observer] than two men who look like Hulk Hogan and Charles Bronson kissing each other passionately." The point may be debatable, but I am after the deeper implication of this statement. The writer implicitly sees the man in a dress to be in the realm of "gender" whereas two men kissing are in the realm of "sexuality." The contention that the practice of two men kissing is not understandable within an analytical scheme called gender is not a natural fact but a constructed set of understandings of what practices and identities are seen best to be described by the category *sexuality* and what are best understood as emanating from experiences of gender.

Two men kissing or engaging in anal sex could as easily be understood as gendered acts as they could sexual acts. But in the historical distancing of gay male identities from concepts of femininity—and the general U.S. cultural devaluation of femininity—the former explanation has been devalued, and gay has been increasingly understood as being purely "about sexuality," the private, the unseen, and that which, if hidden, can make a gay person "the same" as a heterosexual person in realms of political, social, and economic influence. This model, flowing from a gay male model, has formed much of what the unmarked category *gay* carries as meaning. Lesbian experiences of gender and sexuality have been drawn upon less in this formulation, while at the same time their experiences are conceptualized along the same lines. Further, many of those marginalized along lines of gender, class, race, and cultural background are also marginalized within the category *gay.* Those who are gender-variant have been required by the political force of this discourse to create their own identity politics with its claims of ontological distinctiveness. The irony is that many of those whom transgender-identified activists claim as constituents do not understand themselves through this framework and so become unrepresentable.

Despite the differences, disputes, and debates within a broadly conceived queer community, these ideas still hold sway. The task for anthropologists is to investigate all these possibilities, including the one that forms the (shaky) basis for our disciplinary claims, that of the primacy of sexuality and sexual desire as the unifying basis for scholarship and politics.

Queer anthropology is perhaps most valuable in the possibilities it offers for opening its own terms for investigation. The issues I have raised have implications not only for how we think about gendered and sexual categories of personhood but also for experiences of class, race, and cultural difference. If queer anthropology is to address queerness, it needs to examine the underlying assumptions of the categories *gay* and *transgender,* not only cross-culturally but also within the United States. Perhaps most important, we need to investigate how gender and sexuality as categories themselves are described and used in theory, ethnography, and politics. Only then can we begin to examine the tensions and political possibilities that lie between occupying identity categories and opening them for a wider understanding of how all categories of personhood are contextually produced and reproduced.

Notes

Thanks to Donna Cartwright, Robert Lubar, Stacey Lutz, Bambi Schieffelin, Salvador Vidal-Ortiz, and Riki Anne Wilchins for helpful comments on earlier drafts of this essay and also to Gayle Rubin, Don Kulick, and Stephen Murray for their comments and input and to Ellen Lewin and Bill Leap for including the essay in this collection. Special thanks to Deb Amory for including the first version of this essay in the COLGIA panel at the 1997 American Anthropological Association meetings and for her extensive and thoughtful comments. Thanks also to Ellen Lewin, Esther Newton, Mary Porter, and Evie Blackwood for their input on the SOLGA vote and to Louise Lamphere and Mary Weismantel, who reviewed the manuscript and made useful comments. I am deeply in debt to Rosalyne Blumenstein and Barbara Warren of the Lesbian and Gay Community Services Center for their mentorship and for making this fieldwork possible. The research upon which this essay is based was assisted by a fellowship from the Sexuality Research Fellowship Program from the Social Science Research Council with funds provided by the Ford Foundation.

1. I, too, use "queer" in this way to describe, as widely as possible, the lives and experiences of people who might personally take on identities as gay, lesbian, bisexual, transgender, intersex, questioning, and other as yet unnamed but no doubt soon-to-be coined identity categories. I *also* use it to describe people who are queered by their gender expression although they may not take on one of the more common markers of queer identity. Queer, in this sense, becomes a locale rather than a marker of innate identity. A friend who is a car designer has told me that engineers in the plant where he works refer to the designers as the "hairdressers." We could use a queer framework to investigate such gender relations, although "queer identity" is unlikely to be claimed by any of those designers. "Queer" also has heuristic value, but as with any heuristic one must constantly be on guard that the usefulness of the idea does not come to stand for a self-evident or innate truth about the idea.

2. The changes in SOLGA's bylaws were prompted by SOLGA's acceptance into the American Anthropological Association as an official section in 1997 and 1998 and the structural changes that were required of the society in order to be included. The inclusion of the new identity terms seems to have been a feature of the historical moment of their writing.

3. The ballot on this issue failed by one vote. Sixty-eight of three hundred ballots were returned in time to be counted. Sixty-three voted yes to the amended bylaws, four voted no, and one abstained. On the question of the name change, thirty-four voted to keep the name SOLGA, and thirty-three voted to change it by adding more identity categories although there was no consistent choice. Anthropologists who responded to my queries gave several reasons for why they had voted no. The most common was institutional in that some members felt that the battle to achieve recognition of SOLGA within the AAA had taken so long that retaining the name was necessary in order to build on name recognition and retain and gain support within

the AAA. The links with the HRC's position, which I will discuss later, suggest a similar political strategy.

4. I use the prefix *trans* in constructions such as "transpeople," "transcommunities," and "translives" as well as constructions like "transgender people." This language is used within activist and intellectual circles in New York and nationally and is a usage I will follow.

5. The spelling of "transexual" with one *s* is a response to certain discourses within the activist community in which I conducted this study. The one *s* spelling is a textual tactic that transgender activists use to mark a difference—and implicit opposition—to medical meanings of the term, meanings that imply mental disorder and illness. I will also follow this usage throughout the text.

6. GenderPAC was the main force behind the Second National Gender Lobby Day. Other organizations involved, some of which were represented in May 1997, include the Intersex Society of North America (ISNA), International Foundation for Gender Education (IFGE), Renaissance Education Foundation, American Educational Gender Information Service (AEGIS), It's Time America! (ITA), and the International Conference on Transgender Law and Employment Policy (ICTLEP). ICTLEP had conducted its own lobby day in February 1997.

7. This paraphrases the position of the HRC with respect to issues of gender identity and gender expression in terms of their inclusion in ENDA. Although it is not a direct quotation from any HRC staffer, as far as I know GenderPAC members use it to sum up the HRC's basic position.

8. The reaction to the HRC's endorsement of D'Amato was a heated debate between elements of the gay community that see such issues as being linked and those who applauded the HRC's political "pragmatism."

9. Jason Cromwell (personal communication, 1998) has noted that he first heard the term *transgender* as a collective term in San Francisco as early as the mid-1980s. Virginia Prince is generally credited with coining the phrase *transgenderist* to describe a person like herself: Someone who lives full time in a gender different from the one assigned at birth but without surgical or hormonal interventions. I have heard "transgender" used to refer to such identities, but much more often during my fieldwork it was touted as a collective term.

10. The term *intersex* is increasingly used by individuals previously referred to as "hermaphrodites" in the medical literature. It usually marks a politicized identity and attitude toward the medical practices surrounding intersex infants, as with the organization Intersex Society of North America (ISNA). Intersex activists are increasingly making political links with transgender activists. A group of six ISNA members were present at the Second National Gender Lobbying Day described in this essay.

11. The program has seen more than a thousand clients since its beginnings in 1989 (Barbara Warren, personal communication, 1996) and is directed by Rosalyne Blumenstein, who supervises a number of transgender peer counselors and group facilitators.

12. I have seen both "femme" and "fem" used as adjectives in the context of the balls, but "fem," a usage I will follow, is more frequent.

13. In particular, those people are clients of, or peer educators for, social service agencies that do outreach to the transgender community.

14. That is not to imply that Rubin does not see the complex set of interrelations between experiences of gender and sexuality but rather that the effects of her and others' arguments have been to solidify in practice what was intended as only an analytic separation. My thanks to Gayle Rubin for helping to clarify these issues with me.

15. From my reading, County is not referring to heterosexual identity but rather to gender expression; the implication, however, is clear.

16. Many of these arguments hold no water for lesbian experiences. Indeed, one of the interesting features of the deployment of "transgender" is that some butch lesbians have found it empowering as a term in describing gender issues with which they must cope in the broader lesbian community (Rubin 1992). I do argue, however, that "gay" in the sense of referring more broadly to homosexual desire has been de-gendered through a deployment of white, middle-class, gay male concerns in national discourses on homosexuality.

17. The national attention to the sexual relationship between President Bill Clinton and White House intern Monica Lewinsky serves as an example. Although some of the president's detractors considered this activity itself cause enough for his removal from office, most House and Senate Republicans who called for his resignation or removal specifically cited the fact that he had lied about the affair in Grand Jury testimony as the reason, not the affair itself. The investigation, impeachment, and eventual acquittal of the president could be seen as a case study in the meanings attached to sex, sexuality, and the realm of the private in the United States.

18. One participant's (tongue-in-cheek) coinage is LGBTQQIW (lesbian, gay, bisexual, transgender, queer, questioning, intersex, and whatever).

References Cited

Amory, Deborah P. 1996. "Club Q: Dancing with (a) Difference." In *Inventing Lesbian Cultures in America,* ed. Ellen Lewin, 145–60. Boston: Beacon Press.

Badgett, M. V. Lee. 1998. *Income Inflation: The Myth of Affluence among Gay, Lesbian, and Bisexual Americans.* Washington, D.C.: The Policy institute of the National Gay and Lesbian Task Force and the Institute for Gay and Lesbian Strategic Studies. Web-site at <http://www.ngltf.org/downloads/income.pdf>.

Bawer, Bruce, ed. 1996. *Beyond Queer: Challenging Gay Left Orthodoxy.* New York: Free Press.

Butler, Judith. 1990. *Gender Trouble: Feminism and the Subversion of Identity.* New York: Routledge.

Castells, Manuel. 1983. "Cultural Identity, Sexual Liberation and Urban Structure: The Gay Community in San Francisco." In *The City and the Grassroots: A Cross-Cultural Theory of Urban Social Movements,* 138–72. Berkeley: University of California Press.

Chauncey, George. 1994. *Gay New York: Gender, Urban Culture, and the Makings of the Gay Male World.* New York: Basic Books.

County, Jayne (with Rupert Smith). 1995. *Man Enough to Be a Woman.* New York: Serpent's Tail.

D'Emilio, John. 1983. *Sexual Politics, Sexual Communities: The Making of a Homosexual Minority in the United States, 1940–1970.* Chicago: University of Chicago Press.

Elliston, Deborah A. 1995. "Erotic Anthropology: 'Ritualized Homosexuality' in Melanesia and Beyond." *American Ethnologist* 22(4): 848–67.

Herdt, Gilbert, ed. 1992. *Gay Culture in America: Essays from the Field.* Boston: Beacon Press.

Katz, Jonathan Ned. 1976. *Gay American History: Lesbians and Gay Men in the USA.* New York: Thomas Y. Crowell.

Kennedy, Elizabeth L., and Madeline D. Davis. 1993. *Boots of Leather, Slippers of Gold: The History of a Lesbian Community.* New York: Routledge.

Kulick, Don. 1998. *Travesti: Sex, Gender, and Culture among Brazilian Transgendered Prostitutes.* Chicago: University of Chicago Press.

Lewin, Ellen. 1993. *Lesbian Mothers: Accounts of Gender in American Culture.* Ithaca: Cornell University Press.

———. 1998. *Recognizing Ourselves: Ceremonies of Lesbian and Gay commitment.* New York: Columbia University Press.

Levine, Martin P. 1998. *Gay Macho: The Life and Death of the Homosexual Clone.* New York: New York University Press.

Manalansan, Martin F. 1997. "In the Shadows of Stonewall: Examining Gay Transnational Politics and the Diasporic Dilemma." In *The Politics of Culture in the Shadow of Capital,* ed. Lisa Lowe and David Lloyd, 485–505. Durham: Duke University Press.

Minter, Shannon. n.d. "Do Transsexuals Dream of Gay Rights?" Unpublished manuscript.

Morris, Rosalind. 1995. "All Made Up: Performance Theory and the New Anthropology of Sex and Gender." *Annual Review of Anthropology* 24: 567–92.

Newton, Esther. 1979 (1972). *Mother Camp: Female Impersonators in America.* Chicago: University of Chicago Press.

Newton, Esther. 1993. *Cherry Grove, Fire Island: Sixty Years in America's First Gay and Lesbian Town.* Boston: Beacon Press.

Rotello, Gabriel. 1997. *Sexual Ecology: AIDS and the Destiny of Gay Men.* New York: Dutton.

Rubin, Gayle. 1984. "Thinking Sex: Notes for a Radical Theory of the Politics of Sexuality." In *Pleasure and Danger: Exploring Female Sexuality,* ed. Carole S. Vance, 267–319. New York: Routledge.

———. 1992. "Of Catamites and Kings: Reflections on Butch, Gender, and Boundaries." In *The Persistent Desire: A Femme-Butch Reader,* ed. Joan Nestle, 466–82. Boston: Alyson Press.

Shokheid, Moshe. 1995. *A Gay Synagogue in New York.* New York: Columbia University Press.

Sullivan, Andrew. 1995. *Virtually Normal: An Argument about Homosexuality.* New York: Alfred A. Knopf.

Vaid, Urvashi. 1995. *Virtual Equality: The Mainstreaming of Gay and Lesbian Liberation.* New York: Doubleday.

Valentine, David. n.d. "Gender Identity Project: Report on Intake Statistics, 1989–April 1997." Unpublished manuscript.

———. 2000. "'I Know What I Am': The Category 'Transgender' in the Construction of Contemporary USAmerican Conceptions of Gender and Sexuality." Ph.D. diss., New York University.

Warner, Michael, ed. 1993. *Fear of a Queer Planet: Queer Politics and Social Theory.* Minneapolis: University of Minnesota Press.

Weston, Kath. 1991. *The Families We Choose: Lesbians, Gays, Kinship.* New York: Columbia University Press.

Wilchins, Riki Anne. 1997. *Read My Lips: Sexual Subversion and the End of Gender.* Ithaca: Firebrand Books.

NINE

A Queer Itinerary: Deviant Excursions Into Modernities

Martin F. Manalansan IV

i-tin-er-ar-y noun: a line of travel, route, detailed plan for a journey esp. places
to visit; an account of a journey; a guidebook for travelers.
—*Random House Dictionary*

One lazy afternoon in November 1998, I ventured into the Different Light Bookshop in New York City, which sells gay- and lesbian-oriented literature, and stumbled upon a tall bookshelf on which a sign indicated "Gay Travel." From established travel guides like *Fodor's* to makeshift renegade presses, gays and lesbians are being enticed and cajoled into exploring what is touted as an ever-expanding queer world.

This essay is in part seduced by such invitations and by a spirit of wanderlust. It is characterized by its listlessness and topical itinerancy.[1] Airports, visas, and other artifacts of traveling cultures punctuate my narrative, in addition to private and seemingly "localized" spaces such as households or apartments and bars. Multiple places are evoked often simultaneously— Manila and Manhattan frequently follow each other in a bifocal fabulation of queer lives. These seductions are based on my interest in examining how globalization, as evident in the processes of immigration, tourism, migration, and other forms of travel, have reshaped gay modernity if not totally transformed its contours.

Using a multi-sited ethnographic study of Filipino gay/queer men in Manila and New York City, I will examine the limits and possibilities of "gay community-building" by arguing that there is no one, monolithic, modern, gay identity.[2] Rather, to focus on experiences of diasporic Filipino men, there is an emergence of "alternative modernities" (Appadurai 1996; Ong 1999) or, more appropriately, alternative and abject forms of queer modernity. Such multiplicity of queer formations reflects not only the transnational crossings of gay cultures but also the concomitant and systematic proliferation of technologies, inequalities, and bodies that are part of postcolonial struggles in the third world, labor migration, and the political and economic struggles within communities of U.S.–based people of color.

It is imperative to note that the underlying yearning for transnational queer parallel comradeship that permeates this essay is tempered by the sociopolitical and economic realities of globalization. I am concerned with articulating the unholy trinity of gay identity, capitalism, and modernity as expressed in the experiences of Filipino queer/gay men.[3] I will also discuss and critique research on the transnational/global gay movement by demonstrating ways in which transnational processes and interconnections are implicated in community-building and identity formation, both within and across gender and sexual cultures.

The main body of this essay is haunted by the specter of home. Various constructions of home are both the catalysts and the results of cross-national navigation of political and cultural engagement of Filipino in various spaces. Home, which focuses on the poetics and politics of belonging, is never just about the nostalgic, utopian emblems of love and safety. It also concerns violence, betrayal, and endless maneuvering. That idea follows closely what lesbian Chicana theorist Gloria Anzaldúa (1987:19–20) facetiously yet meaningfully suggests: Homophobia is "the fear of going home." Rather than focus on a fixed spatial site or anchor for identity and belonging, I note the possibility of multiple sites for articulating difference and affinity.

Home, in this formulation, can be represented pictorially by a traffic jam in a busy intersection. The ethnographic interviews I conducted in New York City, for example, focus on the clash (if not head-on collision) of transgender politics in America, *bakla* cultural practices, and efforts at cultural translation. My focus is on the cultural dissonance that Filipino queer men who live in New York City and Manila face in relation to the gendering dynamics of racial politics in mainstream and gay America, transnational gay cultural circuits, and translocal conditions. Within this "cultural traffic jam," I will interrogate the ways Filipino gay men both in the Philippines and in America attempt to make sense of, elude, maneuver around, and create unique forms of engagement between gender and sexual politics in queer political organizing and culture.

An emerging body of scholarship since the early 1990s has attempted to engage with what is seen as a queer or gay/lesbian globalization and created a significant turn in LGBT studies. Suddenly, LGBT scholars found the world around (and the "worlds" beyond) the Euro-American gay and lesbian meccas and arenas. Immigrant, diasporic, and traveling individuals of dissident gender and sexual orientation have slowly flooded the academic seas. But what does the queer house of anthropology have in its coffers—or more appropriately its arsenal—that may enable a sensitive if not adequate response? In a world of globalizing processes and traveling cultures, how can anthropology, traditionally the space within the disciplines for the study of "incarcerated natives," allow a more comprehensive understanding of former colonials, racial, economic, and political others as they confront sexual and gendered marginalization? How can contemporary LGBT/queer anthropology navigate this bend on the road?

Still more recent work from other social sciences, including sociology and political science, has characterized anthropology as being a wayward discipline, particularly in terms of understanding the globalization and transnational circulation of gay cultures and practices. For instance, Dennis Altman (1996) misrepresents anthropology as dwelling on the local while other social sciences (namely his own field, political science) focus on the global. At the same time, he constructs the global through meandering anecdotes and musings on gay activism in Asia. In Adam, Duyvendak, and Krouwel (1998), queer globalization is presented as a panoramic survey of national social movements. The work is both admirable and troubling. Although there is need to take stock of what is happening to various national gay and lesbian movements, there is even greater need to be more mindful of those who fall outside those movements and exist in the interstices of the nation, both figuratively and literally.

Both works represent the emerging body of literature on queer globalization and reify the nation and the national. At the same time, they do not adequately examine the dynamics of diaspora and travel among those who are outside organized political movements. I do not imply the death of the nation and the beginning of the postnational in queer cultures. Rather, I will supplement and complicate the ideas suggested by Altman and Adam, Duyvendak, and Krouwel by focusing on the translocal circulation of identities and practices of Filipino gay men, both in the Philippines and in the diaspora.

My intention is to position the national on the margins and center the "global" or the "mobile." The nation is within the processes of travels and moorings that are implicated within and between national spaces. One way of negotiating these issues, and one of the pivotal contributions of contemporary LGBT anthropology, is through examination of conjunctures or the "conjuncturalism" of identities (Lavie and Swedenburg, eds. 1996). Most recent works in queer globalization fail to document and analyze the creative potentials and political possibilities of displacement and the critical negotiations at the intersection of competing national and cultural traditions.

To go back to the traffic metaphor as a critical intervention, I will map the critical maneuvers that Filipino gay men who are outside organized political movements in various sites need to create and execute for survival. In doing so, I argue that the bakla is a figure of Filipino modernity. The word *bakla* is the Tagalog gloss for hermaphroditism, effeminacy, cross-dressing, and homosexuality. Scholarly and popular works have constructed bakla as a premodern form of gender/sexual inversion and thus an archeological artifact or remnant of Filipino tradition.[4] Therefore, I will go against the postulation of bakla as a mere point of departure in a teleological narrative of progress toward gay modernity. I will establish the modernity of the concept of bakla through examination of Filipino national and diasporic queer experiences.

From Manhattan to Manila and Beyond: Home, Travels, and Moorings

Noong nag-go ako sa tate, akala ko magiging international beauty queen. Pero maraming mga disappointments, marami din namang saya. Pag minsan, dumarating nang parang bagyo sa isip ko ang mga naiwan ko sa atin. [When I came to America, I thought I was going to be the international beauty queen. But there have been disappointments as well as a lot of happiness. Sometimes, I feel a wave of nostalgia and the images of things back home hit me like a typhoon.]
    —Filipino gay immigrant informant, New York City

Ano? Mga kapwa bakla sa America—nagdo-do? Ay kanibalan! [What? Bakla have sex with other bakla in America? Oh, cannibalism!]
    —Filipino queer informant, Manila

In the performance piece *Cinema Verité* by Ralph Pena, a Filipino gay immigrant writer, the protagonist, who is initially denied a tourist visa to America by the consular officer, chains himself to a post in the U.S. Embassy in Manila and proclaims, "Long Live Christine Jorgensen." With that ploy he is finally granted a visa.

The protagonist's strategic deployment of the transgender icon Christine Jorgensen to enable himself to cross the political borders between the United States and the Philippines is a tactic that informs this essay in a myriad of ways. My interest is in the kinds of anchors—moorings if not chainings of identities—that immigrant (specifically, Filipino) "men" use when they live in New York City, having arrived with various baggage consisting of sexual and gender traditions, legal impediments, and economic strife. By "moorings," I refer to the important dynamics of nonmovement that communities of color must assume and create in order to survive.[5]

This section is based on a series of ethnographic interviews I conducted among transgender Filipino men between 1996 to 1999. The interviews supplemented my doctoral research on Filipino gay men and were forays into the seemingly binary issue of transgender practice and identity. The New York City–based Filipino men whom I interviewed are part of several communities of immigrants of color that are located in eccentric if not unusual places in relation to transgender identity politics and culture.

In trying to describe and examine these men's predicaments, I present a preliminary formulation of home—the metaphor of choice in transgender scholarship, biography, and debate.[6] Home in this context is a vexed, troubled space where the racialized, gendered, sexualized, demonized, and marginalized bodies of immigrants of color are placed and displaced. It is not a utopian summit—a climax of a teleological narrative of progress and triumph. Rather, home is fraught with power dynamics and is more than anything provisional and multiply inflected by position and stakes.

The travails of immigrant life intersect with cross-gender practices. Carl, popularly known as "Virginia Slims," works in a novelty restaurant in downtown Manhattan famous for its cross-dressing wait staff.[7] He obtained a permanent residency or green card through his parents. Once he got into trouble when a former employer asked for working papers to determine Carl's eligibility for employment. He provided the green card, forgetting that he had added an *a* to his name. The boss, furious, warned Carl about mutilating official government documents. "I don't know what the problem is," Carl recalled. "Isn't this the land of the free? I guess not."

Other Filipino gay men talked about the difficulty of presenting cross-gendered personas to employers and other "officials." Terry, another green card–holder, told me about his "transformation" or transition each time he arrives in the United States from a trip abroad. An hour before the airplane lands on U.S. territory, he goes into the toilet to remove any vestiges of make-up, tie his long hair into a ponytail, and tuck it under a baseball cap. The whole operation is conducted for the benefit of the immigration officer, who will need a living facsimile of a male in front of him to approximate the "male" or "man" represented on the green card. Terry reports being detained for several hours at airport immigration offices when he arrives in semi-drag. He has learned his lesson, he said. After his passport is stamped, he goes to the baggage section. As he does so, he takes off his cap, unties his ponytail, and loosens his hair.

Terry's predicament was challenged by a group of three interviewees who said that they, as Asians, can get away with being "a little effeminate." Elly or Elisa noted that many non-Asians consider most Asian men to be quite feminine. He described a famous Filipino female impersonator who had gone into a green-card marriage: "So Ms. Eartha Kitt (that's the stage name) went to his interview with those thin, plucked eyebrows—I wonder what the immigration officer said." Exotica, another interviewee, interjected, "Maybe the immigration person didn't care, or maybe Ms. Kitt was just another short, slim, Asian man."

Carla described a kind of M. Butterfly situation. A Frenchman had fallen in love with him after they bumped into each other on a sidewalk. They dated for several months without—Carla insisted with a wink— actual or real sex. "Call me the original Monica Lewinsky," he joked. One night, however, the boyfriend found out and became distraught. The couple still dated after that, Carla said, but "it was the beginning of the end." Whether fictional or true, Carla's narrative points to the growing self-consciousness among these men around the intricate links between race, sexuality, and gender.

For others, the role of gender becomes a matter of survival and located along other axes of identity. Ernie, for example, exclaimed in the middle of an interview, "I wish there were no need for working papers, visas and passports. One can go anywhere one likes—in Europe, the Middle East. I wish I was a citizen of the world!" Ernie, who had immigrated from the Philippines, blurted out these words after talking about his life in the United States. He would later tell me that he was an illegal alien, although he did not resemble any of the pitiful stereotypes of such a person. Ernie worked as a personnel supervisor, managing to rise through the ranks with his command of English and excellent work skills. Ironically, one of his duties was to verify the immigration and work status of each applicant and potential hire, yet he lived in fear of being discovered and his real status exposed. More recently, he has called to report that he found the best solution to his predicament—marrying an old college friend. By "putting on the clothes and assuming at least on paper, the image of a heterosexual man—a real normal man," he is now eligible to become a naturalized U.S. citizen in a few years. Ernie's wishful reflection is symptomatic of particular kinds of citizenship and belonging that are founded on the impossibility of specific kinds of border crossings.

Other issues of survival are equally compelling. Several informants have been involved in sex work, and most of them report being physically abused or threatened with violence by clients. Elly recalled a client who threatened to report him/her to the Immigration and Naturalization Service (INS). "How are you sure that I am not an American citizen?" Elly asked. The client sniped back that Elly looked, acted, and spoke like an "alien."

The informants betray what I suspect is true for many queer immigrants of color who are involved in transgendered practices and have marginal connections with established transgender/transexual organizations and cultural practices. They all had networks of gay-identified friends and sometimes lovers. There are slippages when they are asked to overtly identify, and most would perfunctorily identify as gay. Upon further prodding, however, all expressed disenchantment, disaffection, and alienation with gay identity. The terms *transgender* or *transexual* were mostly used to designate bars or parties and very rarely if ever to refer to themselves. The word *bakla* was used to differentiate themselves from others, mostly white gay and trangendered men.

The predicament of these queer immigrants of color points to delicate issues of belonging, citizenship, and identity. Performances of gender-crossing pose questions of survival. Whether confronted by an immigrant officer, an employer, an irate client or boyfriend, or even by various U.S. queer communities, queer immigrants of color are compelled to submit to various official and unofficial oppressive regimes of race, gender, sexuality, and nationality. In trying to settle into and find a new physical, psychic, and cultural home, they are redirected to listless and itinerant routes. The routes do not immediately or smoothly lead to a utopian homeland but rather to various arenas of struggle and contestation.

New York City–based informants who are Filipino and cross-dressers marveled at the kind of "market" and degree of valorization of *dragons* or *mujeristas* in the United States.[8] I first suspected that the informants saw America as the primary source of innovation and the arbiter of queer progress and gay modernity. I was wrong, however. Although there were discourses of America, the former colonial master, as the queer model par excellence, there were also moments of ambivalence that open spaces for critical engagement.

Many informants, for example, saw continuity with, if not recuperation of, bakla traditions. Roldan thought that leaving the Philippines would have allowed him to become fully gay, that is, a full citizen in the gay cultural and political world of America. Yet he found to his dismay that corporeal and racial politics created a kind of erotic recession. For most gay men, he became a marginal figure. He also found, to his astonishment, increased marketability—or, more appropriately, erotic currency—in cross-dressing. There were bars in Manhattan where he was courted by masculine-looking men and even offered money. During one conversation he realized that although he had come to the United States to avail himself (he thought) of gay life, he had instead stumbled upon aspects of the bakla life he thought he left behind.

Many cross-dressing informants like Roldan do not see their predicament as a utopic culmination of desire. Their narratives, although at times filled with hilarity and a celebration of queer freedom, are fraught with ambivalence and the realization that they need to create their own kind or "version" of queerness (i.e., their own formation of queer identity). This ambivalence is marked by a homelessness and fluidity noticeable not only by the queer possibilities of diasporic life but also by its limits and contradictions. For example, Carla used the word *biyuti* (beauty), which at first glance may seem to be about aesthetically pleasing features and experiences. In Filipino queer-speak, however, biyuti is about self-hood and its mercurial and contingent qualities and moorings. During our interview Carla stopped his usual chatter when I asked what he thought about life in the United States. He paused for a while and then sighed, "Sometimes, I know that my biyuti here is better off [than in the Philippines] but then, things happen. My boyfriend beats me up. My mother gets passed over for promotion because of her thick accent. Or my bakla friends are afraid of getting caught by the INS. Sometimes the drama is too much. My biyuti needs to go elsewhere. Maybe back to the Philippines. Who knows?"

The Filipino queers I interviewed in Manila echoed an almost similar ambivalence. In August 1998 I conducted several interviews with thirty Manila-based men.[9] I also observed various queer sites in the greater Manila area. Although the cohort of informants in New York City was greater in number, their average age was the same. There was a wider range of socioeconomic status, from lower middle class to upper class, within the Manila cohort.

In the next section I will present the results of the Manila study, not so much for comparison of two sites but rather to highlight the continuities and discontinuities of translocal queer practices and subjectivities. The exercise curtails any thought that a queer narrative of progress exists from the third-world city of Manila to the global city of New York or vice versa. Rather, a more detailed and critical understanding of the every-day travails and alternative politics of queer subjects of globalization should occur and run counter to and remain outside of more prominently represented political discourses of gay and transgender movements.

Nostalgic Longings: The Queer Erotics of Home

> Dapat ka bang mag-ibang bayan? Dito ba'y wala kang mapaglagyan? Bakit pa iiwanan ang lupang tinubuan? Dito ka natuto ng iyong mga kalokohan. . . . Mas magaganda ang mga Pinay. Sa bahay man sila mahuhusay. [Do you really have to go abroad? Do you not have your own niche here? Why do you have to leave your homeland? This is where you learned all of your mischief . . . Filipinas are more beautiful. They are also good in the house.]
> —Florante (Filipino folk/pop singer)

> Libog lang ba ang rason para magpirme ka dito? [Is lust the only reason for you to stay here (in the Philippines)?]
> —Filipino queer informant

Florante created what was considered the anthem of Filipino immigration and migration in the 1970s and 1980s. Focusing on what was seen as a male-centered flow of human labor and capital, Florante exhorted his heterosexual compatriots to think in terms of their privileges as men, including the right to have the "most beautiful women." That heterosexist admonition can be seen as a "natural" part of the rhetoric of immigration and migration until the tides changed—and an increasingly female outflow became very evident. Still, apart from the obvious kind of heteronormative reading that constructs the heterosexual male as being rooted to (if not a natural appendage of) the national body, a counter-construction happens outside the song, that of a figure of national abjection—the Filipino queer.

In this section, I explore how Filipino queers navigate their predicament, personas, and positionalities within and outside the nation and in the diaspora, specifically as those processes articulate the creation and negotiation of homes. The construction of alternative forms and a sense of belonging and citizenship is predicated on queer erotics and desire. Moreover, I am interested in the queer negotiation between the nation and the diaspora or, as some people would have it, the global. Two pivotal events during a visit to Manila in July 1998 helped unravel many of the issues under discussion.

Raffy, my long-lost high school classmate, tracked me down and visited me at my parents' house in Manila. The moment my mother left the room and we were alone, he lost his manly demeanor and started to speak the native tongue, *swardspeak* (Filipino gay slang). "Darling," he said, "it is totally different to come from America—right stateside—your biyuti is truly PX—as in made in America . . . American woman . . . American gay balikbayan."

How was the scene in Manila? I asked. "What scene?" he replied. *"Atse* [big sister], we might be the third world, but we do have the gay bars—darling, there is Giraffe—it is like—what was that bar you took me in my last trip to New York—oh yes, that glorious Splash! Too many queens with attitude—the same thing here except our own version has a dress code. Mama, you better believe it—whether it is a hot 110 degrees or a cool 80 . . . you need to be wearing a shirt with a collar. Darling, we don't kid around here. We don't wear T-shirts to the bars like your beloved Chelsea boys—we are decent queens!"

When I asked what else there was, he thought for a second and then in a modulated scream so as not to startle my mother in the next room said, "Massage! Massage parlors! Masseurs galore! You came right in time. Recession and the Asian stock market crash—your dollars are quite strong and will buy you a lot of meat. Big sister, for around eleven American dollars you can have your pick. Let's see, most of them will include the masseur charges, a cubicle, and your choice of towel, lotion, or powder. And darling for that price—you won't just get a massage—and who cares about a massage anyway. There are so many of them now." He rattled off the names of a few parlors. Many, strangely enough, had the names of pre-Spanish native nobility and royalty, such as *Lakan* (prince, in loose translation) and *Maginoo* (a nobleman).

While we were talking, the television blared with the inauguration of the new Philippine president, Joseph Estrada, and debates in the Philippine congress about allowing U.S. armed forces to conduct war games on Philippine soil. Raffy's only comment was, "Oh GIs! Here comes Victory Joe!" After we had talked for almost an hour, the television, which was on at the same time, shrilled out a news item about bakla who have converted to being heterosexual. Fanny Serrano, a famous female impersonator and hair stylist, was being interviewed. As he tried to dab tears from heavily mascaraed eyes, he declared that he was no longer gay. "Oh he is just being born again today," Raffy retorted. "Tomorrow he will be back at the massage parlors—I can guarantee you that!"

The particular route that my visit had taken brought several questions as well as an avalanche of competing images from different times and places. My conversation with Raffy elicited thoughts of GIs at American military bases, men long gone but pictured in gray photographs from the turn of the century or covered by the *lahar* (lava) of Mt. Pinatubo in more recent memory. I also realized that a trend among Chelsea gay boys was to wear military fatigue pants. Stringing those images together in a kind of linear connection would be too easy and neat.

Yet Raffy's shrill, funny voice and his welcoming gesture to so-called foreign forces drowned out the voices of Filipino congressmen strongly opposing the "rape of Philippine soil." The United States figures not only in nationalist sentiments but also in particular forms of longing for unbridled sexual fantasies and the creation of queer cultures. In this conjunction of events and images, Filipino queers, at first glance, seem to join other abjected figures, including female sex workers and mail order brides for whom America remains as the pinnacle of modernity. The United States seems to be the fulfillment of a yearning or lust for America, a virtual and real utopia for marginal people. My field interviews, however, created a more complicated reality according to those who must stay in the Philippines or have returned there.

The distance between Chelsea and Manila queer cultures is measured not only by miles but also, and more important, by disparate material realities and positionalities. In Manila, both Raffy and I are confronted with economic and political conditions that enable us as upper-middle-class men to avail ourselves of the pleasures of the city's burgeoning male sex work industry. In Chelsea and Manhattan in general, both of us, like my New York City cohort, are confronted with the racialized divisions of New York City gay life. Categorized as Asians, we are the minority in many bars. Because we have "Oriental bodies," our desirability and sexual images are either erased or fetishized in extreme ways.

Where does home figure in these gaps? Can I consider Manila, with its dramatic class cleavages, a home? Or is Chelsea, a mere six blocks from my present physical lodging, the quintessential home? Perhaps after years of study and work in America I have finally come to realize the inevitability of a queer homecoming. The choice is not mine alone. Many diasporic Filipino queers find themselves in this liminal position, which is neither temporary nor a final and utopian point. Instead, it is a dangerous space full of opportunities. Although Filipino gay men's abjection from the nation is fraught with oppression, there is also—as in any hegemonic struggle—opportunity for resistance, moments for unbinding ties and limits, and, most important, the creation of new spaces and new forms of being and belonging that depart from and go against prevailing norms. My Manila fieldwork experiences opened another space in which I can situate postcolonial yearnings and expatriate desires in the midst of fertile translocal processes of modernity.

Among the Manila informants, Odgie, a hairdresser in a small beauty parlor (the most stereotypical and maligned occupation in the Philippine queer world), stands out. He talked about how the city's newly emerging gay public politics has slowly constructed a world that might be—at most—ambivalent toward cross-dressing, effeminate bakla. At times he felt like a relic, unlike the upper-class couplings of some "masculine" men who he thought merely copied Western gay models. At the same time, he was optimistic about the changes, no matter how distant from his own experience. He was excited about the egalitarian possibilities of gay, yet he deplored many of its cultural and political underpinnings, particularly those around consumption and identity politics.

Odgie longs not for America but for the promise of a queer life imbued with some kind of equality between partners. He has been dissatisfied with a series of boyfriends, most of whom wanted compensation for sex and "affection." Yet he thinks (despite the monetary transactions) that these men actually felt deep affection if not love for him. He hopes for a day when the only kind of currency that would pass between him and his beloved would be of an emotional kind. Odgie believes that will never be possible unless economic conditions improve considerably. In the meantime, he seems, at least in his words, resigned to the particular social order of erotic things in Manila.

At the same time, Odgie is adamant, like several other Manila informants, that the shifts in arrangements he seeks are not the kind where the bakla just becomes the native gay or a gay facsimile. Odgie and several other informants who were well informed about developments in gay practices in America, Europe, and Australia did not feel colonialist nostalgia for the glamour of the West. Instead, they were suspicious, especially with the kind of open and public forms of queer identities. They also saw recent "copies" of queer life in Manila as more quaint than innovative. At the same time, many informants mentioned that unlike the early 1990s, when baklas were portrayed in emerging gay scholarship as historical or archeological artifacts, the attitudes of urban queers have changed and become more accommodating if not celebratory toward bakla.

Odgie's nostalgic longing for a specific queer future was not shared by ten informants who told me they were not looking for equality. They revel in the kind of transactions that occur between bakla and "boyfriends."[10] A bakla may indeed not have the economic resources to sustain a strictly monetary relationship, but, as several of them contend, there have been ongoing relationships that have survived such situations.

Elmer, another informant, claims that dreams such as Odgie's seem to deny the fact that there are advantages to be had, although some things may seem unequal or unjust. In monetary transactions, for example, a bakla can call the shots and make the boyfriend do his bidding. In other words, several informants did not find the egalitarian promise of Western gay modernity all that alluring. At the same time, they see the bakla as an active participant in his destiny and not "trapped" by "pathetic" longings. They mentioned and deplored the fact that much recent gay political writing has urged bakla to desire and relate only to other bakla.[11] Not only was that "unnatural," they said, but it was again trying to "mimic" Western gay relationships. "I do not believe," one informant told me, "that good relationships are based on sameness and equality. The real thrill is how to 'dramatize' your difference and get the upper hand when you need to."[12]

Commenting on Manila's Gay Pride Parades, which began in the mid-1990s, Arnel, a bank clerk, declared that he felt this form of queer life would not last long. When pressed further, he said, "Gay pride parades are fun. A lot of giggling and carousing. But after it was over, we are back to the same thing." Arnel was concerned with the class cleavages that divide queers in Manila. When I countered with the fact that a queer movement may bring about a kind of coalition or comradeship, he sighed and mentioned that it would just follow the same fate of the people power movement that toppled the Marcos dictatorship in the 1980s. People in power changed, but the conditions of the people did not. He was wary of the kinds of promises that queer political organizing may bring.

The words of the Manila informants echo in many ways the experiences of Filipino queers in New York City. Both attempt to recuperate particular versions of the bakla and at the same time contend with specific racial, economic, political, and cultural conditions. Nevertheless, they provide clues to the struggle for queer modernity in both sites.

Migrancy, Modernity, and the Mobile Queer: Alternative Formations

Everywhere, at every national/cultural site, modernity is not one but many; modernity is not new, but old and familiar; modernity is incomplete and necessarily so.
—Dilip Parameshwar Gaonkar (1999)

In this section, I read the ethnographic experiences in the two sites against the grain of a Philippine-based film production, *Miguel/Michelle.* The airport is the pivotal space that frames the film. It is the liminal space of comings and goings, of leaving home and homecoming—the iconic space of traveling cultures. Marc Auge (1995) suggests that in "supermodern" spaces such as airports and highways ("non places," as he calls them) community is absent if not impossible, and such spaces are incapable of nurturing any form of community affiliation. That idea implies a diminishing importance of community formation in the age of traveling cultures.

As the film opens, Miguel, the protagonist, is leaving, and in typical Filipino fashion his family and nearly a dozen of his friends come to the airport to see him off. Like thousands of Filipinos who have crossed the corridors and runways of the Ninoy Aquino International Airport for so-called greener pastures in different parts of the word, Miguel reenacts what has been seen as both inevitable and most sought-after: the performance of leaving home. The performance goes against the popular ideology Filipinos perpetuate of extended families or "sticking close to home."

Miguel, unbeknown to his family, has undergone an operation in the United States and is now Michelle. After several successful years in the United States, now-Michelle returns, ostensibly to receive an award from his/her old high school as its outstanding graduate and citizen.[13] What transpires after the airplane lands in Manila is a quintessential story about queer subjectivities and modernities in the third world.

Michelle rushes to greet his/her mother, who does not recognize him/her. She faints, and in the middle of the chaos that follows Michelle's sister asks whether gender transformation is part of the fashion in America. The town is soon abuzz with vitriolic gossip. From people who hang out in the neighborhood store to the puritanical women in Michelle's mother's group of friends, people try to understand this new, bizarre, and foreign being.

Michelle, having been imposed with the status of cultural and biological "alien," struggles to wrest her rightful place of respect. The film is about the efforts of Michelle and Michelle's family, friends, and hometown to become situated not only in terms of Michelle's new body but within a shifting discourse and the categories of bakla, transsexual, transgender, and gay. The struggle is not merely an attempt to pigeonhole a body or a person but to situate themselves according to elusive modernity.

When Michelle's old high school attempts to rescind the award, the board member who supported the nomination counters insulting innuendoes by saying that the board has no choice but to go ahead. They are, after all, "modern." The statement represents an attempt to grapple with a situation in which America is not only an arbiter or primary space for mediating modernity. The Philippines also can be a space for the kind of alternative modernity that exists, with vestiges of tradition or the pre-modern, for example, the Catholic church.

In Michelle's hometown, the church, the embodiment of tradition, co-exists with queer spaces such as beauty parlors and beauty pageants. A beauty parlor in Filipino queer cartography is the paradigmatic space of bakla, so much so that *parlorista* is another slang term for an overt, screaming bakla. In one pivotal scene, Michelle visits his gang of parloristas and is welcomed with open arms. In the conversation that ensues, the friends situate themselves within corporeal politics and reality. Comparing themselves to Michelle, they sigh that they are doomed to anal intercourse, or as they put it in swardspeak, "kimbash" (Kim Basinger). The star's name is used in reference to an act that amplifies what they lack. At the same time, they consider the West as a space for queer authenticity, proof of which is Michelle's surgically constructed vagina. Although their own local situation is seen within through Hollywood idioms, the parloristas are adamant about their commitment to a claimed space.

The conversation in the parlor traverses borders when categories are exchanged, bakla for gay and vice versa. Categories collide as in a cultural traffic jam. The semantic maneuvers the parloristas deploy are testament to their struggle with local conditions as they marvel at and deploy translocal and transnational icons and ideas. The parloristas are unabashedly bakla. They are situated in the interstitial and liminal space between modernity and tradition.

More important, a bakla is characterized in this situation as someone who crosses borders more efficiently than Michelle, who for the parloristas embodies Western queer modernity. Therefore, bakla, as amplified in their conversation and in the ensuing beauty contest, exist and survive the onslaught of the West and the burden of traditions. At the same time, the film, despite its utopic, naïve ending, and the parloristas portray home as a vexed space fraught with struggle. In the end, it is not the figure of Michelle the "transsexual" that emerges triumphant but rather the modern figure of the bakla, standing at the crossroads of nation and world.

In both Manila and New York City, there is a kind of reconfiguration and recuperation of bakla, not only as a reaction against the onslaught of Western gay and transgender discourses but also as a construction of difference and modernity. They are struggling to create modernity that is founded on a strong, culturally legible, figure of the bakla. The question remains, however, of how to harness the energy behind these struggles into a more fruitful social endeavor.

Queer political organizing in Philippine and Filipino American contexts has long been seen to involve separate processes and to work under different conditions. For many people, a kind of coalitional politics or convergence of these two seemingly disparate experiences (those in the diaspora and those who dwell in the homeland) seem impossible. In other words, how can these experiences converge in a project or projects of modernity? Gaonkar (1999) suggests that alternative modernities of non-Westerners can potentially work with and work against axes of similarity and difference. I am optimistic that this is possible in the face of the kinds of hybrid engagements that Filipino queer subjects in New York City and Manila are creating for themselves usually outside organized political movements.

An incident that made me hopeful about future possibilities occurred one day during my Manila fieldwork as I walked around the neighborhood where I grew up. I noticed that my crew cut, long sideburns, and clothes were attracting stares from people in corner stores. "Is he from around here?" a woman who tended the store asked loudly enough for me to hear. "I have not seen him here before." A man dressed in a frilly blouse, his eyebrows plucked, stepped out of the shade of the store's roof. He stood, arms akimbo, and said with a wink, "No, I have seen him before. I think I recognize him."

Notes

1. I am inspired by Louisa Schein's work (1998) on itinerant ethnography and cosmopolitanism from the margins, although I do not directly base my conceptions of terms on her work.

2. For a detailed discussion of multi-sited or multi-locale ethnography, see George Marcus (1998).

3. I use both "queer" and "gay" for the two groups of Filipino men in Manila and New York City. Queer is used to signify the wide range of identities and practices that go beyond the category *gay*. At the same time, I use "gay" to signal that this category is used, even if provisionally, by these groups. My informants never used "queer" in interviews, either as an identity or as regular terminology. I use "men" because although some informants did cross-dress and perform femininity in various ways, they all referred to the fact that they were men. No one in the New York City cohort was a transsexual. All reported having no surgical procedures done to their sexual organs. Two did report having taken hormone therapy in the past. I also do not use "queer" or "transgender" as self-avowed identities for these men. My use of *bakla* and "queer" parallels Morris's (1998) formulation of *kathoey* and "queer" in Thailand.

4. For a detailed review and critique of such works, see Manalansan (1995).

5. In a discussion that follows Clifford (1992), Homi Bhabha counterposes a dynamic of "non-movement" that most people in the margins must deploy in order to survive.

6. For an example of the uncritical use of home and borders, see Hale (1998); for an excellent counter-example that provides an illuminating critique of this stance, see Halberstam (1998).

7. All names are fictitious, and several identifying markers have been changed to protect all informants' identities.

8. These terms are used to describe cross-dressers in Filipino "queerspeak" or "swardspeak."

9. The average age of these men was thirty-one, and most reported to being lower middle to middle class. Three were beauticians, and twenty were white-collar workers, including clerks, lower-level managers, and salespersons.

10. For an almost parallel situation, see Don Kulick's (1997) study of *travestis* and their "straight boyfriends."

11. A critique of the Philippine gay political writing of the early 1990s appears in Manalansan (1995).

12. This translated statement from swardspeak and Taglish uses the idiom of drama, which for Filipino queers denotes—in this situation—a kind of negotiation and play.

13. My use of both male and female pronouns amplifies the dilemma of gender assignation and the pitfalls of translation. Tagalog pronouns do not inflect gender.

References Cited

Adam, Barry D., Jan Willem Duyvendak, and André Krouwel, eds. 1998. *The Global Emergence of Gay and Lesbian Politics: National Imprints of a Worldwide Movement.* Philadelphia: Temple University Press.

Altman, Dennis. 1996. "Rupture and Continuity? The Internationalization of Gay Identities." *Social Text* 14(3): 77–94.

Anzaldúa, Gloria. 1987. *Borderlands/*La Frontera: *The New Mestiza.* San Francisco: Spinsters/Aunt Lute Books.

Appadurai, Arjun. 1996. *Modernity at Large: Cultural Dimensions of Globalization.* Minneapolis: University of Minnesota Press.

Auge, Marc. 1995. *None Places.* London: Verso Press.

Clifford, James. 1992. "Traveling Cultures." In *Cultural Studies,* ed. Lawrence Grossberg, Cary Nelson, and Paula Treichler, 96–115. New York: Routledge.

Gaonkar, Dilip Parameshwar. 1999. "On Alternative Modernities." *Public Culture* 11(1): 1–18.

Halberstam, Judith. 1998. "Trangender Butch: Butch/FTMBoder Wars and the Masculine Continuum." *GLQ* 4(2): 287–310.

Hale, C. Jacob. 1998. "Consuming the Living: Dis(re)membering the Dead in the Butch/FTM Borderlands." *GLQ* 4(2): 311–48.

Kulick, Don. 1997. "A Man in the House: The Boyfriends of Brazilian *Travesti* Prostitutes." *Social Text* 15(3–4): 133–60.

Lavie, Smadar, and Ted Swedenburg, eds. 1996. *Displacements, Diasporas and Geographies of Identity.* Durham: Duke University Press.

Manalansan, Martin. 1995. "In the Shadows of Stonewall: Examining Gay Transnational Politics and the Diasporic Dilemma." *GLQ* 2(4): 425–38.

Marcus, George. 1998. *Ethnography through Thick and Thin.* Princeton: Princeton University Press.

Morris, Rosalind. 1998. "Educating Desire: Thailand, Transnationalism and Transgression." *Social Text* 15(3–4): 53–79.

Ong, Aihwa. 1999. *Flexible Citizenship: The Cultural Logics of Transnationality.* Durham: Duke University Press.

Schein, Louisa. "Forged Transnationality and Oppositional Cosmopolitanism." In *Transnationalism from Below,* ed. M. P. Smith and L. E. Guarnizo, 291–313. New Brunswick: Transaction Press.

TEN

Do We All "Reek of the Commodity"?
Consumption and the Erasure of Poverty
in Lesbian and Gay Studies

Jeff Maskovsky

Paulie (sometimes Paulina) sat across from me at a corner table at
the Street Eats Diner, a greasy spoon located in the heart of Philadelphia's
downtown gay neighborhood.[1] He lit a cigarette, took a sip of coffee, and,
with much flamboyance and flair, began his life story, which he told in the
style of the jaded drag queen:

> My name is Paulie Robertson. I'm thirty-four years old. I'm the youngest
> of seven children. I grew up in North Philadelphia in a fairly nice home, nice
> parents. Two-parent home until I was about fifteen. Then, at last, there was
> just mom and seven children. Went all the way through school. Graduated
> from school. And decided to start working. Then decided I wanted to hang
> with the in-crowd because those were the disco days and all that. I was fifteen
> years old. Phony ID and everything. I would just party hardy. I would go to
> Center City and party. I would go to West Philly to the Olympia Ballroom.
> Wherever the party was, that's where I went. To be in with the in-crowd, that
> included drinking and smoking cigarettes and smoking reefer, just a total

wild, crazy life. So, that was that. Sowing my oats, not knowing whether I wanted men or women. All that good old happy stuff.

In many respects, Paulie's life history resembles that of many lesbians and gay men, particularly gay men and lesbians of color who have come of age, and come out, in major U.S. cities. Indeed, as Paulie continued he noted the importance of the sexual-minority "community" in his pursuit of self-discovery and sexual freedom:

> In the long run, we all find out exactly who we are after a little while. The in-crowd, where I was going back in those days, was where you could just go and let your hair down and dance with other men and all that other stuff back then. You thought you were hot stuff back then. Didn't need that much money like you do now. And then I got with the transgender community, those girls in dresses. I went from the in-crowd to finding the transgender crowd, and "Oh, doll, you'll look good in make-up and hair and a wig and all that. And smoke some of this good stuff right here, and it will make you feel good, and you'll be Diana Ross." It was crazy but it was fun.

Yet for Paulie, the pursuit of community and personal liberation do not always index happiness and well-being. In fact, as Paulie told me, the more liberated he became, the more integrated into community, the faster his descent into material immiseration:

> So I thought it was fun. And one thing led to another. You start off with pot. You get tired of smoking pot. Then you want to drink beer. You get tired of beer. Do you want vodka? You get tired of vodka. Then crack came along. So you want to try that too. Back again, trying to be with the in-crowd. And things just got crazier and crazier. At that time, I was working in different restaurants in town, waiting tables or bussing tables. I worked in just about every restaurant, every good restaurant in Center City, from one to another. After you start doing a drug you're scamming this one and scamming that one. You scam enough people, and then you move on to the next place. Then when I started really doing hard drugs, which was crack, then it became prostitution time, because no matter how many jobs you've had, or how much money you had coming in, if you needed to put on a skirt and go in a corner to make some money, there I was. That led to about eight or nine years . . . eight or nine years doing that. Still working two jobs, still standing on the corner turning tricks, and it was just crazy. Losing jobs and losing apartments. And mother putting you out. And all that good stuff. "Get out. Come back when you get yourself together."

Paulie's life history is but one reminder that sexual minorities are not immune to poverty.[2] Although cities are traditionally described as places of sexual freedom, expression, and community for sexual minorities in the United States, the same political economic developments that have facilitated the growth of these liberated communities have also caused economic deprivation and immiseration for many sexual minorities.

In this chapter, I will place poor sexual minorities like Paulie at the center of analysis. This focus represents a shift from current preoccupations in the field of lesbian and gay studies that privilege narrow, consumption-based theories of identity formation and ignore class-based differences within the categories of lesbian and gay. Bringing poor sexual minorities into view requires rethinking many prevailing assumptions about sexual-minority identities, communities, and politics. In particular, this chapter demonstrates the need to attend to the ways in which ideologies and institutional practices of work and social welfare create cultural and material boundaries between poor sexual minorities and their more affluent counterparts.It sheds light on the heretofore ignored status of poverty in lesbian and gay communities.

I will locate the question of poverty within the larger context of neoliberal restructuring in the United States. Neoliberalism is the post-Keynesian model of the social order that champions unhindered market forces as the most effective means toward achieving economic growth and guaranteeing social welfare (Bourdieu 1999; Sanchez-Otero 1993). Coming to prominence after the economic downturns of the 1970s shattered the New Deal–Great Society coalition, neoliberalism has flowered into a broad political and ideological phenomenon. Among its hallmarks are the erasure from public discussion of race, class, gender, and other markers of inequality and antagonism; the cultural dissemination of market-based identities to co-opt and replace the social and political identities of the civil rights era; and a market triumphalism that places struggles for (and analyses of) social and economic justice and public welfare in the dustbin of history. "Free-market" ideologies of neoliberal consumerism are implicated not only in shaping the contours of gay and lesbian identity, community, and politics but also in the theories we use to explain them.

In this essay, I will raise three related issues. First, I will take a critical look at how the concept of consumption has been developed in lesbian and gay studies. Consumerism (consumption's ideological correlate) needs to be understood more broadly and more critically than has been heretofore acknowledged in most contemporary literature in lesbian and gay studies, including queer theory. Rather than treating sexual-minority identities as unitary identities forged in relation to acts of consumption in the "free market," I direct attention to the class dynamics that complicate and undercut the deceptively simple view of gay and lesbian identity under capitalism. Second, I will emphasize the connection between the production of poverty and the production of sexual-minority identities, communities, and politics. I stress how the welfare state produces different obligatory consumption modes for poor sexual minorities. Through the analysis of three case studies, I will show that consumption practices and commercial contexts are central in the lives of poor sexual minorities, but they operate very differently than for middle-class lesbians and gay men. The communities that poor lesbians and gay men form within commercial contexts are communities of workers not consumers. But when poor lesbians and gay men adopt consumer identities, they do so in relation to the welfare state not the ever-expanding world of retail goods and services. I will conclude by considering the ironic and even perverse consequences of neoliberal political developments, which include the tempered yet increasingly popular embrace of gay consumer culture, for poor sexual minorities.

Consumption, What's Your Function?

Foundational works by historians, anthropologists, and other scholars have identified the importance of urban-based consumerism to the development of gay and lesbian identities, communities, and politics (D'Emilio 1983; D'Emilio and Freedman 1988; Duberman, Vicinus, and Chauncey, eds. 1989). They have shown how sexual-minority identities and politics are consolidated and transformed through social relations forged in commercialized leisure sites such as bars, clubs, and theaters (Beemyn 1997; Chauncey 1994; Newton 1993). Kennedy and Davis (1993), for example, explore how working-class lesbian communities built around the bar culture of the 1940s and 1950s in Buffalo, New York, were precursors of the lesbian and gay liberation movement. It was in these bars, they argue, that lesbian identity was first consolidated and then transformed into political consciousness. Other related work in the field of lesbian and gay studies focuses on sites of commercial consumption—and for good reason. For most gay men and lesbians, workplaces were, and continue to be, the sites of extreme homophobia, heterosexism, and harassment. It is only in locations outside work, in spaces where gays and lesbians are relatively but by no means entirely free from harassment, that gay and lesbian identity, community, and politics have been forged.

Yet this approach sometimes overlooks the important fact that the commercialized sites of lesbian and gay consumption, whether bars, theaters, or even street corners, are also workplaces.[3] The bars and theaters that have helped to consolidate lesbian and gay communities are sustained by the labor practices of other sexual minorities, who typically are of different socioeconomic status than the patrons they serve. In other words, sexual-minority identities are constituted not only through the consumption practices of customers but also through the labor practices of workers. Failure to attend to labor practices has created an uneven view of identity and community formation in lesbian and gay studies. It has prevented the exploration of how relations of exploitation—based on the inequitable use of labor power for profit and, in the United States, structured along class lines that have racial and gender dimensions—shape the construction and politicization of sexual-minority identities.

Queer theory has offered an important theoretical intervention that is more suspicious of the identity—political underpinnings of community studies. As such it offers at least a partial critique of the consumptionist framework. In an often-cited queer theoretical statement on the connection between capitalism and gay identity, for instance, Michael Warner observes, "Gay culture in [its] most visible mode is anything but external to advanced capitalism and to precisely those features of advanced capitalism that many on the left are eager to disavow. Post-Stonewall urban gay men reek of the commodity. We give off the smell of capitalism in rut, and therefore demand of theory a more dialectical view of capitalism than many people have imagined for" (1993:xxxi).

For Warner, this more "dialectical" view involves elaboration of a politics of queer identity and theory as a challenge to "the regimes of the social" under advanced capitalism. "The social," as Warner understands it, is modernity's preeminent site of normalization, a discursive domain in which subjects are constituted as either normal or deviant. More than just defining itself against what has come to be considered "normal" behavior, queer politics and theory challenge the process of normalization itself. In this way, queer identity and theory offer the possibility of unmasking broader assumptions about the economy and the state:

> The social realm, in short, is a cultural form, interwoven with the political form of the administrative state and with the normalizing methodologies of modern social knowledge. Can we not hear in the resonances of queer protest an objection to the normalization of behavior in this broad sense, and

thus to the cultural phenomenon of societization? If queers, incessantly told to alter their "behavior," can be understood as protesting not just the normal behavior of the social but the *idea* of normal behavior, they will bring skepticism to the methodologies founded on that idea. (Warner 1993:xxvii, emphasis in the original)

As for others, for whom queer theory and politics have become de rigueur, Warner envisions the politics of desire as a challenge to the dominant organization of sex and gender, which in turn translates into a paradigmatic blow against society itself.

But do we all in fact reek of the commodity? And if so, how can the politics of desire release us from commodification as it is variously constituted under the regimes of the social? In answer to that question, I will make two points. First, Warner's assertion that gay men reek of the commodity because we are implicated in advanced capitalism's rampant consumerism is rooted in the conflation of the working-class people of color who rioted at Stonewall with the white, middle-class, "post-Stonewall urban gay men" who came to assume political prominence in the aftermath of the riots. What Warner provides is a narrative of upward mobility that sidesteps the race and class dynamics through which gay communities and politics are forged. As such, this narrative is entirely consistent with the ideology of neoliberalism. It is as if there is a monolithic gay community that, once racially diverse and economically disenfranchised in the 1970s, has since become white and middle class in the age of rampant commodification.

Second, positing queer subjectivity as an alternative to gay and lesbian subjectivity is hardly a solution. As Donald Morton (1995:194) has argued, a queer subject is also a commodified subject and thus an inadequate political alternative in and of itself: "Under the ideological regime of Queer Theory, the subject is—first, last, and always—the *subject of desire* who takes the form of Warner's 'cruising' (commodified/ commodifying) subject and Deleuze and Guattari's 'desiring machine' and lives for the 'intensities' of the moment. The queer subject is utterly distrustful (incapable?) of rational calculations which inevitably "constrain" desire. The queer subject is, in other words, the model 'consuming' subject for the regime of late capitalism."

Queer theory and queer politics are just as incapable as lesbian and gay identity politics of transcending the market relations that brought them into being. Moreover, they do not attend to the most fundamental feature of market society: class relations. Like lesbian and gay subjects, queer subjects are not only consuming subjects but also producing and laboring subjects.

It is in these realms that we can best understand the formation of sexual-minority communities and the trajectory of sexual-minority politics under late capitalism.

To take seriously the investigation of the relations of difference and inequality that adhere in class-based social formations requires specifying the ways sexual identity formation and politicization occurs in connection with the political economic processes of commodification. In what follows, I specify the class (as well as race and gender) dimensions of poor and working-class sexual-minority experiences and identities. The ethnographic data demonstrate that poor and working lesbians and gay men do reek of the commodity but not universally as consumers in a gay marketplace, as Warner's assertion implicitly suggests. Rather, poor and working sexual minorities experience commodification as workers who must sell their labor power to gay business owners or as "consumers" of publicly funded social services. What becomes clear is the importance of the role of the state in the production of sexual-minority communities, particularly those at the bottom end of the social ladder. Although certain forms of consumerism are out of reach to poor lesbians and gay men, others become imposed on them by the state.

Sexual Minorities in the New Urban Poverty

The growth of lesbian and gay neighborhoods and commercial zones since the mid-1970s must be viewed in connection with wider neoliberal developments affecting cities throughout the United States. Manufacturing plants left major mid-Atlantic, northeastern, and midwestern cities since the 1950s and 1960s, first for the Sunbelt and then for other countries. The shift had two major results. First, the number, quality, wages, and security of low-skill and semi-skill jobs decreased tremendously nationwide, especially in large urban centers. Second, the high-skill service and financial sector grew to manage, coordinate, and speed production processes that have become nationally and globally dispersed to an unprecedented degree as production has been relocated across the globe. As a result, many cities are marked by what Neil Smith (1991) calls "uneven development" (see also Brenner 1998).

In this situation, service and finance firms cluster in central business districts, sometimes accompanied by gentrified housing for employees and retail outlets that employ low-end service workers. Older, formerly industrial, neighborhoods are marked by declining social services, decaying housing stock, and concentrated poverty. Faced with budget deficits, declining bond ratings, declining amounts of federal assistance, and a loss of population and businesses, municipal leaders have been forced to pump a disproportionate share of public resources into relatively small targeted areas in the hope of jump-starting the local economy. "Uneven development," observes Smith (1991:5), "is social inequality blazoned into the geographical landscape, and it is simultaneously the exploitation of that geographical unevenness for certain socially determined ends"—in this case, neoliberal efforts to improve cities' images and, by extension it is hoped, their economic fortunes.

An emerging body of literature locates development of lesbian and gay communities within the dynamic of uneven development. One strand of the literature argues that gay men—and to a lesser extent lesbians—often take advantage of economic and social opportunities in developing urban areas by becoming urban pioneers and gentrifiers. They form residential and commercial enclaves that help insulate them from many forms of anti-gay discrimination (Castels 1983; Ettorre 1978; Lauria and Knopp 1985; Levine 1979; see also Bell and Valentine, eds. 1995).

Others, however, have challenged the putatively progressive, identity-based premise underlying this argument to show how gay and lesbian developers and small business owners place their class interests above the interests of a community based on sexual identity. Knopp (1997), for example, describes how gay neighborhood development in New Orleans was structured by class interests. Developers, many of whom were gay, sought to profit by building luxury housing in a gay neighborhood. This strategy of capital accumulation pitted them against middle- and low-income gay residents, with the consequence that the community became more stratified along class lines. Similarly, Weston and Rofel (1997:40) argue for a view of class as "property relations and the division of labor [that] continuously generates class divisions" in their discussion of class struggle between lesbian workers and owners in an auto mechanic shop.

These studies explore the class-based contradictions that emerge in formation of gay and lesbian communities and politics, and they do so by approaching class not exclusively as the outgrowth of consumption practices. Rather, they connect class to sexuality by examining how sexualized identities, communities, and politics are forged in contexts shaped, first and foremost, by the objective political economic processes that produce class relations. This view of community and politics—forged out of class and its connection to sexuality—provides the basis for my discussion of gay and lesbian poverty.[4]

Building on the work of Knopp and of Weston and Rofel, this discussion will show how the economy and the state (through the provision of social welfare) have become key features in the growth of community and politics for poor lesbians and gay men. I discuss several examples drawn from my fieldwork in Philadelphia that describe the making of poverty for lesbians and gay men. These examples highlight the importance of large-scale economic restructuring and the role of welfare-state policies in shaping lesbian and gay identities, communities, and politics among the poor.

Gay Ghetto Service Work and the Construction of Gay Identity

Drew is an African American gay man in his fifties. He did not come to Philadelphia from a small town in the Midwest, unlike the subjects of the migration narratives that are widespread in the literature on community-building in lesbian/gay studies. He grew up in North Philadelphia in a black neighborhood outside the city center. This neighborhood has been hit hard since the 1970s by the elimination of manufacturing jobs, disastrous urban planning, and the withdrawal of social services.[5] Drew left home at sixteen in search of "community" and began hanging out on Thirteenth Street, the heart of Philadelphia's main gay neighborhood. Several gay-oriented adult bookshops are located on the street, as is Philadelphia's largest gay bar and disco. Over the years, Thirteenth Street has become a major site of sex work for black gays and transgender men and women. For Drew, it quickly became a primary site of community as well as work; he soon began working at a gay bar as a female impersonator.

Drew was very successful as a professional drag queen and eventually earned enough money and notoriety to take his show on the road. For twenty years he toured as a headliner and helped other young gay men by hiring them to perform with him. Despite his relative fame, however, Drew always had difficulty making ends meet. Although the pay was good, the expenses associated with being a professional drag queen are quite high. He had to pay the other drag queens out of his own pocket, and he also incurred expenses for travel, lodging, and the materials used in making elaborate costumes. After twenty years on the road, Drew still struggled to get by.

Eventually, Drew stopped touring. Audiences, he said, lost interest in drag, and life was too hard on the road. The young men he hired often left without warning, and they often stole from him. He returned to Philadelphia and performed infrequently at local gay bars, which, he complains, now prefer go-go boys to drag queens. His connections in the community got him a job as a short-order cook at the Street Eats Diner, which is less than two blocks from where he used to hang out on Thirteenth Street. He makes about $250 a week, without health or retirement benefits, vacation pay, or sick leave. He has moved into a one-bedroom apartment nearby. Drew lives on the edge of impoverishment. So long as he can keep his job, or another one like it, he will avoid total destitution, but old age with minimal Social Security payments (his income was mostly off the record) will likely push Drew below the poverty line. Despite all this, he is still very positive about the gay community. "I learned to be gay on Thirteenth Street," he says. "I brought other young ones from there with me and taught them the business. It was crazy and there was a lot of fighting, but it was just my way of giving them a little fame."

Yet Drew is somewhat ambivalent about his work situation. As he explains, "I am the same as everyone else who comes in here [to the coffee shop] or who watches my shows, except I have a little bit more fame. The only thing that I don't like is that sometimes [the owners] don't pay you. They don't know how to run a restaurant or a bar, so they run out of money and you are out of luck."

Drew's story points to a number of important issues relating to sexual minorities at the low end of the labor market. First, his experience accords with what Weston and Rofel (1997:27–30) call "bridging the public and private" in the workplace. For Drew, as for the lesbians who worked at the garage where Weston and Rofel did fieldwork, working in a gay-owned business breaks down the binary opposition between work and leisure by bringing gay identity—so often theorized only in the context of leisure activities in the private sphere—into the public sphere of the workplace. It would be a mistake, however, to conclude that doing so is seamless or easy, as Weston and Rofel also demonstrate. As Drew's experience confirms, the politics of gay community mask economic inequalities in the workplace. His attitudes exemplify the uneasy coexistence of gay identity and class. By viewing himself as "just like everyone else," he deploys a universal gay identity. In nearly the same breath, however, he also recounts the relations of class exploitation that differentiate him from his employers and the (mostly white and middle-class) clientele he serves.

The story also calls into question the primacy of consumption practices in shaping lesbian and gay community. Drew's role as a female impersonator and his efforts to train younger gay men as apprentices provide an example of the importance that workers play in the consolidation of lesbian and gay community in commercial locales. It is often the sex workers, bartenders, barbacks, go-go boys, go-go girls, and other performers—usually from different racial groups and class positions than the consumers they serve— who become central figures in gay and lesbian communities and struggles. In Philadelphia's downtown gay community, for instance, Drew plays a pivotal role in a network of politically involved lesbians and gay men. His sense of community is thus an integral part of their identity—political practice.

Moreover, Drew's work history exemplifies the experiences of many men and women of color who find jobs in the low-wage, low-end service sector of the gay and lesbian economy. Gay and lesbian business owners often exploit wider labor-market trends with nary a second thought as to the effect on equality and solidarity within "the community." Drew's comments suggest that he has experienced a life-time of exploitation, including the refusal of several employers to pay him for work. In the name of the gay community, employers exercise entrepreneurial spirit on the backs of their workers, thereby reinforcing race, class, and gender divisions within sexual-minority communities.

Poverty and Lesbian and Gay Community Formation

What about lesbians and gay men who, because of constraints on labor markets, spend time outside the paid work force? For them, social welfare institutions play a significant role in the formation of community. In fact, publicly funded service programs often form the crucible in which community is formed.

Dawn and Sandi, both African American lesbians, grew up in poor neighborhoods in Newark and Atlantic City, New Jersey, respectively. Hit hard by the economic crises affecting inner-city residents in the Northeast, they experienced family lives characterized by extreme deprivation, violence, and abuse. When Dawn was fifteen she was institutionalized for a month and then thrown out of the house after her mother discovered her in flagrante delicto with a female babysitter. For her part, Sandi ran away from home when her father, after initiating her into drug use, pressured her to return to high school.

Both were addicted to street drugs by the time they were in their mid-teens. For decades they worked in the informal drug economies of Newark, Atlantic City, and Philadelphia. Dawn then moved to Philadelphia to get clean. She entered the New Directions Treatment Center (NDTC), an inpatient detox program, after several other attempts at recovery had failed. Sandi spent eight years in prison and agreed to enter rehab as a condition of her parole. Dawn had arrived at NDTC before Sandi entered the program. They met at a dance party sponsored by a recovery group spun off from NDTC. A few weeks later, Sandi volunteered to be Dawn's detox counselor. Thus, it was through the institutional practices associated with recovery—Narcotics Anonymous meetings, recovery dances, and peer-based drug counseling—that Dawn and Sandi's intimacy was forged.

Although the quasi-institutional settings of detox and recovery programs are seldom sites of anti-homophobic practice, sexual minorities such as Dawn and Sandi can sometimes take advantage of the presumption of heterosexuality to form gay and lesbian community ties there. Detox was a harrowing experience for Dawn. One of its advantages, however, was forced segregation between men and women, a situation that helped her get to know other women:

> For the first couple of days I laid in my own pee. I was a mess. And I had the shakes. I could hardly talk. The thing there was we don't talk to the men. . . . I didn't mind that part about not speaking to the men. I was real happy that the women could not talk to the men because I was gay and that only left me for them to talk to. And that was real good to me. So that stipulation didn't bother me at all. They [the men] walked on one side of the wall, and we had to walk on the other side of the wall. . . . And in the program I learned who I was. And I learned that I wasn't really really a bad person. I just never had a chance to pull it together. And I learned that I was an alcoholic. And I learned that I was also a part of Gambler's Anonymous. And, you know, I learned a lot about me. When I left the program I left there with more friends than I had made in my whole life, I mean, real friends.

I want to make two related points about Dawn's experience. First, for Dawn, recovery is interpolated through her racialized and gendered class position, which has compelled her to overcome drug addiction inside a detox and recovery program like NDTC (in contrast to, say, the Betty Ford Clinic). Inside NDTC, contact between drug users—most of whom are poor, black, inner-city residents—is highly regimented and severely constrained. This practice accords with wider cultural assumptions about the inner-city poor, the so-called underclass whose (hetero)sexuality is pathologized as one aspect of the "culture of poverty." The sexuality of the black poor—often implicitly characterized in poverty studies as "lacking monogamy" or, worse, "hypersexual"—is viewed as a causal factor in preventing their upward mobility (Wilson 1987; for a critique of this view of "underclass" sexuality, see di Leonardo [1997]). It is no surprise then that detox programs would segregate client populations along gender lines. What is surprising is that the presumption of heterosexuality—based in this case on racialized and gendered categorizations of poverty—affords sexual minorities like Dawn a limited agency to pursue same-sex desires.

For Dawn, gay identity has become articulated with the recovery narrative. The identity of the "recovering addict" signifies redemption and personal responsibility through the performance of one's mastery over antisocial desires. For poor sexual minorities, identifying as a recovering addict offers opportunity to refute "underclass" blame ideologies that pathologize the poor as lazy, violent, and sexuality deviant. It also enables them to forge gay identity as an aspect of the new legitimacy and respectability ordained as distinguishing features of recovery. This illustrates an aspect of the political economy of desire that has not been attended to by queer theorists who celebrate desiring subjects without reference to race, class, and gender. Moreover, it shows how the subjectivities of poor sexual minorities become implicated in wider neoliberal discourses of personal responsibility, for is not the recovering "addict"—a subject constituted through the embrace of the moral values of personal uplift, rehabilitation, and accountability—a model neoliberal subject?

The example of Dawn and Sandi also demonstrates the importance of race and class in shaping the cultural politics of controversial practices such as gay marriage. After their discharge from detox, Dawn and Sandi became central figures in a gay and lesbian community of poor, black, recovering "addicts." Their wedding, a ritual that occurred in a downtown Unitarian church in March 1992, served as an important symbol of lesbian and gay community for the poor. In a description of the wedding ceremony, which was published as "The Wedding of the Century" (Williams 1992) in a locally produced newsletter read by many poor sexual minorities, note how Dawn and Sandi offer the community an image of tasteful consumption. The account promotes gay respectability at the same time that it challenges the representation of poor blacks as deviant and pathological members of America's "underclass":

The royal court has assembled in the great hall. The women are flawlessly dressed in their finest attire. The men are handsomely modeling two and three piece suits in colors that shame the most brilliant of rainbows. The atmosphere is charged with laughter, joy, and a sense of celebration. The crowd waits anxiously for the arrival of the bride and groom in anticipation of the wedding of the century.

This is not the wedding of English Royalty or the climax of some happily ever after fairy tale, but the wedding of two lesbian women. On March 7, 1992 at 1:00, before family, friends and many well wishers, Dawn Sampson and Sandi Jones affirmed their love for each other. Their vow was to love each other with the seven types of love. The ceremony brought tears to this writer's eyes as the soloists moved the souls of the audience (which sent accolades rising to the rafters). Then we all vowed to support and nurture their union. At that moment I moved from awestruck spectator to an active participant in the support of not only a marriage but the affirmation of our Gay lifestyle itself . . .

My sincerest thanks go to Dawn and Sandi for allowing me to be a part of their celebration of love, and for being a positive example of our gay and lesbian community. The affirmation of self experienced at their wedding was outstanding. In a world where negative forces and homophobia abound, where racism, oppression, suppression and hatred are the norm (no matter how subtly); It is truly a blessing to be a part of what binds us together and encourages our triumphant survival as Gay and Lesbian MEN AND WOMEN. (Williams 1992:5–6, emphasis in original)

The wedding ceremony, as described, recapitulates bourgeois expectations of respectable desires that serve as the basis for neoliberal norms of consumer activity. Yet more important, the elaboration of community-building through gay marriage shows that poor sexual minorities are in a contradictory relationship to the social norms that seek to justify and excuse their impoverishment. On the one hand, Dawn and Sandi's wedding, although it displaces popular representations of sexual minorities as outside the normative assumptions about marriage and family, can nonetheless be seen as a capitulation to the bourgeois values of marriage that are sanctioned by the very state that oppresses them. This is particularly so because state institutions serve as major sites in the formation of poor sexual-minority communities and hence are much more implicated, in a pernicious way, in community-building practices of that group than in the community-building practices of their more affluent counterparts. On the other hand, the overwhelmingly affirmative tone of the report refutes the abjection that is often considered to be the essential

condition of urban poverty just as the respectability of the wedding ceremony disrupts the retrograde assumption that gay marriages like Dawn and Sandi's are further evidence of pathological familial dysfunction among the inner-city poor. Thus, the uncritical and arguably conservative embrace of gay
marriage in this instance disrupts the "culture of poverty" argument. It provides an important, albeit contradictory, basis for the poor, who are doubly
oppressed by social norms (in the sense that they are asked to conform to them
but their ability to do so is then put under intense scrutiny), to legitimatize
themselves in the face of a wide array of racist and classist cultural valuations that seek to blame them for their own impoverishment.

Poverty, Sexual Politics, and Sexual Citizenship

It might be assumed that poor sexual minorities do not participate
in lesbian and gay identity politics and hence are not political. My research
in Philadelphia, however, suggests that poor lesbians and gay men are indeed political. The dynamics of their politicization, however, vary significantly from those of their middle-class counterparts. Often, excluded from
leisure activities associated with the arenas of retail-oriented consumption
from which lesbian and gay identity politics was born, the politicization of
poor lesbians and gay men nonetheless relates to their consumer identities.
For the poor, those identities are forged in relation to the services of the
welfare state. A case in point concerns participation of poor sexual minorities in AIDS politics. In the following example, AIDS politics provide an
opportunity for political mobilization involving poor lesbians and gay men.

In Philadelphia, competition for funding between white-led and black-
led AIDS organizations has manifested itself in a political discourse pitting
"black providers" against "gay providers." The discourse was framed by the
state's model of structuring competing claims to political authenticity and
community leadership, which required emphasis of key social markers (e.g.,
gay, black, and Latino, women) in the name of communities affected by HIV.
This selective, asymmetrical, and nonsensical emphasis on sexuality versus
race as the central political struggle affecting the provision of life-supporting AIDS services had a number of consequences for poor HIV-positive
people. The harnessing of social identities conventionally used in political
mobilizations to "provider" identities has displaced a class-based discourse
and allowed those who identify as "providers" (the professional staff mem-

bers of AIDS service organizations) to gain prominence in the political field. As a result, HIV-positive people who are poor have been forced to adopt the identity of "consumers" of AIDS services in the context of battles over AIDS service provision. Although the adoption of this identity tends to mask issues of poverty, deprivation, and political exclusion by treating the receipt of life-supporting health services as a matter of consumer choice, it has nonetheless fostered and sustained key forms of political action among poor people with AIDS (PWAs), such as when they demanded an adequate HIV standard of health care as their "consumer" right.

The situation, however, has impeded poor sexual minorities from elaborating their demands to the state as sexualized political subjects. In fact, the emergence of consumer identities in the realm of the AIDS services system must be viewed as part of the state's effort to use service provision in combination with neoliberal ideologies of "empowerment" and "consumer choice" to promote self-regulation and quell dissent among PWAs. One aspect of this strategy of incorporation is that consumerism delinks gay and lesbian identity from consumer identity by linking it instead with provider identities. This makes poor people into desexualized political subjects in the language of the state. Said differently, the state effectively forces poor lesbians and gay men to sacrifice their sexual identities in order to gain access to the political process as consumers. Similarly, lesbians and gay men who rely on other public services are increasingly being recast in public discussion as consumers, thereby erasing their sexual identities at the same time that consumer-based political constituencies are formed.

Yet despite the desexualization of poverty in AIDS politics, many poor people nevertheless continue to see themselves as sexualized political subjects. Many, for example, refer to themselves as lesbian and gay activists after becoming involved with We The People, Philadelphia's largest coalition of HIV-positive people and one comprised predominantly of low-income people of color who are active and recovering "addicts." One such activist, Rose Williams, spoke to a group of low-income PWAs attending an educational program at a local AIDS organization:

> When I was in my addiction I didn't think of anyone but me. Now I think of myself and other people. I made a big change. I am proud of myself from where I've come to where I am today. I'm a lesbian, I am proud to say that. I'm one of the biggest lesbian activists in the city. I fight for us. You figure, you're black, lesbian, poor, got AIDS. They don't care about us, so you got to do it yourself. We have to empower ourselves. A couple of years ago they

would have said here lies a dope fiend who would have killed anyone who got in her way. Now I joined We The People and am an actively involved woman, helping people get food stamps, get medications, get health care. We all have a message, I don't know how long I will be here, but while I'm here I got something to do. My higher power has allowed me to be the type of person I am today, to try to help you help yourselves.

It is important to recognize that Rose's political subjectivity is complex. Her politicization as a lesbian is linked to her politicization as a PWA, as a recovering drug user, as a poor person, as an African American, and as a woman. This is but one example of how poor sexual minorities invent overlapping (or, to use the postmodern term, fragmentary) political identities born out of historically contingent and institutionally defined circumstances.

This leads me to emphasize the role of class in enabling and constraining gay citizenship in relation to AIDS politics. The AIDS mobilization effort of the 1980s brought about the establishment of publicly funded social services provided through organizations formed largely by activists who had fought for their creation. Most of these organizations went through a process of professionalization, where activists developed service-provision skills and certification and imposed professional hierarchies following increasingly formalized standards.

The process of formalization has had a contradictory effect on the promotion of gay citizenship within such organizations. Brown (1997) argues that AIDS organizations, formed initially as voluntary organizations located in civil society and then transformed into bureaucratized agencies of service provision, are important sites of gay citizenship because they serve as gay community-centered associations where volunteers come to participate as members of the gay political community. He adds, however, that these organizations have also become bureaucratic entities that disempower citizens by treating them as clients.

As Rose's story suggests, AIDS service organizations have, at least to a certain extent, became sites in the expression of gay citizenship for the poor. In these institutional contexts, however, the poor respond to the pressure to assume formal roles as clients, professional staff, or board members differently than their more affluent counterparts. There exists a wider array of privately controlled institutional locations in which it is possible for the middle class to pursue gay citizenship and for whom it is possible to take on a number of professional or voluntary roles within state-funded organizations. The poor have few options, however. They are more reliant on public institutions for services, and as these organizations become more bureau-cratized, ongoing professional participation and volunteerism by middle-class gay men and lesbians are more likely than they are among the poor. A disproportionate share of poor sexual minorities is forced into the disempow-ering "client" role in many AIDS organizations. Gay citizenship, as it is constituted in state-funded organizations, is a particularly tricky business for the poor because it is determined, first and foremost, along class lines struc-tured and reproduced by the state. Still, these organizations tend to serve as important sites of community formation for poor lesbians and gay men, even if they ultimately discourage gay citizenship by promoting clientism, or rath-er consumerism, among the poor.

Toward a Lesbian/Gay Poverty Studies

In this essay, I have attempted to flesh out the link between politi-cal economic processes of commodification and the formation of poor peo-ple's sexual-minority identities, communities, and politics. The implications of this argument for lesbian and gay identity politics and queer politics are significant. It is time to recognize that the liberatory dimension of lesbian and gay identity politics that was operative in decades past has been replaced in the era of neoliberalism by a politics of desire that remains largely un-critical of the commodification of sexual-minority identities. Likewise, al-though queer identity may be a necessary condition for building progressive political communities, it, too, is not wholly sufficient. Whereas the challenge to normalization envisioned in queer theory's politics of desire does move us beyond the minoritizing strategies of lesbian and gay identity politics, it does so through a heady idealism that replaces old political boundaries within sexual-minority communities with new ones. Whether one believes that gay consumer power (represented, for instance, by the Martina Navartilova Visa card or gay-oriented Budweiser advertising) will lead to increased tolerance and acceptance or that the rejection of sex or gender identity under the ban-ner of queer politics represents a radical transgression, both positions (which, tellingly, are not necessarily mutually exclusive in concrete political prac-tice) encourage the creation of commercialized sexual-minority subcultures. These subcultures—or, in neoliberal parlance, marketing niches—work in their own ways to mask the objective political economic processes that frag-ment sexual-minority communities along class lines.

That point is particularly salient in the present political context. The rise of domestic neoliberalism has been marked by a shift in health and welfare policy designed to regulate the poor through surveillance rather than supportive services. The shift is likely to have an increasingly negative effect on the community-building strategies of poor sexual minorities. Voluntary detox programs, recovery programs, subsidized housing, and other supportive social and health services have been scaled back as funding for health and social services associated with the welfare state has been withdrawn. In addition, public funding has been diverted toward expansion of the prison industrial complex and development of welfare-to-work programs. This shift places more poor people in daily contact with institutions that are, for various reasons, sites of increasingly coercive state control. Concomitantly, the collective survival strategies of the poor have been undermined by these shifts in social welfare policy, which have worked in tandem with wider economic restructuring to suppress wage levels for low-end workers to near-historic lows (Piven 1999). As a consequence, the poor are forced into even more dire social and economic circumstances. The pattern is likely to exacerbate tensions among various groups of poor people, particularly in the context of public institutions, with increased harassment perpetrated against poor and homeless sexual minorities a likely result.

Given that likelihood, it is vital that we make our theories and politics more meaningful for poor and working-class sexual minorities. This requires the reversal of decades-long trends in social theory and politics that have disavowed the importance of class, downplayed the importance of the role of the state, and avoided direct challenges to capitalism itself. Ironically, Michael Warner's "demand" for a more dialectical view of capitalism with respect to sexual identity can only be met by providing a more dialectical view of sexual identity with respect to class under capitalism. Politically, this will offer an opportunity to align lesbian and gay studies more closely with the working-class struggles that are once again on the move in the United States and abroad. In the current neoliberal climate, poverty is becoming invisible in both popular and academic treatments of urban life.

We should do our utmost to avoid collaborating with this new regime of disappearance. If we fail to contend with the material basis of poverty, and with the neoliberal ideologies and policies that mask increased inequalities within and without sexual-minority communities, our work will continue to ignore poverty as an issue that an increasingly large number of sexual minorities have no choice but to face in their everyday lives. But if we meet the challenge of a lesbian and gay poverty studies, our future contains the potential for a historical realignment with the perspectives and needs of a major segment of the population in whose name we carry out our work.

Notes

This essay was written based on research supported by grants from the National Science Foundation (Grant SBR-9632878) and the Wenner Gren Foundation for Anthropological Research (Grant 6107). A version of this essay was presented at the session "Lavender Language and Space: Multiple Locations" at the sixth annual Conference on Lavender Languages and Linguistics, September 13, 1998, at American University, Washington, D.C. I wish to thank Jennifer Alvey, Sidney Donnell, Bill Leap, Ellen Lewin, and Rudolph Gaudio for helpful comments and feedback on earlier drafts of this paper. I owe special thanks and a large intellectual debt to Sarah Hill and Matt Ruben, who helped me develop many of the ideas in this essay and who read and commented on many drafts. An earlier version was published as "Sexual Minorities and the New Urban Poverty" in *Cultural Diversity in the United States: A Critical Reader,* edited by Ida Susser and Thomas Patterson (Oxford: Blackwell Publishers, 2000).

1. All of the names that appear in this essay are pseudonyms. All place names have been changed as well.

2. A joint report published by the Policy Institute of the National Gay and Lesbian Task Force and the Institute for Gay and Lesbian Strategic Studies (Badgett 1999) suggests that gay men and lesbians are found across the spectrum of income distribution and may earn less than their heterosexual counterparts. One survey discussed in the report found that approximately 20 percent of lesbians and gay men earned less than $15,000 per year (compared to almost 12 percent of heterosexuals); another found that household income is less than $10,000 for 7 to 8 percent of lesbians and gay men (and approximately 12 percent for heterosexuals).

3. Lesbian and gay community studies, reflecting the dominant post-Marxist trends of the 1980s, tend to take as their starting point the highly dubious theoretical claim that consumption, not production, is primary under late capitalism (Bocock 1993; Featherstone 1991; Miller 1994, ed. 1995; Shields, ed. 1992). For a critique of this view, see Fine and Leopold (1993) and Smith (1996).

4. This approach departs not only from the dominant understanding of sexual identity in lesbian and gay studies but also from the typical treatment of poverty by anthropologists and other scholars and policy makers. As economic inequality increases in the United States, old assumptions about the causes of poverty have reemerged and are once again fueling new attacks against the poor by politicians, policy experts, and media pundits. Underlying popular and political responses to poverty since the 1970s is the well-known "culture of poverty" thesis. Originally formulated by anthropologist Oscar Lewis (1966) and disseminated widely through the Moynihan Report (Moynihan 1965), this thesis argues that impoverished people's anti-social

cultural practices prevent their upward mobility. The culture of poverty thesis, although thoroughly critiqued by progressive policy makers and scholars, continues to hold sway and has been resurrected and promoted most enthusiastically in more recent years, both in policy circles and among large segments of the American public. A more useful approach treats poverty as a political and economic problem affecting working-class neighborhoods, communities, and workplaces. Building on the work done by social scientists who challenged Oscar Lewis's original formulation, a new generation of scholars are challenging the newest versions of the culture of poverty thesis. By using theoretical approaches that situate different groups' experiences of poverty in dialectical relation to global, national, state, and local political and economic change and in relation to the interconnected ideologies of race, class, gender, sexuality, and nation, the new poverty studies treat poverty not as a static condition but as a dynamic, historically contingent process (Goode and Maskovsky 2001; Susser 1982, 1996; Williams 1988).

5. See Adams et al. (1991) for a description of these political economic developments.

References Cited

Adams, Carolyn, David Bartelt, David Elesh, Ira Goldstein, Nancy Kleniewski, and William Yancey. 1991. *Philadelphia: Neighborhoods, Divisions and Conflict in a Post-Industrial City.* Philadelphia: Temple University Press.

Badgett, M. V. Lee. 1999. *Income Inflation: The Myth of Affluence among Gay, Lesbian, and Bisexual Americans.* Washington, D.C.: The Policy Institute of the National Gay and Lesbian Task Force and the Institute for Gay and Lesbian Strategic Studies. Web-site at <http://www.ngltf.org/downloads/income.pdf> accessed February 6, 2000.

Beemyn, Brett. 1997. "A Queer Capital." In *Creating a Place for Ourselves: Lesbian, Gay, and Bisexual Community Histories,* ed. Beemyn, 183–210. New York: Routledge.

Bell, David, and Gill Valentine, eds. 1995. *Mapping Desire: Geographies of Sexualities.* New York: Routledge.

Bocock, Robert. 1993. *Consumption.* New York: Routledge.

Bourdieu, Pierre. 1998. *Acts of Resistance: Against the Tyranny of the Markets.* New York: New Press.

Brenner, Robert. 1998. "The Economics of Global Turbulence." *New Left Review* 229: 1–265.

Brown, Micahel P. 1997. *Replacing Citizenship: AIDS Activism and Radical Democracy.* New York: Gilford Press.

Castells, Manuel. 1983. *The City and the Grassroots: A Cross-Cultural Theory of Urban Social Movements.* Berkeley: University of California Press.

Chauncey, George. 1994. *Gay New York: Gender, Urban Culture, and the Makings of the Gay Male World, 1890–1940.* Chicago: University of Chicago Press.

D'Emilio, John. 1983. *Sexual Politics, Sexual Communities: The Making of a Homosexual Minority in the United States, 1940–1970*. Chicago: University of Chicago Press.

———, and Estelle B. Freedman. 1988. *Intimate Matters: A History of Sexuality in America*. New York: Harper and Row.

di Leonardo, Micaela. 1997. "White Lies, Black Myths." In *The Gender/Sexuality Reader: Culture, History, Political Economy*, ed. Roger N. Lancaster and Micaela di Leonardo, 53–70. New York: Routledge.

Duberman, Martin B., Martha Vicinus, and George Chauncey, eds. 1989. *Hidden from History: Reclaiming the Gay and Lesbian Past*. New York: New American Library.

Ettorre, E. M. 1978. "Women, Urban Social Movements, and the Lesbian Ghetto." *International Journal of Urban and Regional Research* 2(3): 499–520.

Featherstone, Michael. 1991. *Consumer Culture and Postmodernism*. Newbury Park, Calif.: Sage.

Fine, Ben, and Ellen Leopold. 1993. *The World of Consumption*. New York: Routledge.

Goode, Judith, and Jeff Maskovsky, eds. 2001. *The New Poverty Studies: The Ethnography of Policy, Politics, and Impoverished People in the United States*. New York: New York University Press.

Kennedy, Elizabeth Lapovsky, and Madeline D. Davis. 1993. *Boots of Leather, Slippers of Gold: The History of a Lesbian Community*. New York: Routledge.

Knopp, Lawrence. 1997. "Gentrification and Gay Neighborhood Formation in New Orleans: A Case Study." In *Homo Economics: Capitalism, Community, and Lesbian and Gay Life*, ed. Amy Gluckman and Betsy Reed, 45–64. New York: Routledge.

Lauria, Mickey, and Lawrence Knopp. 1985. "Towards an Analysis of the Role of Gay Communities in the Urban Renaissance." *Urban Geography* 6: 152–69.

Levine, Martin P. 1979. "Gay Ghetto." *Journal of Homosexuality* 4(4): 363–77.

Lewis, Oscar. 1966. "The Culture of Poverty." *Scientific American* 215(4): 19–25.

Miller, Daniel. 1994. *Modernity, an Ethnographic Approach: Dualism and Mass Consumption in Trinidad*. Oxford: Berg.

———, ed. 1995. *Acknowledging Consumption: A Review of New Studies*. New York: Routledge.

Morton, Donald. 1995. "Queerity and Ludic Sado-Masochism: Compulsory Consumption and the Emerging Post-al Queer." In "Post-Ality: Marxism and Postmodernism," special issue of *Transformation* 1: 189–215.

Moynihan, Daniel P. 1965. *The Negro Family: The Case for National Action*. Washington, D.C.: U.S. Department of Labor.

Newton, Esther. 1979 (1972). *Mother Camp: Female Impersonators in America*. Chicago: University of Chicago Press.

———. 1993. *Cherry Grove, Fire Island: Sixty Years in America's First Gay and Lesbian Town*. Boston: Beacon Press.

Piven, Frances Fox. 1999. "Welfare Reform and the Economic and Cultural Reconstruction of Low Wage Labor Markets." *City and Society* (annual review): 21–37.

Sanchez-Otero, German. 1993. "Neoliberalism and Its Discontents." *NACLA Reports on the Americans* 26(4): 18–24.

Shields, Rob, ed. 1992. *Lifestyle Shopping: The Subject of Consumption.* New York: Routledge.

Smith, Neil. 1991. *Uneven Development: Nature, Capital and the Production of Space.* Cambridge: Basil Blackwell.

———. 1996. *The New Urban Frontier: Gentrification and the Revanchist City.* New York: Routledge.

Susser, Ida. 1982. *Norman Street: Poverty and Politics in an Urban Neighborhood.* New York: Oxford University Press.

———. 1996. "The Construction of Poverty and Homelessness in U.S. Cities." *Annual Review of Anthropology* 25: 411–35.

Warner, Michael. 1993. Introduction. In *Fear of a Queer Planet.* Minneapolis: University of Minnesota Press.

Weston, Kath, and Lisa B. Rofel. 1997. "Sexuality, Class and Conflict in a Lesbian Workplace." In *Homo Economics: Capitalism, Community, and Lesbian and Gay Life,* ed. Amy Gluckman and Betsy Reed, 25–44. New York: Routledge.

Williams, Brett. 1988. *Upscaling Downtown: Stalled Gentrification in Washington, DC.* Ithaca: Cornell University Press.

Williams, Rodney. 1992. "The Wedding of the Century." *Alive and Kicking,* no. 6: 5–6.

Wilson, William J. 1987. *The Truly Disadvantaged: The Inner City, the Underclass and Public Policy.* Chicago: University of Chicago Press.

ELEVEN

Anthropology's Queer Future: Feminist Lessons from Tahiti and Its Islands

Deborah Elliston

At the beginning of the new millennium, numerous signs indicate that lesbian and gay anthropology, or lesbian, gay, bisexual, and transgendered (LGBT) studies, has become an increasingly legitimate subfield of sociocultural anthropology. In 1998 the Society of Lesbian and Gay Anthropologists (SOLGA) finally gained section status in the American Anthropological Association after twenty-five years of operating as a kind of organizational back room for lesbian and gay anthropologists and our friends. SOLGA-sponsored sessions at the annual anthropology meetings draw increasing numbers of presenters and attendees, indexing both expanding scholarly interest and accomplishment. And anthropologists can now much more easily than before publish works in lesbian and gay anthropology. There are recognized audiences to whom some publishing houses rather eagerly market our books, and a variety of journals and their editors interested in bringing this work into print. Although most anthropology departments have yet to designate tenure-track lines in LGBT studies (a fact that, combined with homophobias, makes job security now as earlier precarious for many scholars), there can be little disputing that the subfield and its practitioners are not nearly as marginal as we were in the early 1990s.

These are substantial and rather amazing accomplishments, and they have all taken place in the relatively short space of about twenty-five years. Before the 1970s and with a few notable exceptions—Margaret Mead (1928) comes to mind—homosexuality had a sordid history of rarely being studied by anthropologists. It was covered, when it was addressed, in tiny footnotes, lonely references to "perversions," or small handfuls of sentences fairly bleeding with dismissiveness.[1]

Of course, the community norms of earlier generations of anthropologists and the shifting particulars of Eurocentric homophobias before the 1970s deeply structured the quality and quantity of the possible representations of homosexuality as well as the contexts in which such representations could be made. Homosexuality was, at worst, the stuff of hallway conversations at professional meetings, sharing the corridors with tall tales of sexual adventures in the field and other gossip coded as illicit. In light of these squeaky silences, steadfast omissions, and uncritical complicities between Eurocentric homophobias and ethnographic analysis, work by scholars of homosexuality since the mid-1970s has fundamentally shifted the discursive frameworks within which homosexuality can be represented.

Credit for the increased legitimacy of LGBT studies in anthropology lies largely with those anthropologists who forged ahead in studying homosexualities in earlier, much more difficult, periods, often at great professional and personal cost. Without compromising their profound contributions and successes, in this essay I will consider a particular problematic emergent in the historical trajectory of lesbian and gay anthropology. With the goal of critically reconsidering what kind of future we want to shape for the subfield, what concerns me is a problematic engendered by the ways homosexuality has been inscribed and theorized. When it comes to studying homosexuality, we have come to think we know what it is we are looking for.[2] Instead of the earlier dynamic of Eurocentric homophobias setting the framework for understandings of homosexuality, for how and what (if anything) to write about homosexuality, it is Eurocentric homosexualities that have come to set the framework for recognizing, interpreting, and inscribing homosexualities cross-culturally.

An irony lies at the heart of this development. Although it may seem the very embodiment of progress that the subfield of LGBT studies exists in anthropology, many ethnographies of homosexualities cross-culturally bear more likeness to ethnographies written a generation or more ago than to the contemporary work of colleagues in anthropology. As part of the project of gaining legitimacy for LGBT studies, we have extended a category—homosexuality—to encompass an enormous variety of social practices, cannibalizing and generalizing that variety to fit its diversity beneath the sign of homosexuality. Yet in this same period, most anthropologists have been moving in the opposite analytical direction: deconstructing and further specifying the social practices that their (and our) predecessors had overly generalized under such categories as "kinship," "religion," and "politics." It is time for scholars in LGBT anthropology to do some deconstructing of our own.

In addition, and paradoxically in light of our discipline's historical commitment to specifying cultural differences, studies of homosexuality have by and large been complicitous in assuming certain features of Western homosexualities as fundamental starting points for our investigations and reference points in our analyses. The extent to which this has been the case makes it all too likely that anthropologists have been aborting research possibilities and sacrificing theoretical creativity by sticking too closely to Western homosexuality and looking cross-culturally for its cognates, relatives, and analogs. This is not to say that there has been no critical analysis of the terms and significances of the homosexualities we have studied. The development of paradigms that separate age-structured homosexuality from ritualized homosexuality from role-structured homosexuality, for example, attest to a serious concern with the varying social significances and structurings of what has been studied under the sign of homosexuality.[3] In this essay, however, I will argue for more rigorous critique and more skeptical consideration of the "homosexual practices" out of which such typologies, paradigms, and theories have been built: sex.

In making this argument I raise the potentially heretical possibility that, like "blood" or the genealogical grid in kinship studies, "sex" in LGBT studies in anthropology may well turn out to be a Eurocentric metonym. Its relevance to understanding what are currently counting as "homosexualities" cross-culturally may depend on and derive from Eurocentric theories of sex and everything with which sex is culturally made to connect—desire, erotics, intimacy, power, illegitimate relationship, and the like—to such an extent that it is of only the most limited use cross-culturally.

The counterintuitive question motivating this essay, then, is whether sexual practice is the appropriate touchstone for identifying and entering into the analysis of homosexualities. To give a classic example from Gilbert Herdt's (1981, 1984) work with the pseudonymically memorialized "Sambia," when young boys suck older boys' penises to get semen, motivated by fear of violence and the sudden news (forcefully presented by their elders) that without that semen the boys will remain forever "puny and small," is that sex?[4] In this essay I advocate reconsidering and renegotiating, at a more fundamental level than we have so far, the linguistic, conceptual, and symbolic disjunctures between practices that seem patently sexual to us in light not only of the local significances of those practices but also of the other practices that may, in other places, be used to convey erotics, desire, intimacy, commitment, illegitimate relationship, or any of the other various significances commonly attached to sex in Euro-American contexts. The problematic on which I focus in this essay is the iconic value given to sex in adjudicating the boundaries of LGBT studies in anthropology.

Heresy indeed. If not sex, then what? Here is where the emergence of queer scholarship and queer politics strikes me as of substantial use to anthropologists. Notwithstanding the (at times) enormous variety of positions and claims staked out as queer, at the heart of the best of queer academic work is a resolute refusal to establish a singular, foundational basis for queer identity and practice. And at the heart of the best of queer political practice is a guerrilla politics of tactics and moments rather than a unifying ideology and movement. These, it seems to me, are what anthropologists need right now. Embracing these tenets of queer work, I adopt the category *queer anthropology* as the framework for expanding the purview of LGBT studies, beyond acts and identities and into a much more open-ended set of concerns with, and approaches to, the ways in which sexuality, gender, power, and culture are produced and brought into relationship.

The various changes in the naming of our subfield and its practitioners since the mid-1970s have indexed shifts in objects of inquiry as well as in our self-understandings: from the anthropology of homosexuality, to lesbian and gay anthropology, to LGBT studies, to more recent debates over changing the name of the Society of Lesbian and Gay Anthropologists to better include its transgendered and bisexual members. Moving away from the identity-based, Eurocentric epistemology of lesbian and gay anthropology and into a future queer anthropology would seem to offer a promising framework for an expanded, more flexible project of studying the variable forms, terms, significances, and interrelations of sexuality, gender, power, and culture.

The vehicle for my argument for a reconsideration of the iconic value given to sex in queer anthropology is an examination of the complex relationships between sex and sexual symbolic economies among Polynesians in the Society Islands of French Polynesia, an overseas territory of France in the South Pacific commonly known as "Tahiti and Its Islands."[5] During my fieldwork in the Society Islands in the mid-1990s, Polynesians had a considerable variety of categories that could include the expression of same-sex sexual practices—that is sex between people who have the same sexed-body status (both female or both male in Euro-American terms).[6] They had the Tahitian-language gender terms *vahine* (woman), *tane* (man), and *māhū* (translated as "half-man, half-woman"), as well as the non-gender Tahitian-language terms *raerae* and *petea*. Polynesians also had the French-language terms *travesti* (transvestite, used by some as a synonym for "raerae"); *homosexuel/homosexuelle* (homosexual); *pédé* (pedophile, abbreviated but in common use a colloquial term equivalent to "gay [male]"); *lesbienne* (lesbian); and *gouine* (dyke). Although all of these categories allowed for empirically identical same-sex sexual practices, Polynesians were relatively embracing toward some of the categories and the same-sex sex these allowed. Toward yet other categories and the same-sex sex they allowed, however, they took stances that ranged from ambivalence to animosity. A central question motivating the ethnographic analysis that follows is, Why?

To address this question, I turn to what I gloss as Polynesian interpretive frameworks for understanding sexuality and, more specifically, the logical and productive relationships Polynesians forge between gender and sexuality. In this chapter, I aim to map some of the regions in the discursive field within which same-sex sexuality gains its meanings for Polynesians and, in light of this, to investigate why and how some significations of same-sex sexuality have recently emerged as problematic in the Islands whereas others retain a morally unproblematic status.[7]

In what follows, I detail the ways that interactions between local and transnational symbolic sexual economies provide both the resources and the contexts for Polynesians' interpretive contests around and differential moral evaluations of same-sex sexuality. In other words, the discursive fields within which same-sex sexualities gain their meanings are shifting as new sexual ontologies and epistemologies become available for local uses—and by "uses" I mean these produce subject positions that Polynesians inhabit today. Specifically, Polynesians have recently innovated categories for, and new configurations of, same-sex sexuality in relation to transnational discourses of lesbian and gay identities and politics. In what follows, I argue that the basis of the different (moral) evaluations Polynesians ascribe to empirically identical sex practices that appear on each side of a line dividing the morally unremarkable from the morally problematic lies in the disjuncture between the ontological and epistemological organizing premises of local (compared to translocal) symbolic economies of sexuality. These different organizing premises structure a conflict between, on one hand, Polynesians' privileging of practice or experience in adjudicating the onto-logical validity of same-sex sexualities and, on the other hand, the way the recently introduced and innovated same-sex sexualities are organized through an ontology of sexual essentialism (Rubin 1984) or "sexual identity."

Like most other anthropologists working on LGBT studies cross-cultur-ally, I began my thinking about homosexuality in the Society Islands with sex—who was doing what with whom. My narrative trajectory in the body of this essay recapitulates that starting point and the logics that flow from it in order to undermine it. By weaving into the following analysis counterpoints and critical reflections that destabilize the analytical primacy given to sex as a start-ing point, my goal is to sabotage the resilience and naturalized location of sex as the arbiter of homosexual versus non-homosexual cultural productions. Although I site this destabilizing project in the Society Islands, focusing on the complex and multivalent meanings of sex in Polynesians' current negoti-ations within divergent and overlapping symbolic economies, my arguments are intended to further the larger project of critically reconsidering the future theoretical status that sex should have in queer anthropology.

In what follows, then, I aim first to demonstrate that sex, as an arbiter of the boundaries of LGBT analyses, is of far more limited use than previous-ly thought for analyzing the complex negotiations, at multiple levels, of sex-ual meanings, genders, identities, and related cultural productions in the Society Islands and beyond them. Second, and flowing out of the complex relationship between sexuality and gender in the Society Islands, I aim to demonstrate the possibilities of reframing the study of sexuality, gender, culture, and power as queer anthropology. Sexuality, gender, culture, and power, of course, have been the bread and butter of feminist analyses in anthropology, with feminist work in LGBT studies specifically highlighting gender. Since the mid-1970s, feminist anthropologists have waged guerril-la war on the masculinist boundaries around and significances of gender in the study of homosexualities cross-culturally, reshaping in that process our most fundamental understandings of gender and "sex-gender systems" (Ru-bin 1975). Through that body of work, gender has become a central prob-lematic and tool for analyzing the forms, textures, structures, practices, and significances of homosexualities within anthropological studies and theories. In a bid to open further the conversation about what queer anthropology can become, I suggest in what follows that sex, in addition to gender, is another frontier meriting feminist intervention.

(Re)Configuring Māhū

I focus on Polynesian māhū to begin to analyze Polynesian interpretive frameworks for conceptualizing same-sex sexualities.[8] The category *māhū,* which is indigenous to the Society Islands but also found in the
Hawaiian Islands, was translated by people I knew as meaning "half-man,
half-woman."[9] Unlike the other categories that allow for same-sex sexuality (raerae, petea, and the various French-language terms used in the Islands),
references to māhū are found throughout the earliest voyager and chronicler
accounts of social life in the Society Islands, beginning in the late eighteenth
century. Such historical references, however, usually refer only to male-bodied māhū; female-bodied māhū are practically absent from chronicler accounts.[10] Gunson is one of the few scholars who has allowed that māhū historically could have been female-bodied as well as male-bodied: "The
relatively high proportion of transsexual or effeminate men, particularly in
the Society Islands and Samoa, may well have been balanced by a similar
phenomenon amongst women" (1987:145).[11] Most scholars, however, have
assumed that the absence of chronicler references to female-bodied māhū
has meant that "māhū" as a category has been available only to male-bodied Polynesians.

Such omissions, however, do not preclude the possibility—even the likelihood—that the category has historically been available to females as well.
Conflicting with the scholarly assumption that māhū have been exclusively
male, during my research in the Society Islands I found that Polynesians use
the category *māhū* to refer both to male-bodied and female-bodied persons.
One woman I knew explained the availability of the category to both females
and males by citing the very meaning of māhū: "Māhū, that can be a man or
woman because that's what it means, someone who's both." Although it lies
beyond the scope of this essay to provide a historical argument for the availability of this category to female-bodied persons in the early contact period, there are several possible explanations for the dearth of references to
female-bodied māhū in the historical record—other than the prevailing one
that they did not exist.

First, there are clear sociocultural logics that explain what and how māhū
are, and these logics are not only equally available to male- and female-bodied persons now but also articulate epistemological and ontological positions
and theories of the person that are found historically and today in Polyne-

sian societies. Second, skepticism is requisite for evaluating early voyagers' perceptions and interpretations of encounters with Polynesians. In this regard I want specifically to highlight the problematic of the visibility or noticeability of female-bodied māhū, both historically and currently, to foreigners. The ships' captains and other European and American men who narrated Polynesian social life in earlier periods, on whose narratives most ethnohistorical analyses depend, may well have been unable to discern a difference between female māhū and men in some cases and unable to discern a difference between female māhū and women in others.

At issue is the wide range of practices and behaviors in which Polynesian women historically engaged, and may still engage, and yet be considered women. For adult and older women in the contemporary Society Islands, gender performances are not stridently circumscribed.[12] Because of the wide range of behaviors and self-presentations Polynesian women can deploy while still being identifiable as women, the behaviors and self-presentations of female-bodied māhū do not always stand out. Even during my fieldwork, and despite the fact that I was actively looking for them, female-bodied māhū were far less visible to me (although not to Polynesians) than were male-bodied māhū.

Female-bodied māhū extend the meanings of what Thomas (1987) has theorized as "gender misrecognition" and in some important senses may iconify the problems of reading the significances of gender differences and their performances not only in the past but also in the present. Such gender misrecognition may well be the primary reason why female-bodied māhū have not only been largely absent from historical accounts of Polynesian social life but also why they have been absent from most ethnographic works on the Islands. In his influential ethnography of the Society Islands, for example, Robert Levy (1973:141) has written, *"Māhū* is considered by many to be misused for describing female homosexuals."

My research, however, indicates that Levy is both right and wrong. He is right to identify it as a misuse to translate "māhū" as "female homosexual," because, as I argue subsequently, the meanings of "māhū" for males and for females revolve not around homosexuality but around gender. He is wrong, however, to imply that females do not identify as or are not recognized by other Polynesians as māhū. If they "behave in the manner of men" people recognize female māhū as māhū. In all likelihood it was precisely female-bodied māhū whom Levy was unknowingly describing when he acknowledged that "women dressing and living somewhat as men and playing [*sic*] western-type lesbian roles have been known in the island of Tahiti for some generations at least" (1973:140).

And not only on Tahiti. A female-bodied māhū and her vahine partner had been living together as a married couple for many years in one of the smaller villages on the outer Society Island where I lived during my field-work. The nature of their relationship, however, was not widely recognized—or at least not widely referred to—outside of their village. But it was also true during my fieldwork that female-bodied māhū as well as Polynesian lesbiennes and vahine who slept with women seemed much more likely to migrate to the urban center of the Islands, the city of Papeete on Tahiti Island, rather than live on the outer islands. The female-bodied māhū and lesbiennes with whom I worked and who had migrated to Tahiti explained that they felt life was more difficult for them in small, outer-island villages because, they said, people gossip incessantly. Conversely, they described their lives as easier in Papeete, where their sexual relationships with women were as a rule kept hidden from friends and co-workers. Yet female-bodied māhū and lesbiennes who had chosen to reside on outer islands routinely dismissed the claim that their lives were more difficult. Rua, for example, who lived on an island that had a population of fewer than two thousand, emphasized that she had "no problems" and that people treated her no differently because she has vahine lovers. "I'm me," she said. "I'm the one who lives my life."[13]

As the translation "half-man, half-woman," may suggest, māhū is a gender category for persons who deploy and participate in complex combinations of masculine and feminine gender signs and practices. Māhū adopt styles of dress, work, and/or embodied expressions (gestures, stances, speaking styles, and voice pitch) that, while incorporating both masculine and feminine associations, privilege one set of gender associations over the other. The set of associations privileged, moreover, is that of the gender opposite to the one coordinating with the māhū's own sexed-body status. Female-bodied māhū, for example, are thought to "behave in the manner of men," as Polynesians I knew phrased it. Some undertake work culturally coded as men's. They work as drivers, for example, or at *fa'a'apu* (subsistence gardening or cultivation). They may also use embodied expressions and wear clothing culturally coded as masculine. For example, in a society where most Polynesian women grow their hair long, many female-bodied māhū cut theirs quite short.[14] Male-bodied māhū, in analogous form, are thought to behave "in the manner of women." They commonly undertake work culturally coded as women's (such as sewing crafts, working at hotels and restaurants, or caring for children); they often move, talk, and/or gesture in stylized ways that are coded as an exaggerated femininity; and many grow their hair long and wear *pareu* (Polynesian sarongs), both forms of bodily adornment practiced by women.[15]

Polynesians' evaluations of māhū are, on the whole, accepting. People describe them as "natural," with "naturalness" authorized largely through reference to the māhū's history of "being that way." Māhū are thought to show signs that they are māhū at a very young age; that is, they are thought to begin demonstrating māhū styles of self-presentation or preferences for transgendered work when they are still children. Boys may be identified as māhū at the onset of displaying these behaviors. For girls, however, the links between styles of self-presentation, work/activity preferences, and māhū designation may be more retrospective. Female-bodied māhū, for example, were often described as having been "tomboys" (Fr., *garçon manqué*) during their childhood or adolescent years. The naturalization of māhū through appeals to a consistent personal history introduces the importance of experience for authorizing and explaining gender categorization among Polynesians, and more broadly points to the ontological primacy given to experience and behavior in the formation of the socialized Polynesian person.

While the gender-coded meanings attached to māhū were consistently foregrounded by the men, women, and māhū I knew, the sexuality of māhū was consistently backgrounded. Polynesians with whom I worked commonly assumed that male-bodied māhū have sex with men, particularly with young men in the *taure'are'a* period of the Polynesian life-cycle (adolescence through young adulthood, roughly from the ages of fifteen to thirty). Most of the male-bodied māhū I knew or heard about took men, particularly young men (*taure'are'a tane*), as lovers. But many also had had women lovers. Several were in long-term relationships with women when I knew them and fathers to the children born of these relationships.[16] Still others were celibate. Female-bodied māhū are generally assumed to have sex with women. Among those I worked with and learned about, most had taken women as their lovers, but many had also at some time taken men as lovers, while others were single and celibate.

The Heterosexual Matrix

Same-sex sexuality, whether between a māhū and a man or between a māhū and a woman, is culturally configured in terms of the māhū's gender categorization as "half-man, half-woman." It is, for example, through a female-bodied māhū's characterization as "half-man" that her sexual desires for women are rendered culturally intelligible. One of the corollaries of the complex relationship between gender and sexuality in the Society Islands is that the lovers of māhū are either men or women. Māhū do not sleep with other māhū, that is, they do not take sexed-body-same māhū as lovers. Female-bodied māhū behave, in Polynesian terms, "in the manner of men" and this means that, as for men, the focus of a female-bodied māhū's sexual desires may be a woman. Female lovers of female-bodied māhū are characterized socially and unproblematically as vahine. They deploy the Polynesian signs of femininity—in styles of dress, work, and/or embodied expression—and are considered by other people to be women. The women lovers of female-bodied māhū, then, unlike female-bodied māhū, are not linguistically or socially marked as anything other than women, even though they have sexual relationships with female-bodied māhū.[17]

This is a telling dimension of the ways in which gender and sexuality are both separated and interrelated in the Society Islands. Māhū is primarily meaningful as a gender category. As such, it is not tied to sexed-body status. Rather, gender and sexed-body status are disaggregated, with gender difference made contingent on gender performance—that is, on behavior. It is, then, an individual's participation in or practice of particular gendered codes and behaviors that determines inclusion in the gender categories *vahine, māhū*, or *tane.*

This was made clear to me during a conversation with Aimata, a woman in her mid-thirties who had taken female-bodied māhū as well as men as lovers. During a conversation about whether male-bodied māhū usually sleep with men, Aimata rather impatiently told me, "If one dresses like a woman, of course it's someone who wants to sleep with a man. Why would anyone dress like a woman if he wasn't wanting to sleep with a man?" In her explanation, Aimata makes a telling series of logical links between practice (dressing as a woman), gender (being "like a woman"), and sexuality (women have sex with men). Given Aimata's own history of having sexual relationships with both female-bodied māhū and with men, her insistence on the unambiguous location of gender difference in determining sexual desire and practice becomes particularly compelling.

Moreover, and as Aimata's explanation suggests, it is most accurately and reliably an individual's practice-based participation in a particular gender category that is thought to produce the individual's sexual desires and practices. Gender, then, is not understood by Polynesians as contingent on or derived from sexual practices; rather, Polynesians appear to conceptualize gender difference as productive of sexuality.[18] Sexual practice here has no essential primacy for adjudicating either gender status or the terms of inclusion or exclusion in what American scholars might want to bound categorically as "homosexuality." Further evidence of this lies in Polynesians' disinterest in marking—linguistically or socially—women who have sex with female-bodied māhū as different from women who have sex with men. They also do not mark men who have sex with male-bodied māhū as different from men who have sex with women. What stands the female-bodied māhū apart from women, and the male-bodied māhū apart from men, is the māhū's gender-coded self-presentation and gender-coded behaviors.

With the complex sets of masculine and feminine gender signs and practices that produce māhū gender difference come the possibility of taking lovers who are same-sex-bodied but of the "opposite" gender. The cultural intelligibility of māhū sexuality lies in a māhū's designation as "like a man" or "like a woman." In more theoretical terms, māhū sexuality relies on and articulates a vision of heterosexuality as a particular configuration of sexual desires produced by and through gender difference, what I think of as a "heterosexual matrix." Māhū sexuality does not, correlatively, articulate a configuration of sexual desires indelibly or prediscursively aligned with sexed bodies nor a configuration in which sexual desire produces gender difference.

Within this matrix, same-sex sexuality is configured in gendered terms rather than sexed-body terms. Relatedly, same-sex sexuality can never be same-gender sexuality. Instead, same-sex desire always relies on a gender difference between woman/man, man/māhū, or māhū/woman. Given that, it becomes clearer why the women whose lovers are female-bodied māhū (and the men whose lovers are male-bodied māhū) are not marked by their same-sex sexual practices. In this logic, sex is not endowed with any experiential or essential power to define gender status. Nor is sexual practice empowered to negotiate inclusion (or exclusion) in the category *homosexuality,* in part because that category cannot adequately capture the complex geography of genders and sexualities in this society. Women who are lovers with female-bodied māhū are operating in terms of, and in accordance with, a heterosexual matrix that coordinates sexual practice through gender difference. They are taking as their lovers persons who are of a different gender, persons who behave "in the manner of men" in a social context where gender is produced through behavior and experience and not through sexed-body status. In the logic of this symbolic sexual economy, the sex these women have with their female-bodied māhū lovers as well as their relationships are, for all intents and purposes, heterosexual.[19]

Raerae, Petea, and Lesbiennes

Compared with their acceptance of māhū, and of the tane and vahine who are the lovers of māhū, many Polynesians articulate substantial ambivalence about, and even animosity toward, the other categories circulating in the Society Islands today that allow for same-sex sexuality. One afternoon, for example, I was with three taure'are'a (a man and two women, all in their early twenties) who were talking about a raerae they knew. During the conversation, the young man repeatedly stated that in his view raerae and petea should be "exterminated." People made disparaging comments—particularly about raerae and petea—as a matter of course, and yet these same people often had warm friendships with raerae or petea. I once asked Mahare, a middle-aged woman who had raerae and petea friends with whom she regularly socialized, how she would feel if her eight-year-old son was raerae or petea. She responded, "I'd get a rope and tie it to a high tree branch, stick his neck in a loop at the other end, and that would be the end of him. . . . Not in my family." The subject of lesbiennes did not seem to prompt such visceral reactions, but ambivalent and distancing statements ("I've never heard of that here [on this island]," for example) were standard.

Relative to the other categories that allow for same-sex sexuality, people privilege māhū as the older and most authentically Polynesian category, commonly making reference to its availability to and use by their ancestors centuries ago. In contrast, the other categories are held to be recent innovations or else recent arrivals (from France). For example, when I asked Tefatua about the difference between a lesbienne and a (female) māhū, this middle-aged married man who worked as a cultural expert on Polynesian history and culture answered, "Lesbienne is a universal thing, but māhū is just here, just in Polynesia. . . . It's only here you find māhū . . . we've always had them." Among other Polynesians, lesbiennes are viewed as foreign, assumed to be either French themselves or Polynesians who have been overly influenced by the French. Either way, they are cast as not "truly Polynesian." A married woman I knew once reflected, "I think that lesbiennes didn't exist here in the old times. . . . It's since they brought porno films here that it's increased . . . now there are more . . . I think that before, there were hardly any."

Not surprisingly, Polynesian lesbiennes and "women who sleep with women" do not see themselves as foreign or Frenchified. Neither do they see themselves as sexual innovators, rebels, or radicals. One of the few common themes to emerge across the conversations I had with Polynesian lesbiennes and women who slept with women was that almost unanimously they located same-sex sexuality as something of little or no import, insignificant and unremarkable. Almost without exception they saw themselves as no different from other Polynesian women. Residing in a large city like Papeete, as most of them did, they were assisted in this project of unremarking by their ability to keep their same-sex sexual practice out of the realm of the spoken in their friendships and work lives.

While "lesbienne" was interpreted as a foreign category brought to the Islands by the French, the category *petea* was held to be a recent indigenous innovation. A Tahitian-language word, "petea" has taken on new meaning by being applied to males who have sex with other males. People offered a variety of definitions for the term, but all of them had valences that shaded the category with sexual meanings. "Petea" was variously defined as "a white bird that runs away when you come up to it" and as "a boy who's scared of things—scared to climb trees, scared of everything—cowardly." One person linked these definitions and explained, "It's the name of a bird, really, but now it means—the person you call that, he sleeps only with men." As that explanation indicates, "petea" is a sexual category (rather than a gender category) for referring to any sexed-body male who has sex with other males. The term's privileged focus on sex between males has resulted in both semantic and conceptual flexibility that affects other gender and sexual categories. One hears male-bodied māhū, as well as raerae, occasionally (and derisively) referred to as petea.

As with the recent innovation of the category *petea,* I was told that the category *raerae* had not been around very long, "perhaps a generation or two," according to one man I knew. (The term *raerae* is considered to be somewhat older than *petea,* although not much older.) Many people felt that the numbers of raerae, most of whom are thought to reside in Papeete, had increased substantially since the early 1980s. "When I was growing up," a man in his late twenties told me, "you'd see raerae only rarely in Papeete, like at night, but nothing—nothing—like you see them now. All over Papeete, daytime, night time . . . it's really changed."

Raerae differ from māhū in several important respects. First, unlike māhū, who can be male-bodied or female-bodied, raerae are exclusively male-bodied; the category is not used to refer to females.[20] Second, raerae are not only transgendered but also sometimes transsexual. Although only a few raerae have had sex change operations, many take female hormones and thus have some female secondary sex characteristics such as breasts. Moreover, raerae transgender practices are organized around what might best be described as a specifically Eurocentric form of white femininity. Although raerae might dress in pareu around the house, for example, in public they usually wear European women's fashions, particularly those that are more revealing: miniskirts, skimpy shorts, halter tops, and high heels. Polynesian women I knew routinely admired raerae for their ability to wear such clothing well. Typical of women's statements about raerae was the comment, "Raerae look better in women's clothes than we do." The raerae's more proximate production of the kind of white European femininity idealized in mass-media productions throughout this French territory (from advertisements on the state-run television station, to billboards in Papeete, to fashion magazines) enabled Polynesian women to make comments along the lines of those of one young woman who told me in honest admiration, "They're very pretty, much prettier than us." Her friend made gestures of puffing her hair up on one side, in exaggerated imitation of a raerae's exaggerated imitation of this gesture, saying, "They're more like women than we women are!"

A third way the category *raerae* differs from mãhū is that *raerae* is both a gender and a sexual category. In addition to signifying transgender practices, the category *raerae* has explicit and unambivalent sexual meanings. Raerae have sex with tane. Moreover, in a society in which female prostitution is almost unknown, most raerae work part time as prostitutes, earning some of their money by having sex with men or by stealing from prospective men clients. In addition to part-time prostitution, many raerae also engage in work along the lines of that done by Taia, a raerae I knew in Papeete. They provide labor to the households in which they reside in exchange for being fed and cared for, a prevalent form of exchange in the Islands.[21] When I asked Taia if all raerae work as prostitutes, for example, she responded, "Yes, like me: I work for Mama [the head of the household] here—sweep the floor, clean the house, do the laundry . . . I work here, for Mama, and then in the evenings I do what I want." Raerae sex work, then, is only part-time and usually done at night but not every night. Taia, for example, went out most nights but worked as a prostitute on only some of those nights and usually for only parts of a night. In between, Taia socialized with friends (many of whom were also raerae) at clubs or apartments or while taking scenic drives around the island. A good deal of the money that raerae make in relation to their prostitution comes not from sex work but from their renowned skill at stealing from prospective and actual clients.

Finally, "raerae" is a category that Polynesians consider raerae as having chosen to take on. Taia, for example, told me she had "started off as a petea" and then "become a raerae." She had also, before and during these categorical transitions, fathered three children with a woman. In contrast, Polynesians do not talk about māhū as something people have chosen to be or changed into. Rather, they authorize māhū gender difference by reference to early signs that the māhū was "by nature" a māhū: a girl was a tomboy as a child, or a boy showed early preferences for women's work. Being a māhū is premised on a set of practices and preferences that appear when a child is young, and those attributes stay with a child. It is not something one changes, in part because as a child grows she/he experiences and reexperiences the social world as a māhū and is treated by others as a māhū. As a result, people say that māhū "have always been that way." Produced through experience, māhū gender is understood as fixed or stable in the same way that vahine and tane gender is fixed. These gender categories are authorized by and grounded in the gendered experiences of growing up, in social history and social contexts and practices.

Conflicting Sexual Symbolic Economies

To the extent that it is premised on a sexuality unmoored from gender difference, in some important sense same-sex sexuality is neither a culturally intelligible nor a culturally persuasive construct in the Society Islands. Of course, a same-sex sexuality that stands on its own is somewhat intelligible to the raerae, petea, and lesbiennes who use these categories to name or describe themselves. But even these Polynesians may voice ambiguity about the extent to which the categories apply to them. Some lesbiennes I knew, for example, periodically referred to themselves as māhū, and I worked with some raerae who also occasionally referred to themselves and their friends as māhū. Such flexible forms of self-naming could be attempts to borrow authority from māhū as a morally unproblematic or unremarkable category relative to the others. Alternatively or additionally, flexible self-naming may point to a larger ambivalence about the categories these Polynesians have available to them, including ambivalence about the ontologies the categories assume and promote.

Such ambivalence would take root in conflicts with the logics that naturalize māhū sexuality through gender. Each of the various other categories circulating in the Society Islands that allow for same-sex sexuality and are problematically evaluated by Polynesians organizes, to varying degrees, gender and sexuality through a contrasting Euro-American sexual symbolic economy. In these other configurations, sexuality is disaggregated from gender difference and located within the socially decontextualized individual, or even, at some level, within the individual's sexed body. Raerae, for example, is both a gender and a sexual category. Instead of gender producing raerae same-sex sexuality, however, it is both gender and same-sex sexuality that are seen as producing raerae. This configuration, by giving equal weight to gender difference and same-sex sexuality, confounds the logical and unidirectional relationship in which gender difference produces sexuality.

The category *lesbienne* goes a step further. It is constituted as a sexual category that combines sexual practice with sexed-body status (through sexed-body sameness). This configuration thus has no necessary relationship to gender, let alone a relationship in which gender produces lesbian sexuality. Petea, in similar form, has no necessary relationship to gender. Like "lesbienne," "petea" references sexuality, and it does so in terms of sexed bodies rather than gender difference.

In each of these configurations, sexuality does not rely on gender for its meanings or for its production. Rather, it relies on a sexually essentialist understanding of the person. This Euro-American sexual symbolic economy conflicts with what I have glossed as Polynesian interpretive frameworks. In the Polynesian configuration, vahine and tane are gender categories that produce sexuality through a heterosexual matrix organized around and through the gender difference tane/vahine. In this matrix, gender structures sexuality. Sexuality is produced through and is an outgrowth of the practices of gender difference. As a gender category, māhū also works within that matrix to produce māhū same-sex but opposite-gender sexuality. Because māhū are "half-man, half-woman," the sexuality that their gender designation produces may be oriented toward either men or women. Female-bodied māhū have at times had relationships with men, and male-bodied māhū have at times had relationships with women. Whether a māhū engages in sexual relationships with a man or with a woman, māhū sexuality remains heterosexual in the sense that it is invariably directed at someone who is, in the heterosexual matrix, of the "opposite gender."

In addition, māhū are thought to demonstrate gender difference (like vahine and tane) from an early age. That helps authorize their gender difference as "natural" and in turn makes their sexuality intelligible. The other configurations, in contrast, introduce personal choice and sudden change as ontological possibilities. Raerae, for example, is something one is thought to choose to become. Raerae come to identify themselves not in terms of a (locally) naturalized progression inaugurated in childhood but rather according to their personal desires or motivations in what is usually viewed as a sudden change. Such choices confound the logical and unidirectional relationship in which long-term experience produces gender. The logic productive of raerae, and of petea and lesbienne, thus unties gender and sexuality from social practice, social experience, and social history. In so doing, it violates an epistemological claim laced throughout this and much of Polynesian social life: the priority Polynesians give to behavior and experience for determinations of legitimacy.

Polynesians subscribe, then, to a sexual symbolic economy in which gender difference is productive of sexuality, and gender difference is itself produced through practice or experience. Thus do māhū, vahine, and tane gain their contrasts with other gender and sexual categories (raerae, petea, and lesbienne), first through the productive relationship of experience to gender (i.e., experience produces gender) and second through the productive relationship of gender to sexuality (i.e., gender produces sexuality). My argument has been that such contrasts shape Polynesians' ambivalence about these other gender and sexual categories. The ambivalence stems from the disjunctures between a locally salient logic that constructs gender as produced by experience and gender as productive of sexuality and a competing logic—which produces categories like raerae, petea, and lesbienne—that disaggregates and omits these necessary links between experience, gender, and sexuality. These disjunctures, moreover, index an ontological conflict over the alternative logic premised on a de-gendered reading of sexed bodies, one that locates sexuality within sexed bodies and as the product not of experience or gender difference but of pre-social or socially de-contextualized selves.

Queering the Future of Sex

Although sex gains its meanings in relation to a varied range of discursive formations, feminist anthropologists working on the cross-cultural study of sexualities have demonstrated that one of the more important of these discursive formations is the nexus of discourses organized and articulated as gender difference. Gender difference, and the hierarchies often built out of gender difference, commonly plays a vital role in producing and structuring same-sex sexualities in general and female same-sex sexual possibilities in particular; in structuring women's sexual possibilities; and in structuring the nested links that may be forged between gender and other locally persuasive social differences.[22]

Building on these feminist insights, this essay aims to show another way in which gender may be involved in the production of same-sex sexualities. Gender difference may mediate among culturally specific ontologies, epistemologies, and theories of the person on the one hand and, on the other, the shape of legitimate same-sex sexualities and the frameworks within which people negotiate the local legitimacy of translocal sexual symbolic economies.

My ethnographic project here has been to ask about logics that render some configurations of same-sex sexuality morally problematic and other configurations morally unremarkable. The puzzle, in the larger framework of developing the future of queer anthropology, stems from recognizing that in the Society Islands, and across all of these configurations, the sexual practices involved are empirically identical. That points to the dangers of taking sexual practice as having cross-culturally transparent meaning. Yet clearly it also raises questions about the common object of analysis contained within the subfield of LGBT studies in anthropology. What, precisely, might the referent of "homosexual" be when the same "sex" may be homosexual in some contexts or for some people and non-homosexual in other contexts or for other people. In the Society Islands, sex between people who have the same genitals (i.e., between females or between males) is not a reliable point of entry into understanding what "homosexuality" is or may be for Polynesians. More broadly, there may be no such beasts as "homosexual practices" that can be found cross-culturally and made to set, lie, or grind together on the bed of queer anthropology. In other words, there may be no homosexual practices that could form the basis for theorizing homosexualities cross-culturally or serve as a reliable object of inquiry for queer anthropology.

The ethnographic arguments of this essay also reemphasize and clarify a point made by other feminist scholars. As Biddy Martin (1992:106) has succinctly written, "Sexuality has no meaning outside of the cultural contexts in which it appears."[23] Sex is always about signs and signifying practices and is always the site of cultural interpretation and contestation. In this essay I have analyzed some of the forms that contestation can take by focusing on particular collisions between Polynesian interpretive frameworks for understanding sexuality and recently emerged uses by Polynesians of foreign sexual symbolic economies. Through such a focus, I have tried to show that culturally specific ontologies, theories of the person, and epistemologies are in some cases more central than "sex" for producing meaningful interpretive frameworks for understanding not only sexual practices and desires but also the moral standing of their practitioners.

That argument bears emphasizing for the project of developing theoretical frameworks useful for queer anthropology and also in the context of contemporary academic fashions. Contrary to other work in queer theory, for example, particularly work informed by poststructuralist literary theory, "sex" is not a free-floating signifier available for any social project that comes along. It is structured, embedded, and motivated. As a vital sign in divergent yet interacting sexual symbolic economies, the sign of sex is always simultaneously produced anew and motivated by the internal logics of the sign systems within which it is made to signify and the social contexts through which it gains coherent cultural meanings. Anthropologists, moreover, are ideally positioned to analyze and evidence the processes and social relations through which sex is structured, embedded, and motivated and to build and nuance analyses of the logics involved in the cultural production of sex. Anthropologists are also well positioned to question whether sexual practice is even at issue in determinations of social identities in the production of differences of gender, power, and culture.

If we vest sex with the power to adjudicate the boundaries of queer anthropology—to define who falls within and who falls without the purview of such studies—we stand to misrepresent, misconstrue, and misanalyze the social significances of what Polynesians, and probably many other people, think they are doing and who they think they are in relation to (or not in relation to) what they are doing or who they are doing it with. That is in part because the privileged siting of sex as the adjudicator of homosexuality seems to be a specifically Euro-American way of carving up the lived and messy map of erotics, desire, identities, and bodies. A less cannibalizing methodology might theorize the different sexual symbolic economies within which sexual practices are produced locally as meaningful—including the ways Eurocentric ideologies, or transnational Eurocentrisms, may pose on-the-ground and new challenges to the symbolic economies with which they come into contact and conflict. The Euro-American privileging of sex as the core feature of homosexuality (homosexuals have sex with same-sex bodies) may create moral ruptures, even crises, when this sexual configuration enters arenas in which the organizing bases and interpretive frameworks for what Western scholars want to identify as homosexualities do not privilege sex.

In the Society Islands, Euro-American and Polynesian interpretive frameworks are in uneasy and fraught relationship. Each is available for negotiating the moral meanings of same-sex sexual practices and the moral standing of their practitioners. The complexities and intricacies of this case study point to some of the possibilities offered up by holding back the desire to use sex as the touchstone for claiming lesbian or gay practices. Call it a queer politics of cultural respect. In refusing to locate same-sex sex as the foundation for queer cross-cultural inquiry we can come to understand a topography of erotic desires that gains its meanings in specific social histories and experiences through non-essentialized theories of the person and diverse approaches to the production of legitimate knowledge and understanding. That holds the promise of a more varied and richer set of questions about and approaches to the ways sexuality, gender, power, and culture are produced and brought into relationship.

Notes

Research in the Society Islands and support for writing the dissertation out of which this essay developed was generously provided by the Wenner-Gren Foundation for Anthropological Research (predoctoral grant, 1994–95), the Social Sciences and Humanities Research Council of Canada (doctoral fellowship, 1994–95, 1995–96), and New York University (Dean's Grant for pre-dissertation research, summer 1993, and Dean's Dissertation Fellowship, 1995–96). For conversations that shaped my understandings of same-sex sexualities in the Society Islands I am most grateful to the Polynesians who both tutored and challenged me, and I also thank J. Kehaulani Kauanui, Evie Blackwood, Lanuola Asiasiga, Stephen Eisenman, and Kate Riley for other illuminating exchanges. Fred Myers, Faye Ginsburg, and Annette Weiner gave intellectual fellowship and sustenance throughout the development of my understandings of Polynesian social life. Finally, I thank Ellen Lewin, Bill Leap, and the reviewers of the manuscript for this volume for helpful commentaries. Earlier incarnations of this essay were presented at the 1997 meetings of the American Anthropological Association in the invited session "Queer Challenges: Lesbian/Gay/

Bisexual/Transgender Issues in Anthropology" and published as, "Negotiating Transnational Sexual Economies: Female Māhū and Same-Sex Sexuality in 'Tahiti and Her Islands,'" in *Female Desires: Same-Sex Relations and Transgender Practices across Cultures,* ed. Evelyn Blackwood and Saskia E. Wieringa (New York: Columbia University Press, 1999).

1. One of my favorites, for example, is William Lessa's (1966:91) scarce phallus account of lesbianism on Ulithi atoll in Micronesia: "Women of mature age, usually because of involuntary incontinence [heterosexual abstinence], are sometimes said to resort to mutual masturbation, but only as a substitute for the normal sexual congress being denied them."

2. Not only what we are looking for, but what we are looking at, since we also look in culturally coded ways. One of the more problematic aspects of the ways of looking prevalent in the history of the anthropology of homosexuality is its masculinist orientation and androcentrism. By and large, it is males who have been seen and females who have been actively un-seen. A particularly striking example of this is the more than four hundred page volume by Stephen O. Murray, boldly entitled *Oceanic Homosexualities,* in which male homosexual practices take up all but thirteen pages (a tally that includes the blank page separating the nine-page "Introduction" to female homosexualities from the two-and-a-half-page chapter that follows) which are tacked on to the very end of the volume.

3. I say "somewhat" more critical or reflexive because these typologies are disappointingly androcentric. They have been generated out of research on male homosexualities yet their authors and endorsers usually make the claim, either explicitly or by implication, that they apply equally well to female homosexualities. On the typologies, see the early formulation by Adam (1986) and the endorsements and refinements elaborated by, for example, Greenberg (1988), Herdt (1993), and Murray (1992). For a short critique, see Elliston (1993).

4. For a critical analysis of these practices and their theoretical containment in the construct of "ritualized homosexuality," see Elliston (1995).

5. I use the term *Polynesians* to refer specifically to Polynesians living in the Society Islands of French Polynesia and clarify in the text the few occasions on which I mean the term in a more extensive sense (that is, as referencing Polynesians throughout the Polynesian triangle). My use of this term for people of the Society Islands reflects the preferences and practices of the people with whom I worked, who most often referred to themselves as Polynesians (Fr., *Polynésiens*). Although the more common scholarly term for people of the Society Islands is *Tahitians,* that term derives from a privileging of Tahiti Island in the identification of the people. The generalization from Tahiti Island to all other Society Islands (embedded in the term *Tahitians*), however, was regularly criticized by people of the other Society Islands as both inaccurate and problematic. This is in part because, as I have analyzed elsewhere (Elliston 2000), such a generalization erases and conflicts with the social importance of islands of origin, which Polynesians treat as vital and powerful reference points for individual and social identities.

6. I should clarify the meanings I am attaching to some of the terms I use in this essay. The terms *male* and *female,* for example, as well as *male-bodied, female-bodied,* and *sexed bodies,* are deployed for purposes of analytical clarity and in recognition of the predominantly American audience for this essay. These terms distinguish particularly marked bodies from the gender categories in which those bodies participate and comprise a necessary analytical clarification in order to draw out the significances of sexuality, gender, and desire in their Polynesian forms to an American readership. My use of these terms directs attention to the ways genitals and what is known in the clinical literature as "secondary sex characteristics" may be given primacy for gendering bodies among Americans. Their meanings for Polynesians, however, as I discuss in subsequent sections, are far more various.

7. The criteria for determining the moral standings of these disparate significations now lies at the crossroads of multiple discursive formations, not all of which I can treat in this essay. Among these, for example, is the Tahitian Protestant church's condemnations of same-sex sexuality. Although church discourses on same-sex sexuality are certainly available to Polynesians, they are of limited effect. These and other church teachings that focus on practices identified as "sinful"—any sex outside of marriage, for example—are considered by most Polynesians to be largely impracticable edicts. On Protestant church teachings about sexuality and marriage and their practical significance, see, in particular, chapters 5 and 6 in Elliston (1997). See also Saura (1993) for analysis of broader questions about the relationships between religion and politics in the Islands.

A second discursive formation is the French colonial contribution to local meanings of same-sex sexuality. Although these are complex and also lie beyond the scope of this essay, I want at least to note that in a French "overseas territory," where most Polynesians are ambivalent about their rulers, it should not be surprising that the same-sex sexualities associated with the French may also be met with some ambivalence.

8. In this essay I have opted not to anglicize Tahitian-language nouns; that is, not to mark plurality or singularity through the manipulation of a final *s.* In the Tahitian language, plurality is usually deduced from a noun's context of use, and I leave it to the reader to deduce a noun's singularity or plurality from its context of appearance and use in the text. In the footnoted sentence, for example, māhū is plural.

9. See Morris (1990) on the possibility that Kānaka Maoli (Hawaiians) borrowed the term *māhū* from the Society Islands. Other societies in the Polynesian triangle have gender categories the meanings and practices of which scholars have usually analyzed as similar to mahu: *fa'atama* (for females) and *fa'afāfine* (for males) in Samoa (Mageo 1992); *fāfine tangata* or *fakatangata* (for females) and *fakafefine* or, more recently, *fakaleitī* (for males) in Tonga (James 1994). Besnier (1993) examines these Polynesian categories as a group under his coined term *gender liminality.* Linguistically, however, the causative prefixes in these words—the *fa'a* prefix in Samoan, for example, or the *faka* prefix in Tongan—render the meanings of these categories more along the lines of "to become male" or "to become female." Neither the Tahitian nor the Hawaiian languages have constructions that parallel these Samoan or Tongan terms. In Hawaiian, for example, likely constructions would be

ho'ovahine or *ho'okane,* but these words either do not exist or do not have the same meanings. In Tahitian, the causative prefixes *fa'a* or *ha'a* (enabling the terms *fa'avahine* or *ha'avahine, fa'atane* or *ha'atane*) would be the likely candidates, but as with Hawaiian, these words are not used for these meanings or do not exist. Rather, in the Hawaiian and Tahitian languages speakers use a linguistically and etymologically distinct word: *māhū.* This suggests that māhū should probably not so easily be treated as a gender category on par with the "third gender" categories in other Polynesian societies. I thank J. Kehaulani Kauanui (personal communications) for conversations about these distinctions that helped clarify their import.

10. References to and descriptions of male-bodied mahu are found in many of the published journals of Europeans who traveled in the Society Islands in the late eighteenth and early nineteenth century, including Captain Cook, Louis Antoine de Bougainville, and William Bligh. Descriptions of male-bodied māhū are also peppered throughout books written by the numerous European and American men who came to the Islands for extended visits over the course of the nineteenth century—as well as in the disapproving accounts penned by missionaries of various persuasions. Douglas Oliver (1974) has pulled together descriptions provided by some of these sources in his *Ancient Tahitian Society.* See Besnier (1993) and Watts (1992) for more recent scholarly works that reference and detail some of the historical accounts of male-bodied māhū. For a critical analysis of the import of colonialism (and the import of using colonist- and missionary-authored historical sources) for understanding same-sex sexuality in Polynesia, and female same-sex sexuality in the Pacific, see Hall and Kauanui (1994).

11. I would caution against accepting several premises embedded in Gunson's suggestion, however: first, that transsexuality and effeminacy are accurate descriptive terms for māhū; second, that it is useful or meaningful to quantify māhū as a "proportion" of a population (a move also made by Levy [1971] in his claim that there is one and only one [male-bodied] māhū per village); third, that it is meaningful to speak of a "relatively" high number of effeminate and/or transsexual persons; and, fourth, that one can draw clear links between the presence of transgender males and the likelihood that there are transgender females.

12. This is not to say gender is undifferentiated. Robert Levy takes the latter position when he interprets Polynesians' insistence that "there are no general differences" between women and men (1973:237) as producing an almost pathological gender system marked by gender "blurring" and "blending," by gender "crossover behaviors" (232–39). The pathological part of this appears in Levy's (1971) essay arguing that male-bodied māhū "persist" (12) largely to provide Polynesian men with a clear image of the boundaries of masculinity: Male-bodied māhū show men what not to be. Levy concludes that the blurring, blending, and crossovers "suggest that the doctrines stressing women's similarity to men, their lack of any special basic qualities setting them off from men, involve denial by men of anxiety-producing aspects of women" (238).

Levy's is not an interpretation I endorse. In referring to the wide range of behaviors in which Polynesian vahine may engage, the claim I am making is that gender difference and the performance of vahine/woman gender by females is not stridently policed. The availability and practice of a wide range of behaviors by female Polynesians made it difficult for me as a foreigner to see which behaviors were relevant to "recognizing" someone as a female-bodied māhū rather than as a woman. Such recognitions did not, however, seem to be a problem for Polynesians.

13. The individual names by which I identify Polynesians I worked with are pseudonyms.

14. Long hair is a potent symbolic form that Polynesians associate with femininity and sexuality. Most adolescent and adult women grow their hair long, although they usually wear it braided, particularly outside of the household. Loose hair connotes, I was told, a kind of loose womanhood as well. It is associated, for example, with the sexuality of Polynesian dance, and although it is viewed as entirely appropriate for young women to wear their long hair loose when dancing, this may shade into the risqué and even the morally compromised in other public contexts. For a comparative case, see Mageo (1994) on the symbolics of hair in Samoa.

15. Polynesian pareu are sarong-type garments similar to others found throughout the Pacific—for example, in Samoa and Fiji as well as in Indonesia—and historically related to the barkcloth (*tapa*) sheets Polynesians wore as draped garments in the early contact period. In the contemporary Society Islands, pareu are most often worn by women, but they are also worn by some men. Some nationalists and cultural activists who are men, for example, wear pareu as a statement of cultural pride.

16. My reference to "long-term relationships with women" indicates common-law marriages as well as formal marriages and should not be interpreted as a form of domestic partnership that is in any sense compromised. Most Polynesians practice common-law marriage at some point in their lives, and many practice it for extended periods or even the entirety of their adult lives.

17. One of the more difficult dynamics within relationships between female-bodied māhū and their women partners, however, stems precisely from the ways gender and sexuality are disaggregated and coordinated. The sexuality of the women in these relationships may be viewed, by their female-bodied māhū partners especially, as insecurely tied to the female-bodied māhū, because women who desire female-bodied māhū as their lovers are culturally understood as equally capable of desiring men as their lovers. Female-bodied māhū, on the other hand, view themselves and are viewed by others as more likely to desire women sexually than they are to desire men sexually; that is, as having their sexuality more securely focused on women. As my phrasing might suggest and as I describe in more depth subsequently, none of these sexual dynamics is set in stone. The only constant across the gender categories of tane, māhū, and vahine is that of gender difference between sexual partners.

18. This suggests, and rightly I believe, that Polynesians' cultural configuration of both gender difference and sexuality is dynamically forged through, and conceptually dependent upon, not only social practices but also social contexts. Polynesians' emphasis on the place of gender difference in producing sexuality, in combination with their emphasis on practice/experience as productive of gender difference itself, requires that the cultural processes through which gender difference and sexuality

are produced be foundationally tied to social contexts. See chapter 6 in Elliston (1997) for further analysis of the context-dependencies of sexuality and its links to Polynesian concepts of the person. For comparative cases, see Shore (1982) on the context-dependencies of personhood and social action in Samoa and Kirkpatrick (1983) on the Marquesa Islands (also part of French Polynesia); see also White and Kirkpatrick (1985).

19. I am not suggesting that vahine who have sex with female-bodied māhū are "homosexual," nor that the sex they have should be categorized under the heading *homosexuality*. My strategy in this essay has been to track "sex" between persons of the same sexed-body status in order to analyze the dissonance between the categories that sex leads to using a Euro-American approach and the categories that sex does not lead to among Polynesians. This strategy reveals that the category *homosexuality* is both too broad and too narrow to account for the ways these vahine think about themselves, their sexual lives, and their partners. The same is true for the communities in which these vahine live.

20. During separate conversations about māhū and raerae, two people with whom I worked offered variations on the term *raerae* that created a female variant. One offered *"tamahine* raerae" (*tamahine* is a Tahitian-language term meaning girl or daughter); the other said she had heard "women who sleep with women" referred to as "vahine raerae" (women raerae). I do not include these terms in my main analysis, however, because neither appears to be widely known or used.

21. Giving labor in exchange for being cared for or "fed" is the predominant framework within which and through which Polynesians conceptualize relationships within a household. It structures kinship (for example, relationships between parents and children) as well as (in the case of Taia) relationships between "patrons" and "clients" in a household. For analyses of this practice, see, for example, Elliston (1997), Finney (1965), Levy (1973), and Oliver (1981).

22. On the interrelationships between gender difference, gender hierarchy, and female same-sex sexualities, see in particular Blackwood (1984, 1986) and Blackwood and Wieringa, eds. (1998). On the interrelationships between gender difference, racial hierarchies, and female same-sex sexualities, see, for example, Anzaldúa (1987), Hall and Kauanui (1994), Lorde (1984), and Moraga (1983). On the interrelationships between gender difference, class hierarchies, and female same-sex sexualities, see, for example, Kennedy and Davis (1993).

23. The feminist anthropological scholarship on the social construction of sexuality is at this point extensive, but for useful points of entry see Altman et al. (1989), Blackwood and Wieringa, eds. (1999), Caplan, ed. (1987), Kulick and Willson, eds. (1995), Lewin, ed. (1996), Ortner and Whitehead, eds. (1981), Vance, ed. (1984), and Weston (1993). Key theoretical formulations in feminist anthropological work on sexuality and gender include, in particular, Blackwood (1984, 1986), Morris (1994), Rubin (1984), and Vance (1991).

References Cited

Adam, Barry D. 1986. "Age, Structure, and Sexuality." *Journal of Homosexuality* 11(3–4): 19–33.

Altman, Dennis, et al. 1989. *Homosexuality, which Homosexuality? Essays from the International Scientific Conference on Lesbian and Gay Studies.* London: Gay Men's Press.

Anzaldúa, Gloria. 1987. *Borderlands/*La Frontera: *The New Mestiza.* San Francisco: Spinsters/Aunt Lute.

Besnier, Niko. 1993. "Polynesian Gender Liminality through Time and Space." In *Third Sex, Third Gender: Beyond Sexual Dimorphism in Culture and History,* ed. Gilbert Herdt, 285–328. New York: Zone Books.

Blackwood, Evelyn. 1984. "Sexuality and Gender in Certain Native American Tribes: The Case of Cross-Gender Females." *Signs* 10(1): 27–42.

———. 1986. "Breaking the Mirror: The Construction of Lesbianism and the Anthropological Discourse on Homosexuality." In *The Many Faces of Homosexuality: Anthropological Approaches to Homosexual Behavior,* ed. Blackwood, 1–18. New York: Harrington Park Press.

———, and Saskia Wieringa, eds. 1999. *Female Desires: Same-Sex Relations and Transgender Practices Across Cultures.* New York: Columbia University Press.

Caplan, Pat, ed. 1987. *The Cultural Construction of Sexuality.* New York: Tavistock Publications.

Elliston, Deborah A. 1993. "Review of *Oceanic Homosexualities.*" *Journal of the History of Sexuality* 4(2): 319–21.

———. 1995. "Erotic Anthropology: 'Ritualized Homosexuality' in Melanesia and Beyond." *American Ethnologist* 22(4): 848–67.

———. 1997. "En/Gendering Nationalism: Colonialism, Sex, and Independence in French Polynesia." Ph.D. diss., New York University.

———. 2000. "Geographies of Gender and Politics: The Place of Difference in Polynesian Nationalism." *Cultural Anthropology* 15(2): 171–216.

Finney, Ben R. 1965. "Polynesian Peasants and Proletarians: Socio-Economic Change among the Tahitians of French Polynesia." *Journal of the Polynesian Society* 74(3): 269–328.

Greenberg, David F. 1988. *The Construction of Homosexuality.* Chicago: University of Chicago Press.

Gunson, Niel. 1987. "Sacred Women Chiefs and Female 'Headmen' in Polynesian History." *Journal of Pacific History* (special issue on "Sanctity and Power: Gender in Polynesian History") 22(3–4): 139–73.

Hall, Lisa Kahaleole Chang, and J. Kehaulani Kauanui. 1994. "Same-Sex Sexuality in Pacific Literature." *Amerasia Journal* 20(1): 75–81.

Herdt, Gilbert. 1981. *Guardians of the Flutes: Idioms of Masculinity.* New York: McGraw-Hill.

———, ed. 1984. *Ritualized Homosexuality in Melanesia.* Berkeley: University of California Press.

————. 1993. Introduction to the Paperback Edition. In *Ritualized Homosexuality in Melanesia,* ed. Herdt, vii–xliv. Berkeley: University of California Press.

James, Kerry E. 1994. "Effeminate Males and Changes in the Construction of Gender in Tonga." *Pacific Studies* 17(2): 39–69.

Kennedy, Elizabeth Lapovsky, and Madeline D. Davis. 1993. *Boots of Leather, Slippers of Gold: The History of a Lesbian Community.* New York: Routledge.

Kirkpatrick, John. 1983. *The Marquesan Notion of the Person.* Ann Arbor: UMI Research Press.

Kulick, Don, and Margaret Willson, eds. 1995. *Taboo: Sex, Identity, and Erotic Subjectivity in Anthropological Fieldwork.* New York: Routledge.

Lessa, William A. 1966. *Ulithi: A Micronesian Design for Living.* New York: Holt, Rinehart and Winston.

Lewin, Ellen, ed. 1996. *Inventing Lesbian Cultures in America.* Boston: Beacon Press.

Levy, Robert I. 1971. "The Community Function of Tahitian Male Transvestism: A Hypothesis." *Anthropological Quarterly* 44(1): 12–21.

————. 1973. *Tahitians: Mind and Experience in the Society Islands.* Chicago: University of Chicago Press.

Lorde, Audre. 1984. *Sister Outsider.* Trumansburg: The Crossing Press.

Mageo, Jeannette Marie. 1994. "Hairdos and Don'ts: Hair Symbolism and Sexual History in Samoa." *Man* 29(2): 407–32.

Martin, Biddy. 1992. "Sexual Practice and Changing Lesbian Identities." In *Destabilizing Theory: Contemporary Feminist Debates,* eds. Michèle Barrett and Anne Phillips, 93–119. Stanford: Stanford University Press.

Mead, Margaret. 1928. *Coming of Age in Samoa.* New York: Morrow Quill.

Moraga, Cherríe. 1983. "A Long Line of Vendidas." In *Loving in the War Years,* 90–149. Boston: South End Press.

Morris, Robert J. 1990. *"Aikāne:* Accounts of Hawaiian Same-Sex Relationships in the Journals of Captain Cook's Third Voyage (1776–1780)." *Journal of Homosexuality* 19(4): 21–54.

Morris, Rosalind C. 1994. "Three Sexes and Four Sexualities: Redressing the Discourses on Sex and Gender in Contemporary Thailand." *Positions* 2(1): 15–43.

Murray, Stephen O. 1992. *Oceanic Homosexualities.* New York: Garland Publishing.

Oliver, Douglas L. 1974. *Ancient Tahitian Society.* 3 vols. Honolulu: University Press of Hawai'i.

————. 1981. *Two Tahitian Villages: A Study in Comparison.* Honolulu: Institute for Polynesian Studies.

Ortner, Sherry B., and Harriet Whitehead, eds. 1981. *Sexual Meanings: The Cultural Construction of Gender and Sexuality.* New York: Cambridge University Press.

Rubin, Gayle. 1975. "The Traffic in Women: Notes on the 'Political Economy' of Sex." In *Toward an Anthropology of Women,* ed. Rayna R. Reiter, 157–210. New York: Monthly Review Press.

————. 1984. "Thinking Sex: Notes for a Radical Theory of the Politics of Sexuality." In *Pleasure and Danger: Exploring Female Sexuality,* ed. Carole S. Vance, 267–319. New York: Routledge.

Saura, Bruno. 1993. *Politique et religion à Tahiti.* Pirae, Tahiti: Editions Polymages-Scoop.

Shore, Bradd. 1982. *Sala'ilua: A Samoan Mystery.* New York: Columbia University Press.

Thomas, Nicholas. 1987. "Complementarity and History: Misrecognizing Gender in the Pacific." *Oceania* 57(4):261–70.

Vance, Carole S., ed. 1984. *Pleasure and Danger: Exploring Female Sexuality.* London: Pandora Press.

————. 1991. "Anthropology Rediscovers Sexuality: A Theoretical Comment." *Social Science and Medicine* 33(8): 875–84.

Watts, Raleigh. 1992. "The Polynesian Mahu." In *Oceanic Homosexualities,* ed. Stephen O. Murray, 171–84. New York: Garland Publishing.

Weston, Kath. 1993. "Lesbian/Gay Studies in the House of Anthropology." *Annual Review of Anthropology* 22: 339–67.

White, Geoffrey M., and John Kirkpatrick, eds. 1985. *Person, Self, and Experience: Exploring Pacific Ethnopsychologies.* Berkeley: University of California Press.

Contributors

Evelyn Blackwood was a student of life in the lesbian community of San Francisco in the 1970s. Entering graduate school in 1978, she devoted her research to the study of female same-sex relations, publishing a number of works on the topic, including work on Native American female two-spirits and, more recently, *tombois* in West Sumatra. The *tomboi* research grew out of a larger project on a rural Minangkabau village in West Sumatra. She is the coeditor, with Saskia E. Wieringa, of *Female Desires: Same-Sex Relations and Transgender Practices across Cultures* (1999) and editor of *The Many Faces of Homosexuality: Anthropological Approaches to Homosexual Behavior* (1986). She is associate professor of anthropology and women's studies at Purdue University.

Deborah Elliston's research in the Society Islands of French Polynesia (1993–95) has focused on the locations and meanings of gender and other social differences in contemporary cultural politics and the Polynesian nationalist struggle to gain independence from France. Her work in queer anthropology includes research on Islanders' productions of gender and sexuality and a feminist reanalysis of the scholarship on "ritualized homosexuality" that appeared in *American Ethnologist*. She is an assistant professor of anthropology at Binghamton University/SUNY.

Benjamin Junge is a doctoral candidate in the Department of Anthropology at Emory University in Atlanta, Georgia, where he studies sexuality and gender, medical anthropology, and poststructuralist trends in contemporary social thought. He worked for several years as a public health researcher in Baltimore, Maryland, focusing on HIV/AIDS prevention among injection drug users. His dissertation research examines male sexuality and gender in dialogue with emergent ideologies of citizenship and human rights in Porto Alegre, Brazil.

Elizabeth Lapovsky Kennedy is professor and head of women's studies at the University of Arizona. She received her Ph.D. in social anthropology from Cambridge University, England, in 1972 based on her research about the Waunan of Choco Province, Colombia. Kennedy was a founding member of women's studies at the State University of New York at Buffalo, where she taught for twenty-eight years. Her research pioneered the study of lesbian history, a subject on which she has published widely, including the prize-winning *Boots of Leather, Slippers of Gold: The History of a Lesbian Community*. She has also written about the development of women's studies as a field, including *Feminist Scholarship: Kindling in the Groves of Academe* (1983, with Ellen DuBois et al.).

William L. Leap is professor of anthropology at American University, Washington, D.C., where he regularly teaches courses in linguistics, applied anthropology, and race/gender/social justice studies. He is the author of *Word's Out: Gay Men's English*, editor of *Beyond the Lavender Lexicon* and *Public Sex/Gay Space*, and (with Ellen Lewin) *Out in the Field: Reflections of Lesbian and Gay Anthropologists*. His current research explores intersections of sexuality, place, and space in Washington, D.C., Cape Town, South Africa, and Havana, Cuba. He coordinates the annual American University Conference on Lavender Languages and Linguistics and has been active in supporting LGBTQ-centered research—and researchers—in anthropology, linguistics, and other fields.

Ellen Lewin is professor of women's studies and anthropology and chair of the women's studies department at the University of Iowa. She has worked in feminist anthropology since the early 1970s, specializing in the study of lesbian/gay cultures in relation to issues of reproduction, family, and kinship. Her *Lesbian Mothers: Accounts of Gender in American Culture* (1993) explored the way lesbian mothers incorporate maternal identity into their constructions of self. *Recognizing Ourselves: Lesbian and Gay Ceremonies of Commitment* (1998) discussed the emergence of same-sex wedding rituals in terms of the symbolic agendas they enact. Lewin is also the editor of *Inventing Lesbian Cultures in America* and the coeditor (with William L. Leap) of *Out in the Field: Reflections of Lesbian and Gay Anthropologists.* Her current research focuses on gay fathers in a midwestern community.

Martin F. Manalansan IV is assistant professor of anthropology at the University of Illinois, Urbana-Champaign, where he also teaches in Asian American studies and the Unit for Criticism and Interpretive Theory. He is author of the forthcoming *Global Divas: Filipino Gay Men in the Diaspora;* editor of a collection of essays, *Cultural Compass: Ethnographic Explorations of Asian America* (2000); and (with Arnaldo Cruz-Malve) is coediting an anthology on queer globalization. His current research explores Asian American culinary modernity, racism, and multiculturalism. His essays on queer transnationalism and globalization have appeared in several journals and anthologies.

Jeff Maskovsky is an assistant professor at Montclair State University in New Jersey. His writing and research focus on neoliberalism, grass-roots activism, and poverty in the United States. He is currently engaged in a postdoctoral study of the effects of state policies and economic restructuring on civic participation in three poor neighborhoods in Philadelphia. He is coeditor (with Judith Goode) of *New Poverty Studies: The Ethnography of Power, Politics, and Impoverished People in the United States.*

Esther Newton is a professor of anthropology and Kempner Distinguished Professor at Purchase College, State University of New York, where she is co-chair of the Lesbian and Gay Studies Program. She is the author of three books: *Mother Camp: Female Impersonators in America* (1979), *Cherry Grove, Fire Island: Sixty Years in America's First Gay and Lesbian Town* (1993), and *Margaret Mead Made Me Gay: Personal Essays, Public Ideas* (2000). She lives in New York City in a traditional lesbian family that includes her partner, Holly Hughes, two standard poodles, and two cats.

Gayle Rubin, an itinerant anthropologist, was recently Norman Freehling Visiting Professor at the University of Michigan. She has also taught at the University of California at Berkeley and Santa Cruz. Her research interests include the ethnography of sexual populations, the history of sexological theory, urban sexual geography, and the politics of sexuality. She is the author of many essays, including "The Traffic in Women," "Thinking Sex," and "Elegy for the Valley of the Kings." She been a visiting fellow in sexualities and culture at the Australian National University and was a postdoctoral fellow in the Sexuality Research Fellowship Program of the Social Science Research Council.

Robert A. Schmidt is a visiting lecturer with the Archaeological Research Facility at the University of California, Berkeley. He coedited *Archaeologies of Sexuality* (2000), the first volume to collect original archaeological research on sexuality. His research focuses upon the intersections of gender, biological sex, and sexuality in several contexts, including the Mesolithic of southern Scandinavia.

David Valentine received his Ph.D. in 2000 from the Department of Anthropology at New York University for his work on the genealogy of the category "transgender" and its relationship to contemporary American understandings of gender and sexuality. He teaches at Sarah Lawrence College.

Index

Achilles, Nancy, 30, 31–33, 51, 96, 105n10
Adam, Barry, 79
Advocate, The, 213n21
Africa, 79, 82–83
African, 85
Afrikaner, 145
AIDS, 52, 102, 106n23, 113, 115, 148n9, 191–92, 196, 212n11, 278–79, 281; epidemic, 189; politics, 280
AIDS/HIV, 112
AIDS Prevention Action League (APAL), 192–93
Althusser, Louis, 57n20
Altman, Dennis, 248
alyhu. See Mohave *alyhu*
American Anthropological Association (AAA), 13, 100, 103, 105n17, 106nn21, 132, 135, 241nn2, 3, 287
American Educational Gender Information Service (AEGIS), 242n6
American English, 132
American Psychiatric Association, 21
Amory, Deb, 235
anal sex, 186, 189, 190, 192, 194–95, 199, 200, 202–4, 207–8, 210
Ancient Tahitian Society (Oliver), 310n10

Anderson, Nels, 25
Annual Review of Anthropology, 13, 52
Anthropological Research Group on Homosexuality (ARGOH), 3, 99, 106n21, 135, 148n11
Anthropology and the Colonial Encounter (ed. Asad), 2
Anthropology as a Cultural Critique (Marcus and Fischer), 2
anti-vice organizations, 23
Anzaldúa, Gloria, 247
argot, 138
Armstrong, Walter, 211n6
at-risk groups, 195
Australia, 79, 82–83, 134, 171, 212n14; Australians, 84, 144, 170, 179
authenticity, 143
Azande, 75, 79, 82, 84–85

Baker, Cornelius, 214n27
bakla, 115, 145, 247, 249, 252–53, 255, 257–58, 260–61, 262n3
Balibar, Etienne, 57n20
bareback sex, 186–217
Barrett, Rusty, 140
Bayer, Ronald, 198
Beach, Frank A., 19–20–37, 78, 82, 111

Becker, Howard, 22, 26–27, 47, 51, 53, 56n11, 57n13, 96
berdache, 76, 80, 82, 94, 104n4, 147n2, 171
Berger, Peter, 36
Berkeley Women and Language Conference, 132
Bérubé, Allan, 96, 213n15
Besnier, Niko, 309n9
Bhabha, Homi, 262n5
Binford, Louis, 157–8
bisexual, 10–11, 13, 140
biyuti, 253, 255
Blackwood, Evelyn, 52, 112, 114
Bligh, William, 310n10
Blumer, Herbert, 36
Bohuslän, 167–8
Bolton, Ralph, 114, 215n30
Boots of Leather, Slippers of Gold (Kennedy and Davis), 94, 97–99, 100, 107n24. *See also* Davis, Madeline; Kennedy, Elizabeth
Boston, 95
Boswell, John, 35, 180n2
de Bougainville, Louis Antoine, 310n10
Brazil, 114
Brazilian, 115
brideprice, 71
Bronze Age, 167–68
Brown, Michael P., 142, 280
Bucholtz, Mary, 135
Buffalo, 97–98, 107n24, 118, 133, 232, 267
Buffalo Women's Oral History Project, 95
"bug-chaser," 202, 206
"bug-chasing," 212n9
Burgess, Ernest W., 24, 25, 56n11
butch, 70, 98, 100, 107n24, 120, 227
butches, 95, 228–31
butch-fem, 97, 105n15, 232
butch lesbians, 230
butch queens, 229, 235
Butler, Judith, 48, 131, 159, 174

California, 172
Cameron, Deborah, 132, 149n22
camp, 131, 136, 143
Capetown, South Africa, 144
capitalism, 268–70; dialectical view of, 282; late capitalism, 283n3
Captain Cook, 310n10
Caribbean, 78
Carrier, Joseph, 78–79, 105n17, 112
Casella, Eleanor, 170, 178–79

Centers for Disease Control and Prevention, 192
ceramic, 169
chastity belt, 72
Chauncey, George, 104n3, 232, 237
Cherry Grove, 100, 107n24, 118, 133, 232
Chesebro, James W., 132
Chicago, 24, 26–28, 44, 58n22
Chicago Vice Commission, 23
Chinese, 81, 83; sisterhoods, 74, 83–85
Chumash (Native American group), 172–74
citizenship, 252, 254. *See also* gay citizenship
class, 6–8, 30, 49, 51, 113, 232–34, 236, 240, 269–71, 273–74, 276; importance to social theory and politics, 282; role in gay citizenship, 280
Clatts, Michael, 148n9, 196, 210
Clifford, James, 262n5
Clinton, Bill, 243n17
clitoridectomies, 72
clone, 234
code, 146n1
coming out, 10, 12, 101
Coming Out: Homosexual Politics in Britain, from the Nineteenth Century to the Present (Weeks), 37–38
Commission on Lesbian, Gay, Bixesual, and Transgender Issues in Anthropology (COLGIA), 12, 13, 106n23
commodification, 281
community studies, 8, 97
compulsory heterosexuality, 72–74, 76, 86n4
condomless anal sex, 191–93, 211n6, 214n28; among HIV-positives, 211n8; increase in, 212n14
condoms, 186–87, 189–90, 197, 199–200, 203–5
condom usage, 195, 212n11; promotion of, 193, 213n17
Construction of Homosexuality, The (Greenberg), 78
construction of sexual meaning, 86
consumer choice, 279
consumerism, 266–67, 269, 281
consumption, 264–86
Cook, Blanche Wiesen, 58n27
County, Jayne, 233, 235, 238, 243n15
Craven, Christa, 148n15
Cromwell, Jason, 148n15, 87n7, 242n9
cultural consumption, 7
cultural production, 7

cultural studies, 7, 10
culture, 6, 7, 8
culture-historical approach to archaeology, 157

D'Amato, Alfonse, 227, 233, 242n8
Davies, Peter M., 207, 215n32
Davis, Katherine Bement, 20
Davis, Madeline, 52, 95, 100, 117, 118, 133, 232, 267, 312n22. *See also Boots of Leather, Slippers of Gold*
Davis, W. R., 148n9
Deleuze, Gilles, 168
Delph, Murray Stephen, 131
D'Emilio, John, 95, 101, 105n10
De Vall, William B., 33
Devereaux, George, 87n15, 147n2
deviance, 26
dialect, 138, 146n1
diaspora, 7, 247, 254, 261
direct historical approach, 177–78
disclosure, 30
discrimination, 13
Douglas, Mary, 200
drag, 48–49, 51, 118–19, 227, 237, 272–73
drag balls, 228
drag queens, 46, 118, 131, 230
Drexel, Allen, 25
Dubois, Ellen, 96

economic anthropology, 41
Edel, Deb, 96
Ellis, Havelock, 22
Elovich, Richard, 201, 210, 213n14
Employment Non-Discrimination Act (ENDA), 227, 236–37, 239, 242n7
Erikson, Kai, 56n11
Escoffier, Jeffrey, 22
ethnographic analogy, 177–78
ethnography, 261n2; of communication, 131
Europe, 70, 73, 76
European, 176
European Mesolithic, 175
Evans-Pritchard, E. E., 75, 79, 85

Faderman, Lillian, 104n3
Farmer, Paul, 196, 214n25
Farrell, Ron, 130
fem, 98, 100, 107n24, 242n12
female impersonation, 47
female impersonators, 48–50, 118

female infanticide, 72
female same-sex relations, 70; practices, 74
feminism, 99–102, 105n15, 106n19, 115, 122
feminist; anthropologists, 42, 292; anthropology, 13, 83, 110–11, 121–22, 124; archeologies, 180n3; archeologists, 159–60; focus on gender, 123; movements, 95, 99, 118; perspective, 120–21; politics, 116; scholarship, 106n22; theory, 69
fem queens, 228–31, 235
Ferguson, Ann, 72
Filipino, 115, 134, 145, 234, 247–52, 254
Fine, Gary Alan, 58n22
Fire Island, 19
foot-binding, 71
Ford, Clellen, 19–20, 37, 78, 82, 111
formalism, 41
Forsyth, Craig J., 212n9
Fortes, Meyer, 97
Foucault, Michel, 35–36, 40, 58n21, 87n11, 96, 202, 216n40
Freidson, Eliot, 56n11
French theory, 39
Freud, Sigmund, 71
Frye, Marilyn, 124

Gagnon, John, 28–29, 33, 36–38, 40–41, 43–44, 53, 58n22, 97. *See also Sexual Conduct; Sexual Deviance; The Sexual Scene*
Galliher, John, 26
Gaudio, Rudolf, 133, 134
Gauthier, Dean, 212n9
gay, 75, 95, 231–34, 235–38, 254, 257, 262n3; bars, 30–32, 50, 53; citizenship, 280–81; communities, 49, 57n15; desires, 8; identity, 276; marriage, 209, 276–78
Gay American History (Katz), 94
"gaydar," 142
Gay and Lesbian HIV Prevention Activists (GALHPA), 192
gay and lesbian movements, 96, 99; in the U.S., 223
gay rights, 118; movement, 77, 94, 125n2
gender, 239–40; blending, 310n12; blurring, 310n12; crossover behaviors, 310n12; misrecognition, 294
Gender Identity Project (GIP), 226, 229–31, 236
Gender Public Advocacy Coalition (Gender-PAC), 226–28, 242nn6, 7
Gendin, Stephen, 203

gift-giver, 202, 206

Gil, 216n42

globalization, 6–7, 144, 246–48, 254

Goffman, Erving, 22, 27, 36, 47–48, 51, 56n11, 96, 105n11, 197, 200–201

Goodwin, Joseph, 131–32

Gough, Kathleen, 71

gouine, 291

Grahn, Judy, 140

Greek, 80, 82

Greenberg, David, 35, 78–79, 308n3

Greenwich Village, 19

Guattari, Félix, 168

Gunson, 293, 310n11

Gusfield, Joseph, 25

Halberstam, Judith, 262n6

Hale, C. Jacob, 262n6

Hall, Kira, 134, 135, 137

Halperin, David, 35

Hansen, Bert, 43, 58n27

Haraway, Donna, 58n27

harems, 82

Harlem, 119

Harry, Joseph, 33

Hart, Donn V., 82, 87n15

Hate Crimes Statistics Act, 227

Hausa, 134

Hawaiian language, 309–10n9

Hawkes, C. F., 155, 162

Hawkeswood, William, 119

Hayes, Joseph, 136

Hay, Harry, 105n13

Heap, Chad, 25

Henry, George, 20

Herdt, Gilbert, 9, 52, 78, 81, 112–13, 133, 147n3, 160, 166, 168, 289, 308n3

heterosexual marriage, 76, 84. *See also* gay marriage

heterosexual matrix, 298, 303

Hidatsa, 171–72

Higgins, Ross, 142

high-risk groups, 195, 197

hijra, 134

historical archeologists, 179

history, 39

History of Sexuality (Foucault), 36, 39–40

HIV, 6, 145, 186, 188, 190–95, 198, 200–201, 204, 206, 209–10, 212nn10, 11, 14, 234, 278–79; epidemiology of, 187

HIV/AIDS prevention programs, 115

HIV-negative(s), 199, 203–5, 207, 212nn9, 14

HIV-positive(s), 199, 203, 205, 207, 211n8, 212n9

Hodder, Ian, 158

Hoffman, Martin, 96

Hollibaugh, Amber, 72–73

Hollimon, Sandra, 172–74, 178

home(s), 247, 250, 252, 254, 256, 259, 261, 262n6

homophile movement, 232

homophobia, 14

homosexual: community, 32; practices, 289

Homosexualities (Bell and Weinberg), 59n30

homosexuality: anthropology of, 69

"Homosexual Role, The" (McIntosh), 36

homosexuel/homosexuelle, 291

Hooker, Evelyn, 22, 29, 31, 47, 51, 55n5, 96

House of Xtravaganza, 228–29

Hughes, Everett, 56n11

Human Relations Area Files, 20, 37, 82

Human Rights Campaign (HRC), 227–28, 231, 233, 236–37, 242nn3, 7, 8

Human Sexual Behavior (Marshall and Suggs), 19, 20, 21. *See also* Marshall, Donald; Suggs, Robert

hustlers, 33

Hymes, Dell, 106n20

identity labels, 231

immigrant, 250

immigration, 246

impersonators, 51. *See also* female impersonators

India, 134

inequality/inequalities, 266, 271, 273, 283n4

Institute for Gay and Lesbian Strategic Studies, 283n2

Institute for Sex Research, 27

International Association for Applied Linguistics, 132

International Association for the Study of Sexuality, Culture, and Society, 3

International Conference on Transgender Law and Employment Policy (ICTLEP), 242n6

International Conferences on World Englishes, 134

International Foundation for Gender Education (IFGE), 242n6

International Language and Gender Association (ILGA), 133–34

Intersex Society of North America (ISNA), 242nn6, 10
intersex, 230, 242n10
It's Time America! (ITA), 242n6

Jackson, Peter, 134, 148–49n20
Jacobs, Sue-Ellen, 147n2, 176
Jagose, Annamarie, 40
Janeway, Elizabeth, 71
Japanese, 119–20
Johnson, David K., 25
Jorgensen, Christine, 250
Joyce, Rosemarie, 169–70, 174, 178

Karshch-Haak, Ferdinand, 87n18
Katz, Jonathan, 39–40, 96, 105n13
Kennedy, Elizabeth, 52, 117–118, 133, 232, 267, 312n22. See also Boots of Leather, Slippers of Gold.
Kenya, 74
Kinsey, Alfred, 20, 22, 36–37, 47, 55n5, 56n12, 57nn16, 18, 97, 111
Kinsey Institute, 22, 28
kinship, 84–85, 116–17, 119
Kitsuse, John, 56n11
Kreiger, Susan, 59n30
Kuhn, Thomas, 1
Kulick, Don, 10, 11, 114–15, 134, 143, 148nn13, 15, 262n10
Kutsche, Paul, 105n17

Labeja, Junior, 228–29, 231, 235
labor, 268
Lacan, Jacques, 168
Ladder of Inference. See Hawkes, C. F.
Lakoff, Robin, 132
Langness, L. L., 105n17
language, 146n1
language-centered research, 138
Latin America, 105n17, 134, 145
Lavender Languages Conference, 3, 133–34, 140
leather communities, 227
Lee, John Allan, 59n30
Legends' Ball, 228
lesbian, 70; desires, 8; identity, 8, 72; separatism, 233. See also gay desires; gay identities
lesbian continuum, 72
Lesbian and Gay Community Services Center, 226, 230

Lesbian Herstory Archives, 96
Lesbian Mothers. See Lewin, Ellen
lesbienne, 291; 299; in Polynesia, 300, 303, 304
Lesotho, South Africa, 75
Lessa, William, 308n1
Levine, Martin, 59n30
Levi-Strauss, Claude, 71
Levy, Robert, 294, 310nn11, 12
Lewin, Ellen, 52, 100, 117, 119, 133
Lewinsky, Monica, 243n17, 251
Lewis, Oscar, 283n4
Leznoff, Maurice, 29–30, 47–48, 51
Liang, Anita, 135
liberation movements, 95
Linguistic Society of America, 132
linguistics of contact, 140
Livia, Anna, 135, 137
Livingstone, Jenny, 228
London, 144
Los Angeles, 31, 95
Luckmann, Thomas, 36

māhū, 291, 293; female-bodied, 295, 297, 298, 299, 302, 303, 304, 311n17, 312n19; male-bodied 310nn10, 12, 312n20; meanings of 294, 296
mainstreaming, 232
Making of the English Working Class, The (Thompson), 42
Making of the Modern Homosexual, The (Plummer), 36
Manalansan, Martin IV, 134, 149n21, 234
Manila, 246–47, 250, 253–58, 261, 262n3
Mann Act, 23
mannish woman, 95
Marquesa Islands, 312n18
marriage, 73–74, 234. See also gay marriage; heterosexual marriage
Marshall, Donald, 111
Martin, Biddy, 306
Marx, 71
Marxism, 58n25
Marxist, 99
masculinist, 69–70, 77, 80–81, 83, 85–86, 86n1, 135, 308n2
material culture, 155
mati work, 120
Mattachine Society, 232
Matthews, Keith, 178
Maya, 169–70

McIntosh, Mary, 36–37, 40, 81, 96, 105n10; *The Homosexual Role,* 38

Mead, George Herbert, 56n11

Mead, Margaret, 94, 104n4, 112, 288

medical anthropology, 101

Melanesia, 79, 82

Mesolithic, 176–77, 180n4

Micronesia, 308n1

Middle Stone Age, 175

migration, 246

Minter, Shannon, 232

Modern Homosexualities (Plummer), 36

modernity, 6, 7, 247, 249, 252, 256, 258, 260–61, 268

moffie, 144–45

Mohave, 161

Mojave *alyhu,* 9

Mohave *hwame,* 87n15

Mombasa, 87n20

monogamy, 209

Moonwoman, Birch, 132–33, 137–39, 143

Moraga, Cherríe, 72–73

Morris, Rosalind, 262n3

Morton, Donald, 269

Mother Camp (Newton), 45–48, 51–52, 94–95, 104n5, 105n17, 118, 131, 147n6

Moynihan Report, 283n4

multiple gender, 160

multiple sex, 160

multiple sex/gender paradigm, 161, 166

multi-sited, 261n2

Mumford, Kevin, 25

"mummies" and "babies" in Lesotho, 75, 78, 84–85

Murray, Stephen, 52, 57n15, 105n17, 112, 134, 308n2

Muslim societies, 75

Mutschler, Kevin M., 196

Nader, Laura, 2

National Association of Persons with AIDS, 214n27

National Gay and Lesbian Task Force (NGLTF), 225, 227, 236

Native American, 82, 85, 161, 171–72; cultures, 76

Native American Graves Protection and Repatriation Act (NAGPRA), 165

Navajo, 161

Navartilova, Martina, 281

negotiated safety, 214n24

neoliberal, 267, 270–71; discourses, 276; ideologies, 279; norms, 277

neoliberalism, 266, 269, 281; domestic, 282

Nestle, Joan, 96

new archeologists, 158

new archeology, 157, 159, 161

New Guinea, 19, 53, 55n4, 80–81, 98, 105n17, 112, 133

Newton, Esther, 5, 10, 46–49, 51–3, 98, 100, 105n11, 107n24, 117–18, 133, 232

New York, 95, 118, 192–93, 246–47, 250, 252, 255–56, 258, 261, 262n3

Nicaragua, 145

North America, 19, 35, 49, 53, 55n4, 70, 73, 84, 174

North American, 83

North Americans, 84

North Dakota, 171

Ocamb, K., 204, 211n6

Oceania, 55n4

Odets, Walt, 193

O'Hara, Scott, 192

Oliver, Douglas, 310n10

Oliver, Gerrit, 134

oral histories, 102

oral history, 93, 97

O'Shea, John, 176

Ötzi, 162–66. *See also* Tyrolean Iceman

Out in the Field (Lewin and Leap), 3, 4, 5, 10, 11

OUTIL list-serv, 134–35

outness, 10, 12, 14

Padgug, Robert, 43, 58n27

Papeete, 295, 300–301

Paris Is Burning (film), 228

Park, Robert E., 24, 25, 51, 53, 56n11

Parsons, Talcott, 214n23

passing women, 76, 87n7

patriarchal, 70, 75

patriarchy, 71–73

pédé, 291

peers, 34

Pena, Ralph, 249

Penelope, Julia [Stanley], 131–32, 136, 148n14

performance, 47–48, 103

performative, 121

performativity, 102, 224

Perry, Elizabeth, 174, 178

petea, 291, 293, 300, 302, 303, 304
Philadelphia, 8, 95
Philippine, 255
Philippines, 83, 87n15, 114, 248, 250–51, 253
Plant, Aaron, 202
Plummer, Kenneth, 28, 35–37, 40
Policy Institute of the National Gay and Lesbian Task Force, 283n2
political economies, 47–48, 52
Polynesian 297; interpretive frameworks, 293, 303; *māhū,* 9; men, 310n12; sexual symbolic economies, 303–6
Polynesians, 291–292, 310n12; common-law marriage, 311n16; cultural configuration of, 311n18; encounters with, 294, 296, 298–99, 302, 304–6, 308n5, 309nn6, 7, 311nn13, 14
Ponse, Barbara, 59n30
pornography, 72
post-AIDS, 188
postcolonial, 7, 70, 247
postmodern, 69
postprocessualist, 158–59, 161, 167, 178
poverty, 266–67, 272, 276, 282, 283n4; culture of, 276, 278, 283n4
POZ Magazine, 197, 213n21
Pratt, Mary Louise, 140, 148n17
prehistoric rock art, 167–68
Prince, Virginia, 242n9
Prine, Elizabeth, 171, 178
processual archeology, 157
processualist, 158, 161
promiscuity, 209
protease inhibitors, 188, 191–92
pueblo, 174
purdah, 71

queen, 98
Queen, Robin, 137
queer, 121–22, 238–39, 241n1, 262n3
queer anthropology, 290, 292, 305
queerness: spaces of, 141; spatial, 142
queers, 34
queer theorists, 224
queer theory, 10–11, 12, 14, 58n23, 121, 131, 135, 140–41, 159–60, 268–69, 306; politics of desire, 281

race, 6, 7, 119, 232, 234, 236, 240, 269, 274, 276

racial divisions, 8
radical feminist, 69, 70–74, 77, 85
Radical History Review, 43
Radicalesbians, 125n1
raerae, 291, 293, 300–302, 304, 312n20; sex work, 301; *tamahine raerae,* 312n20
Read, Kenneth, 52, 94, 98–99, 104n7, 105n17, 106n24, 131
recovery, 275; narrative of, 276
recovery programs, 275, 282
recreational drugs, 216n43
referential semantics, 143
register, 138, 146n1
Reinstein, Julia Boyer, 106n18
Reinventing Anthropology (ed. Hymes), 2
Reiss, Albert J., 22, 30, 33–35, 51, 58n22
Renaissance Education Foundation, 242n6
resistance, 72–76, 81, 85, 95–96, 98, 111, 116, 132, 144, 170–71, 257
Rich, Adrienne, 71–72, 74, 81, 124n1
Ricks, Ingrid, 216n39
risk factor(s), 194, 214n22; *see also* at-risk groups; high-risk groups
risk-group categories, 196
ritual, 84
Robertson, Jennifer, 119
Robinson, Paul, 56n12
rock art. *See* prehistoric rock art
Rofes, Eric, 213n18
Roscoe, Will, 101, 104n3, 160
Ross, Ellen, 58n27
Ross Female Factory (Australian prison), 170
Rotello, Gabriel, 193, 199, 213n21
Rubin, Gayle, 10, 71, 83, 95, 97, 100, 111, 156, 158, 231, 243n14
Russia, 175

safer sex, 191, 194, 198–99, 210, 229; guidelines, 206; ideology, 188, 195, 207–8
Sambia, 80, 81, 168, 289
same-gender sexuality, 298
same-sex sexual practices, 29–91
Samoa, 293, 309n9; context-dependencies in, 312n18; symbol of hair in, 311n14
San Francisco, 30, 32, 95, 106n23, 117, 212n14
San Francisco Gay and Lesbian History Project, 95
Sawyer, Ethel, 96, 105n10
Schein, Louisa, 261n1
Schmidt, Robert, 178

Schneider, David, 46–47
Schur, Edwin, 96
Schwartz, Judith, 96
Sedgwick, Eve Kosofsky, 101
semiotics, 131, 143
seroconversion, 204–7
sex and gender, 159
sexed-body status, 290, 295, 297–99, 303
sex/gender, 160–61, 179
sex/gender system, 156–57, 158, 162, 166, 223; reshaping understandings of, 292
Sex Panic (group), 193
Sexual Behavior in the Human Male (Kinsey), 37, 57n16
Sexual Conduct (Gagnon and Simon), 29, 36, 57n13
Sexual Deviance (Gagnon and Simon), 29, 33, 44
sexuality, 239
Sexual Scene, The (Gagnon and Simon), 29
Sexual Stigma: An Interactionist Account (Plummer) 36, 38
sex wars, 72
shamans, 176–77
Shanks, Michael, 158
Sheon, Nicolas, 202
Shepherd, Gill, 75
Siberia, 176
Siegal, C., 207
Signorile, Michelangelo, 193, 213nn17, 21
Simes, Gary, 134
Simon, William. *See* Gagnon, John
slang, 136
Smith, Neil, 270–71
Smith-Rosenberg, Carol, 125n1
Snitow, Ann Barr, 58n27
social construction, 36, 39, 41, 43, 54, 59n28, 74, 80
social constructionist, 58 n.23, 159, 180n2
Social Construction of Reality, The (Berger and Luckmann), 36
Social Organization of Gay Men, The, 59n30
Social Problems (journal), 26, 27, 30, 56n11
Social Science Research Council, 147n9
Society for the Study of Social Problems, 27
Society Islands of French Polynesia, 290–94, 297, 305, 307, 308n5, 310n10, 311n15
Society of Lesbian and Gay Anthropologists (SOLGA), 3, 99–100, 105n17, 106nn21, 23, 125n2, 135, 148n11, 225, 241nn2, 3, 287, 290

sociocultural anthropology, 287
socioeconomic status, 253
sociolect, 138
sociology of deviance, 47
sodomy, 144
Solomon Islands, 82
Sonenschein, David, 43–47, 129–30
Sothern, J. L., 148n9
South Africa, 134
South African, 145, 149n22
South Pacific, 53
Southwest, 174
speaking style, 146n1
speech community, 141
Spender, Dale, 132
spiritual desire, 76
Spivak, Gayatri, 141
STD, 215n28
stigma, 27, 30, 36, 46–47, 49, 50–51, 58n22, 119, 197, 200–201
Stigma: Notes on the Management of Spoiled Identity (Goffman), 27
Stonewall, 50, 129, 143, 268–69
Strauss, Anselm, 56n11
substantivism, 41
Suggs, Robert, 111
Suriname, 120
Sutton, Lurel, 135
Sweden, 167
systems theory, 158

Tagalog, 249
Tahiti, 291, 295
Tahitian language, 291; prefixes of, 310n9
Tahitians, 308n5
takarazuka, 119–20
tane, 291, 297, 304
Tan, Michael, 114–15
Tannen, Deborah, 131
Taylor, Clark, 105n17
Tearoom Trade (Humphreys), 59n30
textual authenticity, 142
Thailand, 134, 149n20
third gender, 9, 101, 144, 160, 171, 177
third sex, 9, 160
third-world women, 73
Thomas, Wesley, 22–24, 56n11, 149n21, 294
Thompson, E. P., 42, 58n27
Thorne, Barrie, 56n10
Tilley, Christopher, 158
tomboy, 70, 296, 302

Tonga, 309n9
tourism, 246
Toward an Anthropology of Women (Reiter), 2
trans, 140
transgender, 6, 10, 11, 13, 78, 82–83, 85–86, 101
trans-gendered, 102, 114, 174
transgenders, 100
transnational, 247–48
transsexual, 102, 252, 260
Transexual Menace (group), 228
travel, 246–47, 249
travesti, 134, 148n15
Treichler, Paula, 148n9
Trumbach, Randolph, 104n3
Turner, Dwayne, 112–13
Turner, William, 40
two spirit, 76, 82, 85, 87n8, 94, 171–73
Tyrolean Iceman, 162

University of Chicago, 22, 25, 46
unprotected anal intercourse, 212n10
urban, 53
urban gay, 46
urban homosexual subculture, 38
Urban Life and Culture (journal), 56n11
urban societies, 45

vahine, 291, 295, 297, 304, 310n12
Vaid, Urvashi, 227, 232, 237
Vance, Carole B., 41n4, 57n19, 59n28, 105n17
variety, 146n1
veiling, 72
verbal style, 143
vice, 24
Vicinus, Martha, 86n4
violence, 34–35
Vivien, Renee, 95
Voss, Barbara, 180n3

Walkowitz, Daniel, 58n26
Walkowitz, Judith, 42, 58n26

Walters, Suzanna, 122
wame. See Mohave *hwame*
Warner, Michael, 215n31, 268–69, 282
Warren, Barbara, 230
Washington, 95
We The People (group), 279–280
Weeks, Jeffrey, 35, 37, 39–40, 58n27
Wekker, Gloria, 120
Wenner-Gren Foundation for Anthropological Research, 147n9
West Hollywood, 19
Westley, William A., 22, 30, 47–48, 51, 58n22
Weston, Kath, 5, 13, 52, 100, 106n24, 111, 117
White, Edmund, 136
Wilchins, Riki Anne, 148n15, 228, 230
Williams, Walter, 112
Wolf, Deborah Goleman, 52
Wolitski, R., 215n29
Woman, Culture and Society (ed. Rosaldo and Lamphere), 2
Women in the Field (Golde), 4
women's sexuality, 69
women's studies, 93, 99
Women Writing Culture (ed. Behar and Gordon), 2–3
working-class, 99, 100, 107n24, 118
Writing Culture (ed. Clifford and Marcus), 2

xhosa, 145

Yates, Tim, 159, 167–68, 178

Zita, Jacquelyn, 72, 121
Znaniecki, Florian, 22
Zorbaugh, 25
Zulu, 145
Zuni, 161, 174
Zvelebil, Marek, 176–77
Zwicky, Arnold, 133–34

The University of Illinois Press
is a founding member of the
Association of American University Presses.

University of Illinois Press
1325 South Oak Street
Champaign, IL 61820-6903
www.press.uillinois.edu